THE HOLY ROMAN EMPIRE

JAMES BRYCE

The Holy Roman Empire

INTRODUCTION BY HANS KOHN

SCHOCKEN BOOKS · NEW YORK

CONTENTS

v

CHAPTER IV

RESTORATION OF THE EMPIRE IN THE WEST

CHAPTER V

EMPIRE AND POLICY OF CHARLES

CHAPTER VI

CAROLINGIAN AND ITALIAN EMPERORS

CHAPTER VII

THEORY OF THE MEDIAEVAL EMPIRE

CHAPTER VIII

THE ROMAN EMPIRE AND THE GERMAN KINGDOM

CHAPTER IX

SAXON AND FRANCONIAN EMPERORS

CHAPTER X

STRUGGLE OF THE EMPIRE AND THE PAPACY

CHAPTER XI

THE EMPERORS IN ITALY: FREDERICK BARBAROSSA

CHAPTER XII

IMPERIAL TITLES AND PRETENSIONS

CHAPTER XIII

FALL OF THE HOHENSTAUFEN: RENEWED STRIFE OF PAPACY AND EMPIRE

CHAPTER XVI

THE CITY OF ROME IN THE MIDDLE AGES

CHAPTER XVII

THE EAST ROMAN EMPIRE

CHAPTER XVIII

THE RENAISSANCE: CHANGE IN THE CHARACTER OF THE EMPIRE

CHAPTER XIX

THE REFORMATION AND ITS EFFECTS UPON THE EMPIRE

CHAPTER XX

THE PEACE OF WESTPHALIA: LAST STAGE IN THE DECLINE OF THE EMPIRE

CHAPTER XXI

FALL OF THE EMPIRE

CHAPTER XXII

SUMMARY AND REFLECTIONS

INTRODUCTION

INTRODUCTION

In a long, rich and productive life James Bryce wrote only one book which can properly be called a historian's work. Yet this book immediately established itself as a classic. It has served until today—that is, for almost a century—as the main source from which students all over the world have gained deeper understanding of the ideas underlying the political thought of the Middle Ages. Although these ideas now belong to the past, yet, like so many other relics, they continue to exercise an often subterranean influence on the thought, emotion and actions of peoples. Thus Bryce's *The Holy Roman Empire* not only informs the reader about the nature of the medieval mind and the continuation and transformation of the Roman idea as it survived in the Roman Church and the German Empire; it also sharpens his awareness of the survival of this idea, in adulterated forms, in some of the "modern" movements of our day.

Bryce's classic book was a work of his youth. It originated in a prize essay which the twenty-four year old student, newly elected a Fellow of Oriel College in Oxford, submitted in 1862. Two years later it was published as a slender volume of one hundred and seventy pages. It was immediately hailed as one of the most remarkable studies in the history of ideas—comparable to *Die Kultur der Renaissance in Italien* which the then forty-two year old Swiss historian, Jacob Burckhardt, had published four years before. In subsequent editions *The Holy*

Roman Empire grew into a volume of more than 450 pages. It went through thirty-five printings—the latest in 1956—and was translated into many languages.

The changes and enlargements in the editions of 1873 and especially that of 1904 were made not merely to accommodate new scholarly insights; under the impact of Bismarck's establishment of the Second German Empire Bryce went further and added new chapters on the history of German nationalism, a subject hardly connected with the ideas underlying the Holy Roman Empire. For, in truth, the Holy Roman Empire was in origin and substance the representation of a non-nationalist age, in fact the very antithesis of nationalism. To confound it with later German nationalist developments obscured their true character and helped to bring about disastrous consequences. But when Bryce's book appeared in the 1860's, its analysis of the inner meaning and significance of the Holy Roman Empire attracted attention because of the almost simultaneous sequence of events through which Bismarck raised Prussia to a paramount position in Europe.

This new German Empire, whose creation and basic idea really ran counter to both German traditions and the nature of the Holy Roman Empire, was often identified in German historiography and public opinion with the Empire, which had existed for one thousand years, from 800 to 1806. The identification gave rise to misleading myths and dreams. This "Second Empire" of Bismarck lasted less than half a century. It was followed, under Hitler, by a supposedly "Third Empire" or "Reich" which in a dangerous way mixed the most objectionable features of the "First" and "Second" Empires, while overlooking or rejecting whatever good features and traditions they possessed. Hitler's "Third Empire," which claimed that it would last for one thousand years as had the "First Empire," collapsed after only twelve years of existence and buried in its ruins whatever remnants there were of the Holy Roman Empire or of Bismarck's Reich. Thus this collapse may have brought to an end the dangerous influence which the imperial idea, the idea of the Reich, exercised upon the German mind.

II

Burckhardt's classic treatise on the Renaissance stressed a sharp difference between the Renaissance, which inaugurated a new era, and the thought and society of the period which preceded it. Like Goethe, Burckhardt went back, beyond the Middle Ages and Rome, to the humanism of the Greeks, and celebrated its rebirth in fifteenth century Italy. His book was not a narrative history of events, but an analysis of underlying ideas, of the intellectual and moral climate of the period. The same can be said of Bryce's treatise on the Holy Roman Empire. It is an essay on the history of ideas. However, Bryce's work is not limited, as is Burckhardt's, to one century and one country. It covers the long period from the Barbaric Invasions to the Napoleonic Age, and treats of lands and orders which have "almost wholly passed away from the world." To make his book more readily accessible to the student of history Bryce rightly added some account of the great events and territorial shifts which marked the growth and decay of the idea of the Holy Roman Empire.

Burckhardt's and Bryce's approaches to the history of ideas differ also in another point: the former puts emphasis on civilization and the arts, the latter on political systems and institutions. Burckhardt was fascinated by Greece; Bryce, by Rome. Rome meant not a creative explosion of the arts and sciences as did the Greek city-states, but the cultivation of law and of political and administrative institutions which helped to unify its immense territory within an order of peace and justice.

This difference in interest follows indeed from the different backgrounds of the two scholars. Burckhardt was a burgher living a retired life in the small, and quiet city-republic of

Basel; Bryce was a citizen of a mightily expanding empire, himself actively interested in politics, law and diplomacy, holding high positions in the most varied fields. Burckhardt traveled extensively in Italy, which he loved deeply; her ancient art centers became his spiritual home. Bryce too loved Italy and Rome, but he traveled throughout the civilized world.

This typically British familiarity with the world at large and with the ways and responsibilities of public office gave Bryce's writing a density and sustained interest seldom found in historical treatises. He was a master of English style. His language is lucid and often rises to passages of great beauty. Thus he succeeds in evoking for the student of today the importance in universal history of an idea whose power and fascination modern minds can scarcely apprehend.

III

James Bryce (1838-1922) was born in Belfast, Ulster province, of Scottish parents. His father was headmaster of the High School in Glasgow, and Bryce studied at the University of Glasgow. He excelled in classical studies as well as law and modern history. In 1857 he was elected to a scholarship at Oxford. This coincided with the start of a decade whose great intellectual and political transformations agitated the minds of mid-Victorian England. In 1859 Darwin's *On the Origin of the Species by Means of Natural Selection* appeared; its whole first edition was sold out on the day of issue. In 1867 the broadening of suffrage was widely discussed, and with the second Parliamentary Reform Bill the age of democracy dawned in Britain. On all these issues Bryce took his stand on the side of liberalism and democracy.

In 1867 he contributed a chapter to *Essays on Reform,* the collective effort of a group of academic Liberals. When his opponents cited examples from ancient Greece, Rome and contemporary France to point out the evils of democracy, Bryce replied by showing that the Greek republics were all slave states ignorant of the brotherhood of man. While England was closer to Rome than to Greece, Rome too was never a democracy. And as for contemporary France, he simply quoted Tocqueville's remark "that France did not demonstrate the evils of democracy but the evils of a democratic state of society without a democratic government." To exemplify the merits of democracy Bryce referred to the United States and Switzerland. Class government, he maintained, was inherently bad because inherently selfish. "The real danger of England now is not from the working class," he wrote, "for no working class in any country was ever more peaceably disposed than ours is, but from the isolation of classes." The century which has since passed has born out his confidence in British democracy.

In 1870 Bryce was appointed Regius professor of Civil Law at Oxford, a chair he held until 1893. That same year he made his first visit to the United States. In the late 1870's he wrote articles for the New York weekly, The Nation, then brilliantly edited by Edwin Lawrence Godkin, in which he attacked the foreign policy of Disraeli's Conservative government. Bryce bitterly castigated the Turkish persecution of the Armenians and followed his leader, Gladstone, in advocating Irish home rule.

In 1888 he was elected to the House of Commons and in later years joined several Liberal cabinets. He revisited the United States in 1881 and in 1883, and as a result of his studies and observations wrote his second great work, *The American Commonwealth,* published in 1888, half a century after Tocqueville's *Démocratic en Amérique.* The two men approached the subject in different ways. Tocqueville was less interested in the United States itself than in democracy in general, less in forms and institutions of government than in the conditions of social life. Bryce discussed social conditions only in the third volume of his work, where he analyzed the impact of public opinion and social institutions on politics. He was able, as Tocqueville was not, to discuss institutions in the United States from the viewpoint of a constitutional lawyer, for in contrast to Tocqueville he was deeply familiar with English history and the working of English institutions. He was rightly convinced that the whole American fabric was founded, in the first instance, upon English constitutional and legal traditions.

He went to the United States as a convinced democrat and his studies and experiences there confirmed his faith. "America marks the highest level," he wrote, "not only for material well-being but of intelligence and happiness, which a race has yet attained." He clearly saw the dangers in American democracy but remained confident about the outcome. "The Americans have fortunately the power of recognizing, trusting and following a strong and honest man. In this quality, coupled with that instinct for order, that sense of justice, that freedom from class bitterness which belong to the native American, we may perhaps find the best ground for hope for the future of the nation."

In 1907 Bryce was appointed ambassador to the United States, the first non-professional diplomat to fill this coveted post. At his retirement in 1913 he was created a viscount. He availed himself of his experiences in the United States and his travels in Canada, Latin America, Australia and New Zealand, to publish in 1921, at the age of eighty-three, the two volumes of his *Modern Democracies*. After a general historical introduction, in which he also discussed Spanish America, Bryce devoted most of the book to an anlysis of the forms of government in six countries—France, Switzerland, Canada, the United States, Australia, and New Zealand. In his concluding remarks Bryce expressed certain fears about the future of democracy: "Democracy has become, all over Europe, and to some extent even in North America also, desired merely as a means, not as an end, precious in itself because it was the embodiment of liberty. It is now valued, not for what it is, but for what it may be used to win for the masses. When the exercise of their civil rights has brought them that which they desire, and when they feel sure that what they have won will remain with them, may they not cease to care for the further use of those rights? . . . If that which the masses really desire should turn out to be the extinction of private property or some sort of communistic system, and if in some countries such a system should ever be established, the whole character of government would be changed, and that which is now called democracy would become a different thing altogether, perhaps an industrial bureaucratic oligarchy."

But these doubts in no way diminished his faith in the vitality and fecundity of American democracy. He firmly believed in the soundness of its institutions and in its future. He rejected, and tried to refute, the widespread belief in the tyranny and fickleness of the majority and in democratic incapacity for energetic action. He was in no way convinced that the higher education of the upper class was a safer guide in politics than the political sentiments of the masses who, though more slowly, arrive more frequently at the right decision.

During the First World War Lord Bryce, while taking his stand whole-heartedly on the side of democracy, adhered to the great liberal tradition of which he was one of the best representatives. In his Presidential Address, delivered to the British Academy on June 30, 1915, he warned that "Time modifies our judgment as it cools our passions. Neither the friendships nor the enmities of the nations are exempt from change. It is better that nothing should be said today in an address to the Academy which any one of its members, to whatever country he may belong, would feel pain in reading ten or twenty years hence. Newspapers and pamphlets will convey to posterity sufficiently, and even more than sufficiently, the notions and fancies and passions of the moment." In another Presidential Address the following year, on July 14, 1916, he insisted that "the study of philosophy and history has done little for those of us who pursue it if it has not extended their vision beyond their own country and their own time, pointing out to them that human progress has been achieved by the united efforts of many races and many types of intellect and character, each profiting by the efforts of the others, and also reminding them that for further advance this co-operation is essential. To restore it is at this moment impossible. But let us at least do nothing to retard its return in happier days."

His love for the United States, his faith in democracy, his desire for peace inspired the course of his lectures on his last visit to America. He appealed to Americans "to take their share in the great task of raising international relations to a higher plane." He would not venture to prescribe the mode in which Americans should do it, for that must be left to them, but he asked them to take their share, each assuming his responsibility as the citizen of a great nation in helping to form public opinion. The lectures appeared in book form under the title *International Relations* in 1922, shortly after Lord Bryce's death.*

IV

Most of Lord Bryce's great works, based on keen observation of political realities, bear out his training and experience as a British lawyer and politician. They may be called thoroughly practical in character. *The Holy Roman Empire* shares with them the erudite scholarship, the philosophic insight, and the judicial temperament of the author. But it deals less with the concrete workings of a state and its institutions than with a "wonderful" and, to the modern reader, perplexing, "system of

* The Standard Biography of Lord Bryce was written by H. A. L. Fisher (1865-1940), who, like Bryce himself, was an Oxford man, a Liberal, a historian and a man of letters, a member of the House of Commons and of the Cabinet. The book appeared in 1927.

ideas." To the modern mind, which has been trained since the seventeenth century to think critically and practically, these ideas may appear absurd or fantastic. As far as this writer knows, there is no other work which brings to the modern student a similar grasp of the power of the ideas which dominated the medieval mind.

Medieval thinkers, enthralled by the majesty of their own theory, a theory which existed outside the sphere of fact, were not disturbed by facts inconsistent with it. Their conception of a universal Christian commonwealth was a part of that imaginative vision and mystic sense, on which even our own imagination, poetry and legend still feed. It was founded upon the earlier reality of Roman domination. But more important even than the reality of Roman rule—although Bryce does not stress this sufficiently—was the assimilation by Rome of the Greek Stoic philosophy of cosmopolitanism. For under the impact of this philosophy the Roman Empire changed. Had it been dynastic or national or attached to its own center, it would have fallen with the destruction of the city or with the defeat of the ruling tribe; but it was not so limited or localized. "It was imperishable because it was universal; and when its power had ceased, it was remembered with awe and love by the races whose separate existence it had destroyed, because it had granted equal rights to all, and closed against none of its subjects the path of honourable ambition. When the military power of the conquering city had departed, her sway over the world of thought began . . . The magic of her name remained, and she held a sway over the imagination which the passing of century after century scarcely reduced. She had gathered up and embodied in her literature and institutions all the ideas and all the practical results of ancient thought. Embracing, organizing and propagating the new religion, she made it seem her own. Her language, her theology, her laws, her architecture made their way where the eagles of war had never winged their flight."

The Middle Ages accepted the idea of the universal dominion of Empire and Papacy, based upon the imprescriptible rights of Rome, without regard to the actions of individual emperors or popes or the actual exercise of their power. The human spirit was then "prostrated before authority and tradition" and the exercise of private judgment "was impossible to most and sinful to all." Life, with its ferocity, violence and disorder was made bearable by the passion for unity. The modern insistence on verification, individualism, and pluralism was unthinkable.

It is the story of this persistence of the Roman idea within ever-changing historical contexts which Bryce unfolds with style and clarity. This idea shaped Europe, or at least Western Europe, until, contemporaneously with the settlement of the New World, there emerged the philosophy of life and government upon which the United States is based. That Bryce's penetrating vision could embrace both the Holy Roman Empire of the Middle Ages and the United States, which from its beginnings was the most modern nation, testifies to the catholicity of his education and understanding.

When the Roman Empire was destroyed by the barbaric invasions, the conception of this Empire as a necessary part of the world's order did not vanish. The idea was admitted by the very conquerors who destroyed its representation on earth. It was accepted in its fullness by the Roman Church. It was cherished by the peoples who had formerly been vanquished by Rome and who now looked back upon it as a golden age of peace and order. The dark ages came to an end, when in 800 A.D. Charlemagne and the Pope restored the Empire in the west. Thereby they laid the foundation for the emergence of the Western world of Latins and Germans. This world remained the center of our understanding of history, until the eighteenth century, when Russia and the Near East entered into active partnership with it, and broadened its basis. Even this basis has become too narrow in our own day. The revitalization of Asia and Africa have transformed the idea of a single world history and world order, as envisaged by the Roman Empire, into an incipient reality.

Yet within the very narrow frame of the Stoic Roman Empire and the Christian Western Empire the idea of unity and universal order shone with an all-pervasive splendor of which our age shows no trace. For then this idea had its foundation, it was believed, in the very nature of the divine universe, in which an exact correspondence of heaven and earth reigned. The Holy Roman Church and the Holy Roman Empire were one and the same thing, seen from different sides. Both rested upon the universality of Rome. Their mystic dualism corresponded to the two natures of the Founder of the Church, he who was born into his earthly existence by divine providence under the reign of Augustus, the founder of the Roman Empire. Accordingly, it was believed that men's souls were entrusted to the Pope; their bodies to the Emperor.

At no time did factual reality correspond to theory. But this discrepancy was characteristic of the age and was not felt as such. "At no time in the world's history," Bryce writes, "has theory, professing all the while to control practice, been so utterly divorced from it. Ferocious and sensual, the age worshipped humility and asceticism; there has never been a purer ideal of love, nor a grosser profligacy of life." Magnificent theories were proclaimed which no one attempted to carry out. "While everyone believed in the rights of the Empire as a part of divine truth, no one would yield to them where his own passions or interests interfered. Resistance to God's Vicar might be, and indeed was, admitted to be a deadly sin, but it was one which few hesitated to commit." At no time was the theory of the Holy Roman Empire more strikingly set forth than in the treatise *De Monarchia* which Dante, the greatest and most representative mind of the age, wrote at the very moment when the last shred of real power was torn from the imperial dignity.*

V

Even at the height of the Middle Ages the idea of one Empire and one Church, as glorified by Dante, hardly took note of the fact that the Roman Empire continued in Constantinople, the new or second Rome, where Constantine the First had transferred and consecrated the capital. The truly Holy Roman Empire was there, for its history started not with a pagan Rome but with a city consecrated by Christian bishops. This eastern Roman Empire lasted for over one thousand years, from the accession of Arcadius in 395, when the real separation of East and West began, to the conquest of Constantinople by the Turks in 1453. The civil and military administration of the Eastern Empire was much superior to that of its western rival. Until recently scant attention was paid by Western thinkers and historians to the Roman Empire which continued in a legitimate line in Constantinople. Its advanced civilization has been carefully studied only since Bryce first published his book. After the fall of Constantinople the princes and people of Moscow, who were as much a religious as a political community, claimed the succession to the eastern, or true, Roman Empire. Moscow was proclaimed the new or Third Rome, which was to stand to the end of history, for a fourth Rome was regarded as inconceivable.

This eastern Empire was not disturbed by the conflict which raged in the West, where in the thirteenth century each of three different parties asserted itself as the true source of the imperial office: the Emperor, the Pope and the people of Rome.

---

*Dante's treatise is probably the most revealing single document of the medieval concept of the Empire. See in this book pp. 278-284 and the translation by Herbert W. Schneider, *On World-Government or De Monarchia* by Dante Alighieri (New York: The Liberal Arts Press, 1950).

In the thirteenth century the papal and imperial claims reached their high point. With the fall of the Hohenstaufen dynasty the imperial glory began to decline rapidly, never to recover. Fifty years later, the Popes removed their court from Rome to Avignon and this "Babylonish captivity" lasted for 70 years, to be followed immediately by the great Schism which lasted another forty years. The city of Rome has scarcely a building to commemorate this period; to her "they were times of turmoil and misery, times in which the shame of the present was embittered by recollections of the brighter past."

After the fourteenth century the Holy Roman Empire, in theory a world empire, became more and more a purely Germanic Empire. Yet the myth of its former glory survived as an illusion. The imperial dignity was extolled by writers whose imaginations were enthralled by the glories of a legendary past. "The Germans," Bryce writes, "had confounded the two characters of their sovereign so long, and grown so fond of the style and pretensions of a dignity whose possession appeared to exalt them above the other peoples of Europe, that it was now too late for them to separate the local from the universal monarch."

The most powerful of the Hohenstaufen emperors, Frederick Barbarossa, was believed to lie asleep deep down in the Kyffhäuser Mountain in central Germany. If Germany were ever in need of a saviour, he would rise and lead her to the glory of a new golden age. Compared with this certainty of salvation the actual events of German history and the realities of the world outside paled. In their hearts the Germans felt that their true ruler, the *heimliche Kaiser,* was ever ready to come to their rescue. Under the spell of such legends, Germans were sometimes in danger of losing sight of political realities and of abandoning themselves to wistful dreams.

The Reformation destroyed the very basis of an imperial idea which was founded on the assumption that the limits of Church and State were co-extensive. The united Christendom which the Empire was created to represent had now vanished. After exulting for centuries in the heritage of Roman rule, half of the Germans now turned against it to exult in Arminius, the barbaric prince who defeated the Romans. In the treaty of Westphalia of 1648 "the last link which bound Germany as a whole to Rome was snapped, the last of the principles by which the Empire had existed was abandoned." But the fiction and illusion continued for another one hundred and fifty years.

The official end came in August, 1806 when the last Holy Roman Emperor resigned the imperial dignity. A new claimant to the imperial title had arisen: Napoleon Bonaparte, who regarded himself as Charlemagne's successor and as lawful emperor of the West. His imperial throne, based on the two capitals of Paris and Rome, seemed the first on earth. Like Charlemagne, he wished to found the empire in collaboration with the Roman Church yet without allowing it to be weakened by papal claims. To the Ecclesiastical Committee, Napoleon declared on March 16, 1811: "The present epoch carries us back to the time of Charlemagne. All the kingdoms, principalities, and duchies which formed themselves out of the debris of the Empire have been rejuvenated under our laws. The Church of my empire is the Church of the Occident and of almost the whole of Christendom." In 1811 this Empire, with its frontiers on the Elbe, the Ebro and the Adriatic Sea, was practically coextensive with that of Charlemagne.

This new empire of the west collapsed when it challenged the empire of the east. The new Rome of Moscow turned back the new Rome of Napoleon. But the real victor was modern Britain. In the liberal nineteenth century a revival of Rome, whether in the west or in the east, was an anachronism. Napoleon's liberal opponent, Benjamin Constant, in his *De l'esprit de conquête et de l'usurpation dans leurs rapports avec la civilization européenne* (1813), saw in imperial wars the instrument of the past, and in commerce that of modern civilization.

"Carthage, fighting with Rome in ancient times, had to succumb; it had the force of circumstances against it. But if the fight between Rome and Carthage were taking place today, Carthage would have the universe on its side. *Elle aurait pour alliés les moeurs actuelles et le génie du monde.* (Carthage would have as her allies present-day morality and the spirit of the world)."

In 1806 the history of the Holy Roman Empire itself came to an end. Less than ten years later Napoleon's effort to assume its succession ended in disaster. At that point Bryce's original book ended too. Yet the imperial glory of the past continued to haunt the three peoples—Germans, French and Italians—who in various ways regarded themselves as its heirs. The century from 1850 to 1950 was filled with unfortunate attempts to revive the imperial idea, to fight the commercial spirit of the modern West on behalf of Roman virtue. The fascination of the myth of the past misled these peoples and their attempts at revival ended in disaster. In two additional chapters Lord Bryce told in the 1904 edition of his book, of the beginnings of this revival of the imperial idea. These two chapters, which are omitted in the present edition, no longer show the penetrating insight of the preceding chapters. They are filled with the spirit of an unfounded optimism about the trends which led to the renewal of the imperial idea, an optimism typical of British liberal thought in the second half of the nineteenth century as it contemplated developments on the European continent.

VI

The forty years between the first publication of Bryce's book (1864) and its final revision (1904) witnessed the unification of Italy and Germany, the two countries in which the idea of the Holy Roman Empire had found its terrestrial foundation. In one and the same year, 1870, Bismarck established the new German Empire on the victory of the Prussian army over imperial France, and the new Italian kingdom took possession of Rome, the ancient imperial seat with all its haunting memories. Bryce was in full sympathy with this trend of events. Without much hesitation he followed the official line taken at the time by German and Italian national historiography.

Bismarck's German Empire or Reich was, in spite of many differences, regarded by Bryce as being "in a real sense the representative" of the Holy Roman Empire. Bismarck's creation gave, according to Bryce, "a new and more cheerful meaning to all that has gone before. It is, in a moral and intellectual sense, the offspring of the old Empire." This was the theory then being proposed by the Prussian school of German historiography. Under the impact of the Prussian victories it was soon generally accepted, but it was an entirely new interpretation of German history and represented a break with the main line of German tradition.

This new interpretation shifted the center of German history from the west, that is, the Rhineland, to Prussia in the northeast. It made Protestantism its dominant and creative religion, and based this religion upon a strictly nation-centered concept. Its outlook was not only anti-Roman but anti-Western. It held that following the fall of the mighty Hohenstaufen, German history reached a new climax in the Prussian-led War of Liberation against France, and a fulfillment in Prussia's victory over France in 1870. Speaking of Prussia's rulers, the German historian Johann Gustav Droysen declared in 1848: "To the Hohenzollern belongs the place which has been empty since the days of the Hohenstaufen."

At the time of the great flowering of the German mind in the second half of the eighteenth century no German historian or representative thinker would have accepted this thesis. Prussia then appeared alien to the German mind. Its garrison-spirit was repugnant to the pacifist, cosmopolitan ideology of the average German intellectual. Travelling in southern Germany in the later years of the reign of Frederick the Great of Prussia, Friedrich Nicolai, the well-known Berlin bookseller and publisher, wrote that "these free people look down upon us poor people from Brandenburg as slaves." Eleven years before, Gotthold Ephraim Lessing, on August 25, 1769, wrote to Nicolai: "Don't tell me of your Berlin freedom of thinking and writing. It reduces itself exclusively to the liberty of saying as much nonsense about religion as one wishes. And by now the honest man must be ashamed to make use of this liberty. But let anyone in Berlin try to . . . tell the truth to the noble Court rabble there as Sonnenfels did in Vienna; let anyone in Berlin raise his voice for the rights of the subjects against exploitation and despotism, as is now being done even in France and Denmark, and you will soon learn which country is even today the most enslaved in Europe."

The great art historian, Johann Joachim Winckelmann, a Prussian subject, escaped to Rome and wrote in 1763 that he shuddered from head to foot whenever he thought of the Prussian despotism and of Frederick. This slave driver of peoples would transform his country into an abomination for men; "better to be a circumcised Turk than a Prussian." Another Prussian subject, Johann Gottfried Herder, advocated the dismemberment of Prussia for the happiness of its people and prophesied that Frederick's work would remain sterile and his Empire disintegrate.*

The paradoxical identification of Bismarck's Prussian Germany with the old Reich which had fascinated the imagination of the Middle Ages, had dangerous consequences for German political thought. "It was the tradition of the glorious past," Bryce writes, "when Germany led the world that made the Germans again a united people, the central power of continental

---

*On the interpretation of German history see Hans Kohn, *The Mind of Germany* (New York: Charles Scribner's Sons, 1960) and *The Idea of Nationalism* (Seventh Printing, New York: Macmillan, 1958) ch. VII.

Europe." The consciousness of being heirs to the Reich made the Germans feel much superior to the other peoples of Europe, a feeling entirely unknown to Kant or Goethe. The Germans made the mistake of regarding the temporary superiority of Bismarck's diplomacy and of Prussian arms as something permanent, something inherent in the national character and in history. In reality it was a passing phenomenon and the feeling of superiority only helped to make it more passing. But when the Bismarckian Prussian Empire collapsed in 1918, the Germans not only clung to its fundamental concept of a Berlin-centered Reich—the republican constitution of Weimar maintained the official title Deutsches Reich—but intensified it in proud defiance of the West.

The assumed heritage of the Roman Empire confused not only the Germans but also the Italians. It burdened the young and weak Italian nation with a legacy of the past which like a will-o'-the-wisp drew it from the patient mastering of reality to the world-embracing dreams of Roman ghosts. Giuseppe Mazzini, the prophet of Italian nationalist regeneration, wished to found it on the rock of eternal Rome. Twice Rome had guided mankind in the past, under the Caesars and under the Popes. Would not a third Rome, the Rome of the People, rise to even greater heights in the future? Writing in 1871, Mazzini demanded the creation of a vast colonial empire over the southern shores of the Mediterranean. "The Roman standard did float over those lands in the days when, after the fall of Carthage, the Mediterranean was named our sea. We were masters of the whole of that region up to the fifth century." This identification of present-day Italy with the Roman past haunted many Italians until 1945.*

---

*See Hans Kohn *Prophets and Peoples. Studies in Nineteenth Century Nationalism* (Fourth Printing, New York: Macmillan, 1957) ch. III, and Guido de Ruggiero, *The History of European Liberalism,* tr. by R. G. Collingwood (London: Oxford University Press, 1927) pp. 298-324.

A British contemporary, Lord Acton (1834-1902) recognized more clearly than did Bryce the dangers inherent in modern nationalism and the identification of this nationalism with past stages of history. In an article written in 1862 Acton warned that a state which identifies itself too closely with one nationality or one class tends to become absolute. Diversity, he wrote, is a corrective against intolerance. Deeply trained in the German method of scientific history which he helped to introduce in Britain, he had no illusions about the Prussian German Reich established in Berlin. As Regius Professor of Modern History in the University of Cambridge, he delivered a course of lectures on modern history in the academic years 1899 to 1900 and 1900 to 1901. Speaking of the Prussian government, he stressed its fundamental difference from the western type of government. "Government so understood is the intellectual guide of the nation, the promoter of wealth, the teacher of knowledge, the guardian of morality, the mainspring of the ascending movement of man. That is the tremendous power, supported by millions of bayonets, which grew up in the days of which I have been speaking at Petersburg, and was developed by much abler minds, chiefly at Berlin; and it is the greatest danger that remains to be encountered by the Anglo-Saxon race."*

No finality can be claimed for any historical idea or any historical form of government. The collapse of the Third Reich in Berlin and of the Third Rome on the Tiber may have laid the ghost of the Holy Roman Empire to its rest. Its two last representations were unholy travesties of a great idea of the past. Today the myth of the Reich seems to have lost its fascination for the German mind. There is no longer a Deutsches Reich but a Federal Republic of Germany. The center of

*See John Emerich Edward Dalberg-Acton, First Baron Acton, *Lectures on Modern History* (10th Printing, London: Macmillan, 1950; New York: Schocken Paperbacks, 1961) pp. 289, 314.

gravity has shifted from Prussia in the northeast, westward to the Rhine where it has traditionally belonged. The intellectual and social orientation of Germany is today no longer self-centered and turned against the West. Rather, Germany has again become part of the common Western development. The state of Prussia no longer exists and its former dominant class has been uprooted. The city of Königsberg, in eastern Prussia, where in 1701 the Electors of Brandenburg assumed the newly created royal crown of Prussia, has been renamed Kaliningrad. Thus the last sentence with which Bryce concluded his book in 1864 can, in slightly varied form, be applied to the Germans of today. The Reich, the Holy Roman Empire, which to the Germans of 1860 to 1945 loomed so large on the horizon of the past, will to the Germans of today sink lower and lower as they journey onward into the future. But its importance for the past history of Europe it can never lose.

New York, Fall 1960   HANS KOHN

THE HOLY ROMAN EMPIRE

THE HOLY ROMAN EMPIRE

CHAPTER I

INTRODUCTORY

OF those who in August, 1806, read in the newspapers that the Emperor Francis II had announced to the Germanic Diet his resignation of the imperial crown there were probably few who reflected that the oldest political institution in the world had come to an end. Yet it was so. The Empire which a note issued by a diplomatist on the banks of the Danube extinguished was the same which the crafty nephew of Julius had won for himself, against the powers of the East, beneath the cliffs of Actium; and which had preserved almost unaltered, through eighteen centuries of time, and through the greatest changes in extent, in power, and in character, a title and pretensions from which their ancient meaning had long since departed. Nothing else so directly linked the old world to the new — nothing else displayed so many strange contrasts of the present and the past, and summed up in those contrasts so much of European history. From the days of Constantine till far down into the Middle Ages it was, conjointly with the Papacy, the recognized centre and head of Christendom, exercising over the minds of men an influence such as its material strength could never have commanded.

It is of this influence and of the causes that gave it power rather than of the external history of the Empire that the following pages are designed to treat. That history is indeed full of interest and brilliancy, of grand characters and striking situations.   But it is a subject too vast for any single canvas.   Without a minuteness of detail sufficient to make its scenes dramatic, and give us a lively sympathy with the actors, a narrative history can have little value and still less charm.   But to trace with any minuteness the career of the Empire, would be to write the history of Christendom from the fifth century to the twelfth, of Germany and Italy from the twelfth to the nineteenth ; while even a narrative of more restricted scope, which should attempt to disengage from a general account of the affairs of those countries the events that properly belong to imperial history, could hardly be compressed within reasonable limits.   It is therefore better, declining so great a task, to attempt one simpler and more practicable though not necessarily inferior in interest ; to speak less of events than of principles, and endeavour to describe the Empire not as a State but as an Institution, an institution created by and embodying a wonderful system of ideas.   In pursuance of such a plan, the forms which the Empire took in the several stages of its growth and decline must be briefly sketched.   The characters and acts of the great men who founded, guided, and overthrew it must from time to time be touched upon.   But the chief aim of the treatise will be to dwell more fully on the inner nature of the Empire, as the most signal instance of the fusion of Roman and Teutonic elements in modern civilization : to shew how such a combination was possible ; how Charles and Otto were led to revive the imperial title in the West ; how far during the reigns of their successors it preserved the memory of its origin, and influenced the European commonwealth of nations.

Strictly speaking, it is from the year 800 A.D., when a King of the Franks was crowned Emperor of the Romans

by Pope Leo III, that the beginning of the Holy Roman
Empire must be dated. But in history there is nothing
isolated, and just as to explain a modern Act of Parliament or a modern conveyance of lands we must go back
to the feudal customs of the thirteenth century, so among
the institutions of the Middle Ages there is scarcely one
which can be understood until it is traced up either to
classical or to primitive Teutonic antiquity. Such a mode
of inquiry is most of all needful in the case of the Holy
Empire, itself no more than a tradition, a fancied revival
of departed glories. And thus one who seeks to explain
out of what elements the imperial system was formed,
might be required to scrutinize the antiquities of the
Christian Church, to survey the constitution of Rome in
the days when Rome was no more than the first of the
Latin cities, nay, to travel back yet further to that Jewish
theocratic polity whose influence on the minds of the
mediaeval priesthood was necessarily so profound. Practically, however, it may suffice to begin by glancing at the
condition of the Roman world in the third and fourth centuries of the Christian era. We shall then see the old
Empire with its scheme of absolutism fully matured; we
shall mark how the new religion, rising in the midst of a
hostile power, ends by embracing and transforming it;
and we shall be in a position to understand what impression the whole huge fabric of secular and ecclesiastical
government which Roman and Christian had piled up
made upon the barbarian tribes who pressed into the
charmed circle of the ancient civilization.

CHAPTER II

THE ROMAN EMPIRE BEFORE THE ENTRANCE OF THE BAR-BARIANS

THAT ostentation of humility which the subtle policy of Augustus had conceived, and the jealous hypocrisy of Tiberius maintained, was gradually dropped by their successors, till despotism became at last recognized in principle as the government of the Roman Empire. With an aristocracy decayed, a populace degraded, an army no longer recruited from Italy, the semblance of liberty that yet survived might be swept away with impunity. Republican forms had never been known in the provinces, and the aspect which the imperial administration had originally assumed there soon reacted on its position in the capital. Earlier rulers had disguised their supremacy by making a slavish senate the instrument of their more cruel or arbitrary acts. As time went on, even this veil was with-

drawn; and in the age of Septimius Severus the Emperor stood forth to the whole Roman world as the single centre and source of political power and action. The warlike character of the Roman State was preserved in his title of Commander (*Imperator*); his provincial lieutenants were military governors; and a more terrible enforcement of the theory was found in his practical dependence on the army, at once the origin and the support of his authority. But, as he united in himself every function of government, his sovereignty was civil as well as military. Laws ema-

nated from him; all officials acted under his commission; Chap. II.
the sanctity of his person bordered on divinity. This increased concentration of power was mainly required by the
necessities of frontier defence, for within there was more
decay than disaffection. Few troops were quartered
through the country: few fortresses checked the march
of armies in the struggles which placed Vespasian and (a
century later) Severus on the throne. The distant crash
of war from the Rhine or the Euphrates was scarcely
heard or heeded in the profound calm of the Mediterranean
coasts, where, after the extinction of piracy, fleets had
ceased to be maintained. No quarrels of race or religion
disturbed that calm, for all national distinctions were becoming merged in the idea of a common Empire. The
gradual extension of Roman citizenship through the *Obliteration*
founding of *coloniae*, first throughout Italy and then in *of national distinctions.*
the provinces, the working of the equalized and equalizing
Roman law, the even pressure of the government on all
subjects, the movements of population caused by commerce and the slave traffic, were steadily assimilating the
various peoples. Emperors who were for the most part
natives of the provinces cared little to cherish Italy or
even, after the days of the Antonines, to conciliate Rome.
It was their policy to keep open for every subject a career
by whose freedom they had themselves risen to greatness,
and to recruit the senate from the most illustrious families
in the cities of Gaul, Spain, and Asia. The edict by A.D. 211–217.
which Caracalla extended to all natives of the Roman
world the rights of Roman citizenship, though prompted
by no motives of generosity, proved in the end a boon.
Annihilating distinctions of legal status among freemen, it
completed the work which trade and literature and toleration to all beliefs but one were already performing, and
left, so far as we can tell, only one nation still cherishing

a national feeling.[a] The Jew was kept apart by his religion : but the Jewish people was already dispersed over the world. Speculative philosophy lent its aid to this general assimilation. Stoicism, with its doctrine of a universal system of nature, made minor distinctions between man and man seem insignificant : and by its teachers the idea of a world-commonwealth whereof all men are citizens was for the first time proclaimed. Alexandrian Neo-Platonism, uniting the tenets of many schools, and bringing the mysticism of Egypt and the East into connection with the logical philosophies of Greece, had opened up a new ground of agreement or controversy for *The capital.* the minds of all the world. Yet the commanding position of the Roman city was scarcely shaken. The actual power of her assemblies had indeed long since departed. Rarely were her senate and people permitted to choose the sovereign : more rarely still could they influence his policy. Neither law nor custom raised the inhabitants of the city above other subjects, or accorded to them any advantage in the career of civil or military ambition. As in time past Rome had sacrificed domestic freedom in making herself the mistress of others, so now in becoming the Universal State,[b] she, the conqueror, had descended to the level of the conquered.[c] But the sacrifice had not wanted its reward. From her came the laws and the language that had overspread the world :[d] at her feet

[a] As to this gift of citizenship, reference may be made to an essay on the Extension of Roman and English Law throughout the World in the author's *Studies in History and Jurisprudence*, Vol. I.

[b] As it was said, *Urbs fiebat Orbis.*

[c] Under Diocletian, the provincial land tax and provincial system of administration were introduced into Italy, and the four imperial residences were Milan, Treves, Sirmium (in Pannonia), and Nicomedia (in Bithynia).

[d] Condita est civitas Roma per quam Deo placuit orbem debellare terrarum et in unam societatem reipublicae legumque longe lateque pacare. — St. Augustine, *De Civit. Dei*, xviii. 22.

the nations laid the offerings of their labour : she was the CHAP. II.
head of the Empire and of civilization, and in riches, fame,
and splendour far outshone as well the other cities of
that time as the fabled glories of Babylon or Persepolis.

Scarcely had these slowly-working influences brought
about this unity, when other influences began to threaten
it. New foes assailed the frontiers ; while the loosening
of the structure within was shewn by the long struggles
for power which followed the death or deposition of each
successive emperor. In the period of anarchy after the
fall of Valerian, generals were raised by their armies in *A.D. 253–270.*
every part of the Empire, and ruled great provinces as
monarchs apart, owning no allegiance to the possessor
of the capital. The breaking-up of the Western half of
the Empire into separate kingdoms might have been
anticipated by two hundred years had the barbarian tribes
on the borders been bolder, or had there not arisen in
Diocletian a prince active and skilful enough to bind up *Diocletian,*
the fragments before they had lost all cohesion, meeting *A.D. 284–305.*
altered conditions by new remedies. The policy he adopted
of dividing and localizing authority recognized the fact that
the weakened heart could no longer make its pulsations
felt to the body's extremities. He parcelled out the
supreme power among four monarchs, ruling as joint-
emperors in four capitals, and then sought to give it a
factitious strength by surrounding it with an oriental pomp
which his earlier predecessors would have scorned. The
sovereign's person became more sacred, and was removed
further from the subject by the interposition of a host of
officials. The prerogative of Rome was menaced by the
rivalry of Nicomedia, and the nearer greatness of Milan.
Constantine trod in the same path, developing the system *Constantine,*
of titles into a sort of nobility, separating the civil from *A.D. 306–337.*
the military functionaries, placing counts and dukes along

the frontiers and in the cities, making the household larger, its etiquette stricter, its offices more dignified, though to a Roman eye degraded by their attachment to the monarch's person. The crown became, for the first time, the fountain of honour.

These expedients proved insufficient to prop the tottering fabric of imperial administration. Taxation, which grew always heavier as the number of persons who bore it was reduced, depressed the aristocracy : [e] population decreased, agriculture withered, serfdom spread : it was found more difficult to raise native troops and to pay any troops whatever. The removal by Constantine of the imperial residence to Byzantium, if it prolonged the life of the Eastern half of the Empire, shook the Empire as a whole, by accelerating the separation of East and West. By that removal Rome's self-abnegation that she might Romanize the world was completed ; for though the new capital preserved her name, and followed her customs and precedents, yet now the imperial sway ceased to be connected with the city which had created it. Thus did the idea of Roman monarchy become more universal ; for, having lost its local centre, it subsisted no longer by historic right only, but, so to speak, naturally, as a part of an order of things which a change in external conditions seemed incapable of disturbing. Henceforth the idea of a Roman Empire might stand unaffected by the disasters of the city. And though, after the partition of the Empire had been confirmed by Valentinian I, and finally settled on the death of Theodosius the Great, the seat of the Western government was removed first to Milan and then to Ravenna, neither event destroyed Rome's prestige, nor

---

[e] According to the vicious financial system that prevailed, the *curiales* in each city were required to collect the taxes, and when there was a deficit, to supply it from their own property.

the notion of a single imperial nationality common to all CHAP. II.
her subjects.   The Syrian, the Pannonian, the Briton, the
Spaniard, still called himself a Roman.[f]

For that imperial nationality was now beginning to be *Christianity.*
supported by a new and vigorous power.   The emperors
had indeed opposed Christianity as disloyal and revolutionary : had more than once put forth their whole strength
to root it out.   But the unity of the Empire, and the ease
of communication through its parts, had favoured the
spread of the new faith : persecution had scattered the
seeds more widely, had forced on it a firm organization,
had given it martyr-heroes and a history.   When Constantine, partly perhaps from a genuine moral sympathy,
yet doubtless also in the well-grounded belief that he had
more to gain from the zealous support of its professors
than he could lose by the aversion of those who still
cultivated a languid paganism, extended toleration to
Christianity and ultimately embraced it himself, it was
already a great political force, able, and not more able *Its alliance*
than willing, to repay him by aid and submission.   Yet *with the*
the league was struck in no mere mercenary spirit, for *State.*

[f] See the eloquent passage of Claudian, *In secundum consulatum Stilichonis,*
129 sqq., and especially the following lines (150–160) :
      ‘ Haec est in gremio victos quae sola recepit,
        Humanumque genus communi nomine fovit,
        Matris, non dominae, ritu ; civesque vocavit
        Quos domuit, nexuque pio longinqua revinxit.
        Huius pacificis debemus moribus omnes
        Quod veluti patriis regionibus utitur hospes :
        Quod sedem mutare licet : quod cernere Thulen
        Lusus, et horrendos quondam penetrare recessus :
        Quod bibimus passim Rhodanum, potamus Oronten,
        Quod cuncti gens una sumus.   Nec terminus unquam
        Romanae ditionis erit.’
St. Patrick (a younger contemporary of Claudian), in his Epistle to Coroticus,
speaks of the Christians of Gaul as Romans.

the league was inevitable.   Of the evils and dangers incident to such an alliance of the civil and the ecclesiastical authority as that which grew up in the century after Constantine, there was as yet no experience : of that antagonism between Church and State which to a modern appears so natural, there was not even an idea. In the Psalms and the historical books of the Old Testament (the influence of which on the early Christians was profound) the unity of the nation stands based upon religion : Israel is the people of Jehovah, owes Him collective as well as individual worship, conquers and prospers by His help.   Among the Romans religion had been an integral part of the political constitution, a matter far more of national or tribal or family feeling than of personal devotion to a spiritual power.[g]   Both in Israel and at Rome the mingling of religious with civic patriotism had been harmonious, giving strength and elasticity to the whole body politic.   So perfect a union was now no longer possible in the Roman Empire, for the Christian community had already a governing body of its own in those rulers and teachers on whom the growth of sacramentalism, and of sacerdotalism its necessary consequence, was every day conferring more and more power, while marking them off more sharply from the mass of the Christian people.   Since therefore the ecclesiastical organization could not be identical with the civil, it became its counterpart.   Suddenly called from danger and ignominy to the seat of power, and finding her inexperience perplexed by a sphere of action vast and varied, the Church was compelled to continue the process on which she had already entered of framing her government upon the model of the secular administration.   Where her own machinery was defective, as in the case of doctrinal dis-

[g] In the Roman jurisprudence, *ius sacrum* is a branch of *ius publicum*.

putes affecting the whole Christian world, she sought the
interposition of the Sovereign; in all else she strove not
to sink into, but to reproduce for her own ecclesiastical
purposes, the imperial system.   And just as with the
extension of the Empire all the independent rights of
districts, towns, or tribes had disappeared, so now the
primitive freedom and diversity of individual Christians
and local churches, already circumscribed by the frequent
struggles against heresy and schism, was finally overborne
by the idea of one Visible Catholic Church, uniform in
faith and ritual; uniform too in her relation to the civil
power and the increasingly oligarchical character of her
government.   Thus, under the combined force of doctrinal
theory and practical needs, there shaped itself a hierarchy
of patriarchs, metropolitans, and bishops, their jurisdiction,
although still chiefly spiritual, recognized, and after a time
enforced, by the laws of the State, their provinces and
dioceses usually corresponding to the administrative divisions of the Empire.   As no patriarch yet enjoyed more
than an honorary supremacy, the earthly head of the
Church — so far as she could be said to have a head —
was virtually the Emperor himself.   The presumptive
right to intermeddle in religious affairs which he had in
heathen times derived from the office of Pontifex Maximus, regularly assumed by the successors of Augustus,
was readily admitted; and the clergy, preaching the duty
of obedience now as it had been preached even in the
days of Nero and Decius,[h] were well pleased to see him

[h] 'Let every soul be subject unto the higher powers.   For there is no
power but from God: the powers that be are ordained of God.   Whosoever
therefore resisteth the power, resisteth the ordinance of God' (Rom. xiii. 1).
'Submit yourselves to every ordinance of man for the Lord's sake: whether
it be to the Emperor as supreme; or unto Governors, as unto them that are
sent by him for the punishment of evildoers, and for the praise of them that
do well' (1 Pet. ii. 13).   So Tertullian, writing circ. A.D. 200, says: 'Sed

preside in General Councils, issue edicts against heresy, and testify even by arbitrary measures his zeal for the advancement of the faith and the overthrow of pagan rites.[1] But though the tone of the Church remained humble, her strength waxed greater, nor were occasions wanting which revealed the future that was in store for her. The resistance to the Emperor of St. Athanasius (Archbishop of Alexandria), and his final triumph in the long struggle against the Arians, proved that the new society could put forth a power of opinion such as had never been known before: the abasement of Theodosius the Emperor before Ambrose the Archbishop admitted the supremacy of spiritual authority. In the decrepitude of old institutions, in the barrenness of literature and the feebleness of art, it was to the Church that the life and feelings of the people sought more and more to attach themselves; and when in the fifth century the horizon grew black with clouds of ruin, those who watched with despair or apathy the approach of irresistible foes, fled for comfort to the shrine of a religion which even those foes revered.

It embraces and preserves the imperial idea.

But that which we are above all here concerned to remark is, that this church system, demanding a more rigid uniformity in doctrine and organization, making more and more vital the notion of a visible body of worshippers united by participation in the same sacraments, maintained

---

quid ego amplius de religione atque pietate Christiana in imperatorem quem necesse est suspiciamus ut eum quem Dominus noster elegerit. Et merito dixerim, noster est magis Caesar, ut a nostro Deo constitutus.' — *Apologet.* cap. 34.

[1] Eusebius describes Constantine as a sort of 'Summus episcopus': οἷά τις κοινὸς ἐπίσκοπος ἐκ Θεοῦ καθεσταμένος συνόδους τῶν τοῦ Θεοῦ λειτουργῶν συνεκρότει. And Constantine (according to Eusebius) described himself to the bishops in a similar way : ὑμεῖς τῶν εἴσω τῆς ἐκκλησίας ἐγὼ δὲ τῶν ἐκτὸς ὑπὸ Θεοῦ καθεσταμένος ἂν εἴην.

and propagated afresh the feeling of a single Roman people CHAP. II.
throughout the world.   Christianity as well as civilization
became conterminous with the Roman Empire.[j]   To be
a Roman was to be a Christian : and this idea soon passed
into the converse.   To be a Christian was to be a Roman.

[j] See the book of Optatus, Bishop of Milevis (circ. A.D. 370), *Contra Dona-tistas.* 'Non enim respublica est in ecclesia, sed ecclesia in republica, id est, in imperio Romano, cum super imperatorem non sit nisi solus Deus' (p. 999 of vol. ii of Migne; *Patrologiae Cursus completus*).   The treatise of Optatus is full of interest, as shewing the growth of the idea of the visible Church, and of the primacy of Peter's chair, as constituting its centre and representing its unity.   In the end of the fifth century, the only Christian countries outside the limits of the Empire were Ireland and Armenia, and Armenia, maintaining a precarious existence beside the great Persian monarchy of the Sassanid kings, had been for a long time virtually dependent on the Roman power.

CHAPTER III

THE BARBARIAN INVASIONS

UPON a world so constituted did the barbarians of the North descend. From the dawn of history they shew as a dim background to the warmth and light of the Mediterranean coasts, changing little while kingdoms rise and fall in the South, only thought on when some hungry swarm comes down to pillage or to settle. It is always as foes that they are known. The Romans never forgot the invasion of Brennus; and their fears, renewed by the irruption of the Cimbri and Teutones, could not let them rest till the extension of the frontier to the Rhine and the Danube removed Italy from immediate danger. A little more perseverance under Tiberius, or again under Hadrian, would probably have reduced all Germany as far as the Baltic and the Oder. But the politic or jealous advice of Augustus [a] was followed, and it was only along the frontiers that Roman arts and culture affected the Teutonic races. Commerce was brisk; Roman envoys penetrated the forests to the courts of rude chieftains; adventurous barbarians entered the provinces, sometimes to admire, oftener, like the brother of Arminius,[b] to take service under the Roman flag, and rise to a distinction in the legion which some

---

[a] 'Addiderat consilium coercendi intra terminos imperii, incertum metu an per invidiam.' — Tac. *Ann.* i. 11.

[b] Tac. *Ann.* ii. 9.

14

feud denied them at home. This was found even more convenient by the hirer than by the hired; till by degrees barbarian mercenaries came to form the largest, and certainly the most efficient, part of the Roman armies. The bodyguard of Augustus had been so composed; the praetorians were generally selected from the bravest frontier troops, most of them German; the practice could not but increase with the extinction of the free peasantry, the growth of villenage, and the effeminacy of all classes. Emperors who were, like Maximin, themselves sprung from a barbarian stock, encouraged a system by whose means they had risen, and whose advantages they knew. After Constantine, the levies from outside the Empire form the majority of the troops; after Theodosius, a Roman is the exception. The soldiers of the Eastern Empire in the time of Arcadius are almost all Goths, vast bodies of whom had been settled in the provinces; while in the West, Stilicho [c] can oppose Rhodogast only by summoning the German auxiliaries from the frontiers. Along with this practice there had grown up another, which did still more to make the barbarians feel themselves members of the Roman State. The pride of the old republic had been exclusive, but under the Empire the maxim was accepted that neither birth nor race should exclude a subject from any post which his abilities deserved. This principle, which had removed all obstacles from the path of the Spaniard Trajan, the Thracian Maximin, the Arabian Philip, was afterwards extended to the conferring of honour and power on persons who did not even profess to have passed through the grades of Roman service, but remained leaders of their own tribes. Ariovistus had been soothed by the title of Friend of the Roman People; in the third century the insignia of the

Admitted to Roman titles and honours.

A.D. 405.

[c] Stilicho, the bulwark of the Empire, seems to have been himself a Vandal by extraction.

consulship[d] were conferred by Gallienus on Naulobatus a Herulian chief: Crocus and his Alemanni entered as an independent body into the service of Rome; along the Rhine whole tribes received, under the name of Laeti, lands within the provinces on condition of military service; and the foreign aid which the Sarmatian had proffered to Vespasian against his rival, and Marcus Aurelius had indignantly rejected in the war with Cassius, became the usual, at last the sole support of the Empire, in civil as well as in external strife.

Thus in many ways was the old antagonism broken down — Romans admitting barbarians to rank and office, barbarians catching something of the manners and culture of their neighbours. And thus when the final movement came, and the Teutonic tribes slowly established themselves through the provinces, they entered not as savage strangers, but as settlers knowing something of the system into which they came, and not unwilling to be considered its members; despising the degenerate provincials who struck no blow in their own defence, but full of respect for the majestic power which had for so many centuries confronted and instructed them.

Their feelings towards the Roman Empire.

Great during all these ages, but greatest when they were actually traversing and settling down in the Empire, must have been the impression which its elaborate machinery of government and mature civilization made upon the minds of the Northern invaders. With arms whose fabrication they had learned from their foes, these children of the forest conquered well-tilled fields, and entered towns whose busy workshops, marts stored with the productions of distant countries, and palaces rich in monuments of

---

[d] Not the consulship itself, but the *ornamenta consularia*. An Aquitanian chieftain was legate of Central Gaul (Lugdunensis) under the name of Julius Vindex in A.D. 68.

art, equally roused their wonder.   To the beauty of statuary
or painting they might often be blind, but the rudest mind
must have been awed by the massive piles with which
vanity or devotion, or the passion for amusement, had
adorned Milan and Verona, Arles, Treves, and Bordeaux.
A deeper awe would strike them as they gazed on the
crowding worshippers and stately ceremonial of Christianity, most unlike their own rude sacrifices.   The exclama-
tion of the Goth Athanarich, when led into the market-place
of Constantinople, may stand for the feelings of his nation :
'Without doubt the Emperor is a God upon earth, and he
who attacks him is guilty of his own blood.' [e]

The social and political system, with its cultivated language and literature, into which they came, would impress
fewer of the conquerors, but by those few would be admired beyond all else.   Its regular organization supplied
what they most needed and could least construct for themselves, and hence it was that the greatest among them
were the most desirous to preserve it.   Except Attila the
Hun, there is among these terrible hosts no destroyer ;
the wish of each leader is to maintain the existing order,
to spare life, to respect every work of skill and labour,
above all to perpetuate the methods of Roman administration, and rule the people as the deputy or successor of
their Emperor.   Titles conferred by him were the highest
honours they knew : they were also the only means of ac-
quiring something like a legal grant of authority, a claim
to the obedience of the provincial subject, and of turning
a patriarchal or military chieftainship into the regular
sway of an hereditary monarch.   Civilis had long since
endeavoured to govern his Batavians as a Roman general.[f]
Alarich became master-general of the armies of Illyricum.
Clovis exulted in the bestowal of an honorary consulship ;

Their desire to preserve its institutions.

[e] Jordanes, *De Rebus Geticis*, cap. 28.   [f] Tac. *Hist.* i and iv.

his grandson Theodebert addresses the Emperor Justinian as ' Father.'[g] Sigismund the Burgundian king, created count and patrician by the Emperor Anastasius, professed the deepest gratitude and the firmest faith to that Eastern court, which was powerless to help or to hurt him. ' My people is yours,' he writes, ' and to rule them delights me less than to serve you ; the hereditary devotion of my race to Rome has made us account those the highest honours which your military titles convey ; we have always preferred what an Emperor gave to all that our ancestors could bequeath. In ruling our nation we hold ourselves but your lieutenants : you, whose divinely-appointed sway no barrier bounds, whose beams shine from the Bosphorus into distant Gaul, employ us to administer the remoter regions of your Empire : your world is our fatherland.'[h]

A contemporary historian has recorded the remarkable disclosure of his own thoughts and purposes, made by one of the ablest of the barbarian chieftains, Athaulf the West Goth, the brother-in-law and successor of Alarich. ' It was at first my wish to destroy the Roman name, and erect in its place a Gothic empire, taking to myself the place and the powers of Caesar Augustus. But when experience taught me that the untameable barbarism of the Goths would not suffer them to live beneath the sway of law, and that to abolish the laws on which the state rests would destroy the state itself, I chose the glory of renewing and maintaining by Gothic strength the fame of Rome, desiring to go down to posterity as the restorer of that Roman power

[g] ' Praecellentissimo Domino et Patri.' — Letters printed in Dom Bouquet, iv, *Epp.* 15 and 16.

[h] Letter printed among the works of Avitus, Bishop of Vienne (Migne's *Patrologia*, vol. lix. p. 285).

This letter is obviously the composition not of Sigismund himself, but of Avitus, writing on Sigismund's behalf. But this makes it scarcely less valuable evidence of the feelings of the time.

which I could not replace.   Wherefore I avoid war and
strive for peace.'[1]

The records of the time, scanty as they are, shew us
how valuable was the experience of Roman officials to
princes who from leaders of tribes had become rulers of
wide lands ; and in particular how indispensable the aid of
the Christian bishops, the intellectual aristocracy of their
new subjects, whose advice could alone guide the policy of
the conqueror and secure the good-will of the vanquished.
Not only is this true ; it is but a small part of the truth,
one form of that manifold and overpowering influence
which the old system exercised over the intruding strangers not less than over its own children.   For it is hardly
too much to say that the thought of antagonism to the
Empire and the wish to extinguish it never crossed the
mind of the barbarians.[j]   The conception of that Empire
was too universal, too august, too enduring.   It was everywhere around them, and they could remember no time
when it had not been so.   It had no association of people
or place whose fall could seem to involve that of the whole
fabric ; it had that connection with the Christian Church
which made it all-embracing and venerable.

[1] ' Referre solitus est (sc. Ataulphus) se in primis ardenter inhiasse : ut
obliterato Romanorum nomine Romanum omne solum Gothorum imperium
et faceret et vocaret : essetque, ut vulgariter loquar, Gothia quod Romania
fuisset ; fieretque nunc Ataulphus quod quondam Caesar Augustus.   At ubi
multa experientia probavisset, neque Gothos ullo modo parere legibus posse
propter effrenatam barbariem, neque reipublicae interdici leges oportere sine
quibus respublica non est respublica, elegisse se saltem, ut gloriam sibi de
restituendo in integrum augendoque Romano nomine Gothorum viribus quae-
reret, habereturque apud posteros Romanae restitutionis auctor postquam
esse non potuerat immutator.   Ob hoc abstinere a bello, ob hoc inhiare paci
nitebatur.' — Orosius, vii. 43.

[j] Athaulf formed only to abandon it.

When in A.D. 587 Reccared, king of the West Goths of Spain, renounced
Arianism to adopt the orthodoxy of the Empire, he called himself Flavius.

There were especially two ideas whereon it rested, and from which it obtained a peculiar strength and a peculiar direction. The one was the belief that as the dominion of Rome was universal, so must it be eternal. Nothing like it had been seen before. The empire of Alexander had lasted a short lifetime; and within its wide compass were included many arid wastes, and many tracts where none but the roving savage had ever set foot. That of the Italian city had for fourteen generations embraced all the most wealthy and populous regions of the civilized world, and had laid the foundations of its power so deep that they seemed destined to last for ever. If Rome moved slowly for a time, her foot was always planted firmly: the ease and swiftness of her later conquests proved the solidity of the earlier; and to her, more justly than to his own city, might the boast of the Athenian statesman be applied: that she advanced farthest in prosperity, and in adversity drew back the least. From the end of the republican period her poets, her orators, her jurists, ceased not to repeat the claim of world-dominion, and confidently predict its eternity.[k] The proud belief of his countrymen which Virgil had expressed —

> ' His ego nec metas rerum, nec tempora pono:
> Imperium sine fine dedi ' —

was shared by the early Christians when they prayed for the persecuting power whose fall would bring Antichrist upon earth. Lactantius (a contemporary of Constantine) writes: 'When Rome the head of the world shall have fallen, who can doubt that the end is come of human

[k] See, among other passages, Varro, *De lingua Latina*, iv. 34; Cic. *Pro Domo*, 33; Virg. *Aen.* ix. 448; Hor. *Od.* iii. 30, 8; Tibull. ii. 5. 23; Ovid, *Am.* i. 15. 26; *Trist.* iii. 7. 51; and cf. the Digest of Justinian, book xiv. 2. 9; and i. 1. 33 ('Roma communis nostra patria'). The phrase 'urbs aeterna' appears in a constitution issued by Valentinian III (*Nov. Valent.* 17).

Tertullian speaks of Rome as 'civitas sacrosancta.'

things, aye, of the earth itself. She, she alone is the state by which all things are upheld even until now; wherefore let us make prayers and supplications to the God of heaven, if indeed His decrees and His purposes can be delayed, that that hateful tyrant come not sooner than we look for, he for whom are reserved fearful deeds, who shall pluck out that eye in whose extinction the world itself shall perish.'[1] With the triumph of Christianity this belief had found a new basis. For as the Empire had decayed, the Church had grown stronger: and now while the one, trembling at the approach of the destroyer, saw province after province torn away, the other, rising in stately youth, prepared to fill her place and govern in her name, and in doing so, to adopt and sanctify and propagate anew the notion of a universal and unending state.

The second chief element in this conception was the association of such a state with its absolute and irresponsible head, the Emperor. The hatred to the name of King, which their earliest political struggles had left in the Romans, by attaching to their ruler a new and strange title, marked him off from all the other sovereigns of the world. To the provincials especially he became an awful impersonation of the great machine of government which moved above and around them. It was not merely that he was, like a modern king, the centre of power and the dispenser of honour: his pre-eminence, broken by no comparison with other princes, by the ascending ranks of no titled aristocracy, had in it something almost supernatural. The right of legislation had become vested in him alone: the decrees of the people, and resolutions of the senate, and edicts of the magistrates were, during the last three centuries, replaced by imperial 'Constitutions'; his domestic council, the Consistory, was the supreme

Sanctity of the imperial name.

[1] See Note I at the end.

court of appeal; his interposition, like that of some terrestrial Providence, was invoked, and legally provided so to be, to reverse or overleap the ordinary rules of law.[m] From the time of Julius Caesar and Augustus his person had been hallowed by the office of chief pontiff [n] and the tribunician power; to swear by his head was considered the most solemn of all oaths;[o] his effigy was sacred,[p] even on a coin; to him or to his Genius temples were erected and divine honours paid while he lived;[q] and when, as it was expressed, he ceased to be among men, the title of Divus was accorded to him, after a solemn consecration.[r] In the confused multiplicity of mythologies, the worship of the Emperor was the only worship common to the whole Roman world, and was therefore

[m] For example, by the 'restitutio natalium,' and the 'adrogatio per rescriptum principis,' or, as it is expressed, 'per sacrum oraculum.'

[n] Even the Christian Emperors took the title of Pontifex Maximus, till Gratian refused it as unlawful: ἀθέμιστον εἶναι Χριστιάνῳ τὸ σχῆμα νομίσας. — Zosimus, lib. iv. cap. 36. Pope Gelasius I (*Tractat.* iv. 11), noting that Melchizedek had been both king and priest, says that the Devil imitated this arrangement when he made the Roman Emperors chief pontiffs; but when Christ the true King and Priest came, He provided that the two offices should be thereafter distinct.

[o] 'Maiore formidine et callidiore timiditate Caesarem observatis quam ipsum ex Olympo Iovem, et merito, si sciatis. . . . Citius denique apud vos per omnes Deos quam per unum genium Caesaris peieratur.' — Tertull. *Apolog.* c. xxviii.

Cf. Zos. v. 51: εἰ μὲν γὰρ πρὸς τὸν θεὸν τετυχήκει διδόμενος ὅρκος, ἦν ἂν ὡς εἰκὸς παριδεῖν ἐνδιδόντας τῇ τοῦ θεοῦ φιλανθρωπίᾳ τὴν ἐπὶ τῇ ἀσεβείᾳ συγγνώμην. ἐπεὶ δὲ κατὰ τῆς τοῦ βασιλέως ὀμωμόκεσαν κεφαλῆς, οὐκ εἶναι θεμιτὸν αὐτοῖς εἰς τὸν τοσοῦτον ὅρκον ἐξαμαρτεῖν.

[p] Tac. *Ann.* i. 73; iii. 38, etc.

[q] It is curious that this should have begun in the first years of the Empire. See, among other passages that might be cited from the Augustan poets, Virg. *Georg.* i. 24; iv. 560; Hor. *Od.* iii. 3. 11; Ovid, *Epp. ex Ponto*, iv. 9. 105.

[r] Hence Vespasian's dying jest, 'Ut puto, deus fio.' The title was not conferred upon Emperors of evil memory.

that usually proposed as a test to the Christians on their
trial. Under the new religion the form of adoration vanished, the sentiment of reverence remained : and the right
to control the Church as well as the State, admitted by
the bishops assembled in the first oecumenical council at
Nicaea, and frequently exercised by the sovereigns of Constantinople, made the Emperor hardly less essential to the
new conception of a world-wide Christian monarchy than
he had been to the military despotism of old.

These considerations explain why the men of the fifth
century, clinging to preconceived ideas, and filled with the
belief, drawn from Jewish prophecy, that the great Fourth
Kingdom was to last till the end of the world, refused to
believe in that dissolution of the Empire which they saw
with their own eyes. Because it could not die, it lived.
And there was in the slowness of the change and its
external aspect, as well as in the fortunes of the capital,
something to favour the illusion. The Roman name was
shared by every subject; the Roman city was no longer
the seat of government, nor did her capture extinguish
the imperial power, for the maxim was now accepted,
Where the Emperor is, there is Rome.[8] But her continued existence, not permanently occupied by any conqueror, striking the nations with an awe which the history
or the external splendours of Constantinople, Milan, or
Ravenna could nowise inspire, was an ever new assertion
of the endurance of the Roman race and dominion. Dishonoured and defenceless, the spell of her name was still
strong enough to arrest the conqueror in the moment of
triumph. The irresistible impulse that drew Alarich was
one of glory or revenge, not of destruction : the Hun
turned back from Aquileia with a vague fear upon him :
the Ostrogoth adorned and protected his splendid prize.

[8] ὅπου ἂν ὁ βασιλεὺς ᾖ, ἐκεῖ ἡ Ῥώμη — says Herodian.

In the history of the last days of the Western Empire, two points deserve special remark: its continued union with the Eastern branch, and the way in which its ideal dignity was respected while its representatives were despised. Stilicho was the last statesman who could have saved it. After his death, and after the City had been captured by Alarich in A.D. 410, the fall of the Western throne, though delayed for two generations by traditional reverence, became practically certain. While one by one the provinces were abandoned by the central government, left either to be occupied by invading tribes or to maintain a precarious independence, like Britain and the Armorican cities, by means of municipal unions, Italy lay at the mercy of the barbarian auxiliaries and was governed by their leaders. The degenerate line of Theodosius might have seemed to reign by hereditary right, but after their extinction in Valentinian III it was from the haughty Ricimer, general of the barbarian troops, that each phantom Emperor — Maximus, Avitus, Majorian, Anthemius, Olybrius — received the purple only to be stripped of it

when he presumed to forget his dependence. Though the division between Arcadius and Honorius had definitely severed the two realms for administrative purposes, they were still deemed to constitute a single Empire, and the rulers of the East interfered more than once to raise to the Western throne princes they could not protect upon it. Ricimer's insolence quailed before the shadowy grandeur of the imperial title: his ambition, and that of Gundobald his successor, were bounded by the name of Patrician. The bolder genius of Odoacer,[t] commander of the barbarian

[t] Odoacer or Odovacar, as it seems his name ought to be written, is usually, but incorrectly, described as a King of the Heruli, who led his people into Italy and overthrew the Empire of the West; others call him King of the Rugii, or Skyrri, or Turcilingi, or even of the Goths, for the name 'Goth' was sometimes used to denote the Teutonic invaders generally. The truth

auxiliaries, resolved to abolish an empty pageant, and extinguish the title and office of Emperor in the West. Yet over him too the spell had power; and as the Gaulish warrior had gazed on the silent majesty of the senate in a deserted city, so the Herulian revered the power before which the world had bowed, and though there was no force to check or to affright him, shrank from grasping in his own barbarian hand the sceptre of the Caesars. When, at Odoacer's bidding, Romulus, nicknamed Augustulus, the boy whom a whim of fate had chosen to be the last native Caesar of Rome, had formally announced his resignation to the senate, a deputation from that body proceeded to the Eastern court to lay the insignia of royalty at the feet of the reigning Emperor Zeno. The West, they declared, no longer required an Emperor of its own: one monarch sufficed for the world; Odoacer was qualified by his wisdom and courage to be the protector of their state, and upon him Zeno was entreated to confer the title of Patrician and the administration of the Italian provinces.[u] The Emperor, though he reminded the Senate that their request ought rather to have been made to the lately dispossessed Western Emperor Julius Nepos, granted what he could not refuse, and wrote to Odoacer, address-

Its extinction by Odoacer, A.D. 476.

seems to be that he was not a king at all, but the son of a Skyrrian chieftain (Edecon, possibly the same Edecon as the one whom Attila sent as an envoy to Constantinople), whose personal merits made him chosen by the barbarian auxiliaries to be their leader. The Skyrri were a small tribe, apparently akin to the more powerful Heruli, whose name is often extended to them.

[u] Αὔγουστος ὁ Ὀρέστου υἱὸς ἀκούσας Ζήνωνα πάλιν τὴν βασιλείαν ἀνακεκτῆσθαι τῆς ἕω. . . . ἠνάγκασε τὴν βουλὴν ἀποστεῖλαι πρεσβείαν Ζήνωνι σημαίνουσαν ὡς ἰδίας μὲν αὐτοῖς βασιλείας οὐ δέοι, κοινὸς δὲ ἀποχρήσει μόνος ὢν αὐτοκράτωρ ἐπ' ἀμφοτέροις τοῖς πέρασι. τὸν μέντοι Ὀδόαχον ὑπ' αὐτῶν προβεβλῆσθαι ἱκανὸν ὄντα σώζειν τὰ παρ' αὐτοῖς πράγματα πολιτικὴν ἐχὼν νοῦν καὶ σύνεσιν ὁμοῦ καὶ μάχιμον, καὶ δεῖσθαι τοῦ Ζήνωνος πατρικίου τε αὐτῷ ἀποστεῖλαι ἀξίαν καὶ τὴν τῶν Ἰτάλων τουτῷ ἐφεῖναι διοίκησιν.— *Corp. Scr. Hist. Byzant.*, vol. xix. p. 235 (Excerpta e Malchi *Hist.*).

ing him as Patrician.   Assuming the title of King,[x] Odoacer continued the consular office, respected the civil and ecclesiastical institutions of his subjects, and ruled for fourteen years under the nominal suzerainty of the Eastern Emperor.[y]   There was thus legally no extinction of the Western Empire at all, but only a reunion of East and West.   In form, and to some extent also in the belief of men, things now reverted to their state during the first two centuries of the Empire, save that New Rome on the Bosphorus instead of Old Rome on the Tiber was the centre of the civil government.   The joint tenancy which had been conceived by Diocletian, carried further by Constantine, renewed under Valentinian I and again at the death of Theodosius, had come to an end ; once more did a single Emperor sway the sceptre of the world, and head an undivided Catholic Church.   To those who lived at the time, this year (A.D. 476) was no such epoch as it has since become, nor was any impression made on men's minds commensurate with the real significance of the event.   It is, indeed, one of the most striking instances in history of a change whose magnitude was not perceived until long after it occurred.   For though the cessation of an Emperor reigning in the West did not destroy the Empire in idea, nor wholly even in fact, its consequences were from the first immense.   It hastened the developement of a Latin as opposed to Greek and Oriental forms of Christianity : it emancipated the Popes : it gave a new character

[x] Not king of Italy, as is often said. The barbarian kings did not for several centuries employ territorial titles; *Rex Angliae* is not seen till Henry I : *Rex Franciae* not till Henry IV (of France), and Jordanes and Cassiodorus tell us that Odoacer never so much as assumed the insignia of royalty; but there is a coin on which he appears as ʻrex.'

[y] As to Odoacer and the occurrences of A.D. 476, cf. Hodgkin, *Italy and her Invaders*, vol. ii. p. 518 sqq.

[z] Statues of Zeno as reigning Emperor were set up in Rome.

to the projects and government of the Teutonic rulers of   CHAP. III.
the Western countries.   But the importance of remembering its formal aspect to those who witnessed it will be felt
as we approach the era when the Empire was revived by
Charles the Frank.

Odoacer's monarchy was not more oppressive than were   *Odoacer.*
those of the barbarian kings who were reigning in Gaul,
Spain, and Africa.   But the confederated mercenary troops
who supported it were a loose swarm of predatory tribes :
themselves without cohesion, they could take no firm
root in Italy.   Under his rule no progress seems to have
been made towards the reorganization of society ; and
the first real attempt to blend the peoples and maintain
the traditions of Roman wisdom in the hands of a new
and vigorous race was reserved for a more famous chieftain, the greatest of all the barbarian conquerors, the forerunner of the first barbarian Emperor, Theodorich the
Ostrogoth.   The aim of his reign, though he professed   *Theodorich,*
deference to the Eastern court which had favoured the   A.D. 493-
invasion in which he overthrew Odoacer, and whose titular   526.
supremacy he did not reject,[a] was the establishment of
what would have become a national monarchy in Italy.
Brought up as a hostage in the court of Constantinople,
he learned to know the advantages of an orderly and cultivated society and the principles by which it must be
maintained ; called in early manhood to roam as a warrior-
chief over the plains of the Danube, he acquired along
with the arts of command a sense of the superiority of

[a] 'Nil deest nobis imperio vestro famulantibus,' writes Theodorich to
Zeno : So to Anastasius I, 'Pati vos non credimus inter utrasque respublicas
quarum semper unum corpus sub antiquis principiis fuisse declaratur aliquid
discordiae permanere. . . . Romani regni unum velle, una semper opinio sit'
(Cassiod. *Variar.* i. 1).   Cf. Jordanes, *De Rebus Geticis*, cap. 57.   So in a
letter to the Emperor Anastasius 'Regnum nostrum imitatio vestri' (Cassiod.
Variar. i. 1).

his own people in valour and energy and truth. When the defeat and death of Odoacer had left both Italy and Sicily at his mercy, he sought no further conquest, easy as it would have been to tear away new provinces from the Eastern realm, but strove only to preserve and strengthen the ancient polity of Rome, to breathe into her decaying institutions the spirit of a fresh life, and without endangering the military supremacy of his own Goths, to conciliate by indulgence and gradually raise to the level of their masters the degenerate population of Italy.　The Gothic nation appears from the first less cruel in war and more sage in council than any of their Germanic brethren:[b] all that was noble among them shone forth now in the rule of the greatest of the Amals.　From his palace at Verona,[c] commemorated in the song of the Nibelungs, he issued equal laws for Roman and Goth, and bade the intruder, if he must occupy part of the lands, at least respect the goods and the person of his fellow subject.　Jurisprudence and administration remained in native hands : two annual consuls, one named by Theodorich, the other by the Eastern monarch, presented an image of the ancient state; and while agriculture and the arts revived in the provinces, Rome herself celebrated the visits of a master who provided for the wants of her people and preserved with care the monuments of her former splendour.[d] With peace and plenty men's minds took hope, and the study of letters revived.　The last gleam of classical literature gilds the reign of the barbarian.

By the consolidation of the two races under one wise

[b] ' Unde et paene omnibus barbaris Gothi sapientiores exstiterunt Graecisque paene consimiles.' — Jord. cap. 5.

[c] See Note II at the end.

[d] He restored some of the buildings which were already falling to ruin in the Roman Forum.　Bricks stamped with his name were found in 1902 near the south-west end of the recently uncovered floor of the Basilica Aemilia.

government, Italy might have been spared six hundred years of gloom and degradation. It was not so to be. Theodorich was tolerant, but toleration was itself an offence in the eyes of his orthodox subjects: the Arian Goths were and remained strangers and enemies among the Catholic Italians. Scarcely had the sceptre passed from the hands of Theodorich to his weaker offspring, when Justinian, who had viewed with jealousy the greatness of his nominal lieutenant, determined to assert his dormant rights over Italy and Sicily; its people welcomed Belisarius as a deliverer, and in the long struggle that followed the race and name of the Ostrogoths perished for ever. Thus again reunited in fact, as it had been all the while united in theory, to the Roman Empire, Italy was divided into counties and dukedoms, and obeyed the exarch of Ravenna, viceroy of the East Roman court, till the arrival of the Lombards in A.D. 568 drove him from some districts, and left him only a feeble authority over the Eastern and Southern parts of the peninsula.

Italy and Sicily conquered by Justinian, A.D. 535–553.

Beyond the Alps, though the Roman population had by this time ceased to seek help from the Eastern sovereigns, the Empire's rights were still deemed to subsist, though as respects Gaul they were deemed to have been yielded by Justinian to the Franks.[e] As has been said,

The transalpine provinces.

e Procopius tells us that when the Ostrogoths found themselves unable to defend their territories in South-eastern Gaul, they yielded these to Theodebert, king of the Franks, who thereupon obtained a confirmation of his possession from Justinian. Thus the barbarians obtained Marseilles, and celebrated at Arles the equestrian contest, probably the *ludus Troianus,* which had been instituted by Augustus, καὶ νῦν κάθηνται μὲν ἐν τῇ Ἀρελάτῳ τὸν ἱππικὸν ἀγῶνα θεώμενοι (*Bell. Goth.* iii. 33). He adds that the Franks did not think their acquisition of Gaul secure until it had been formally ratified by the Emperor.

The (almost contemporary) Life of St. Trevirius says that the saint lived 'eo tempore quo Gallia sub imperii iure Iustini consulis (the Emperor Justin I) exstitit,' and refers to the reign of Theodebert as the time when 'reges Gallia-

those rights had been admitted by the conquerors them-selves : by Athaulf, when he reigned in Aquitaine as the vicar of Honorius, and recovered Spain from the Suevi to restore it to its ancient masters; by the West Gothic kings of Spain, when they permitted the Mediterranean cities to send tribute to Constantinople; by Clovis, when, after the representatives of the old government, Syagrius and the Armorican cities, had been conquered or absorbed, and the West Gothic kingdom in Aquitaine had been over-thrown, he received with delight from the Eastern emperor Anastasius the grant of a Roman dignity to confirm his possession. Arrayed like a Fabius or Valerius in the consul's purple robe and senatorial chlamys, the Sicambrian chieftain rode through the streets of Tours, while the shout of the provincials hailed him Augustus.[f] They already obeyed him, but his power was now legalized in their eyes, and it was not without a melancholy pride that they saw the terrible conqueror himself yield to the spell of the Roman name, and do homage to the enduring majesty of their legitimate sovereign.

Lingering influences of Rome.

Yet the severed limbs of the Empire forgot by degrees their original unity. As in the breaking up of the old society, which we trace from the sixth to the eighth cen-tury, rudeness and ignorance grew apace, as language and manners were changed by the infiltration of Teutonic settlers, as men's thoughts and hopes and interests were

rum Francorumque suae ditioni, sublato imperii iure, gubernacula ponerent, et sublata Reipublicae dominatione, propria fruerentur potestate.'—Extract from *Vita S. Trevir.* in Dom Bouquet, iii. 441.

[f] 'Igitur Chlodovechus ab imperatore Anastasio codicillos de consulatu accepit, et in basilica beati Martini tunica blattea indutus est et chlamyde, imponens vertici diadema . . . et ab ea die tanquam consul aut (= et) Augustus est vocitatus.' — Gregory of Tours, ii. 38. He may probably have also received the title of Patrician: a poem in Dom Bouquet, ii. 538, says of him, 'Patricius magno sublimis fulsit honore.'

narrowed by isolation from their fellows, as the organization of the Roman province and the Germanic tribe alike dissolved into a chaos whence the new order began to shape itself, dimly and doubtfully as yet, the memory of the old Empire, its symmetry, its sway, its civilization, must needs wane and fade. It might have perished altogether but for the two enduring witnesses Rome had left — her Church and her Law. The barbarians had at first associated Christianity with the Romans from whom they learned it: the Romans had used it as their only bulwark against oppression. The hierarchy were the natural leaders of the people, and the necessary councillors of the king. Their power grew with the decay of civil government and the spread of superstition; and when the Frank found it too valuable to be abandoned to the vanquished people, he insensibly acquired the feelings and policy of the order which he entered.

Religion.

As the Empire fell to pieces, and the new kingdoms which the conquerors had founded began in their turn to dissolve, the Church clung more closely to her unity of faith and discipline, the common bond of all Christian men. That unity must have a centre, that centre was Rome. A succession of able and zealous pontiffs extended her influence — the sanctity and the writings of Gregory the Great were famous through all the West. Never permanently occupied by barbarians, she retained her peculiar character and customs, and laid the foundations of a power over men's souls more durable than that which she had lost over their bodies.[g] Only second in

Jurisprudence.

g Even so early as the middle of the fifth century, St. Leo the Great could say to the Roman people, 'Isti (*sc.* Petrus et Paulus) sunt qui te ad hanc gloriam provexerunt ut gens sancta, populus electus, civitas sacerdotalis et regia, per sacram B. Petri sedem caput orbis effecta latius praesideres religione divina quam dominatione terrena.' — *Sermon on the Feast of SS. Peter and Paul.* (Opp. *ap.* Migne, tom. i. p. 336.)

importance to this influence was that which was exercised by the permanence of the old law, and of its creature the municipal organization of the cities. The barbarian invaders retained the customs of their ancestors, characteristic memorials of a rude people, as we see them in the Salic law or in the ordinances of Ini and Alfred. But the subject population and the clergy continued to be governed by that elaborate system which the genius and labour of many generations had raised to be the most lasting monument of Roman greatness.

The civil law had maintained itself in Spain and Southern Gaul, nor was it utterly forgotten even in the North, in Britain, on the borders of Germany. Revised collections of extracts from the Theodosian Code and other Roman law books were issued by the West Gothic and Burgundian princes.[h] For some centuries it was the patrimony of the subject population everywhere, and in Aquitaine and Italy has outlived feudalism. The presumption that all men were to be judged by it who could not be proved to be subject to some other law continued to be accepted down to the end of the Middle Ages.[i] Its phrases, its forms, its courts, its subtlety and precision, all recalled the strong and cultivated society which had produced it. Other

[h] The Lex Romana Burgundionum, published by the Burgundian kings at the beginning of the sixth century, and the Lex Romana Visigothorum (*Breviarium Alaricianum*), published in or about A.D. 506, continued to form bodies of written law which were in use for a long time, and became the kernel of the customary law which grew up in South-eastern and Southern Gaul.

Agathias, writing at Constantinople in the middle of the sixth century, says the Franks had adopted much of the Roman administration and law, οἱ Φράγγοι πολιτείᾳ ὡς τὰ πολλὰ χρῶνται Ῥωμαϊκῇ καὶ νόμοις τοῖς αὐτοῖς καὶ τὰ ἄλλα ὁμοίως ἀμφί τε τὰ συμβόλαια καὶ γάμους καὶ τὴν τοῦ θείου θεραπείαν νομίζουσιν (*Hist.* i. 2).

[i] 'Ius Romanum est adhuc in viridi observantia et eo iure praesumitur quilibet vivere nisi adversum probetur,' says Maranta in the sixteenth century.

motives, as well as those of kindness to their subjects, made the new kings favour it ; for it exalted their prerogative, and the submission enjoined by it on one class of their subjects soon came to be demanded from the other, by their own Teutonic customs almost the equals of the prince. Considering attentively how many of the old institutions continued to subsist, and studying the ideas of that time, as they are faintly preserved in its scanty records, it seems hardly too much to say that in the eighth century the Roman Empire still existed in the West : existed in men's minds as a power weakened, delegated, suspended, but not destroyed.

It is easy for those who read the history of an age in the light of those that followed it, to perceive that in this men erred ; that the tendency of events was wholly different ; that society had entered on a new phase, wherein every change did more to localize authority and strengthen the aristocratic principle at the expense of the despotic. We can see that other forms of life, more full of promise for the distant future, had already begun to shew themselves. They, with no type of power or beauty but that which had filled the imagination of their forefathers, and now loomed on them grander than ever through the mist of centuries, mistook (as did many of the great spirits of Italy down to the days of Dante and Rienzo) memories for hopes, and sighed only for the renewal of its strength. Events were at hand by which these hopes seemed destined to be gratified.

CHAPTER IV

RESTORATION OF THE EMPIRE IN THE WEST

IT was towards Rome as their ecclesiastical capital that the thoughts and hopes of the men of the sixth and seventh centuries were constantly directed. Yet not from Rome, feeble and corrupt, nor on the exhausted soil of Italy, was the deliverer to arise. Just when, as we may suppose, the vision of a renewal of imperial authority in the Western provinces was beginning to vanish away, there appeared in the furthest corner of Europe, sprung of a race but lately brought within the pale of civilization, a line of chieftains devoted to the service of the Holy See, and among them one whose power, good fortune, and heroic character pointed him out as worthy of a dignity to which doctrine and tradition had attached a sanctity almost divine.

The Franks. Of the new monarchies that had risen on the ruins of Rome, that of the Franks was by far the greatest. In the third century they appear, with Saxons, Alemanni, and Thuringians, as one of the greatest German tribe leagues. The Sicambri (for it seems probable that this famous race was a chief source of the Frankish nation) had now laid aside their former hostility to Rome, and her future representatives were thenceforth, with few intervals, her faithful allies. Many of their chiefs rose to high places: Malarich receives from Jovian the charge of the Western provinces; Bauto and Mellobaudes figure in the days of Theodosius

34

and his sons; the legendary Merovech (grandfather of
Clovis, and supposed to be the son of a water-sprite),
whose name has given itself to the Merwing dynasty, is
said to have fought under Aetius against Attila in the
great battle of Chalons; his countrymen endeavoured in
vain to save Gaul from the Suevi and Burgundians.   Not
till the Empire was evidently helpless did they claim a
share of the booty; then Clovis, or Chlodovech, chief
of the Salian tribe, leaving his kindred the Ripuarians in
their seats on the lower Rhine, advanced out of Flanders
to wrest Gaul from the barbarian nations which had entered it some sixty years before.   Few conquerors have
had a career of more unbroken success.   By the defeat of
the Roman governor Syagrius he was left master of the
Northern provinces: the Burgundian kingdom in the valley
of the Rhone was in no long time reduced to dependence:
last of all, the West Gothic power was overthrown in one
great battle, and Aquitaine added to the dominions of
Clovis.   Nor were the Frankish arms less prosperous
against the Germans who dwelt beyond the Rhine.   A
victory (supposed to have been won at Tolbiac) led to the
submission of the Alemanni: their allies the Bavarians
followed, and when the Thuringian power had been broken
by Theodorich I (son of Clovis), the Frankish league embraced all the tribes of Western and Southern Germany.
The dominion thus formed, stretching from the Bay of
Biscay to the Inn and the Ems, was of course in no sense
a Gallic empire.   Nor, although the widest and strongest
monarchy that had yet been founded by a Teutonic race,
was it, under the Merovingian kings, a united kingdom at
all, but rather a congeries of principalities, held together
by the predominance of a single tribe and a single family,
who ruled in Gaul as masters over a subject race, and in
Germany exercised a sort of hegemony among kindred and

scarcely inferior tribes. But towards the middle of the eighth century a change began. Under the rule of Pipin of Herstal and his son Charles Martel, mayors of the palace to the last feeble Merovingians, the Austrasian Franks in the lower Rhineland became acknowledged heads of the nation, and were able, while establishing a firmer government at home, to direct its whole strength to projects of foreign ambition. The form those projects took arose from a circumstance which has not yet been mentioned. It was not solely or even chiefly to their own valour that the Franks owed their past greatness and the yet loftier future which awaited them, it was to the friendship of the clergy and the favour of the Apostolic See. The other Teutonic nations, Goths, Vandals, Burgundians, Suevians, Lombards, had been most of them converted by Arian missionaries who proceeded from the Roman Empire during the short period when Arian doctrines were in the ascendant. The Franks, who were among the latest converts, were Catholics from the first, and after the days of Clovis, whom the clergy had welcomed as a sort of new Constantine, gladly accepted the clergy as their teachers and allies. Thus it was that while the hostility of their orthodox subjects had weakened the Vandal kingdom in Africa and the East Gothic kingdom in Italy, the eager sympathy of the priesthood helped the Franks to vanquish their Burgundian and West Gothic enemies, and made it comparatively easy for them to blend with the Roman population in the provinces. They had done good service against the Saracens of Spain; they had aided the English Winfrith (St. Boniface) in his mission to the heathen of Germany;[a] and at length, as the most power-

[a] 'Denique gens Francorum multos et foecundissimos fructus Domino attulit, non solum credendo, sed et alios salutifere convertendo,' says the Emperor Lewis II in A.D. 871.

ful among Catholic nations, they attracted the eyes of the *CHAP. IV.*
ecclesiastical head of the West, now sorely bested by
domestic foes.

Since the invasion of Alboin, Italy had groaned under *Italy: the*
a complication of evils.   The Lombards who had entered *Lombards.*
along with that chief in A.D. 568 had settled in considerable numbers in the valley of the Po, which became the
seat of their kingdom, and had founded the duchies of
Spoleto and Benevento, leaving the Adriatic coast as well
as Rome and the Southern provinces to be governed by
the exarch of Ravenna as viceroy of the Eastern crown.
This subjection was, however, little better than nominal.
Although too few to occupy the whole peninsula, the invaders were yet strong enough to harass every part of it
by inroads which met with little resistance from a population unused to arms, and without the spirit to use them in
self-defence.   More cruel and repulsive, if we may believe
the evidence of their enemies, than any other of the
Northern tribes, the Lombards were certainly singular in
their aversion to the clergy, never admitting them to the
national councils.   Tormented by their repeated attacks,
Rome sought help in vain from Constantinople, whose
forces, scarce able to repel from her walls the Avars and
Saracens, could give no support to the distant exarch of
Ravenna.   The Popes were the Emperor's subjects; they *The Popes.*
awaited his confirmation, like other bishops; they had
more than once been the victims of his anger.[b]   But as
the city became more accustomed to a practical independence, and the Pope rose to a predominance, real if not yet
legal, his tone grew bolder than that of the Eastern patriarchs.   In the controversies that had raged in the Church,
he had had the wisdom or good fortune to espouse (though

[b] This befel Pope Martin I, as in earlier days Sylverius.

not always from the first)[c] the orthodox side : it was now by another quarrel of religion that his deliverance from an unwelcome yoke was accomplished.

The Emperor Leo, born among the Isaurian mountains, where a simpler faith may yet have lingered, and stung by the Mohammedan taunt of idolatry, determined to abolish the worship of images, which seemed to be fast obscuring the more spiritual part of Christianity. An attempt which had been sufficient to cause tumults among the submissive populations of the East excited in Italy a fiercer commotion. The people rose with one heart in defence of what had become to them more than a symbol : the exarch was slain : the Pope, though unwilling to sever himself from the lawful head and protector of the Church, must yet resist and rebuke the prince whom he could not reclaim from so hateful a heresy.[d] Liudprand, king of the Lombards, improved his opportunity. Falling on the Exarchate as the champion of images, on Rome as the pretended ally of the Emperor, he overran the one, and all but succeeded in capturing the other. Overawing Liudprand by the majesty of his office, the Pope escaped for the moment, but he saw his peril. Placed between a heretic and an invader, he turned his gaze beyond the Alps, to a Catholic chief who had just achieved a signal deliverance for Christendom by his defeat of the Spanish

Musulmans on the field of Poitiers. Gregory II, though his reluctance to break with the Eastern Empire led him to dissuade the North Italians from the notion of setting up an Emperor against Leo,[e] had already opened commu-

[c] Vigilius in the days of Justinian, and Honorius I in those of Heraclius, had lapsed for a time into error.

[d] See Note III at end.

[e] 'Ammonebat ne a fide vel amore imperii Romani desisterent.' — *Liber Pontificalis*, ed. Duchesne, vol. i. p. 407. So Paulus Diaconus (ch. xliv): 'Omnis Ravennae exercitus vel Venetiarum talibus iussis [the command to

nications with Charles Martel, mayor of the palace, and
virtual ruler of the Frankish realm.   As the crisis becomes
more pressing, Gregory III (who had excommunicated the
Iconoclasts in a synod at Rome) finds in the same quarter
his only hope, and appeals to him, in urgent letters, to
hasten to the succour of Holy Church.[f]   Some accounts
add that Charles was offered, in the name of the Roman
people, the office of consul and patrician.   It is at least
certain that here begins the connection of the old imperial
seat with the rising Germanic power : here first the pontiff
leads a political movement, and shakes off the ties that
bound him to his legitimate sovereign.   Charles died
before he could obey the call; but his son Pipin (surnamed the Short) made good use of the new friendship
with Rome.   He was the third of his family who had ruled
the Franks with the full power of a monarch : it seemed
time to abolish the pageant of Merovingian royalty ; yet a
departure from the ancient line might shock the feelings
of the people.   A course was taken whose dangers no one
then foresaw : the Holy See, now for the first time
invoked as an international or supranational power, pronounced the deposition of the feeble Merovingian Chil-   A.D. 750-51.
deric, and gave to the royal office of his successor Pipin a
sanctity hitherto unknown ; adding to the old Frankish
election, which consisted in raising the chief on a shield
amid the clash of arms, the Roman diadem and the
Hebrew rite of anointing.   The compact between the   *Pipin
chair of Peter and the Teutonic throne was hardly sealed,   patrician
when the latter was summoned to discharge its share of   of the
Romans,*
the duties.   Twice did Aistulf the Lombard assail Rome,   A.D. 754.

destroy images] uno animo restiterunt, et nisi eos prohibuisset Pontifex, imperatorem super se constituere fuissent aggressi.'

[f] Letter in *Codex Carolinus*, in Muratori's *Scriptores Rerum Italicarum,*
vol. iii (part 2nd), p. 75, addressed ' Subregulo Carolo.'

twice did Pipin descend to the rescue: the second time at the bidding of a letter written in the name of St. Peter himself.[g] Aistulf's resistance was easily overcome; and the Frank bestowed on the Papal chair all that had belonged to the Exarchate in North Italy, receiving as the meed of his services the title of Patrician.[h]

Import of this title.

As a foreshadowing of the higher dignity that was to follow, this title requires a passing notice. Introduced by Constantine at a time when its original meaning had been long forgotten, it was designed to be, and for awhile remained, the name not of an office but of a rank, the highest after those of emperor and consul. As such, it was usually conferred upon provincial governors of the first class, and in time also upon barbarian potentates whom the imperial court might wish to flatter or conciliate. Thus Odoacer, Theodorich, the Burgundian king Sigismund, Clovis himself, had all received it from the Eastern Emperor; so too in still later times it was given to Saracenic and Bulgarian princes.[i] In the sixth and seventh centuries an invariable

---

[g] Letter in *Cod. Carol.* (Mur. *R. S. I.* iii. [2.] p. 96), a strange mixture of passionate adjurations, dexterous appeals to Frankish pride, and long scriptural quotations: 'Declaratum quippe est quod super omnes gentes vestra Francorum gens prona mihi Apostolo Dei Petro exstitit, et ideo ecclesiam quam mihi Dominus tradidit vobis per manus Vicarii mei commendavi.'

[h] The exact date when Pipin received the title cannot be made out. Pope Stephen's next letter (p. 96 of Mur. iii) is addressed 'Pipino, Carolo et Carolomanno patriciis.' And so the *Chronicon Casinense* (Mur. iv. 273) says it was first given to Pipin. Probably it was not formally conferred on Charles Martel, although one or two documents may be quoted in which it is used of him. As one of these is a letter of Pope Gregory II's, the explanation may be that the title was offered or intended to be offered to him, although never accepted by him. The nature and extent of Pipin's donation (which cannot be found in any extant document) have been much disputed, but some sort of gift was evidently made.

[i] The title of Patrician appears even in the remote West: it stands in a charter of Ini the West Saxon king, and in one given by Richard of Normandy in A.D. 1015. Ducange, *s.v.*

THE EMPIRE RESTORED IN THE WEST

practice seems to have attached it to the East Roman CHAP. IV. viceroys of Italy, and thus, as we may conjecture, a natural confusion of ideas had made men take it to be, in some sense, an official title, conveying an extensive though un-defined authority, and implying in particular the duty of overseeing the Church and promoting her temporal inter-ests.   It was doubtless with such a meaning that the Romans and their bishop bestowed it upon the Frankish kings, acting quite without legal right, for it could emanate only from the Emperor, but choosing it as the title which bound its possessor to render to the Church support and defence against her Lombard foes.   Hence the phrase is always '*Patricius Romanorum*'; not, as formerly, '*Patri-cius*' alone: hence it is usually associated with the terms '*defensor*' and '*protector*.'   And since 'defence' implies a corresponding measure of obedience on the part of those who profit by it, there must have been conceded to the new patrician more or less of positive authority in Rome, although not such as to extinguish either the practical power of the Pope or the titular supremacy of the Em-peror.

So long indeed as the Franks were separated by a hostile kingdom from their new allies, this control of Rome remained little better than nominal.   But when on Pipin's death the restless Lombards again took up arms and menaced the possessions of the Church, Pipin's son Charles, whom we commonly call Charlemagne, swept down like a whirlwind from the Alps at the call of Pope Hadrian, seized King Desiderius in his capital, himself assumed the Lombard crown, and made Northern Italy thenceforward an integral part of the Frankish Empire. Proceeding to Rome at the head of his victorious army, the first of a long line of Teutonic kings who were to experience alternately her love and her hate, he was

Extinction of the Lom-bard king-dom by Charles, king of the Franks.

received by Hadrian with distinguished honours, and welcomed by the people as their leader and deliverer. Yet even then, whether out of policy or from that sentiment of reverence to which his ambitious mind did not refuse to bow, he was moderate in claims of jurisdiction, he yielded to the pontiff the place of honour in processions, and renewed, although in the guise of a lord and conqueror, the gift of the Exarchate and Pentapolis, which Pipin had made to the Roman Church twenty years before.

Charles and Hadrian.

It is with a strange sense, half of sadness, half of amusement, that in watching the progress of this grand historical drama we recognize a mixture of higher and lower motives in the minds of the chief actors. The Frankish king and the Roman pontiff were for the time the two most powerful forces that urged the movement of the world, leading it on by swift steps to a mighty crisis of its fate, themselves guided, as it might well seem, by the purest zeal for its spiritual welfare. Their words and acts, their character and bearing in the sight of expectant Christendom, were worthy of men destined to leave an indelible impress on their own and many succeeding ages. Nevertheless in them too appears the undercurrent of material interests. The lofty and fervent mind of Charles was not free from the stirrings of personal ambition : yet these may be excused as being almost inseparable from an intense and restless genius, which, be it never so unselfish in its ends, must in pursuing them fix upon everything its grasp and raise out of everything its monument. So too in the policy of the Popes the desire to secure spiritual independence was mingled with less noble motives. Ever since the disappearance of an Emperor from Italian soil had virtually emancipated the ecclesiastical potentate from secular control, the most abiding object of his schemes and prayers had been the

acquisition of territorial wealth in the neighbourhood of
his capital.   He had indeed a sort of justification, for
Rome, a city with neither trade nor industry, was crowded
with poor, for whom it devolved on the bishop to provide.[j]
Yet the pursuit was one which could not fail to pervert
the purposes of the Popes and give a sinister character
to their action.   It was this fear for the lands of the
Church more than for religion or the safety of the city,
neither of which was seriously endangered by the Lombard attacks, that had prompted their passionate appeals
to Charles Martel and Pipin; it was now the well-grounded
hope of having these possessions confirmed and extended
by Pipin's greater son that made the Roman ecclesiastics
so forward in his cause.   And it was the same lust after
worldly wealth and pomp, mingled with the dawning prospect of an independent principality, that now began to
seduce them into a long course of guile and intrigue.
For this is probably the very time, although neither the
exact date nor the complicity of any Pope can be established, to which must be assigned the extraordinary forgery
of the Donation of Constantine, whereby it was pretended
that power over Italy and the whole West had been granted
by the first Christian Emperor to Pope Sylvester and his
successors in the Chair of the Apostle.[k]

For the next twenty-four years Italy remained quiet.
The government of Rome was carried on in the name of
the Patrician Charles, although it does not appear that he
sent thither any official representative; while at the same
time both the city and the Exarchate continued to admit
the nominal suzerainty of the Eastern Emperor, employing

[j] Even in Theodorich's days, Cassiodorus had written to the Pope as
guardian of the humbler classes: 'Securitas plebis ad vestram respicit famam,
cui divinitus est commissa custodia.' — *Variar.* ii. 157.

[k] See p. 99, *post*, and Note IV at end.

the years of his reign to date documents.   Southern Italy, which had received only a slight infusion of Teutonic blood, and to which the Greek tongue — its use recently increased by an immigration of Greek refugees during the Iconoclastic troubles — was still familiar, had remained loyal to the East Roman princes, and continued to form part of their realm till the rise of the Norman kingdom in the *Accession of* eleventh century.   In A.D. 796 Leo the Third succeeded *Pope Leo III,* Pope Hadrian, and signalized his devotion to the Frankish *A.D. 796.* throne by sending to Charles the banner of the city and the keys of the holiest of all Rome's shrines, the confession of St. Peter, asking that some officer should be deputed to the city to receive from the people their oath of allegiance to the Patrician.   He had soon need to seek the Patrician's help for himself.   In A.D. 798 a sedition broke out : the Pope, going in solemn procession from the Lateran to the church of S. Lorenzo in Lucina, was attacked by a band of armed men, headed by two officials of his court, nephews of his predecessor ; was wounded and left for dead, and with difficulty succeeded in escaping to Spoleto, whence he fled northward into the Frankish lands.   Charles had led his army against the revolted Saxons : thither Leo following overtook him at Paderborn in Westphalia.   The king received with respect his spiritual father, entertained and conferred with him for some time, and at length sent him back to Rome under the escort of Angilbert, one of his trustiest ministers ; promising to follow ere long in person.   After some months peace was restored in Saxony, and in the autumn of 799 Charles descended from the Alps once more, while Leo revolved deeply the great scheme for whose accomplishment the time was now ripe.

Belief in the Three hundred and twenty-four years had passed since *Roman* the last Caesar of the West resigned his power into the *Empire not* *extinct.* hands of the senate, and left to his Eastern brother the

sole headship of the Roman world.   To the latter Italy
had from that time been nominally subject; but it was
only during one brief interval between the death of Teia
the last Ostrogothic king and the descent of Alboin the
first Lombard that his power had been really effective.
In the further provinces, Gaul, Spain, Britain, it was only
a memory.   But the idea of a Roman Empire as a necessary part of the world's order had not vanished: it had
been admitted by those who seemed to be destroying it;
it had been cherished by the Church; it was still recalled
by laws and customs; it was dear to the subject populations, who fondly looked back to the days when despotism
was at least mitigated by peace and order.   We have seen
the Teuton endeavouring everywhere to identify himself
with the system he overthrew.   As Goths, Burgundians,
and Franks sought the title of consul or patrician, as the
Lombard kings when they renounced their Arianism styled
themselves Flavii, so even in distant England the fierce
Saxon and Anglian conquerors used the names of Roman
dignities, and after a time began to call themselves *imperatores* and *basileis* of Britain.   Within the last century and
a half the rise of Mohammedanism,[1] a vast religious community which was also a vast temporal dominion, had
brought out the common Christianity of Europe into a
fuller relief, while the march of Saracenic invasion exposed
Italy to terrible dangers.   The False Prophet had left one
religion, one Empire, one Commander of the faithful: the
Christian commonwealth needed more than ever an efficient head and centre.   Such leadership it could no wise

---

[1] From A.D. 712, when the Musulmans conquered Spain, till the fall of the
Ommiyad dynasty in A.D. 750, the power of the Khalifate stretched from the
Persian Gulf to the Atlantic.   After A.D. 800 the Roman Empire in the East
and the Romano-Frankish Empire in the West corresponded to the two
Khalifates of Bagdad and Cordova.

find in the Court on the Bosphorus, shaken by the Arab conquests, and growing ever more alien to the West.   The name of 'respublica,' permanent at the elder Rome, had become long since obsolete in the Eastern Empire.   Its government, which had from the first been tinged with a Greco-Asiatic colour, had now drifted away from its ancient traditions into the forms of an Oriental despotism.   Claudian had already sneered at 'Greek Quirites':[m] the general use, since Justinian's time, of the Greek tongue, and the difference of manners and usages, made the taunt now

Motives of the Pope.

more deserved.   The Pope had no reason to wish well to the East Roman princes, who, while insulting his weakness, had given him no help against the savage Lombards, and who for nearly seventy years [n] had been contaminated by a heresy the more odious that it touched not speculative points of doctrine but the most familiar usages of worship. In North Italy their power was extinct: no pontiff since Zacharias had asked their confirmation of his election: nay, the appointment of the intruding Frank to the patriciate, an office which it belonged to the Emperor to confer, was of itself an act of rebellion.   Nevertheless their rights subsisted in theory: they were still, and while they retained the imperial name must so long continue, titular sovereigns of the Roman city.   Even Pope Hadrian had addressed Constantine VI with studied humility.   Nor could the spiritual head of Christendom dispense with the temporal head; without the Roman Empire there could not be a Roman nor by necessary consequence (as was

---

[m] 'Plaudentem cerne senatum
Et Byzantinos proceres, Graiosque Quirites.'
— *In Eutrop.* ii. 135.

[n] Several Emperors during this period had been patrons of images, as was Irene at the moment of which I write: the stain nevertheless adhered to their government as a whole.

believed) a Catholic and Apostolic Church.[o]   For, as will
be shewn more fully hereafter, men could not separate in
fact what was indissoluble in thought : Christianity seemed
to stand or fall along with the great Christian state : they
were but two names for the same thing.   Moved by these
ideas and pressed by these needs the Pope took a step
which some among his predecessors are said to have already contemplated,[p] and towards which the events of the
last fifty years had pointed.   The moment was opportune.
The widowed Empress Irene, famous alike for her beauty,
her talents, and her crimes, had deposed and blinded her
son Constantine VI : a woman, a usurper, almost a parri-
cide, sullied the throne of the world.   By what right, it
might well be asked, did the factions of a distant city in
the East impose a master on the original seat of empire ?
It was time to provide better for the most august of human
offices : an election at Rome was as valid as at Constantinople : the possessor of the real power should be clothed
with the outward dignity also.   Nor could it be doubted
where that possessor was to be found.   The Frank had
been always faithful to Rome : his baptism was the enlist-
ment of a new barbarian auxiliary.   His services against
Arian heretics and Lombard marauders, against the Saracen of Spain and the Avar of Pannonia, had earned him
the title of Champion of the Faith and Defender of the
Holy See.   He was now unquestioned lord of Western

[o] The nature of the connection between the conception of the Roman
Empire and the conception of a Catholic and Apostolic Church — things
which to a modern, remembering the long struggle of Church and State, may
seem naturally antagonistic, will be explained in chapter viii.   The interest
of history lies not least in this, that it shews us how men have at different
times entertained wholly different notions respecting the relation to one
another of the same ideas or the same institutions.

[p] Monachus Sangallensis, *De Gestis Karoli;* in Pertz, *Monumenta Germaniae Historica, Scriptores,* ii. pp. 731 sqq.

Europe, whose subject nations, Celtic and Teutonic, were eager to be called by his name and to adopt his customs.[q] In Charles, the hero who united under one sceptre so many races, and whose religious spirit made him appear to rule all as the vicegerent of God, the pontiff might well see, as later ages saw, the new golden head of a second image,[r] erected on the ruins of that whose mingled iron and clay seemed crumbling to nothingness behind the impregnable bulwarks of Constantinople.

Coronation of Charles at Rome, A.D. 800.

At length the Frankish host entered Rome. The charges brought against the Pope were heard; his innocence, already vindicated by a miracle, was pronounced by the Patrician in full synod; his accusers were condemned in his stead. Charles remained in the city for some weeks; and on Christmas Day, A.D. 800,[s] he heard mass in the basilica of St. Peter. On the spot where now the gigantic dome of Bramante and Michael Angelo towers over the buildings of the modern city, the spot which tradition had hallowed as that of the Apostle's martyrdom, Constantine the Great had erected the oldest and stateliest temple of Christian Rome. Nothing could be less like than was this basilica to those Northern cathedrals, shadowy, fantastic, irregular, crowded with pillars, fringed all round by clustering shrines and chapels, which are to most of us the types of mediaeval architecture. In its plan and deco-

---

[q] So Pope Gregory the Great had written two centuries earlier: 'Quanto caeteros homines regia dignitas antecedit, tanto caeterarum gentium regna regni Francorum culmen excellit.' — Ep. v. 6.

Had the Lombards not been neighbours and enemies of the See of Rome, as well as anti-clerical in their sentiments and habits, the restoration of an Empire in the West would probably have fallen to them instead of to the Franks.

[r] Alciatus, *De Formula imperii Romani.*

[s] Or rather, according to the then prevailing practice of beginning the year from Christmas Day, A.D. 801.

rations, in the spacious sunny hall, the roof plain as that
of a Greek temple, the long row of Corinthian columns,
the vivid mosaics on its walls, in its brightness, its stern-
ness, its simplicity, it had preserved every feature of Roman
art, and had remained a perfect expression of Roman character.[t]   Out of the transept a flight of steps led up to the
high altar underneath and just beyond the great arch, the
arch of triumph as it was called : behind in the semicircular
apse sat the clergy, rising tier above tier around its walls ;
in the midst, high above the rest, and looking down past
the altar over the multitude, was placed the bishop's
throne, itself the curule chair of some forgotten magistrate.[u]   From that chair the Pope now rose, as the reading
of the Gospel ended, advanced to where Charles, who had
exchanged his simple Frankish dress for the sandals and
the chlamys of a Roman patrician, knelt in prayer by the
high altar, and as in the sight of all he placed upon the
brow of the barbarian chieftain the diadem of the Caesars,
then bent in obeisance before him, the church rang to the
shout of the multitude, again free, again the lords and
centre of the world, 'To Charles Augustus, crowned by
God, the great and peace-giving Emperor, be life and
victory.'[x]   In that shout, echoed by the Franks without,
was pronounced the union, so long in preparation, so
mighty in its consequences, of the Roman and the Teuton,
of the memories and the civilization of the South with the
fresh energy of the North, and from that moment modern
history begins.

[t] An elaborate description of old St. Peter's may be found in Bunsen's and
Platner's *Beschreibung der Stadt Rom ;* with which may be compared Bunsen's
work on the Basilicas of Rome.

[u] See Note V at end.

[x] 'Karolo Augusto a Deo coronato magno et pacifico imperatori vita et
victoria.'

CHAPTER V

EMPIRE AND POLICY OF CHARLES

THE coronation of Charles is not only the central event of the Middle Ages, it is also one of those very few events of which, taking them singly, it may be said that if they had not happened, the history of the world would have been different. In one sense indeed it has scarcely a parallel. The assassins of Julius Caesar thought that they had saved Rome from monarchy, but monarchy came inevitable in the next generation. The conversion of Constantine changed the face of the world, but Christianity was spreading fast, and its ultimate triumph was only a question of time. Had Columbus never spread his sails, the secret of the Western sea would yet have been pierced by some later voyager : had Charles V broken his safe-conduct to Luther, the voice silenced at Wittenberg would have been taken up by echoes elsewhere. But if the Roman Empire had not been restored in the West in the person of Charles, it would never have been restored at all, and the endless train of consequences for good and for evil that followed could not have been. Why this was so may be seen by examining the history of the next two centuries. In that day, as through all the Dark and Middle Ages, two forces were striving for the mastery. The one was the instinct of separation, disorder, anarchy, caused by the ungoverned impulses and barbarous ignorance of the great bulk of mankind; the other was that passionate longing of the better minds for a formal unity of government, which had its historical basis in the memories of the old Roman Empire, and its most constant expression in the devotion to a visible and catholic Church. The former tendency was, in secular affairs, the stronger, but the latter, used and stimulated by an extraordinary genius like Charles, achieved in the year 800 a victory whose results were never to be lost.   When the hero was gone, the returning wave of anarchy and barbarism swept up violent as ever, yet it could not wholly obliterate the past: the Empire, maimed and shattered though it was, had struck its roots too deep to be overthrown by force, and when it perished at last, perished from inner decay. It was just because men felt that no one less than Charles could have won such a triumph over the evils of the time, by framing and establishing a gigantic scheme of government, that the excitement and hope and joy which the coronation evoked were so intense.   Their best evidence is perhaps to be found not in the records of that time itself, but in the cries of lamentation that broke forth when the Empire began to dissolve towards the close of the ninth century, in the marvellous legends which attached themselves to the name of Charles the Emperor, a hero of whom any exploit was credible,[a] in the devout admiration wherewith his German successors looked back to, and strove in all things to imitate, their all but superhuman prototype.

[a] Before the end of the tenth century we find the monk Benedict of Soracte ascribing to Charles an expedition to Constantinople and Palestine, with other marvellous exploits. A twelfth-century window in the cathedral of St. Denis represents his reception at Constantinople. The romance which passes under the name of Archbishop Turpin is well known. All the best stories about Charles — and some of them are very good — may be found in the book of the Monk of St. Gall. Many refer to his dealings with the bishops, towards whom he is described as acting like a good-humoured schoolmaster.

As the event of A.D. 800 made an unparalleled impression on those who lived at the time, so has it engaged the attention of men in succeeding ages, has been viewed in the most opposite lights, and become the theme of interminable controversies. It is better to look at it simply as it appeared to the men who witnessed it. Here, as in so many other cases, may be seen the errors into which jurists have been led by the want of historical feeling. In rude and unsettled states of society men respect forms and obey facts, while careless of rules and principles. In England, for example, in the eleventh and twelfth centuries, it signified comparatively little whether an aspirant to the throne was next lawful heir, but it signified a great deal whether he had been duly crowned and was supported by a strong party. Regarding the matter thus, it is not hard to see why those who, writing seven centuries afterwards, judged the actors of A.D. 800 as they would have judged their contemporaries, should have misunderstood the nature of that which then came to pass. Baronius and Bellarmine, Spanheim and Conring, are advocates bound to prove a thesis, and therefore believing it; nor does either party find any lack of plausible arguments.[b] But canonist and civilian alike proceed upon strict ecclesiastical or legal principles, and no such principles can be found in the case, or be fitly applied to it. Neither the instances cited by the Cardinal from the Old Testament of the power of priests to set up and pull down princes, nor those which shew the earlier Emperors controlling the bishops of Rome, really meet the question. Pope Leo acted not as having alone the right to transfer the crown; the practice of hereditary succession and the theory of

[b] Baronius, *Ann.*, ad ann. 800; Bellarminus, *De translatione imperii Romani adversus Illyricum;* Spanhemius, *De ficta translatione imperii;* Conringius, *De imperio Romano Germanico.*

popular election would have equally excluded such a claim.
He was the spokesman of the popular will, which, identifying itself with the sacerdotal power, hated the Easterns and was grateful to the Franks. Yet he was also something more. The act, as it specially affected his interests, was mainly his work, and without him would never have been brought about at all. It was natural that a confusion of his secular functions as leader of the people, and his spiritual as consecrating priest, should lay the foundation of the right claimed afterwards of raising and deposing monarchs at the will of Christ's vicar. The Emperor was passive throughout; he did not, as in Lombardy, appear as a conqueror, but was received by the Pope and the people as a friend and ally. Rome no doubt became his capital, but it had already obeyed him as Patrician, and the greatest fact that stood out to posterity from the whole transaction was that the crown was, if not bestowed, yet at least imposed, by the hands of the pontiff. He seemed the divinely appointed agent through whom the will of God expressed itself.[c]

The best way of shewing the thoughts and motives of those concerned in the transaction is to transcribe the narratives of three contemporary, or almost contemporary annalists, two of them German and one Italian. The Annals of Lauresheim say:— *Contemporary accounts.*

'And because the name of Emperor had now ceased among the Greeks, and their Empire was possessed by a woman, it then seemed both to Leo the Pope himself, and to all the holy fathers who were present in the self-same council, as well as to the rest of the Christian people, that they ought to take to be Emperor Charles king of the Franks, who held Rome herself, where the Caesars had always been wont to sit, and all the other regions which

[c] Cf. Greenwood, *Cathedra Petri*, vol. iii. p. 109.

he ruled through Italy and Gaul and Germany; and inasmuch as God had given all these lands into his hand, it seemed right that with the help of God and at the prayer of the whole Christian people he should have the name of Emperor also. Whose petition king Charles willed not to refuse, but submitting himself with all humility to God, and at the prayer of the priests and of the whole Christian people, on the day of the nativity of our Lord Jesus Christ he took on himself the name of Emperor, being consecrated by the lord Pope Leo.' [d]

Very similar in substance is the account of the Chronicle of Moissac (ad ann. 801):—

'Now when the king upon the most holy day of the Lord's birth was rising to the mass after praying before the confession of the blessed Peter the Apostle, Leo the Pope, with the consent of all the bishops and priests and of the senate of the Franks and likewise of the Romans, set a golden crown upon his head, the Roman people also shouting aloud. And when the people had made an end of chanting the Laudes, he was adored by the Pope after the manner of the emperors of old. For this also was done by the will of God. For while the said Emperor abode at Rome certain men were brought unto him, who said that the name of Emperor had ceased among the Greeks, and that among them the Empire was held by a woman called Irene, who had by guile laid hold on her son the Emperor, and put out his eyes, and taken the Empire to herself, as it is written of Athaliah in the Book of the Kings; which when Leo the Pope and all the assembly of the bishops and priests and abbots heard, and the senate of the Franks and all the elders of the Romans, they took counsel with the rest of the Christian people, that they should name Charles king of the Franks to be Emperor, seeing that

[d] *Ann. Lauresh.*, *ap.* Pertz, *M. G. H.*, *Script.* i. p. 38.

he held Rome the mother of empire where the Caesars and Emperors were always used to sit; and that the heathen might not mock the Christians if the name of Emperor should have ceased among the Christians.' [e]

These two accounts are both from a German source: that which follows is Roman, written probably within some fifty or sixty years of the event. It is taken from the Life of Leo III in the *Vitae Pontificum Romanorum*, which used to pass under the name of Anastasius the papal librarian.

'After these things came the day of the birth of our Lord Jesus Christ, and all men were again gathered together in the aforesaid basilica of the blessed Peter the Apostle: and then the gracious and venerable pontiff did with his own hands crown Charles with a very precious crown. Then all the faithful people of Rome, seeing the defence that he gave and the love that he bare to the Holy Roman Church and her Vicar, did by the will of God and of the blessed Peter, the keeper of the keys of the kingdom of heaven, cry with one accord with a loud voice, "To Charles, the most pious Augustus, crowned of God, the great and peace-giving Emperor, be life and victory." While he, before the holy confession of the blessed Peter the Apostle, was invoking divers saints, it was proclaimed thrice, and he was chosen by all to be Emperor of the Romans. Thereon the most holy pontiff anointed Charles with holy oil, and likewise his most excellent son to be king, upon the very day of the birth of our Lord Jesus Christ; and when the mass was finished then after the mass the most serene lord Emperor offered gifts.' [f]

In these three accounts there is no serious discrepancy as to the facts, although the Italian priest, as is natural, heightens the importance of the part played by the Pope,

[e] *Apud* Pertz, *M. G. H., Script.* i. pp. 305, 306.
[f] *Liber Pontificalis, Vita Leonis III.*

while the Germans are more disposed to rationalize the event, talking of a synod of the clergy, a consultation of the people, and a formal request to Charles, which the silence of Eginhard, as well as the other circumstances of the case, forbid us to accept as literally true. Similarly the Roman narrative passes over the adoration rendered by the Pope to the Emperor, upon which most of the Frankish records insist in a way which puts it beyond

Impression which they convey.

doubt. But the impression which the three accounts leave is essentially the same. They all shew how hard it is to give a technical character to the transaction as an act either of conquest or of election. The Frankish king does not of his own might seize the crown, but rather receives it as coming naturally to him, as the legitimate consequence of the authority he already enjoyed. The Pope bestows the crown, not in virtue of any right of his own as head of the Church : he is merely the instrument of God's providence, which has unmistakeably pointed out Charles as the proper person to defend and lead the Christian commonwealth. The Roman people do not formally choose and appoint, but by their applause accept the chief who is presented to them. The act is conceived of as directly ordered by the Divine Providence which has brought about a state of things that admits of but one issue, an issue which king, priest, and people have only to recognize and obey ; their personal ambitions, passions, intrigues, sinking and vanishing in reverential awe at what seems the immediate interposition of Heaven. And as the result is desired by all parties alike, they do not think of inquiring into one another's rights, but take their momentary harmony to be natural and necessary, never dreaming of the difficulties and conflicts which were to arise out of what then seemed so simple. And it was just because everything was thus left undetermined, resting not on express stipulation but rather on a sort of mutual

understanding, a sympathy of beliefs and wishes which augured no evil, that the event admitted of being afterwards represented in so many different lights. Four centuries later, when Papacy and Empire had been forced into the mortal struggle by which the fate of both was decided, three distinct theories regarding the coronation of Charles will be found advocated by three different parties, all of them plausible, all of them to some extent misleading. The Swabian Emperors held the crown to have been won by their great predecessor as the prize of conquest, and drew the conclusion that the citizens and bishop of Rome had no rights as against themselves. The patriotic party among the Romans, appealing to the early history of the Empire, declared that only by the voice of their senate and people could an Emperor be lawfully created, he being their chief magistrate, the temporary depositary of their authority. The Popes pointed to the indisputable fact that Leo imposed the crown, and argued that as God's earthly vicar it was then his right, and must always continue to be their right, to give to whomsoever they would an office created to be the handmaid of their own. Of these three it was the last view that eventually tended to prevail, yet to an impartial eye it cannot claim, any more than do the two others, to contain the whole truth. Charles did not conquer, nor the Pope give, nor the people elect. As the act was unprecedented, so was it extralegal;[g] it was a revolt of the ancient Western capital

---

[g] It must be remembered that no method of choosing an Emperor ever was prescribed by law either under the earlier Emperors at Rome or the later at Constantinople. So far as the right of choice could be said to reside in any body, it resided in the senate or the army, or (in a still more shadowy way) in the people, first of Old Rome, afterwards of New Rome (Constantinople), but in practice the senate counted for very little : it was a matter *facti potius quam iuris*. Hence the Romans in A.D. 800 might claim that they were

against a daughter who had become a mistress; an exercise of the sacred right of insurrection, justified by the weakness or wickedness of the Eastern princes, hallowed to the eyes of the world by the sanction of Christ's representative, but founded upon no law, nor competent to create any for the future.

Was the coronation a surprise?

It is an interesting and somewhat perplexing question, how far the coronation scene, an act as imposing in its circumstances as it was momentous in its results, was prearranged among the parties. Eginhard tells us that Charles was accustomed to declare that he would not, even on so high a festival, have entered the church had he known of the Pope's intention.[h] Even if the monarch had uttered, the secretary would hardly have recorded a falsehood long after the motive that might have prompted it had disappeared. Of the existence of the motive that has been most commonly assumed, a fear of the discontent of the Franks who might think their liberties endangered, little or no proof can be brought from the records of the time, wherein the nation is represented as exulting in the new dignity of their chief as an accession of grandeur to themselves. Nor can we assume that Charles's disavowal was merely meant to soothe the offended pride of the East

revindicating a right which, originally vested in their ancestors, had been misused at Constantinople, and the more palpably misused because no woman had ever reigned except as consort of an Emperor.

The Franks evidently attached importance to the Roman acclamations, but these would come from the party in Rome which favoured Pope Leo, and we must not suppose any formal election by the people.

h 'Imperatoris et Augusti nomen accepit, quod primo in tantum aversatus est ut adfirmaret se eo die, quamvis praecipua festivitas esset, aecclesiam non intraturum si pontificis consilium praescire potuisset. Invidiam tamen suscepti nominis, Romanis imperatoribus super hoc indignantibus, magna tulit patientia, vicitque eorum contumaciam magnanimitate, qua eis proculdubio longe praestantior erat, mittendo ad eos crebras legationes et in epistolis fratres eos appellando.' — *Vita Karoli*, c. xxxviii.

Roman princes, from whom he had little to fear, and who were none the more likely to recognize his dignity, if they should believe it to be not of his own seeking. Yet it is hard to suppose the whole affair a surprise ; for it was the goal towards which the policy of the Frankish kings had for many years pointed, and Charles himself, in sending before him to Rome many of the spiritual and temporal magnates of his realm, in summoning thither his son Pipin from a war against the Lombards of Benevento, had shewn that he expected some more than ordinary result from this journey to the imperial city. Alcuin moreover, Alcuin of York, the trusted adviser of Charles in matters religious and literary, appears from one of his extant letters to have sent as a Christmas gift to his royal pupil a carefully corrected and superbly adorned copy of the Scriptures, with the words 'ad splendorem imperialis potentiae.' This has commonly been taken for conclusive evidence that the plan had been settled beforehand, and such it would be were there not some reasons for giving the letter an earlier date, and looking upon the word 'imperialis' as a mere magniloquent flourish.[1] More weight is therefore to be laid upon the arguments supplied by the nature of the case itself. The Pope, whatever his confidence in the sympathy of the people, would never have ventured on so momentous a step until previous conferences had assured him of the feelings of the king, nor could an act for which the assembly were evidently prepared have been kept a secret. Nevertheless, the declaration of Charles himself can neither be evaded nor set down to mere dissimulation. It is more fair to him, and on the whole more reasonable, to suppose that Leo, having satisfied himself of the wishes of the Roman clergy and people as well as of

[1] Lorentz, *Leben Alcuins.* And cf. Döllinger, *Das Kaiserthum Karls des Grossen und seiner Nachfolger.*

the Frankish magnates, resolved to seize an occasion and
place so eminently favourable to his long-cherished plan,
while the king, carried away by the enthusiasm of the
moment and seeing in the pontiff the prophet and instrument of the divine will, accepted a dignity which he might
have wished to receive at some later time or in some other
way.[j] If, therefore, any positive conclusion be adopted,
it would seem to be that Charles, who may probably have
given a more or less vague consent to the project, was
surprised and disconcerted by a sudden fulfilment which
interrupted his own carefully studied designs. And although a deed which changed the history of the world
was in any case no accident, it may well have worn to the
Frankish and Roman spectators the air of a surprise. For
there were no preparations apparent in the church ; the
king was not, like his Teutonic successors in the aftertime,
led in procession to the pontifical throne : suddenly, at the
very moment when he rose from the sacred hollow where
he had knelt among the ever-burning lamps before the
holiest of Christian relics — the body of the prince of the
Apostles — the hands of that Apostle's representative
placed upon his head the crown of glory and poured upon
him the oil of sanctification. There was something in this
to thrill the beholders with the awe of a Divine presence,
and make them hail him whom that presence seemed almost visibly to consecrate, the 'pious and peace-giving
Emperor, crowned of God.'

The reluctance of Charles to assume the imperial title
has been variously explained. Some high authorities [k]

[j] A recent writer (Martens, *Beleuchtung der neuesten Controversen über
die römische Frage*) thinks that Charles and Leo had arranged that the coronation should take place, but that the Emperor meant to crown himself, and
then let the Pope anoint him.

[k] Dahn, *Urgeschichte der romanischen und teutonischen Völker*, Hodgkin,
Italy and her Invaders, vol. viii. p. 202 sqq. Dr. Hodgkin suggests another

think that his sagacity stretched far enough into the future to discern the danger of the precedent set by the Pope's action, and the claims which might thereafter be based upon it. True it is that when the time came for his son to be crowned as co-emperor, Charles himself set the crown on the head of Lewis. Yet Pope Leo had been so humble towards Charles, so far from advancing those pretensions to supremacy which, foreshadowed by Pope Nicholas I sixty years later, appeared full-blown under Gregory VII, that we may doubt whether the Emperor could have perceived all that lay involved in the imposition of the crown by papal hands. Eginhard[1] himself seems to hint that Charles feared the jealous hostility of the Eastern Court, which could not only deny his claim to the title, but might disturb by intrigues his dominions in Italy. Accepting this statement, the problem remains, how is this reluctance to be reconciled with those acts of his which clearly shew him aiming at the Roman crown? A probable solution is suggested by a distinguished historian,[m] who argues from a minute examination of the previous policy of Charles, that while it was the great object of his reign to obtain the crown of the world, he foresaw at the same time the opposition of the East Roman Court, and the want of legality from which his title would in consequence suffer. He was therefore bent on getting from the Eastern rulers, if possible, a transference of their crown; if not, at least a recognition of his own: and he appears to have hoped to win this by the negotiations which had been for some time kept on foot with the Empress Irene. Just at this moment came the coronation by

explanation also, the difficulty of securing the city of Rome for Charles's eldest son, who was to be his chief heir, inasmuch as Italy was to be part of the dominions of his younger son.

[1] See the passage quoted in note [h], p. 58.   [m] Döllinger, *ut supra.*

Pope Leo, interrupting these deep-laid schemes, irritating Constantinople, and forcing Charles into the position of a rival who could not with dignity adopt a soothing or submissive tone. Nevertheless, he seems not even then to have abandoned the hope of obtaining a peaceful recognition. He was not, if we may credit Theophanes,[n] deterred by Irene's crimes from seeking her hand in marriage. And when the project of thus uniting the East and West in a single Empire, baffled for a time by the opposition of her minister Aetius, was rendered impossible by her subsequent dethronement and exile, he did not abandon the policy of conciliation until a surly acquiescence in, rather than admission of, his dignity had been won from the Eastern Emperor Nicephorus and confirmed by his successor Michael.[o]

Defect in the title of the Teutonic Emperors.

Whether, supposing Leo to have been less precipitate, a cession of the crown, or an acknowledgement of the right of the Romans to confer it, could ever have been obtained by Charles is more than doubtful. But it is clear that he judged rightly in rating its importance high, for the want of it was the great blemish in his own and his successors' dignity. To shew how this was so, reference must be made to the events of A.D. 476. Both the extinction of the Western Empire in that year and its revival in A.D. 800 have been generally misunderstood in modern times, and

[n] Παρὰ Καρούλλου ἀποκρισιάριοι καὶ τοῦ πάπα Λέοντος πρὸς τὴν Εἰρήνην αἰτούμενοι ζευχθῆναι αὐτὴν τῷ Καρούλλῳ πρὸς γάμον καὶ ἐνῶσαι τὰ Ἑῷα καὶ τὰ Ἑσπέρια. — Theoph., *Chron.* in *Corp. Scr. Hist. Byzant.* vol. xliii. p. 737.

[o] Their ambassadors at last saluted him by the desired title: 'Laudes ei dixerunt imperatorem eum et basileum appellantes.' Eginh., *Ann.*, ad ann. 812. Charles in a letter sent to Michael had addressed the latter as Emperor, and spoken of the peace established 'inter Orientale et Occidentale imperium.' There was thus a sort of reciprocal recognition, but (as will be further explained in chapter XVII) the two Empires did not as a rule admit one another's claims.

although the mistake is not, in a certain sense, of practical importance, yet it tends to confuse history and to blind us to the ideas of the people who acted on both occasions. When Odoacer compelled the abdication of Romulus Augustulus, he did not abolish the Western Empire as a separate power, but caused it to be reunited with or sink into the Eastern, so that from that time there was, as there had been before Diocletian, a single undivided Roman Empire. In A.D. 800 the very memory of the separate Western Empire, as it had stood from the death of Theodosius till Odoacer, had, so far as appears, been long since lost, and neither Leo nor Charles nor any one among their advisers dreamt of reviving it. They too, like their predecessors, held the Roman Empire to be one and indivisible, and proposed by the coronation of the Frankish king not to proclaim a severance of the East and West, but to reverse the act of Constantine, and make Old Rome again the civil as well as the ecclesiastical capital of the Empire that bore her name. Their deed was in its essence illegal, but they sought to give it every semblance of legality: they professed and partly believed that they were not revolting against a reigning sovereign, but legitimately filling up the place of the deposed Constantine the Sixth, the people of the imperial city exercising their ancient right of choice, their bishop his right of consecration.

Their purpose was but half accomplished. They could create, but they could not destroy. They set up an Emperor of their own, whose representatives thenceforward reigned in the West, but Constantinople, which they did not attempt to reduce to obedience, retained her sovereigns as of yore; and Christendom saw henceforth two imperial lines, not as in the time before A.D. 476, the conjoint heads of a single realm, but always rivals and usually enemies, each denouncing the other as a pretender, each professing

CHAP. V.

to be the only true and lawful head of the Christian Church and people. Although therefore we must in practice speak during the next seven centuries (down till A.D. 1453, when Constantinople fell before the Turkish Sultan Mohammed II) of an Eastern and a Western Empire, the phrase is in strictness incorrect, and was one which either court ought to have repudiated. The Byzantines almost always did repudiate it ;[p] the Latins usually; although, yielding to facts, they sometimes condescended to employ it themselves. But their theory was always the same. Charles was held to be the legitimate successor, not of Romulus Augustulus, but of Constantine VI, of his father Leo IV, of Heraclius, Justinian, Arcadius, and the whole Eastern line; and hence it is that in the annals of the time and of many succeeding centuries, the name of Constantine VI, the sixty-seventh in order from Augustus, is followed without a break by that of Charles, the sixty-eighth.

Government of Charles as Emperor.

The maintenance of an imperial line among the Easterns was a continuing protest against the validity of Charles's title. But from their enmity he had little to fear, and in the eyes of the world he seemed to step into their place, adding the traditional dignity which had been theirs to the power that he already enjoyed. North Italy and Rome ceased for ever to own the supremacy of Constantinople; and while the Eastern princes paid a shameful tribute to the Musulman, the Frankish Emperor — as the recognized head of Christendom — received from the Patriarch of Jerusalem the keys of the Holy Sepulchre and the banner of Calvary; the gift of the Sepulchre itself, says Eginhard, from 'Aaron king of the Persians.'[q] Out of this peaceful

[p] Although they occasionally conceded the title of Emperor to the Teutonic sovereign: as in the instances cited in note o, p. 62, and see *post*, ch. XVII.

[q] Harun er Rashid; Eginh., *Vita Karoli*, cap. 16.

intercourse with the famous Khalif the romancers created
a crusade. Within his own dominions the sway of Charles
assumed a more sacred character. Already had his un-
wearied and comprehensive activity made him throughout
his reign an ecclesiastical no less than a civil ruler, summoning and sitting in councils, examining and appointing
bishops, settling by capitularies the smallest points of
church discipline and polity. A synod held at Frankfort in
A.D. 794 condemned the decrees of the second Council of
Nicaea, which had been approved by Pope Hadrian, cen-
sured severely the conduct of the Eastern Emperors in
suggesting them, and without excluding images from
churches, altogether forbade them to be worshipped or
even venerated. Not only did Charles preside in and
direct the deliberations of this synod, although legates from
the Pope were present—he also caused a treatise to be
drawn up stating and urging its conclusions; he pressed
Hadrian to declare Constantine VI a heretic for denouncing doctrines to which Hadrian had himself consented.
There are letters of his extant in which he lectures Pope
Leo in a tone of easy superiority, admonishes him to obey
the holy canons, and bids him pray earnestly for the success of the efforts which it is the monarch's duty to make
for the subjugation of pagans and the establishment of
sound doctrine throughout the Church. Nay, subsequent
Popes themselves admitted and applauded the despotic
superintendence of matters spiritual which he was wont to
exercise, and which led some one to give him playfully a
title that had once been applied to the Pope himself,
'Episcopus episcoporum.'

Acting and speaking thus when merely king, it may be
thought that Charles needed no further title to justify his
power. The inference is in truth rather the converse of
this. Upon what he had done already the imperial title

would naturally follow : the attitude of protection and control which he held towards the Church and the Holy See belonged, according to the ideas of the time, properly and only to an Emperor. His coronation was, therefore, the fitting completion and legitimation of his authority, sanctifying rather than increasing it. We have, however, one remarkable witness to the importance that was attached to the imperial name, and the enhancement which he conceived his office to have received from it. In a great *Capitulary of* A.D. 802. assembly held at Aachen, A.D. 802, the lately-crowned Emperor revised the laws of all the races that obeyed him, endeavouring to harmonize and correct them, and issued a capitulary singular in subject and tone.[r] All persons within his dominions, as well ecclesiastical as civil, who have already sworn allegiance to him as king, are thereby commanded to swear to him afresh as Caesar; and all who have never yet sworn, down to the age of twelve, shall now take the same oath. 'At the same time it shall be publicly explained to all what is the force and meaning of this oath, and how much more it includes than a mere promise of fidelity to the monarch's person. Firstly, it binds those who swear it to live, each and every one of them, according to his strength and knowledge, in the holy service of God; since the lord Emperor cannot extend over all his care and discipline. Secondly, it binds them neither by force nor fraud to seize or molest any of the goods or servants of his crown. Thirdly, to do no violence nor treason towards the holy Church, or to widows, or orphans, or strangers, seeing that the lord Emperor has been appointed, after the Lord and His saints, the protector and defender of all such.' Then in similar fashion purity of life is prescribed to the monks;,

---

[r] Pertz, *M. G. H.* iii. (*Legg.* i) p. 91.

homicide, the neglect of hospitality, and other offences are denounced, the notions of sin and crime being intermingled and almost identified in a way to which no parallel can be found, unless it be in the Mosaic code. There God, the invisible object of worship, is also, by necessary consequence, the judge and ruler of Israel; here the whole cycle of social and moral duty is deduced from the obligation of obedience to the visible autocratic head of the Christian state.

In most of Charles's words and deeds, nor less distinctly in the writings of his adviser Alcuin, may be discerned the working of the same theocratic ideas. Among his intimate friends he chose to be called by the name of David, exercising in reality all the powers of the Jewish king; presiding over this kingdom of God upon earth rather as a second Constantine or Theodosius than in the spirit and traditions of the earlier successors of Augustus. Among his measures there are two which in particular recall the first Christian Emperor. As Constantine founds so Charles erects on a firmer basis the connection of Church and State. Bishops and abbots are as essential a part of rising feudalism as counts and dukes. Their benefices are held under the same conditions of fealty and the service in war of their vassal tenants, not of the spiritual person himself: they have similar rights of jurisdiction, and are subject alike to the imperial *missi*. The monarch often tries to restrict the clergy, as persons, to spiritual duties; quells the insubordination of the monasteries; endeavours to bring the seculars into a quasi-monastic life by instituting and regulating chapters. But after granting wealth and power, the attempt was vain; his strong hand withdrawn, they laughed at control. Again, it was by him first that the payment of tithes, for which the priesthood had long been pleading, was made compulsory in Western

CHAP. V.

*Influence of
the imperial
title in
Germany and
Gaul.*

Europe, and the support of the ministers of religion recognized as a legally binding obligation.

In civil affairs also Charles acquired, with the imperial title, a new position. Later jurists labour to distinguish his power as Roman Emperor from that which he held already as king of the Franks and their subject allies: they insist that his coronation gave him the capital only, that it is absurd to talk of a Roman Empire in regions whither the eagles had never flown.[8] In such expressions there seems to lurk either confusion or misconception. It was not the actual government of the city that Charles obtained in A.D. 800; that his father had already held as Patrician, and he had himself exerted the rights which the title gave. It was far more than the titular sovereignty of Rome which had hitherto been supposed to be vested in the Emperor at Constantinople. It was nothing less than the headship of the world, believed to appertain of right to the lawful Roman Emperor, whether he reigned on the Bosphorus, the Tiber, or the Rhine. As that headship, although never denied, had been in abeyance in the West for several centuries, its bestowal on the king of so vast a realm was a change of the first moment, for it made the coronation not merely a transference of the seat of Empire, but a renewal of the Empire itself, a bringing back of it from faith to sight, from the world of belief and theory to the world of fact and reality. And since the powers it gave were autocratic and unlimited, it must swallow up all minor claims and dignities: the rights of Charles the Frankish king were merged in those of Charles the successor of Augustus, the lord of the world. That his imperial authority was theoretically irrespective of place is clear from his own words and acts, and from all the

[8] Putter, *Historical Development of the German Constitution;* so too Con-ring, and esp. David Blondel, *Adv. Chiffletium.*

monuments of that time. He would not, indeed, have
dreamed of treating the high-spirited Franks as Justinian
had treated his half-Oriental subjects, nor would the
warriors who followed his standard have brooked such an
attempt. Yet even to German eyes his position must
have been altered by the halo of vague splendour which
now surrounded him ; for all, even the Saxon and the
Slav, had heard of Rome's glories, and revered the
name of Caesar. And in his effort to weld discordant *Action of*
elements into one body, to introduce regular gradations *Charles on Europe.*
of authority, to control the Teutonic tendency to localization by his *missi* — officials commissioned to traverse
each some part of his dominions, reporting on and redress-
ing the evils they found — as well as by his own oft-
repeated personal progresses, Charles was guided by the
traditions of the old Empire. His sway is the revival of
order and culture, seeking to fuse the West into a compact whole, whose parts are never thenceforward to lose
the marks of their connection and their half-Roman
character, gathering up all that is left in Europe of intellect knowledge and skill, hurling it with the new force of
Christianity on the infidel of the South and the masses
of untamed barbarism to the North and East. Ruling
the world by the gift of God, and by the transmitted rights
of the Romans and their Caesar whom God had chosen
to conquer it, he renews the original aggressive movement
of the Empire. The civilized world has subdued her
invader,[t] and now arms him against savagery and
heathendom. Hence the wars, not more of the sword
than of the cross, against Saxons, Avars, Slavs, Danes,
Spanish Arabs, where monasteries are fortresses and
baptism the badge of submission. The overthrow

[t] 'Graecia capta ferum victorem cepit,' is repeated in this conquest of the
Teuton by Roman civilization.

of the Irminsûl,[u] in the first Saxon campaign, sums up the changes of seven centuries. The Romanized Teuton destroys the monument of his country's freedom, for it is also the emblem of paganism and barbarism. The work of the Cheruscan Arminius is undone by his successor.

His position as Frankish king.

This, however, is not the only side from which Charles's policy and character may be regarded. If the unity of the Church and the shadow of imperial prerogative was one pillar of his power, the other was the Frankish nation. The empire was still military, though in a sense strangely different from that of Julius or Severus. The warlike Franks had permeated Western Europe; their primacy was admitted by the kindred tribes of Bavarians, Lombards, Thuringians, Alemannians, and Burgundians; the Slavonic peoples on the borders trembled and paid tribute; the Spanish Alfonso of Asturias found in the Emperor a protector against the infidel foe. His influence, if not his exerted power, crossed the ocean : the kings of the Scots sent gifts and called him lord :[x] the restoration of Eardulf to Northumbria, still more of Egbert to Wessex, might furnish a better ground for the claim of suzerainty than many to which his successors had afterwards recourse.

As it was by Frankish arms that this predominance in Europe which the imperial title adorned and legalized had been won, so was the government of Charles Roman in name rather than in fact. It was not by restoring the effete mechanism of the old Empire, but by his own vigorous personal action and that of his great officers, that he strove to administer and reform. With every effort for a strong central government, there is no

[u] See Note VI at end.

[x] Probably the Scots of Ireland. — Eginhard, *Vita Karoli*, cap. 16.

despotism : each nation retains its laws, its hereditary chiefs, its free popular assemblies. The conditions granted to the Saxons after long and cruel warfare, conditions so favourable that in the next century their dukes hold the foremost place in Germany, shew how little he sought to make the Franks a dominant caste. One *General re-* may think of him as a second Theodorich, trying to *sults of his* maintain the traditions of Rome and to breathe a new *Empire.* spirit into the ancient forms. The conception was magnificent ; and it fitted the time better than it had done in the hands of Theodorich, not only because Charles was himself orthodox and pious, but also because the name and dominion of Rome were now more closely associated with Christianity than they had been in days when the recollection of heathen Emperors was still fresh in the memory of men. But two obstacles forbade success. The one was the ecclesiastical, especially the papal power, apparently subject to the temporal, but with a strong and undefined prerogative which only waited the occasion to trample on what it had helped to raise. The Pope might take away the crown he had bestowed, and turn against the Emperor the Church which now obeyed him. The other was to be found in the discordance of the component parts of the Empire. The nations were not ripe for settled life or extensive schemes of polity ; the differences of race, language, manners, over vast and thinly-peopled lands baffled every attempt to maintain their cohesion : and when once the spell of the great mind was withdrawn, the mutually repellent forces began to work, and the mass dissolved into that chaos out of which it had been formed. Nevertheless, the parts separated not as they met, but having all of them undergone influences which continued to act when political connection had ceased. For the work of Charles — a genius pre-eminently creative — was not lost in the anarchy that followed: rather are we to regard his reign as the beginning of a new era, or as laying the foundations whereon men continued for many generations to build.

Personal habits and sympathies.

It is no longer necessary to shew how little the modern French, children of the Latinized Celt, have to do with the Teutonic Charles. At Rome he might assume the chlamys and the sandals, but at the head of his Frankish host he strictly adhered to the customs of his country, and was beloved by his people as the very ideal of their own character and habits. Of strength and stature almost superhuman, in swimming and hunting unsurpassed, steadfast and terrible in fight, to his friends gentle and condescending, he was a Roman, much less a Gaul,[y] in nothing but his culture and his schemes of government, otherwise a German. The centre of his realm was the Rhine; his favourite residences Aachen[z] and Engilenheim;[a] his sympathies — as they are shewn in the gathering of the old hero-lays,[b] the composition of a German grammar, the ordinance against confining prayer to the three languages, Hebrew, Greek, and Latin, — were all for the race from which he sprang, and whose advance, represented by the victory of Austrasia, the true Frankish fatherland along the

[y] He could, however, speak Latin as easily as German, but understood Greek better than he spoke it. He tried to learn to write, but, says Eginhard: 'parum successit labor praeposterus et sero inchoatus.'

[z] Aix-la-Chapelle (called by English writers of the seventeenth century Aken). It is commemorated in the lines (to be found in Pertz's edition of Eginhard) beginning —

> 'Urbs Aquensis, urbs regalis,
> Sedes regni principalis,
> Prima regum curia.'

[a] Engilenheim, or Ingelheim, lies near the left shore of the Rhine between Mentz and Bingen.

[b] 'Barbara et antiquissima carmina quibus veterum regum actus et bella canebantur scripsit memoriaeque mandavit.' — *Vita Karoli*, cap. 29.

lower Rhine, over Neustria (central Gaul) and Aquitaine, spread a second Germanic wave over the conquered countries.

There were in his Empire, as in his own mind, two elements, those two from the union and mutual action and reaction of which modern civilization has arisen. These vast domains, reaching from the Ebro to the mountains of Hungary, from the Eyder to the Liris, were the conquests of the Frankish sword, and, although the army was drawn from all the more warlike races, the imperial governors and officers were mostly of Frankish blood. But the conception of the Empire, that which made it a State and not a mere mass of subject tribes like those great Eastern dominions which rise and perish in a lifetime, the realms of Sesostris, or Attila, or Timur, was inherited from an older and a grander polity, and had in it an element which was Roman rather than Teutonic — Roman in its striving after the uniformity and precision of a well-ordered administration, which should subject the individual to the system and realize perfection through the rule of law.[c]   And the bond, too, by which the Empire was chiefly held together was Roman in its origin, although Roman in a sense which would have surprised Trajan or Severus, could it have been foretold them.   The ecclesiastical body was already organized and beginning to be centralized, and it was in his control of the ecclesiastical body that the secret of Charles's power lay.   Every Christian — Frank, Gaul, or Italian — owed loyalty to the head and defender of his religion : the unity of the Empire was a reflection of the unity of the Church.

[c] These things were not in fact done, but the idea of doing them was involved in the imperial tradition. So he reduced to writing the laws of the various tribes subject to him (probably the Germanic tribes), 'Omnium nationum quae sub eius dominatu erant iura quae scripta non erant describere et literis mandari fecit.' — *Vita Karoli*, cap. 29.

Into a general view of the government and policy of
Charles it is not possible here to enter. Yet his legislation, his assemblies, his administrative schemes, his magnificent works, recalling the projects of Alexander and
Caesar, the zeal for education and literature, which he
shewed in the collection of manuscripts, the founding of
schools, the gathering of eminent men from all quarters
around him, cannot be appreciated apart from his position
as restorer of the Roman Empire. Like most of those
who have led the world, Charles was many great things in
one, and was so great just because the workings of his
genius were so harmonious. He was more than a barbarian warrior, more than an astute negotiator ; there is none
of his qualities which would not be forced out of its place
were we to characterize him chiefly by it. Comparisons
between famous men of different ages are generally as
unprofitable as they are easy : the circumstances among
which Charles lived do not permit us to institute a minute
parallel between his greatness and that of those two to
whom it was once the fashion to compare him, nor to say
whether he was as profound a statesman as Julius Caesar,
as skilful a commander as Napoleon. But scarcely either
to the Roman or to the Corsican was he inferior in that
quality by which both he and they chiefly impress our imagination — the vivid and unresting energy which swept
him over Europe in campaign after campaign, which
sought a field for its workings in theology and science, in
law and literature, no less than in politics and war. As it
was this amazing activity that made him the conqueror of
Europe, so was it by the variety of his culture that he
became her civilizer. From him, in whose wide deep
mind the whole mediaeval theory of the world and human
life mirrored itself, did mediaeval society take the form
and impress which it retained for centuries, and the

traces whereof are among us and upon us to this
day.

The great Emperor was buried at Aachen, in that basilica which it had been the delight of his later years to erect
and adorn with the treasures of ancient art. His tomb
under the dome — where now we see an enormous slab,
with the words 'Carolo Magno' — was inscribed, '*Magnus
atque Orthodoxus Imperator.*' [d] Poets, fostered by his own
zeal, sang of him who had given to the Franks the sway
of Romulus.[e] The gorgeous mists of romance gradually
rose and wreathed themselves round his name, till by
canonization as a saint he received the highest glory the
world or the Church could confer.[f] For the Roman

[d] This basilica was built upon the model of the church of the Holy Sepulchre at Jerusalem, and as it was the first church of any size that had been
erected in those regions for centuries past, it excited extraordinary interest
among the Franks and Gauls. In many of its features it resembles the beautiful church of San Vitale, at Ravenna (also supposed to have been influenced
by that of the Holy Sepulchre), which was begun by Theodorich, and completed under Justinian. Probably San Vitale was used as a pattern by
Charles's architects: we know that he caused marble columns (along with a
statue of Theodorich) to be brought from Ravenna to deck the church at
Aachen. Over the tomb of Charles, below the central dome (to which the
existing Pointed choir was added some centuries later), there hangs a huge
chandelier, the gift of Frederick Barbarossa.

[e] 'Romuleum Francis praestitit imperium.' — Elegy of Ermoldus Nigellus,
in Pertz, *M. G. H.* t. ii. So too Florus the Deacon —

Huic etenim cessit etiam gens Romula genti,
Regnorumque simul mater Roma inclyta cessit:
Huius ibi princeps regni diademata sumpsit
Munere apostolico, Christi munimine fretus.'

(*Ap.* Migne, cxix. p. 251.)

[f] A curious illustration of the influence of the name and fame of Charles,
even on remote nations, is supplied by a story in the Heimskringla of Snorri
Sturluson. Alfhild, a concubine of St. Olaf, had given birth to a child at
night, while Olaf was asleep; and Sigvat his favourite skald, seeing it to be
weak, and fearing it might die, caused it to be baptized at once, and gave
it the name of Magnus. When the king awoke and heard what had been
done, he was angry, and calling Sigvat asked, 'Why hast thou called the child

Church claimed then, as she claims still, the privilege which, in one form or another, humanity seems scarce able to deny itself, of raising to honours almost divine its great departed; and as in pagan times temples had risen to a deified Emperor, so churches were dedicated to St. Charlemagne. Between Sanctus Carolus and Divus Julius how strange an analogy and how strange a contrast!

Magnus, which is not a name of our race?' The skald answered, 'I called him after king Karl Magnus, who I knew had been the best man in the world.' The child grew up to be king Magnus the Good, the most popular and one of the greatest of the Norwegian kings; and from him the name became a common one, as it is to-day, over all the North.

CHAPTER VI

CAROLINGIAN AND ITALIAN EMPERORS

LEWIS the Pious,[a] left by Charles's death sole heir, had been some years before associated with his father in the Empire, and had been crowned by his father's hand in a way which, intentionally or not, appeared to deny the need of papal sanction. But it was soon seen that the strength to grasp the sceptre had not passed with it. Too mild to restrain his turbulent nobles, and thrown by over-conscientiousness into the hands of the clergy, he had reigned few years when dissensions broke out on all sides. Charles had wished the Empire to continue one, under the supremacy of a single Emperor, but with its several parts, Lombardy, Aquitaine, Austrasia, Bavaria, each a kingdom held by a scion of the reigning house. A scheme danger-ous in itself, and rendered more so by the absence or neg-lect of regular rules of succession, could with difficulty have been managed by a wise and firm monarch. Lewis tried in vain to satisfy his sons (Lothar, Lewis, and Charles) by dividing and redividing his dominions: they rebelled; he was deposed, and forced by the bishops to do penance, again restored, but without power, a tool in the hands of contending factions. On his death the sons flew to arms, and the first of the dynastic quarrels of modern Europe was fought out on the field of Fontenay. In the

CHAP. VI.
Lewis the Pious.

[a] Usage has established this translation of 'Hludowicus Pius,' but 'gentle' or 'kind-hearted' would better express the meaning of the epithet.

77

partition treaty of Verdun which followed, the Teutonic principle of equal division among heirs triumphed over the Roman one of the transmission of an indivisible Empire : the practical sovereignty of all three brothers was admitted in their respective territories, while a barren precedence was reserved to Lothar, with the imperial title which he, as the eldest, already enjoyed.   A more important result was the separation of the Gaulish and German nationalities. Their difference of feeling, shewn already in the support of Lewis the Pious by the Germans against the Gallo-Franks and the Church, perhaps an early instance of the aversion of the Teutonic peoples to the pretensions of the spiritual power, took now a permanent shape : modern Germany proclaims the era of A.D. 843 the beginning of her national existence, and celebrated its thousandth anniversary in 1843.   To Charles the Bald was given Francia Occidentalis, that is to say, Neustria and Aquitaine ; to Lothar, who as Emperor must possess the two capitals, Rome and Aachen, a long and narrow kingdom stretching from the North Sea to the Mediterranean, and including the northern half of Italy ; Lewis (surnamed, from his kingdom, the German) received all east of the Rhine, — Franks, Saxons, Bavarians, Austria, Carinthia, with possible supremacies over Czechs in far-off Bohemia and Moravia.   Throughout these regions German or some Slavonic tongue was spoken ; through Charles's kingdom a corrupt language, equally removed from Latin and from modern French. Lothar's, being mixed and having no national basis, was the weakest of the three, and soon dissolved into the separate sovereignties of Italy, Burgundy, and Lotharingia, the name of which is perpetuated in the German Lothringen, the French Lorraine.

On the tangled history of the period that follows it is not possible to do more than touch.   After passing from one branch of the Carolingian line to another,[b] the imperial sceptre was at last possessed and disgraced by Charles the Fat, who united all the dominions of his great-grandfather. This unworthy heir could not avail himself of recovered territory to strengthen or defend the expiring monarchy. He was driven out of Italy in A.D. 887, and his death in 888 has been usually taken as the date of the extinction of the Carolingian Empire of the West. The Germans, still attached to the ancient line, chose Arnulf, an illegitimate Carolingian (grandson of Lewis the German), for their king: he entered Italy and was crowned Emperor by his partisan the Corsican Pope Formosus, in 896. But Germany, divided and helpless, was in no condition to maintain her power over the Southern lands: Arnulf retreated in haste, leaving Rome and Italy to sixty years of stormy independence.

That time was indeed the nadir of order and civilization. From all sides the torrent of barbarism which Charles the Great had stemmed was rushing down upon his Empire. The Saracen wasted the Mediterranean coasts, and sacked Rome herself. The Dane and Norseman swept the Atlantic and the North Sea, pierced France and Germany by their rivers, burning, slaying, carrying off into captivity: pouring through the Straits of Gibraltar, they fell upon Provence and Italy. By land, while Wends and Czechs and Obotrites threw off the German yoke and threatened the borders, the wild Hungarian bands, pressing in from the steppes of the Caspian, dashed over Germany like the flying spray of a new wave of barbarism, and carried the terror of their battleaxes to the Apennines and the ocean. Under such strokes the already loosened fabric

CHAP. VI.
Lewis II.
Charles II
(the Bald).
Charles III
(the Fat).
End of the
Carolingian
Empire of
the West,
A.D. 888.

[b] The dynasty of the region which was to become modern France (Francia occidentalis) had the least share of it. Charles the Bald was the only West Frankish Emperor, and reigned a very short time.

CHAP. VI.

swiftly dissolved. No one thought of common defence or wide organization : the strong built castles, the weak became their bondsmen, or took shelter under the cowl : the governor — count, abbot, or bishop — tightened his grasp, turned a delegated into an independent, a personal into a territorial authority, and hardly owned a distant and feeble suzerain. The grand vision of a universal Christian Empire was being utterly lost in the isolation, the antagonism, the increasing localization of all powers : it might seem to have been but a passing gleam from an older and better world.

The German kingdom.

In Germany, the greatness of the evil worked at last its cure. When the male line of the Eastern branch of the Carolingians had ended in Lewis (surnamed the Child), son of Arnulf, the chieftains chose and the people accepted as king Conrad duke of the Franconians, and after him Henry duke of the Saxons, both representing the female line of Charles. Henry laid the foundations of a firm monarchy,

Henry the Fowler.

driving back the Magyars and Wends, recovering Lotharingia, founding towns to be centres of orderly life and strongholds against Hungarian irruptions. He had meant to claim at Rome the rights of his kingdom, rights which Conrad's weakness had at least asserted by the demand of tribute ; but death overtook him, and the plan was left to be fulfilled by Otto his son.

Otto the Great.

The Holy Roman Empire, taking the name in the sense which it commonly bore in later centuries, as denoting the sovereignty of Germany and Italy vested in a Germanic prince, is the creation of Otto the Great. Substantially, it is true, as well as technically, it was a prolongation of the Empire of Charles ; and it rested (as will be shewn in the sequel) upon ideas essentially the same as those which brought about the coronation of A.D. 800. But a revival is always more or less a revolution : the one hundred and

fifty years that had passed since the death of Charles had
brought with them changes which made Otto's position in
Germany and Europe less commanding and less autocratic
than his predecessor's. With narrower geographical limits,
his Empire had a less plausible claim to be the heir of Rome's
universal dominion ; and there were also differences in its
inner character and structure sufficient to justify us in considering Otto (as he is usually considered by his countrymen) not a mere successor after an interregnum, but rather
a second founder of the imperial throne in the West.

Before Otto's descent into Italy is described, something
must be said of the condition of that country, where circumstances had again made possible the plan of Theodorich,
permitted it to become an independent kingdom, and given
the title of Emperor to its king.

The bestowal of the imperial crown on Charles the Great
was long afterwards described as a 'transference of the
Empire from the Greeks to the Franks.' But it was not
in this light that the men of time regarded it. There was
no conscious purpose of settling the office in one nation or
one dynasty : there was but an extension of that long-
established principle of the equality of all Romans which
had made Trajan and Maximin Emperors. The '*arcanum
imperii*,' whereof Tacitus speaks, '*posse principem alibi
quam Romae fieri*,'[c] had even in heathen days become
alium quam Romanum; and now, the names of Roman
and Christian having grown co-extensive, a barbarian chieftain was, as a Roman citizen, eligible to the office of Roman
Emperor. Treating him as such, the people and pontiff
of the capital had in the vacancy of the Eastern throne
asserted their ancient rights of election, and while attempting to reverse the act of Constantine, had, as it turned out,
re-established the division of Valentinian. The dignity

[c] Tac. *Hist.* i. 4.

was therefore in strictness personal to Charles ; though, in point of fact, and by consent, it tended to become hereditarily transmissible, just as it had formerly been transmitted in the families of Constantine and Theodosius. To the Frankish crown or nation it was by no means legally attached, though the Franks might think it to be so ; it had passed to their king only because he was the greatest European potentate, and might equally well pass to some stronger race, if any such appeared. Hence, when the line of Carolingian Emperors ended in Charles the Fat, the rights of Rome and Italy might be taken to revive, and there was nothing to prevent the citizens and the Pope from choosing whom they would. At that memorable era (A.D. 888) the four kingdoms which this prince had united fell asunder ; West France, where Odo or Eudes then began to reign, was never again united to Germany ; East France (Germany) chose Arnulf ; Burgundy[d] split up into two principalities, in one of which (Transjurane) Rudolf proclaimed himself king, while the other (Cisjurane with Provence) submitted to Boso ;[e] while Italy (*i.e.* Northern and Middle Italy, for Southern Italy still obeyed Constantinople) was divided between the parties of Berengar of

[d] For an account of the various applications of the name Burgundy, see Appendix, Note A.

[e] The accession of Boso took place in A.D. 877, eleven years before Charles the Fat's death. But the new kingdom could not be considered legally settled until the latter date, and its establishment is at any rate a part of that general break-up of the great Carolingian Empire whereof A.D. 888 marks the crisis. See Appendix, Note A.

It is a curious mark of the reverence paid to the Carolingian blood, that Boso, a powerful and ambitious prince, seems to have chiefly rested his claims on the fact that he was husband of Irmingard, daughter of the Emperor Lewis II. Baron de Gingins la Sarraz (*Archiv für Schweizer Geschichte*) quotes a charter of his (drawn up when he seems to have doubted whether to call himself king), which begins, ' Ego Boso Dei gratia id quod sum, et coniux mea Irmingardis proles imperialis.'

Friuli and Guido of Spoleto. The former was chosen
king by the estates of Lombardy; the latter, and on his
speedy death his son Lambert, was crowned Emperor by
the Pope. Arnulf's descent chased them away and vindicated the claims of the Franks, but on his flight the Italians
and anti-German faction at Rome became again free.
Berengar was made king of Italy, and afterwards Emperor.   Lewis of Burgundy, son of Boso, renounced his
fealty to Berengar, and procured the imperial dignity,
whose vain title he retained through years of misery and
exile, till A.D. 928.[f] No one of these Emperors was strong
enough to rule well even in Italy; beyond it they were not
so much as recognized. The crown had become a bauble
with which unscrupulous Popes dazzled the vanity of princes
whom they summoned to their aid, and soothed the credu-
lity of their more honest supporters. The demoraliza-
tion and confusion of the country, the shameless profligacy
of Rome and her pontiffs during this period, were enough
to prevent a true Italian kingdom from being built up on
the basis of Roman choice and national unity. Italian
indeed it could scarcely be called, for these Emperors
were still in blood and manners Teutonic, and akin rather
to their Transalpine neighbours than to their Romanic subjects.   But Italian it might soon have become under a
vigorous rule which would have organized it within and
knit it together to resist attacks from without. And therefore the attempt to establish such a kingdom is remarkable,
for it might have had great consequences; might, if it had
prospered, have spared Italy much suffering and Germany
endless waste of strength and blood. He who from the
summit of Milan cathedral sees across the misty plain the
gleaming turrets of its icy wall sweep in a great arc from

---

[f] Lewis had been surprised by Berengar at Verona, blinded, and forced to
take refuge in his own kingdom of Provence.

North to West, may well wonder that a land which nature has so severed from its neighbours should, since history begins, have been so often the victim of their intrusive tyranny.

In A.D. 924 died Berengar, the last of these phantom Emperors. After him Hugh of Burgundy, and Lothar his son, reigned as kings of Italy, if puppets in the hands of a riotous aristocracy can be so called. Rome was meanwhile ruled by the consul or senator Alberic,[g] who had placed himself at the head of her never quite extinct republican institutions, and in the weakness of the Papacy was almost absolute in the city. Lothar dying, his widow

Adelheid, queen of Italy.

Adelheid[h] was sought in marriage by Adalbert son of Berengar II, the new Italian monarch. A gleam of romance is shed on the Empire's revival by her beauty and her adventures. Rejecting the odious alliance, she was seized by Berengar, escaped with difficulty from the loathsome prison where his barbarity had confined her, and appealed to Otto the German king, the model of that knightly virtue which was beginning to shew itself after the fierce brutality of the last age. He listened,

Otto's first expedition into Italy, A.D. 951.

descended into Lombardy by the Adige valley, espoused the injured queen[i] and forced Berengar to hold his kingdom as a vassal of the East Frankish crown. That prince was turbulent and faithless; new complaints ere long

Invitation sent by the Pope to Otto.

reached his liege lord, and envoys from the Pope offered Otto the imperial title if he would revisit and pacify Italy. The proposal was well-timed. Men still thought, as they had thought in the centuries before the Carolingians, that the Empire was suspended, not extinct; and the desire

[g] Alberic is called variously senator, consul, patrician, and prince of the Romans.

[h] Adelheid was daughter of Rudolf, king of Transjurane Burgundy. She was at this time in her nineteenth year.

[i] Otto's first wife, the English Edith, grand-daughter of Alfred the Great, had died some time before.

to see its effective power restored, the belief that with- CHAP. VI.
out it the world could never be right, might seem better
grounded than it had been before the coronation of
Charles. Then the imperial name had recalled only the *Motives for*
faint memories of Roman majesty and order : now it was *reviving the*
Empire.
also associated with the golden age of the first Frankish
Emperor, when a single firm and just hand had guided
the State, reformed the Church, repressed the excesses of
local power : when Christianity had advanced against
heathendom, civilizing as she went, fearing neither Hun
nor Saracen. One annalist tells us that Charles was
elected ' lest the pagans should insult the Christians, if
the name of Emperor should have ceased among the
Christians.' [j] The motive would be bitterly enforced
by the calamities of the last fifty years. In a time of
disintegration, confusion, strife, all the longings of every
wiser and better soul for unity, for peace and law, for
some bond to bring Christian men and Christian states
together against the common enemy of the faith, were
but so many cries for the restoration of the Roman
Empire.[k] These were the feelings that on the field of
Merseburg broke forth in the shout of ' Henry the
Emperor' : these the hopes of the Teutonic host when A.D. 933.
after the great deliverance of the Lechfeld they greeted

---

[j] *Chron. Moiss.*, in Pertz, *M. G. H.* i. 305. So Pope John VIII, when summoning Charles the Bald into Italy, says, ' Et hanc terram, quae sui imperii
caput est, ad libertatem reducat, ne quando dicant gentes : Ubi est imperator
illius ? ' — Letter in Mansi, *Concil.* xvii. 29.

[k] See especially the poem of Florus the Deacon (printed in the Benedictine
collection and in Migne, cxix. pp. 249–253), a bitter lament over the dissolution of the Carolingian Empire, from which I take four lines (p. 251) : —

> ' Quid faciant populi quos ingens alluit Hister,
> Quos Rhenus Rhodanusque rigant, Ligerisve, Padusve,
> Quos omnes dudum tenuit concordia nexos,
> Foedere nunc rupto divortia moesta fatigant ? '

CHAP. VI.

Condition
of Italy.

Otto, conqueror of the Magyars, as 'Imperator, Pater Patriae.' [1]

The anarchy which an Emperor was needed to heal was at its worst in Italy, desolated by the feuds of a crowd of petty princes. A succession of infamous Popes, raised by means yet more infamous, the paramours and sons of Theodora and Marozia, had disgraced the chair of the Apostle, and though Rome herself might be lost to decency, Western Christendom was roused to anger. The rule of Alberic had been succeeded by the wildest confusion, and calls were heard for the renewal of that imperial authority which all admitted in theory,[m] and which nothing but the resolute opposition of Alberic himself had prevented Otto from claiming in 951. From the Eastern Empire, to which Italy was more than once tempted to turn, nothing could be hoped ; its dangers from foreign enemies were aggravated by the plots of the court and the seditions of the capital ; it was becoming more and more alienated from the West by the Photian schism and the question regarding the Procession of the Holy Ghost, which that quarrel had started. Germany was extending and consolidating herself, had escaped domestic perils, and might think of reviving ancient claims. No one could be more willing to revive them than Otto the Great. His ardent spirit, after waging a successful struggle against the turbulent magnates of his German realm, had engaged him in wars with the surrounding nations, and was now captivated by the vision of a wider sway and a loftier world-embracing dignity. Nor was the prospect which the papal offer opened up less

[1] Widukind, *Annales* (bk. iii. c. 49), in Pertz, *M. G. H., Script.* iii. p. 459. It may, however, be doubted whether the annalist is not here giving a very free rendering of the triumphant cries of the German army.

[m] Cf. esp. the '*Libellus de imperatoria potestate in urbe Roma*,' in Pertz, *M. G. H., Script.* iii. pp. 719–722.

welcome to his people. Aachen, their capital, was the
ancestral home of the house of Pipin : their sovereign, although himself a Saxon by race, titled himself king of the
Franks, in opposition to the Frankish rulers of the Western
branch, whose Teutonic character was disappearing among
the Romanized inhabitants of Gaul.   They held themselves
in every way the true representatives of the Carolingian
power, and accounted the period since Arnulf's death
nothing but an interregnum which had suspended but
not impaired their rights over Rome. 'For so long,' says
a writer of the time, 'as there remain kings of the Franks,
so long will the dignity of the Roman Empire not wholly
perish, seeing that it will abide in its kings.'[n]   The recovery
of Italy was therefore to German eyes a righteous as well
as a glorious design, approved by the Teutonic Church
which had lately been negotiating with Rome on the subject of missions to the heathen, embraced by the people,
who saw in it an accession of strength to their young kingdom.   Everything smiled on Otto's enterprise, and the
connection which was destined to bring so much strife
and woe to Germany and to Italy was welcomed by the
wisest of both countries as the beginning of a better
era.

Whatever were Otto's own feelings, whether or not *Descent of*
misgivings were within him lest he might be sacrificing, as *Otto the*
modern writers have thought that he did sacrifice, the *Great into*
greatness of his German kingdom to the lust of universal *Italy.*
dominion, he shewed no hesitation in his acts. Descending from the Alps with an overpowering force, he was

[n] 'Licet videamus Romanorum regnum in maxima parte iam destructum,
tamen quamdiu reges Francorum duraverint qui Romanum imperium tenere
debent, dignitas Romani imperii ex toto non peribit, quia stabit in regibus
suis.' — *Liber de Antichristo*, addressed by Adso, abbot of Moutier-en-Der,
to Queen Gerberga (circa A.D. 950), *ap.* Migne, ci. p. 1290.

acknowledged as king of Italy at Pavia;[o] and, having first taken an oath to protect the Holy See and respect the liberties of the city, advanced to Rome.   There, with Adelheid his queen, he was crowned in the church of St. John Lateran by John XII, on the day of the Purification, the second of February, A.D. 962.   The details of his election and coronation are unfortunately still more scanty than in the case of his great predecessor.   Most of our authorities dwell chiefly on the Pope's part in the act,[p] yet it is plain that the consent of the people was still thought an essential part of the ceremony, and that Otto rested after all on his host of conquering Saxons.   Be this as it may, there was neither question raised nor opposition made in Rome.   The usual courtesies and promises were exchanged between Emperor and Pope, the latter owning himself a subject, and the citizens swore for the future to elect no pontiff without Otto's consent.

[o] From the money which Otto struck in Italy, it seems that he did occasionally use the title of king of Italy or of the Lombards.   That he was crowned is perhaps not absolutely certain.

[p] 'A papa imperator ordinatur,' says Hermannus Contractus. 'Dominum Ottonem, ad hoc usque vocatum regem, non solum Romano sed et poene totius Europae populo acclamante imperatorem consecravit Augustum.'—*Annal. Quedlinb.*, ad ann. 962. 'Benedictionem a domno apostolico Iohanne, cuius rogatione huc venit, cum sua coniuge promeruit imperialem ac patronus Romanae effectus est ecclesiae.'—Thietmar, ii. c. 7 (Pertz, *M. G. H.*, *Script.* iii. p. 747). 'Acclamatione totius Romani populi ab apostolico Iohanne, filio Alberici, imperator et Augustus vocatur et ordinatur.'—Continuator Reginonis, *s. a.* 962 (Pertz, *M. G. H.*, *Script.* i. p. 625).   And similarly the other annalists.

CHAPTER VII

THEORY OF THE MEDIAEVAL EMPIRE

THESE were the events and circumstances of the time: let us now look at the causes. The restoration of the Empire by Charles may seem to be sufficiently accounted for by the width of his conquests, by the peculiar connection which already subsisted between him and the Roman Church, by his commanding personal character, by the temporary vacancy of the throne at Constantinople. The causes of its revival under Otto must be sought deeper. Making every allowance for the favouring incidents which have already been dwelt upon, there must have been some further influence at work to draw him and his successors, Saxon and Frankish kings, so far from home in pursuit of a barren crown, to lead the Italians to accept the dominion of a stranger and a barbarian, to make the Empire itself appear through the whole Middle Age not what it seems now, a gorgeous anachronism, but an institution divine and necessary, having its foundations in the very nature and order of things. The Empire of the elder Rome had been splendid in its life, yet its judgement was written in the misery to which it had brought the provinces, and the helplessness that had invited the attacks of the barbarian. Now, as we at least can see, it had long been dead, and the course of events was adverse to its revival. Its actual representatives, the Roman people, were a turbulent rabble, sunk in a profligacy notorious even in that rude age. Yet not the less for all this did men cling to the idea, and strive through long ages to stem the irre-sistible time-current, fondly believing that they were breast-ing it even while it was sweeping them ever faster and faster away from the old order into a region of new thoughts, new feelings, new forms of life. Not till the days of the Renaissance and the Reformation was the illusion dispelled.

Mediaeval theories.   The explanation is to be found in the beliefs which filled the human mind during these centuries. To describe those beliefs concisely and yet faithfully is difficult, for although some of their salient features remained substantially the same from the days of St. Augustine almost to the days of Erasmus, no single epoch in that long series of generations can be taken as shewing them in their full and typical com-pleteness. The system of ideas which created and sustained the Holy Empire was in some of its aspects, or some of its parts, constantly growing, in other aspects and other parts constantly decaying, from the fifth century to the fifteenth, the relative prominence of its cardinal doctrines varying from age to age. But, just as the painter who sees the ever-shifting lights and shades play over the face of a wide land-scape faster than his brush can place them on the canvas, in despair at representing their exact position at any single moment, contents himself with painting the effects that are broadest and most permanent, and at giving rather the impression which the scene makes on him than every detail of the scene itself, so here the best and indeed the only practicable course seems to be that of setting forth in its most self-consistent form the body of ideas and be-liefs on which the Empire rested, although this form may not be exactly that which they can be asserted to have worn in any one century, and although the illustrations adduced may have to be taken sometimes from earlier, sometimes from later writers. As the fundamental doc-

trines were in their essence the same during the whole
of the Middle Ages, such a general description as is here
attempted may, *mutatis mutandis*, serve true for the tenth
as well as for the fourteenth century.

The Middle Ages were, as compared with the ages that
preceded and the ages that followed, essentially unpoliti-
cal. Ideas as familiar to the commonwealths of antiquity
as to ourselves, ideas of the common good as the object of
the State, of the rights of the people, of the comparative
merits of different forms of government, were to those
generations, though such ideas often found an unconscious
expression in practical expedients, in their speculative form
little known, and to most men incomprehensible.[a] Feudalism was the one great secular institution to which those
times gave birth, and feudalism was a social and a legal
system, only indirectly and by consequence a political one.
Yet the human mind, so far from being idle, was in certain directions never more active ; nor was it possible for
it to remain without general conceptions regarding the
relation of men to each other in this world. Such conceptions were neither made an expression of the actual present condition of things nor scientifically determined by an
induction from the past ; they were partly inherited from
the imperial scheme of law and government that had preceded, partly evolved from the principles of that metaphysical theology which was ripening into scholasticism.
Now the two great ideas which expiring antiquity bequeathed to the ages that followed were those of a World-
Monarchy and a World-Religion.

Before that great movement towards assimilation which *The World-*
began with the Hellenization of the East and was com- *Religion.*
pleted by the Western and Northern as well as the East-

[a] Political thought, in the modern sense of the word, began to re-emerge
under the influence of Aristotle in the later half of the thirteenth century.

ern conquests of Rome, men, with little knowledge of each other, with no experience of wide political union,[b] had held differences of race to be natural and irremovable barriers. Similarly, religion appeared to them a matter purely local and national; and as there were gods of the hills and gods of the valleys,[c] gods of the land and of the sea, so each tribe rejoiced in its peculiar deities, looking on the natives of another country who worshipped other deities as Gentiles, natural foes, unclean beings. Such feelings, if keenest in the East, frequently shew themselves in the early records of Greece and Italy: in Homer the hero who wanders over the unfruitful sea glories in sacking the cities of the stranger;[d] the primitive Latins have the same word for a foreigner and an enemy: the exclusive systems of Egypt, Hindostan, China, are only more vehement expressions of the belief which made Athenian philosophers look on a state of war between Greeks and barbarians as natural, and defend slavery on the same ground of the original diversity of the races that rule and the races that serve.[e] The Roman dominion giving to many nations a common speech and law, smote this feeling on its political side; Christianity more effectually

---

[b] Empires like the Persian did nothing to assimilate the subject races, who retained their own laws and customs, sometimes their own princes, and were bound only to serve in the armies and fill the treasury of the Great King.

[c] See 1 Kings xx. 23, with which compare 2 Kings xvii. 26.

[d] Od. iii. 72: —

.... ἢ μαψιδίως ἀλάλησθε,
οἷά τε ληϊστῆρες, ὑπεὶρ ἅλα, τοίτ' ἀλόωνται
ψυχὰς παρθέμενοι, κακὸν ἀλλοδαποῖσι φέροντες;

Cf. Od. ix. 39; Il. v. 214 ἀλλότριος φώς; and the Hymn to the Pythian Apollo, l. 274.

[e] Plato, in the beginning of the Laws, represents it as natural between all states: πόλεμος φύσει ὑπάρχει πρὸς ἁπάσας τὰς πόλεις. Even Aristotle deems slavery to be based on a natural distinction, though before his time the orator Alcidamas had said, οὐδένα δοῦλον ἡ φύσις πεποίηκεν.

banished it from the soul by substituting for the variety of local pantheons the belief in One God, before whom all men are equal.[f]

It is on religion that the inmost and deepest life of a nation rests. Because divinity was divided, humanity had been divided likewise; the doctrine of the unity of God now enforced the unity of man, who had been created in His image. The first lesson of Christianity was love, a love that was to join in one body those whom suspicion and prejudice and pride of race had hitherto kept apart. There was thus formed by the new religion a community of the faithful, a Holy Empire, designed to gather all men into its bosom, and standing opposed to the manifold poly-theisms of the older world, exactly as the universal sway of the Caesars was contrasted with the innumerable king-doms and city republics that had gone before it. The analogy of the two movements made them appear parts of one great world-movement towards unity: the coinci-dence of their boundaries, which had begun before Con-stantine, lasted long enough after him to associate them indissolubly together, and make the names of Roman and Christian convertible.[g]

Coincide with the World-Empire.

Men who were already disposed (for reasons set forth above [h]) to believe the Roman Empire to be eternal, came, under influences of far greater power, to believe the Church, founded by the ever-living Son and guided by the ever-present Spirit of God, to be also eternal. Seeing the two institutions allied and conterminous, they took their alli-ance and interdependence to be equally eternal; and went

World-State and the Uni-versal Church.

[f] See especially Acts xvii. 26; Gal. iii. 28; Eph. ii. 11 sqq., iv. 3–6; Col. iii. 11.

[g] 'Romanos enim vocitant homines nostrae religionis,' says Gregory of Tours. In the early Middle Ages, 'Ρωμαῖοι is occasionally used to mean Christians, as opposed to Ἕλληνες, heathens.

[h] See p. 12, *ante.*

on for centuries believing in the necessary existence of the Roman Empire, because they believed in its necessary union with the Catholic Church.

Oecumenical councils, where the whole spiritual body gathered itself from every part of the temporal realm under the presidency of the temporal head, presented the most visible and impressive examples of the connection of the World-Church and the World-State. The language of civil government was, throughout the West, that of the sacred writings and of worship; the greatest mind of his generation consoled the faithful for the fall of their earthly commonwealth Rome, by describing to them its successor and representative, the 'city which hath foundations, whose builder and maker is God.' [1]

Preservation of the unity of the Church. Of these two parallel unities, that of the political and that of the religious society, meeting in the higher unity of all Christians, which may be indifferently called Catholicism or Romanism (since in that day those words would have had the same meaning), that unity only which had been entrusted to the keeping of the Church survived the storms of the fifth century. Many reasons may be assigned for the firmness with which she clung to it. Seeing one institution after another falling to pieces around her, seeing how countries and cities were being severed from each other by the irruption of strange tribes and the increasing difficulty of communication, she strove to save religious fellowship by strengthening the ecclesiastical organization,

[1] Augustine, in the *De Civitate Dei*. His influence, great through all the Middle Ages, was greater on no one than on Charles. — 'Delectabatur et libris sancti Augustini, praecipueque his qui De Civitate Dei praetitulati sunt.' — Eginhard, *Vita Karoli*, cap. 24. One can imagine the impression which such a chapter as that on the true happiness of a Christian Emperor (Book v, chap. 24) would make upon a pious and susceptible mind. It is hardly too much to say that the Holy Empire was built upon the foundation of the *De Civitate Dei*.

by drawing tighter every bond of outward union. Necessities of faith were still more powerful. Truth, it was said, is one, and as it must bind into one body all who hold it, so it is only by continuing in that body that they can preserve it. There is one Flock and one Shepherd. Thus along with the growing rigidity of dogma, which may be traced from the council of Jerusalem to the council of Trent, there had been developed, out of the original and natural attachment to the teaching of the apostles preserved by tradition, the idea that the Church is the divinely-appointed guardian of doctrine, able to supplement as well as to interpret the revealed word: and with this, there had also grown up the habit of exalting the universal conscience and belief above the individual, and allowing the soul to approach God only through the universal consciousness, represented by the sacerdotal order: principles still maintained by one branch of the Christian Church, and for some at least of which reasons could be assigned then, in the paucity of written records and the blind ignorance of the mass of the people, weightier than those on which stress has in later days been laid.

Mediaeval Theology requires One Visible Catholic Church.

There was also another cause yet more deeply seated, and which it is hard adequately to describe. It was not exactly a want of faith in the unseen, nor a shrinking fear which dared not look forth on the universe alone: it was rather the powerlessness of the untrained mind to realize the idea as an idea and live in it: it was the tendency to see everything in the concrete, to turn the parable into a fact, the doctrine into its most literal application, the symbol into the essential ceremony; the tendency which interposed the Virgin Mother and the saints between the worshipper and the spiritual Deity, and could satisfy its devotional feelings only by visible images even of these; which conceived of man's aspirations and temptations as the result of the direct action of angels and devils; which expressed the strivings of the soul after purity by the search for the Holy Grail; which in the Crusades sent myriads to win at Jerusalem by earthly arms the sepulchre of Him whom they found it hard to serve in their own spirit and approach by their own prayers. And therefore it was that the whole fabric of mediaeval Christianity rested upon the idea of the Visible Church. Such a Church could be in nowise local or limited. To acquiesce in the establishment of National Churches, independent and self-sufficing, would have appeared to those men, as it must always appear when scrutinized, opposed to the genius of Christianity as a religion meant for all mankind, defensible, when capable of defence at all, only as a temporary resource in the presence of insuperable difficulties. Had this plan, on which so many have dwelt with complacency in later times, been proposed either to the primitive Church in its adversity or to the dominant Church of the ninth century, it would have been rejected with horror. But since there were as yet no nations, the plan was one which did not and could not present itself. The Visible Church was therefore the Church Universal, the whole congregation of Christian men dispersed throughout the world, the Church held together by one hope, one faith, one baptism.[1]

Idea of political unity upheld by the clergy. Now of the Visible Church the emblem and stay was the priesthood; and it was by them, in whom dwelt whatever of learning and thought was left in Europe, that the second great idea whereof mention has been made — the belief in one universal temporal state — was preserved. As a matter of fact, that state had perished out of the West, and it might seem their interest to let its memory be lost. They, however, did not so calculate their interest. So far

[1] Eph. iv. 4–6.

from feeling themselves opposed to the civil authority in
the seventh and eighth centuries, as many of them came
to do in the twelfth and thirteenth, the clergy were fully
persuaded that its maintenance was indispensable to their
own welfare, and to that of the whole Christian commonwealth. They were, be it remembered, at first Romans
themselves, living by the Roman law, using Latin as their
proper tongue, and imbued with the idea of the historical
connection of the two powers. And by them chiefly was
that idea expounded and enforced for many generations,
by none more earnestly than by Alcuin of York, the adviser of Charles.[k] The limits of those two powers had
become confounded in practice : bishops were princes, the
chief ministers of the sovereign, sometimes even the leaders
of their flocks in war : kings were accustomed to summon
ecclesiastical councils and appoint to ecclesiastical offices.

But, like the unity of the Church, the doctrine of a
universal monarchy had a theoretical as well as an historical basis, and may be traced up to those metaphysical
ideas out of which the system we call Realism developed
itself. The beginnings of philosophy in those times were
logical ; and its first efforts were to distribute and classify :
system, subordination, uniformity, appeared to be that
which was most desirable in thought as in life. The search
after causes became a search after principles of classification,
since simplicity and truth were held to be attainable not by
an analysis of thought into its elements, nor by an observation of the process of its growth, but rather through a
sort of genealogy of notions, a statement of the relations of

Influence of the meta-physics of the time upon the theory of a World-State.

[k] 'Quapropter universorum precibus fidelium optandum est, ut in omnem
gloriam vestram extendatur imperium, ut scilicet catholica fides . . . veraciter
in una confessione cunctorum cordibus infigatur, quatenus summi Regis do-
nante pietate eadem sanctae pacis et perfectae caritatis omnes ubique regat et
custodiat unitas.' — Quoted by Waitz (*Deutsche Verfassungsgeschichte*, ii. 182)
from an unprinted letter of Alcuin.

classes as containing or excluding each other. These classes, genera, or species, were not themselves held to be conceptions formed by the mind from phenomena, nor mere fortuitous aggregates of objects grouped under and called by some common name; they were real things, existing independently of the individuals who composed them, recognized rather than created by the human mind. In this view, Humanity is an essential quality present in all men, and making them what they are: as regards it they are therefore not many but one, the differences between individuals being no more than accidents. The whole truth of their being lies in the universal property, which alone has a permanent and independent existence. The common nature of the individuals thus gathered into one Being is typified in its two aspects, the spiritual and the secular, by two persons, the World-Priest and the World-Monarch, who present on earth a similitude of the Divine unity. For, as we have seen, it was through its concrete and symbolic expression that a thought could then be best apprehended.[1]

Although it was primarily to unity in religion that the clerical body was both by doctrine and by practice attached,

[1] A curious illustration of this tendency of mind is afforded by the descriptions we meet with of Learning or Theology (*Studium*) as a concrete existence, having a visible dwelling in the University of Paris. The three great powers which rule human life, says one writer, the Popedom, the Empire, and Learning, have been severally entrusted to the three foremost nations of Europe : Italians, Germans, French. ' His siquidem tribus, scilicet sacerdotio imperio et studio, tanquam tribus virtutibus, videlicet naturali vitali et scientiali, catholica ecclesia spiritualiter mirificatur, augmentatur et regitur. His itaque tribus, tanquam fundamento pariete et tecto, eadem ecclesia tanquam materialiter proficit. Et sicut ecclesia materialis uno tantum fundamento et uno tecto eget, parietibus vero quatuor, ita imperium quatuor habet parietes, hoc est, quatuor imperii sedes, Aquisgranum, Arelatum, Mediolanum, Romam.' — *Iordanis Chronica;* in Schardius, *Sylloge Tractatuum.* And see Döllinger, *Die Vergangenheit und Gegenwart der katholischen Theologie,* p. 8.

they found this inseparable from the corresponding unity in politics. They saw that every act of man has a social and public as well as a moral and personal bearing, and concluded that the rules which directed and the powers which rewarded or punished must be parallel and similar, not so much two powers as different manifestations of one and the same. That the souls of all Christian men should be guided by a well compacted hierarchy, rising through successive grades to one supreme head, while for their deeds they were answerable to a multitude of local, unconnected, mutually irresponsible potentates, appeared to them necessarily opposed to the Divine order. As they could not imagine, nor value if they had imagined, a communion of the saints without its expression in a Visible Church, so in matters temporal they recognized no brotherhood of spirit without the bonds of form, no universal humanity save in the image of a universal State.[m] In this, as in so much else, the men of the Middle Ages were the slaves of the letter, unable, with all their aspirations, to rise above the concrete, and prevented by the very grandeur and boldness of their conceptions from carrying them out in practice against the enormous obstacles that met them.

Deep as this belief had struck its roots, it might never have risen to maturity nor sensibly affected the progress of events, had it not gained in the pre-existence of the

[m] 'Una est sola respublica totius populi Christiani, ergo de necessitate erit et unus solus princeps et rex illius reipublicae, statutus et stabilitus ad ipsius fidei et populi Christiani dilatationem et defensionem. Ex qua ratione concludit etiam Augustinus (*De Civitate Dei*, lib. xix.) quod extra ecclesiam nunquam fuit nec potuit nec poterit esse verum imperium, etsi fuerint imperatores qualitercumque et secundum quid, non simpliciter, qui fuerunt extra fidem Catholicam et ecclesiam.' — Engelbert (abbot of Admont in Upper Austria), *De Ortu Progressu et Fine Imperii Romani* (circà 1310), *ap.* Goldast, *Politica imperii*, p. 754.

In this ' de necessitate' everything is included.

CHAP. VII.

*The ideal
State sup-
posed to be
embodied in
the Roman
Empire.*

monarchy of Rome a definite shape and a definite purpose. It was chiefly by means of the Papacy that this came to pass at the end of and after the second century. The Roman Church had already begun to be regarded in the West as a specially trustworthy guardian of Christian doctrine. The pre-eminence of the City had given to the Roman bishop a position of influence and authority great even in the days of Irenaeus : and when, under Constantine, the Christian Church was strengthening her organization on the model of the State which thenceforth protected her, the bishop of the capital perceived and improved the analogy between himself and the head of the civil govern- ment. The notion that the chair of Peter was the imperial throne of the Church had dawned upon the Popes very early in their history, and grew stronger every century under the operation of causes already specified. Even before the Empire had fallen in the West, St. Leo the Great could boast that to Rome, exalted by the preaching of the chief of the Apostles to be a holy nation, a chosen people, a priestly and royal city, there had been appointed a spiritual dominion wider than her earthly sway.[n]   In A.D. 476 Rome ceased to be the political capital of the Western countries, and the Papacy, inheriting no small part of the local authority which had belonged to the Emperor's officers, drew to herself the reverence which the name of the city still commanded, until, in the days which followed her emancipation from the control of the Emperors at Constantinople, she had perfected in theory a scheme which made her the exact counterpart of the departed despotism, the centre of the hierarchy, absolute

mistress of the Christian world. The character of that scheme is best set forth in the singular document, most stupendous of all the mediaeval forgeries, which under the

n See note [g], p. 31.

name of the Donation of Constantine commanded for
seven centuries the almost unquestioning belief of mankind.[o] Itself a portentous fabrication, it is unimpeachable
evidence of the thoughts and beliefs of the priesthood
which framed it, some time between the middle of the
eighth and the end of the ninth century. It tells how
Constantine the Great, cured of his leprosy by the prayers
of Pope Sylvester, resolved, on the fourth day from his
baptism, to forsake the ancient seat for a new capital on the
Bosphorus, lest the continuance of the secular government
should cramp the freedom of the spiritual, and how he
bestowed therewith upon the Pope and his successors the
sovereignty over Italy and the countries of the West. But
this is not all, although this is what historians, in admiration of its splendid audacity, have chiefly dwelt upon.
The edict proceeds to grant to the Roman pontiff and his
clergy a series of dignities and privileges, all of them
enjoyed by the Emperor and his senate, all of them showing the same desire to make the pontifical a copy of the
imperial office. The Pope is to inhabit the Lateran palace,
to wear the diadem, the collar, the purple cloak, to carry
the sceptre, and to be attended by a body of chamberlains.
Similarly his clergy are to ride on white horses and receive
the honours and immunities of the senate and patricians.[p]

The notion which prevails throughout, that the chief of
the religious society must be in every point conformed to
his prototype the chief of the civil, is the key to all the
thoughts and acts of the Roman clergy, not less plainly
seen in the details of papal ceremonial than it is in the
gigantic scheme of papal legislation. The Canon law
which the Roman Curia began to build up after Pope

*Interdepen-
dence of
Papacy and
Empire.*

[o] See p. 43, *ante:* and cf. Aegidi, *Der Fürstenrath nach dem Luneviller
Frieden.*

[p] See as to the Donation Note IV at end of this volume.

Hadrian I, and which rose apace in the eleventh and twelfth centuries, with the enlarged activity and growing claims of the Papacy, was intended by its authors to reproduce and rival the imperial jurisprudence. In the middle of the thirteenth century Gregory IX, who was the first to consolidate it into a code, sought the fame and received the title of the Justinian of the Church, and a correspondence was traced between its divisions and those of the Corpus Iuris Civilis. But during the earlier period the wish and purpose of the clergy, even when the temporal power was weak or hostile, was to imitate and rival, not to supersede it, since they held it the necessary complement of their own, and thought the Christian people equally imperilled by the fall of either. Hence the reluctance of Gregory II to break with the East Roman princes, and the maintenance of their titular sovereignty till A.D. 800 : hence the part which the Holy See played in transferring the crown to Charles, the first sovereign of the West capable of fulfilling its duties ; hence the grief with which its weakness under his successors was seen, the gladness when it descended to Otto as representative of the Frankish kingdom.

The Roman Empire revived in a new character. Up to the era of A.D. 800 there had been at Constantinople a legitimate historical prolongation of the Roman Empire. Technically, as we have seen, the election of Charles, after the deposition of Constantine VI, was itself a prolongation, and maintained the old rights and forms in their integrity. But the Pope, though he knew it not, did far more than effect a change of dynasty when he rejected Irene and crowned the barbarian chief. Restorations are always delusive. As well might one hope to stop the earth's course in her orbit as to arrest that ceaseless change and movement in human affairs which forbids an old institution, suddenly transplanted into a new order

of things, from filling its ancient place and serving its CHAP. VII.
former ends. The dictatorship at Rome in the second
Punic war was not more unlike the dictatorships of Sulla
and Caesar, nor the States-general of Louis XIII to the
assembly which his unhappy descendant convoked in 1789,
than was the imperial office of Theodosius to that of
Charles the Frank; and the seal, ascribed to A.D. 800,
which bears the legend ' Renovatio Romani Imperii,' q expresses, more justly perhaps than was intended by its
author, a second birth of the Roman Empire.

It is not, however, from the days of the later Carolingians that a proper view of this new creation can be
formed. That period was one of transition, of fluctuation
and uncertainty, in which the office, passing from one
dynasty and country to another, had not time to acquire a
settled character and claims, and was without the power
that would have enabled it to support them. From the
coronation of Otto the Great a new period begins, in which
the ideas that have been described as floating in men's
minds took clearer shape, and attached to the imperial
title a body of definite rights and definite duties. It is
this latter phase, the Holy Empire, that we have now to
consider.

The realistic philosophy, and the needs of a time when *Position and*
the only notion of civil or religious order was submission *functions of*
to authority, required the World-State to be a monarchy: *the Emperor.*

q The seal is preserved at Paris. There are few monuments of that age whose
genuineness can be considered altogether beyond doubt; but this seal has
many respectable authorities in its favour. See, among others, Le Blanc,
Dissertation historique sur quelques monnoies de Charlemagne, Paris, 1689;
J. M. Heineccius, *De veteribus Germanorum aliarumque nationum sigillis*,
Lips. 1709; Anastasius, *Vitae Pontificum Romanorum*, ed. Vignoli, Romae,
1752; Götz, *Deutschlands Kayser-Münzen des Mittelalters*, Dresden, 1827;
and the authorities cited by Waitz, *Deutsche Verfassungsgeschichte*, iii. 179,
n. 4.

tradition, as well as the continued existence of a part of the ancient institutions, gave the monarch the name of Roman Emperor. A king could not be universal sovereign, for there were many kings: the Emperor must be universal, for there had never been but one Emperor; he had in older and brighter days been the actual lord of the civilized world; the seat of his power was placed beside that of the spiritual autocrat of Christendom.[1] His functions will be seen most clearly if we deduce them from the leading principle of mediaeval mythology, the exact correspondence of earth and heaven. As God, in the midst of the celestial hierarchy, rules blessed spirits in Paradise, so the Pope, His vicar, raised above priests, bishops, metropolitans, reigns over the souls of mortal men below. But as God is Lord of earth as well as of heaven, so must he (the *Imperator coelestis* [8]) be represented by a second earthly viceroy, the Emperor (*Imperator terrenus*), whose authority shall be of and for this present life. And as in this present world the soul cannot act save through the body, while yet the body is no more than an instrument and means for the soul's manifestation, so must there be a rule and care of men's bodies as well as of their souls, yet subordinated always to the well-being of that element which is the

[1] 'Praeterea mirari se dilecta fraternitas tua quod non Francorum set Romanorum imperatores nos appellemus; set scire te convenit quia nisi Romanorum imperatores essemus, utique nec Francorum. A Romanis enim hoc nomen et dignitatem assumpsimus, apud quos profecto primum tantae culmen sublimitatis effulsit,' &c. — *Letter of the Emperor Lewis II to Basil the Emperor at Constantinople,* from *Chron. Salernit., ap.* Pertz, *M. H. G., Script.* iii. p. 523 (c. 106).

[8] 'Illam (*sc.* Romanan ecclesiam) solus ille fundavit, et super petram fidei mox nascentis erexit, qui beato aeternae vitae clavigero terreni simul et coelestis imperii iura commisit.' — Pope Nicholas II, A.D. 1060, in *Corpus Iuris Canonici,* Dist. xxii. c. 1. The expression is not uncommon in mediaeval writers. So 'unum est imperium Patris et Filii et Spiritus Sancti, cuius est pars ecclesia constituta in terris,' in Lewis II's letter.

purer and the more enduring.   It is under the emblem of
soul and body that the relation of the papal and imperial
power is presented to us throughout the Middle Ages.[t]
The Pope, as God's vicar in matters spiritual, is to lead
men to eternal life; the Emperor, as vicar in matters temporal, must so control them in their dealings with one another that they may be able to pursue undisturbed the
spiritual life, and thereby attain the same supreme and
common end of everlasting happiness.   In the view of this
object his chief duty is to maintain peace in the world,
while towards the Church his position is that of Advocate
or Patron, a title borrowed from the practice adopted by
churches and monasteries of choosing some powerful baron
to protect their lands and lead their tenants in war.[u]   The
functions of Advocacy are twofold: at home to make the
Christian people obedient to the priesthood, and to execute
priestly decrees upon heretics and sinners; abroad to
propagate the faith among the heathen, not sparing to use

[t] ' Merito summus Pontifex Romanus episcopus dici potest rex et sacerdos.
Si enim dominus noster Iesus Christus sic appellatur, non videtur incongruum
suum vocare successorem.   Corporale et temporale ex spirituali et perpetuo
dependet, sicut corporis operatio ex virtute animae.   Sicut ergo corpus per
animam habet esse virtutem et operationem, ita et temporalis iurisdictio principum per spiritualem Petri et successorum eius.' — St. Thomas Aquinas, *De
Regimine Principum.*

[u] ' Nonne Romana ecclesia tenetur imperatori tanquam suo patrono, et
imperator ecclesiam fovere et defensare tanquam suus vere patronus? certe
sic. . . . Patronis vero concessum est ut praelatos in ecclesiis sui patronatus
eligant.   Cum ergo imperator onus sentiat patronatus, ut qui tenetur eam de-
fendere, sentire debet honorem et emolumentum.'   I quote this from a curious document, a pamphlet called forth by the great schism of A.D. 1378, in
Goldast's collection of tracts (*Monarchia Imperii*, vol. i. p. 229), entitled
'*Letter of the four Universities, Paris, Oxford, Prague, and the " Romana
generalitas,"* to the Emperor Wenzel and Pope Urban,' A.D. 1380.   The title
or description is obviously untrue, but the document has all the appearance
of being practically contemporary.   It is therefore available as evidence of
the ideas which filled men's minds.

carnal weapons.[x] Thus does the Emperor answer in every point to his antitype the Pope, his power being yet of a lower rank, created on the analogy of the papal, as the papal itself had been modelled after the elder Empire. The parallel holds good even in its details; for just as we have seen the churchman assuming the crown and robes of the secular prince, so now did he array the Emperor in his own ecclesiastical vestments, the stole and the dalmatic, gave him a clerical as well as a sacred character, removed his office from all narrowing associations of birth or country, inaugurated him by rites every one of which was meant to symbolize and enjoin duties in their essence religious. Thus the Holy Roman Church and the Holy Roman Empire are one and the same thing, seen from different sides; and Catholicism, the principle of the universal Christian society, is also Romanism; that is, rests upon Rome as the origin and type of its universality; manifesting itself in a mystic dualism which corresponds to the two natures of its Founder. As divine and eternal, its head is the Pope, to whom souls have been entrusted; as human and temporal, the Emperor, commissioned to rule men's bodies and acts.

Correspondence and harmony of the spiritual and temporal powers.

In nature and compass the government of these two potentates is the same, differing only in the sphere of its

---

[x] So Leo III in a charter issued on the day of Charles's coronation: '. . . actum in praesentia gloriosi atque excellentissimi filii nostri Caroli quem auctore Deo in defensionem et provectionem sanctae universalis ecclesiae hodie Augustum sacravimus.'—Jaffé, *Regesta Pontificum Romanorum*, ad ann. 800.

So, indeed, Theodulf of Orleans, a contemporary of Charles, ascribes to the Emperor an almost papal authority over the Church itself :—

'Coeli habet hic (*sc.* Papa) claves, proprias te iussit habere ;
Tu regis ecclesiae, nam regit ille poli ;
Tu regis eius opes, clerum populumque gubernas,
Hic te coelicolas ducet ad usque choros.'

—In D. Bouquet, v. 415.

working; and it matters little whether we call the Pope a spiritual Emperor or the Emperor a secular Pope. Nor, though the one office is below the other as far as man's life on earth is less precious than his life hereafter, is therefore, on the older and sounder theory, the imperial authority delegated by the papal. For, as has been said already, God is represented by the Pope not in every capacity, but only as the ruler of spirits in heaven: as sovereign of earth, He issues His commission directly to the Emperor. Opposition between two servants of the same King is inconceivable, each being bound to aid and foster the other, the co-operation of both being needed in all that concerns the welfare of Christendom at large. This is the one perfect and self-consistent scheme of the union of Church and State; for, taking the absolute coincidence of their limits to be self-evident, it assumes the infallibility of their joint government, and derives, as a corollary from that infallibility, the duty of the civil magistrate to root out heresy and schism no less than to punish treason and rebellion. It is also the scheme which, granting the possibility of their harmonious action, places the two powers in that relation which gives to each of them its maximum of strength. But by a law to which it would be hard to find exceptions, in proportion as the State became more Christian, the Church, who to work out her purposes had assumed worldly forms, became by the contact worldlier, meaner, spiritually weaker; and the system whose foundations were joyfully laid in the days of Constantine, and which culminated triumphantly in the Empire Church of the Middle Ages, has in each succeeding generation been slowly losing ground, has seen its brightness dimmed and its completeness marred, and sees now those who are most zealous on behalf of its surviving institutions feebly defend or silently desert the principle upon which all must rest.

Union of Church and State.

The complete accord of the papal and imperial powers which this theory, as sublime as it is impracticable, requires, was attained only at a few points in their history.[y] It was finally supplanted by another view of their relation, which, professing to be a developement of a principle recognized as fundamental, the superior importance of the religious life, found increasing favour in the eyes of fervent churchmen.[z] Declaring the Pope sole representative on earth of the Deity, it concluded that from him, and not directly from God, must the Empire be held — held feudally, it was said by many — and it thereby thrust down the temporal power to be the servant instead of the sister of the spiritual.[a] Nevertheless, the Papacy in her meridian, and under the guidance of her greatest minds, of Hildebrand, of Alexander II, of Innocent III, not seeking to

[y] Perhaps at no more than three: in the time of Charles and Leo III; again under Otto III and his two Popes Gregory V and Sylvester II; thirdly, under Henry III; certainly never thenceforth.

[z] The *Sachsenspiegel* (*Speculum Saxonicum*, circ. A.D. 1240), the great North-German law book, says, 'The Empire is held from God alone, not from the Pope. Emperor and Pope are supreme each in what has been entrusted to him: the Pope in what concerns the soul; the Emperor in all that belongs to the body and to knighthood.' The *Schwabenspiegel*, compiled half a century later, subordinates the prince to the pontiff: 'The Pope gives the worldly sword of judgement to the Emperor: the spiritual sword belongs to the Pope that he may judge therewith.' 'Daz weltliche Schwert des Gerichtes daz lihet der Babest dem Chaiser; daz geistlich ist dem Babest gesetzt daz er damit richte.'

[a] So Boniface VIII in the bull *Unam Sanctam* (*Corp. Iur. Canon. Extrav. Commun.* i. 8) will have but one head for the Christian people: 'Igitur ecclesiae unius et unicae unum corpus, unum caput, non duo capita quasi monstrum, Christus videlicet et Christi vicarius Petrus, Petrique successor. . . . In eius potestate duos esse gladios, spiritualem et temporalem, evangelicis dictis instruimur. Nam dicentibus apostolis "Ecce gladii duo hic," in ecclesia scilicet, non respondit Dominus nimis esse sed satis. . . , Uterque gladius, spiritualis et materialis, est in potestate ecclesiae. Sed is quidem pro ecclesia, ille vero ab ecclesia exercendus. Ille sacerdotis, is manu regum et militum, sed ad nutum et patientiam sacerdotis.'

abolish or absorb the civil government, required only its CHAP. VII.
obedience, and exalted its dignity against all save herself.[b]
It was reserved for Boniface VIII, whose extravagant pretensions betrayed the decay that was already at work
within, to show himself to the crowding pilgrims at the
jubilee of A.D. 1300, seated on the throne of Constantine,
arrayed with sword, and crown, and sceptre, shouting
aloud, 'I am Caesar — I am Emperor.'[c]

The theory of an Emperor's place and functions thus *Proofs from*
sketched cannot be definitely assigned to any point of *mediaeval*
time; for it was growing and changing from the fifth *documents.*
century to the fifteenth. Nor need it surprise us that
we do not find in any one author a full account of the
grounds whereon it rested, since much of what seems
strangest to us was then too obvious to need statement or

[b] St. Bernard writes to Conrad III: 'Non veniat anima mea in consilium
eorum qui dicunt vel imperio pacem et libertatem ecclesiae vel ecclesiae
prosperitatem et exaltationem imperii nocituram.' So speaking of the papal
claim to temporal and spiritual authority, he writes in the *De Consideratione*,
addressed to Pope Eugenius III: 'I ergo tu et tibi usurpare aude aut domi-
nans Apostolatum aut Apostolicus dominatum. Plane ab alterutro prohiberis.
Si utrumque simul habere velis, perdes utrumque' (Bk. ii. ch. 6).

[c] Sedens in solio armatus et cinctus ensem, habensque in capite Constantini diadema, stricto dextra capulo ensis accincti, ait: "Numquid ego summus
sum pontifex? nonne ista est cathedra Petri? Nonne possum imperii iura
tutari? ego ego sum imperator." — Fr. Pipinus (*ap.* Murat. *S. R. I.* ix), l.
iv. c. 41. These words, however, are by this writer ascribed to Boniface when
receiving the envoys of the Emperor Albert I, in A.D. 1299. I have not been
able to find authority for their use at the jubilee, but give the current story
for what it is worth.

It is possible that Dante may be alluding to this sword scene in a remarkable passage of the Purgatorio (xvi. l. 106): —
     'Soleva Roma, che 'l buon mondo feo,
        Duo Soli aver, che l' una e l' altra strada
        Facean vedere, e del mondo e di Deo.
    L' un l' altro ha spento, ed è giunta la spada
        Col pastorale: e l' un coll' altro insieme
        Per viva forza mal convien che vada.'

explanation. No one, however, who examines mediaeval writings can fail to perceive, sometimes from direct words, oftener from allusions or assumptions, that such ideas as these are present to the minds of the authors.[d] That which stands out most clearly is the connection of the Empire with religion. From every record, from chronicles and treatises, proclamations, laws, and sermons, passages may be adduced wherein the defence and spread of the faith, and the maintenance of concord among the Christian people, are represented as the function to which the Empire has been set apart. The belief expressed by Lewis II, 'Imperii dignitas non in vocabuli nomine sed in culmine pietatis gloriosae consistit,'[e] appears again in the address of the archbishop of Mainz to Conrad II,[f] as Vicar of God; is reiterated by Frederick I,[g] when he writes to the prelates of Germany, 'On earth God has placed no more than two powers, and as there is in heaven but one God, so is there here one Pope and one Emperor. Divine providence has specially appointed the Roman Empire to prevent the continuance of schism in the Church;'[h] is

[d] See especially Peter de Andlau (*De Imperio Romano*); Dante (*De Monarchia*); Engelbert (*De Ortu Progressu et Fine Imperii Romani*); Landolfo Colonna (*De translatione Imperii Romani*); Marsilius Patavinus (*De translatione Imperii Romani*); Aeneas Sylvius Piccolomini (*De Ortu et Authoritate Imperii Romani*); Zoannetus (*De Imperio Romano atque eius Iurisdictione*); and the writers in Schardius's *Sylloge Tractatuum*, and in Goldast's Collection of Tracts, entitled *Monarchia Imperii*.

[e] Letter of Lewis II to Basil the Macedonian, in *Chron. Salernit.* in Pertz, *M. G. H., Script.* iii. p. 521 (c. 106), also given by Baronius, *Ann. Eccl.*, ad ann. 871.

[f] 'Ad summum dignitatis pervenisti: Vicarius es Christi.' — Wippo, *Vita Chuonradi, ap.* Pertz, *M. G. H., Script.* ii. p. 260 (c. 3).

[g] Letter in Radewic or Rahewin, *ap.* Pertz, *M. G. H., Script.* xx. p. 476 (bk. iv. c. 56).

[h] Lewis IV is styled in one of his proclamations, 'Gentis humanae, orbis Christiani custos, urbi et orbi a Deo electus praeesse.' — Pfeffinger, *Vitriarius Illustratus.*

echoed by jurists and divines down to the days of Charles V.[1] It was a doctrine which we shall find the friends and opponents of the Holy See equally concerned to insist on — the one party to make the transference (*translatio*) of the imperial dignity 'from the Greeks to the Germans' appear entirely the Pope's work, and thereby to establish his right of overseeing or cancelling the election of an Emperor; the others, by setting the Emperor at the head of the whole congregation of Christians, to reduce the bishop of the capital to a place in the world-realm similar to that held by the primate in each of the countries of Christendom.[j] The Emperor's headship was deemed to stand out and be exerciseable chiefly in the two duties already noticed. As Defender of the Faith — the counterpart of the Musulman Commander of the Faithful — he was leader of the Church militant against her infidel foes, was in this capacity summoned to conduct crusades, and in later times recognized chief of the confederacies against the conquering Ottomans. As representative of the whole Christian people, it belonged to him to convoke General Councils, a right not without importance even when exercised concurrently with the Pope, but far more weighty when the object of the Council was to settle a disputed election, or, as at Constance, to depose reigning pontiffs themselves.

No better illustrations can be desired than those to

[1] In a document issued by the Diet of Speyer (A.D. 1529) the Emperor is called 'Oberst Vogt, und Haupt der Christenheit.' Hieronymus Balbus, writing about the same time, puts the question whether all Christians are subject to the Emperor in temporal things, as they are to the Pope in spiritual, and answers it by saying, 'Cum ambo ex eodem fonte perfluxerint et eadem semita incedant, de utroque idem puto sentiendum.'

[j] 'Non magis ad Papam depositio seu remotio pertinet quam ad quoslibet regum praelatos, qui reges suos prout assolent, consecrant et inungunt.' — *Letter of Frederick II* (lib. i. c. 3).

be found in the Office for the imperial coronation at Rome, too long to be transcribed here, but well worthy of an attentive study.[k] The rites prescribed in it are rites of consecration to a religious office: the Emperor, besides the sword, globe, and sceptre of temporal power, receives a ring as the symbol of his faith, is ordained a subdeacon, assists the Pope in celebrating mass, partakes as a clerical person of the communion in both kinds, is admitted a canon of St. Peter and St. John Lateran. The oath to be taken by an elector begins, 'Ego N. volo regem Romanorum in Caesarem promovendum, temporale caput populo Christiano eligere.' The Emperor swears to cherish and defend the Holy Roman Church and her bishop: the Pope prays after the reading of the Gospel, 'Deus qui ad praedicandum aeterni regni evangelium Imperium Romanum praeparasti,[l] praetende famulo tuo Imperatori nostro arma coelestia.' Among the Emperor's official titles there occur these: 'Head of Christendom,' 'Defender and Advocate of the Christian Church,' 'Temporal Head of the Faithful,' 'Protector of Palestine and of the Catholic Faith.'[m]

Very singular are the reasonings by which the necessity and divine right of the Empire are proved out of the Bible. The mediaeval theory of the relation of the civil power to the priestly was profoundly influenced by the account in the Old Testament of the Jewish theocracy, in which the king, though the institution of his office is described as being a derogation from the purity of the older system, appears divinely chosen and com-

---

[k] *Liber Ceremonialis Romanus,* lib. i. sect. 5; with which compare the *Coronatio Romana* of Henry VII, in Pertz, *M. G. H., Legg.* ii. 1, pp. 528–537, and Muratori's Dissertation in vol. i. of the *Antiquitates Italiae Medii Aevi.*

[l] See, for another prayer, Note VIII at end.

[m] See Goldast, *Collection of Imperial Constitutions;* and Moser, *Römische Kayser.*

missioned, and stood in a peculiarly intimate relation to the national religion. From the New Testament the authority and eternity of Rome herself was established. Every passage was seized on where submission to the powers that be is enjoined, every instance cited where obedience had actually been rendered to imperial officials, a special emphasis being laid on the sanction which Christ Himself had given to Roman dominion by pacifying the world through Augustus, by being born at the time of the taxing, by paying tribute to Caesar, by saying to Pilate, 'Thou couldest have no power at all against Me except it were given thee from above.'

More attractive to the mystical spirit than these direct arguments were those drawn from prophecy, or based on the allegorical interpretation of Scripture. Very early in Christian history had the belief formed itself that the Roman Empire — as the fourth beast of Daniel's vision, as the iron legs and feet of Nebuchadnezzar's image — was to be the world's last and universal kingdom. From Origen and Jerome downwards it found unquestioned acceptance,[n] and that not unnaturally. For no new power had arisen to extinguish the Roman, as the Persian monarchy had been blotted out by Alexander, as the realms of his successors had fallen before the conquering republic herself. Every Northern conqueror, Goth, Lombard, Burgundian, had cherished her memory and preserved her laws ; Germany had adopted even the name of the Empire 'dreadful and terrible and strong exceedingly, and diverse from all that were before it.' To these predictions, and to many others from the Apocalypse, were added those which in the Gospels and Epistles foretold the advent of Antichrist.[n] He was to succeed the Roman dominion, and the Popes are more than once warned that by weakening

[n] See Note VII at end.

the Empire they are hastening the coming of the enemy and the end of the world. It is not only when groping in the dark labyrinths of prophecy that mediaeval authors are quick in detecting emblems, imaginative in explaining them. Men were wont in those days to interpret Scripture in a singular fashion. As it did not occur to them to ask what meaning words had to those to whom they were originally addressed, so they were quite as careless whether the sense they discovered was one which the language used would primarily and naturally bear to any reader at any time. No analogy was too faint, no allegory too fanciful, to be drawn out of a simple text; and, once propounded, the interpretation acquired in argument all the authority of the text itself. Melchizedek is both priest and king; therefore the Pope has regal as well as ecclesiastical authority. The two swords of which Christ said, 'It is enough,' are the spiritual and temporal powers, and the grant of the spiritual to Peter involves the supremacy of the Papacy.[o] Thus one writer proves the eternity of Rome from the seventy-second Psalm, 'They shall fear thee as long as the sun and moon endure, throughout all generations;' the moon being of course, since Gregory VII, the Roman Empire, as the sun, or greater light, is the Popedom. Another quoting, 'Qui tenet teneat donec auferatur (he who now letteth will let until he be taken out of the way),'[p] with Augustine's explanation thereof,[q] says, that when 'he who letteth' is removed, tribes and

---

[o] Papalists often insisted that both swords were given to Peter, while Imperialists assigned the temporal sword to John. Thus a gloss to the *Sachsenspiegel* says, 'Dat eine svert hadde Sinte Peter, dat het nu de paves: dat andere hadde Johannes, dat het nu de keyser.'

[p] 2 Thess. ii. 7.

[q] St. Augustine, however, though his commentary states the view (applying the passage to the Roman Empire) which was thereafter generally received, is careful not to commit himself positively to it.

provinces will rise in rebellion, and the Empire to which God has committed the government of the human race will be dissolved. From the miseries of his own time (he wrote under Frederick III) he predicts that the end is near. The same spirit of symbolism seized on the number of the electors : 'the seven lamps burning in the unity of the sevenfold spirit which illumine the Holy Empire.'[r] Strange legends told how Romans and Germans were of one lineage ; how Peter's staff had been found on the banks of the Rhine, the miracle signifying that a commission was issued to the Germans to reclaim wandering sheep to the one fold.[s] So complete does the scriptural proof appear in the hands of mediaeval churchmen, many holding it a mortal sin to resist the power ordained of God, that we forget they were all the while only adapting to an existing institution what they found written long before ; we begin to fancy that the Empire was maintained, obeyed, exalted for centuries, on the strength of words to which we attach in almost every case a wholly different meaning.

It would be a pleasant and profitable task to pass on from the theologians to the poets and artists of the Middle Ages, and endeavour to trace through their works the influence of the ideas which have been expounded above. But it is a task far too wide for the scope of the present treatise ; and one which would demand an acquaintance with those works themselves such as only minute and long-continued study could give. For even a slight knowledge enables any one to see how much still remains to be interpreted in the imaginative literature and in the paintings

Illustrations from Mediaeval Art.

[r] *Iordanis Chronica* (written towards the close of the thirteenth century).

[s] This is really no stranger than the belief long current, and perhaps not wholly extinct, that the coronation stone of Scone (now in Westminster Abbey) is the stone on which Jacob slept at Bethel, and which was afterwards carried to Ireland from Egypt, and from Ireland by the Scots to Dunstaffnage and thence to Scone.

of mediaeval times, and how apt we are in glancing over a piece of work to miss those seemingly trifling indications of the artist's thought or belief which are all the more precious that they are indirect or unconscious. Therefore a history of mediaeval art which shall evolve its philosophy from its concrete forms, if it is to have any value at all, must be minute in description as well as subtle in method. But lest this class of illustrations should appear to have been wholly forgotten, it may be well to mention here two pictures in which the theory of the mediaeval empire is unmistakeably set forth. One of them is in Rome, the other in Florence; every traveller in Italy may examine both for himself.

Mosaic of the Lateran Palace at Rome. The first of these is the famous mosaic of the Lateran triclinium, constructed by Pope Leo III about A.D. 800, which, afterwards restored and moved to its present site, may still be seen over against the façade of the great basilica of St. John Lateran. Originally meant to adorn the state banqueting-hall of the Popes, it is now placed in the open air, in the finest situation in Rome, looking from the brow of a hill across the green ridges of the Campagna to the olive-groves of Tivoli and the glistering crags and snow-capped summits of the Umbrian and Sabine Apennine. It represents in the centre Christ surrounded by the Apostles, whom He is sending forth to preach the Gospel; one hand is extended to bless, the other holds a book with the words 'Pax Vobis.' Below and to the right Christ is depicted again, and this time sitting: on His right hand kneels Pope Sylvester, on His left the Emperor Constantine; to the one He gives the keys of heaven and hell, to the other a banner surmounted by a cross. In the group on the opposite, that is, on the left side of the arch, we see the Apostle Peter seated, before whom in like manner kneel Pope Leo III and Charles the Emperor;

the latter wearing, like Constantine, his crown. Peter, CHAP. VII.
himself grasping the keys, gives to Leo the pallium of an
archbishop, to Charles the banner of the Christian army.
The inscription is, ' Beate Petre donas vitam Leoni PP et
bictoriam Carulo regi donas ; ' while round the arch is
written, ' Gloria in excelsis Deo, et in terra pax omnibus
bonae voluntatis.'

The order and nature of the ideas here symbolized is
sufficiently clear. First comes the revelation of the Gospel, and the divine commission to gather all men into its
fold. Next, the institution, at the memorable era of Constantine's conversion, of the two powers by which the
Christian people is to be respectively taught and governed.
Thirdly, we are shewn the permanent Vicar of God, the
Apostle who keeps the keys of heaven and hell, re-estab-
lishing these same powers on a new and permanent basis.[t]
The badge of ecclesiastical supremacy he gives to Leo as
the spiritual head of the faithful on earth, the banner of
the Church Militant to Charles, who is to maintain her
cause against heretics and infidels.

The second painting is of greatly later date. It is a *Fresco in*
fresco in the chapter-house of the Dominican convent of *S. Maria*
Santa Maria Novella[u] at Florence, usually known as the *Novella at Florence.*
Capellone degli Spagnuoli. It has been commonly as-
cribed, on Vasari's authority, to Simone Martini of Siena,
but an examination of the dates of his life seems to discredit this view.[x] Most probably it was executed between
A.D. 1340 and 1350. It is a huge work, covering one
whole wall of the chapter-house, and filled with figures,
some of which, but seemingly on no sufficient authority,

---

[t] See Note IX at end.

[u] The church in which the opening scene of Boccaccio's *Decameron* is laid.

[x] So Kugler (Eastlake's ed. vol. i. p. 144), and so also Messrs. Crowe and
Cavalcaselle, in their *New History of Painting in Italy,* vol. ii. pp. 85 sqq.

have been taken to represent eminent persons of the time —Cimabue, Arnolfo, Boccaccio, Petrarch, Laura, and others. In it is represented the whole scheme of man's life here and hereafter — the Church on earth and the Church in heaven. Full in front are seated side by side the Pope and the Emperor: on their right and left, in a descending row, minor spiritual and temporal officials; next to the Pope a cardinal, bishops, and doctors; next to the Emperor, the king of France and a line of nobles and knights. Behind them appears the Duomo of Florence as an emblem of the Visible Church, while at their feet is a flock of sheep (the faithful) attacked by ravening wolves (heretics and schismatics), whom a pack of spotted dogs (the Dominicans [y]) combat and chase away. From this, the central foreground of the picture, a path winds round and up a height to a great gate where the Apostle sits on guard to admit true believers: they passing through it are met by choirs of seraphs, who lead them on through the delicious groves of Paradise. Above all, at the top of the painting and just over the spot where his two lieutenants, Pope and Emperor, are placed below, is the Saviour enthroned amid saints and angels. [z]

Anti-national character of the Empire. Here, too, there needs no comment. The Church Militant is the perfect counterpart of the Church Triumphant: her chief danger is from those who would rend the unity of her visible body, the seamless garment of her heavenly Lord; and that devotion to His person which is the sum of her faith and the essence of her being, must on earth be

---

[y] Domini canes. Spotted because of their black-and-white raiment.

[z] There is of course a great deal more detail in the picture, which need not be described. St. Dominic is a conspicuous figure.

It is worth remarking that the Emperor, who is on the Pope's left hand, and so made slightly inferior to him while superior to every one else, holds in his hand, instead of the usual imperial globe, a death's head, typifying the transitory nature of his power.

rendered to those two lieutenants whom He has chosen to govern in His name.

A theory such as that which it has been attempted to explain and illustrate, is utterly opposed to restrictions of place or person. The idea of one Christian people, all whose members are equal in the sight of God — an idea so forcibly expressed in the unity of the priesthood, where no barrier separated the successor of the Apostle from the humblest curate — and in the prevalence of one language for worship and ecclesiastical government, made the post of Emperor independent of the race, or rank, or actual resources of its occupant. The Emperor was entitled to the obedience of Christendom, not as hereditary chief of a victorious tribe, or feudal lord of a portion of the earth's surface, but as solemnly invested with an Office. Not only did he excel in dignity the kings of the earth : his power was different in its nature ; and, so far from supplanting or rivalling theirs, rose above them to become the source and needful condition of their authority in their several territories, the bond which joined them in one harmonious body. The vast dominions and vigorous personal action of Charles the Great had concealed this distinction while he reigned ; under his successors the imperial crown appeared disconnected from the direct government of the kingdoms into which his realm had been divided, existing only in the form of an undefined suzerainty, as the type of that unity without which men's minds could not rest. It was characteristic of the Middle Ages, that demanding the existence of an Emperor, they cared little who he was or how he was chosen, so he had been duly inaugurated ; and that they were not shocked by the contrast between unbounded rights and actual help-lessness. At no time in the world's history has theory, professing all the while to control practice, been so utterly

divorced from it. Ferocious and sensual, that age worshipped humility and asceticism: there has never been
a purer ideal of love, nor a grosser profligacy of life.

The power of the Emperor cannot as yet be called
international, though this became in later times its
most important aspect; for in the tenth century national distinctions had scarcely begun to exist. But
its genius was clerical rather than territorial, Roman
rather than Teutonic: it rested not on armed hosts or
wide lands, but upon the duty, the awe, the love of its
subjects.

CHAPTER VIII

THE ROMAN EMPIRE AND THE GERMAN KINGDOM

THIS was the office which Otto the Great assumed in
A.D. 962. But it was not his only office. He was already *Union of*
a German king; and the new dignity by no means super- *the Roman*
seded the old. The union in one person of two charac- *Empire with*
ters, a union at first personal, then official, and which *the German*
became at last a fusion of the two characters into some- *kingdom.*
thing different from what either had been, is the key to
the whole subsequent history of Germany and the Empire.

Of the German kingdom little need be said, since it *Germany and*
differs in no essential respect from the other kingdoms of *its monarchy.*
Western Europe as they stood in the tenth century. The
five or six great tribes or tribe-leagues which composed
the German nation had been first brought together under
the sceptre of the Carolingians; and, though still retaining marks of their independent origin, were prevented
from separating by community of speech and a common
pride in the great Frankish Empire. When the male line
of Charles the Great ended in A.D. 911, by the death of
Lewis the Child (son of Arnulf), Conrad, duke of the
Franconians, and after him Henry (the Fowler), duke of
the Saxons, were chosen to fill the vacant throne. By his
vigorous yet conciliatory action, his upright character, his
courage and good fortune in repelling the Hungarians,
Henry laid deep the foundations of royal power: under
his more famous son it rose into a stable edifice. Otto's

coronation feast at Aachen, where the great nobles of the realm did him menial service, where Franks, Bavarians, Suabians, Thuringians, and Lorrainers gathered round the Saxon monarch, is the inauguration of a true Teutonic realm, which, though it called itself not German but East Frankish, and claimed to be the lawful representative of the Carolingian monarchy of Charles, had a constitution and a tendency in many respects different.

Feudalism. There had been under the Carolingian princes a singular mixture of the old German local organization by tribes or districts (the so-called Gauverfassung), such as we find in the earliest records, with the method introduced by Charles of maintaining by means of officials, some fixed, others moving from place to place, the control of the central government. In the suspension of that government which followed his days, there grew up a system whose seeds had been sown as far back as the time of Clovis, a system whose essence was the combination of the tenure of land by military service with a peculiar personal relation between the landlord and his tenant, whereby the one was bound to render fatherly protection, the other aid and obedience. This is not the place for tracing the origin of feudality on Roman soil, nor for shewing how, by a sort of contagion, it spread into Germany, how it struck firm root in the period of comparative quiet under Pipin and Charles, how from the hands of the latter it took the impress which determined its ultimate form, how the weakness of his successors allowed it to triumph everywhere. Still less would it be possible here to examine its social and moral influence. Politically it might be defined as the system which made the owner of a piece of land, whether large or small, the governor of those who dwelt thereon : an annexation of personal to territorial authority more familiar to Eastern despotism

than to the free races of primitive Europe.   On this principle were founded, and by it are explained, feudal law and
justice, feudal finance, feudal legislation, each tenant holding towards his lord the position which his own tenants
held towards himself.   And it is just because the relation
was so uniform, the principle so comprehensive, the ruling
class so firmly bound to its support, that feudalism was
able to lay upon society that grasp which the struggles of
twenty generations have, in some parts of Europe, not yet
wholly shaken off.

   Now by the middle of the tenth century, Germany, less *The feudal*
fully committed than France to feudalism's worst feature, *king.*
the bondage of the peasantry, was otherwise thoroughly
feudalized.   As for that equality of all the freeborn save
the sacred line which we find in the Germany of Tacitus,
there had been substituted a gradation of ranks and a concentration of power in the hands of a landholding caste,
so had the monarch lost his ancient character as leader
and judge of the people, to become the head of a turbulent
oligarchy.   He was titular lord of the soil, could exact
from his vassals service and aid in arms and money, could
dispose of vacant fiefs, could at pleasure declare war or
make peace.   But all these rights he exercised less as
sovereign of the nation than as standing in a peculiar
relation to the feudal tenants, a relation which had in its
origin been personal, and whose prominence obscured the
political duties of prince and subject.   And great as these
rights might become in the hands of an ambitious and
politic ruler, they were in practice limited by the corresponding duties he owed to his vassals, and by the difficulty
of enforcing them against a powerful offender.   The king
was not permitted to retain in his own hands escheated
fiefs, must even grant away those he had held before coming to the throne ; he could not interfere with the juris-

diction of his tenants in their own lands, nor prevent them from waging war or forming leagues with each other like independent princes. Chief among the Germanic nobles stood the dukes, who, although their authority was now delegated, theoretically at least, instead of independent, territorial instead of personal, retained nevertheless much of that hold on the exclusive loyalty of their subjects which had belonged to them as hereditary leaders of the tribe under the ancient system. They were, with the three Rhenish archbishops, by far the greater subjects, often aspiring to the crown, sometimes not unable to resist its wearer. The constant encroachments which Otto made upon their privileges, especially through the institution of the Counts Palatine, destroyed their ascendancy, but not their importance. It was not till the thirteenth century that they disappeared with the rise of the second order of

nobility. That order, at this period far less powerful, included the counts, margraves or marquises, and landgraves, originally officers of the crown, now feudal tenants; holding their lands of the dukes, and maintaining against them the same contest which they in turn waged with the crown. Below these came the barons and simple knights, then the diminishing class of freemen, the increasing class of serfs. The institutions of primitive Germany were almost all gone; supplanted by a new system, partly the natural result of the formation of a settled from a half-nomad society, partly imitated from that which had arisen upon Roman soil, west of the Rhine and south of the Alps. The army was no longer the Heerbann of the whole nation, which had been wont to follow the king on foot in distant expeditions, but a cavalry militia of barons and their retainers, bound to service for a short period, and rendering it unwillingly where their own interest was not concerned. The frequent popular assemblies, whereof under the names of the Mallum, the Placitum, the Mayfield, we hear so much under Clovis and Charles, were now never summoned, and the laws that had been promulgated there were in their old form obsolete, though the substance of some was embodied in well established customs.   No national council existed, save the Diet in which the higher nobility, lay and clerical, met their sovereign, sometimes to decide on foreign war, oftener to concur in the grant of a fief or the proscription of a rebel.   Every district had its own rude local usages administered by the court of the local lord : other law there was none, for imperial jurisprudence had in these lately civilized countries not yet filled the place left empty by the disuse of the old barbarian codes.

This condition of things was indeed better than that utter confusion which had gone before, for a principle of order had begun to group and bind the tossing atoms ; and though the union into which it drove men was an imperfect and narrow one, it was something that they should have learnt to unite themselves at all.   Yet nascent feudality was but one remove from anarchy ; and the tendency to isolation and diversity had continued, despite the efforts of the Church and the Carolingian princes, to be all-powerful in Western Europe.   The German kingdom was already a bond between the German races, and appears strong and united when we compare it with the France of Hugh Capet, or the England of Ethelred II ; yet its history down to the twelfth century is little else than a record of disorders, revolts, civil wars, of a ceaseless struggle on the part of the monarch to enforce his feudal rights, a resistance by his vassals equally obstinate and more frequently successful.   What the issue of the contest might have been if Germany had been left to take her own course is matter of conjecture, though the example of every European state except England and Poland may incline the balance in favour of the crown. But the strife had scarcely begun when a new influence was interposed : the German king became Roman Emperor. No two systems can be more unlike than those whose headship became thus vested in one person : the one centralized, the other local ; the one resting on a sublime theory, the other the rude offspring of anarchy ; the one gathering all power into the hands of an irresponsible monarch, the other limiting his rights and authorizing resistance to his commands ; the one demanding the equality of all Christians as creatures equal before Heaven, the other bound up with an aristocracy the proudest, and in its gradations of rank the most exact, that Europe had ever seen. Characters so repugnant could not, it might be thought, meet in one person, or if they met must strive till one swallowed up the other. It was not so. In the fusion which began from the first, though it was for a time imperceptible, each of the two characters gave and each lost some of its attributes : the king became more than German, the Emperor less than Roman, till, at the end of six centuries, the monarch in whom two 'persons' had been united, appeared as a third different from either of the former, and might not inappropriately be entitled 'German Emperor.'[a] The nature and progress of this change will appear in the after history of Germany, and cannot be described here without in some measure anticipating subsequent events. A word or two may indicate how the process of fusion began.

It was natural that the great mass of Otto's subjects, to whom the imperial title, dimly associated with Rome and the Pope, sounded grander than the regal, without being known as otherwise different, should in thought and speech confound them. The sovereign and his eccle-

---

[a] Although this was of course never his legal title. Till 1806 he was 'Romanorum Imperator semper Augustus'; 'Römischer Kaiser.'

siastical advisers, with clearer views of the new dignity
and of the relation of the two offices to one another, found
it impossible to separate them in practice, and were glad
to merge the lesser in the greater. For as lord of the
world, Otto was Emperor north as well as south of the
Alps. When he issued an edict, he claimed the obedience
of his Teutonic subjects in both capacities ; when as Emperor he led the armies of the gospel against the heathen,
it was the standard of their feudal superior that his
armed vassals followed : when he founded churches and
appointed bishops, he acted partly as suzerain of feudal
lands, partly as protector of the faith, charged to guide
the Church in matters temporal. Thus the assumption
of the imperial crown brought to Otto as its first result
an apparent increase of domestic authority ; it made his
position by its historical associations more dignified, by
its religious more hallowed ; it raised him higher above
his vassals and above other sovereigns ; it enlarged his
prerogative in ecclesiastical affairs, and by necessary consequence gave to ecclesiastics a more important place at
court and in the administration of government than they
had enjoyed before. Great as was the power of the bishops and abbots in all the feudal kingdoms, it stood
nowhere so high as in Germany. There the Emperor's
double position, as head both of Church and State, required the two organizations to be exactly parallel. In the
eleventh century a full half of the land and wealth of the
country, and no small part of its military strength, was in
the hands of Churchmen : their influence predominated
in the Diet ; the archchancellorship of the Empire, highest
of all offices, was held by, and eventually came to belong of
right to, the archbishop of Mainz as primate of Germany.
It was by Otto, who in resuming the attitude must repeat
the policy of Charles, that the greatness of the clergy was

thus advanced.   He is commonly said to have wished to weaken the aristocracy by raising up rivals to them in the hierarchy.   It may have been so, and the measure was at any rate a disastrous one, for the clergy soon approved themselves scarcely less rebellious than those whom they were expected to restrain.   But in accusing Otto's judgement, historians have often forgotten in what position he stood to the Church, and how it behoved him, according to the doctrine received, to establish in her an order like in all things to that which he found already subsisting in the State.

Changes in title.   The style which Otto adopted shewed his desire thus to merge the king in the Emperor.[b]   Charles had called himself 'Imperator Caesar Carolus rex Francorum invictissimus'; and again, 'Carolus serenissimus Augustus, Pius, Felix, Romanorum gubernans Imperium, qui et per misericordiam Dei rex Francorum atque Langobardorum.' Otto and his first successors, who until their coronation at Rome had used the titles of 'Rex Francorum,' or 'Rex Francorum Orientalium,' or oftener still 'Rex' alone, discarded after it all titles save the highest of 'Imperator Augustus,' seeming thereby, though they too had been crowned at Aachen and Milan, to claim the authority of Caesar through all their dominions.   Tracing as we are the history of a title, it is needless to dwell on the significance of the change.   Charles, son of the Ripuarian allies of the Emperor Probus, had been a Frankish chieftain on the Rhine ; Otto, the Saxon successor of the Cheruscan Arminius, would rule his native Elbe with a power borrowed from the Tiber.

Nevertheless, the imperial element did not in every

---

[b] Pütter, *Dissertationes de Instauratione Imperii Romani :* cf. Goldast's Collection of Constitutions; and the proclamations and other documents collected in Pertz, *M. G. H., Legg.* ii. p. 19 sqq.

respect predominate over the royal. The monarch might
desire to make good against his turbulent barons the
boundless prerogative which he acquired with his new
crown, but he lacked the power to do so ; and they, disputing neither the supremacy of that crown nor his right
to wear it, refused with good reason to let their own
freedom be infringed upon by any act of which they had
not been the authors. So far was Otto from embarking
on so vain an enterprise, that his rule was even more
direct and more personal than that of Charles had been.
There was no scheme of mechanical government, no
claim of absolutism ; there was only the resolve to make
the energetic assertion of the king's feudal rights subserve
the further aims of the Emperor. What Otto demanded
he demanded as Emperor, what he received he received
as king; the singular result was that in Germany the
imperial office was itself pervaded and transformed by
feudal ideas. Feudality needing, to make its theory
complete, a lord paramount of the world, from whose
grant all ownership in land must be supposed to have
emanated, and finding such a suzerain in the Emperor,
constituted him liege lord of all kings and potentates,
keystone of the feudal arch, himself, as it was expressed,
'holding' the world from God. There were not wanting
Roman institutions to which these notions could attach
themselves. Constantine, imitating the courts of the
East, had made the dignitaries of his household great
officials of the State : these were now reproduced in the
cup-bearer, the seneschal, the marshal, the chamberlain
of the Empire, presently to become its electoral princes.
The holding of land on condition of military service had
been known in Roman days : the divided ownership of
feudal law found its analogies in the Roman tenure of
emphyteusis. Thus while Germany was Romanized the

Empire was feudalized, and came to be considered not the antagonist but the perfection of an aristocratic system. This conception of a suzerainty over minor potentates, since it was adapted to existing political facts, enabled the Empire afterwards to assume an international character. Nevertheless, even while they seemed to blend, there remained between the genius of imperialism and that of feudalism a deep and lasting hostility. And so the rule of Otto and his successors was in a measure adverse to feudal polity, not from knowledge of what Roman government had been, but from the necessities of their position, raised as they were to an unapproachable height above their subjects, surrounded with a halo of sanctity as protectors of the Church. Thus were they driven to seek to reduce local independence, and assimilate the various races through their vast territories. It was Otto who made the Germans, hitherto an aggregate of tribes, a single people, and welding them into a strong political body taught them to rise through its collective greatness to the consciousness of national life, never thenceforth to be extinguished.

The commons.

One expedient against the land-holding oligarchy which old Roman traditions as well as present needs might have suggested it was scarcely possible for Otto to use. He could not invoke the friendship of a Third Estate, for as yet none existed. The Teutonic order of freemen, which two centuries earlier had formed the bulk of the population, was now fast disappearing, just as in England all who did not become thanes were classed as ceorls, and from ceorls sank for the most part, after the Norman Conquest, into villeins. It was only in the Alpine valleys and along the shores of the ocean that small free communities maintained themselves. Town-life there was none, till Henry the Fowler forced his forest-loving people to dwell in

fortresses that might repel the Hungarian invaders; and
the burgher class thus beginning to form was as yet too
small to be a power.   But popular freedom, as it expired,
bequeathed to the monarch such of its rights as could be
saved from the grasp of the nobles; and the crown thus
became what it has been wherever an aristocracy presses
upon both, the tacit ally of the people.   More, too, than
the royal name could have done, did the imperial name
invite the sympathy of the commons.   For in all, however
ignorant of its history, however unable to comprehend its
functions, there yet lived a feeling that it was in some
mysterious way consecrated to Christian brotherhood and
equality, to peace and law, to the restraint of the strong
and the defence of the helpless.

CHAPTER IX

SAXON AND FRANCONIAN EMPERORS

He who begins to read the history of the Middle Ages is alternately amused and provoked by the seeming absurdities that meet him at every step. He finds writers proclaiming amidst universal assent magnificent theories which no one attempts to carry out. He sees men stained with every vice full of sincere devotion to a religion which, even when its doctrines were most obscured, never sullied the purity of its moral teaching. He is disposed to conclude that such people must have been either fools or hypocrites. Yet in so concluding he would greatly err. Every one knows how little a man's actions conform to the general maxims which he would lay down for himself, and how many beliefs he holds without realizing their application, so that his opinions, though they influence his thoughts, do not govern his conduct. Now in the Middle Ages this perpetual opposition of theory and practice was peculiarly abrupt. Men's impulses were more violent and their conduct more reckless than is usually seen in modern communities; while the absence of a criticizing and measuring spirit made them surrender their minds more unreservedly than they would now do to a complete and imposing theory. Therefore it was, that while every one believed in the rights of the Empire as a part of divine truth, no one would yield to them where his own passions or interests interfered. Resistance to God's Vicar might

be and indeed was admitted to be a deadly sin, but it was
one which few hesitated to commit. Hence, in order to
give this unbounded imperial prerogative any practical
efficiency, it was found necessary to prop it up by the
limited but tangible authority of a feudal king. And the
one spot in Otto's empire on which feudality had never
fixed its grasp, and where therefore he was forced to rule
merely as Emperor, and not also as king, was that in
which he and his successors were never safe from insult
and revolt. This spot was his capital. Accordingly an
account of what befel the first Saxon Emperor in Rome
is a not unfitting comment on the theory expounded above,
as well as a curious episode in the history of the Apostolic
Chair.

After his coronation Otto had returned to North Italy, *Otto the*
where the partizans of Berengar and his son Adalbert still *Great in*
maintained themselves in arms. Scarcely was he gone *Rome.*
when the restless Pope, who found too late that in seeking
an ally he had given himself a master, renounced his allegiance, opened negotiations with Berengar, and did not even
scruple to send envoys pressing the heathen Magyars to
invade Germany. The Emperor was soon informed of
these plots, as well as of the flagitious life of the pontiff,
a youth of twenty-five, the most profligate if not the most
guilty of all who have worn the tiara. But he affected to
despise them, saying, with a sort of unconscious irony,
'He is a boy, the example of good men may reform him.'
When, however, Otto returned with a strong force, he
found the city gates shut, and a party within furious
against him. John the Twelfth was not only Pope, but as
the heir of Alberic, the head of a strong faction among
the nobles, and a sort of temporal prince in the city. But
neither he nor they had courage enough to stand a siege:
John fled into the Campagna to join Adalbert, and Otto

entering convoked a synod in St. Peter's. Himself presiding as temporal head of the Church, he began by inquiring into the character and manners of the Pope. At once a tempest of accusations burst forth from the assembled clergy. Bishop Liudprand, a credible although a hostile witness, gives us a long list of them : — 'Peter, cardinal-priest, rose and witnessed that he had seen the Pope celebrate mass and not himself communicate. John, bishop of Narnia, and John, cardinal-deacon, declared that they had seen him ordain a deacon in a stable, neglecting the proper formalities. They said further that he had defiled by shameless acts of vice the pontifical palace; that he had openly diverted himself with hunting; had put out the eyes of his spiritual father Benedict; had set fire to houses; had girt himself with a sword, and put on a helmet and hauberk. All present, laymen as well as priests, cried out that he had drunk to the devil's health; that in throwing the dice he had invoked the help of Jupiter, Venus, and other demons; that he had celebrated matins at uncanonical hours, and had not fortified himself by making the sign of the cross. After these things the Emperor, who could not speak Latin, since the Romans could not understand his native, that is to say, the Saxon tongue, bade Liudprand bishop of Cremona interpret for him, and adjured the council to declare whether the charges they had brought were true, or sprang only of malice and envy. Then all the clergy and people cried with a loud voice, 'If Pope John hath not committed all the crimes which Benedict the deacon hath read over, and even greater crimes than these, then may the chief of the Apostles, the blessed Peter, who by his word closes heaven to the unworthy and opens it to the just, never absolve us from our sins, but may we be bound by the chain of anathema, and on the last day may we stand on the left hand along with those who

have said to the Lord God, "Depart from us, for we will
not know Thy ways."'

The solemnity of this answer seems to have satisfied
Otto and the council: a letter was despatched to John,
couched in respectful terms, recounting the charges
brought against him, and asking him to appear to clear
himself by his own oath and that of a sufficient number of
compurgators. John's reply was short and pithy.

'John the bishop, the servant of the servants of God, to
all the bishops. We have heard tell that you wish to set
up another Pope: if you do this, by Almighty God I excommunicate you, so that you may not have power to perform mass or to ordain no one.'[a]

To this Otto and the synod replied by a letter of humor-
ous expostulation, begging the Pope to reform both his
morals and his Latin. But the messenger who bore it
could not find John: he had repeated what seems to have
been thought his most heinous sin, by going out into the
country to shoot:[b] and after a search had been made
in vain, the synod resolved to take a decisive step. Otto, *Deposition of*
who still led their deliberations, demanded the condemna- *John XII.*
tion of the Pope; the assembly deposed him by acclamation, 'because of his reprobate life,' and having obtained
the Emperor's consent, proceeded in an equally hasty
manner to raise Leo, the chief secretary and a layman, to
the chair of the Apostle.

Otto might seem to have now reached a position loftier
and firmer than that of any of his predecessors. Within

[a] 'Iohannes episcopus, servus servorum Dei, omnibus episcopis. Nos
audivimus dicere quia vos vultis alium papam facere: si hoc facitis, da Deum
omnipotentem excommunico vos, ut non habeatis licentiam missam celebrare
aut nullum ordinare.' — Liudprand, *Historia Ottonis*, c. 13. The 'da' shews
the progress of the change from Latin to Italian. The answer sent by Otto
and the council takes exception to the double negative.

[b] 'In campestria pharetratus abierat.'

little more than a year from his arrival in Rome, he had exercised powers greater than those of Charles himself, ordering the dethronement of one pontiff and the installation of another, forcing a reluctant people to bend themselves to his will.   The submission involved in his oath to protect the Holy See was more than compensated by the oath of allegiance to his crown which the Pope and the Romans had taken, and by their solemn engagement not to elect or ordain any future pontiff without the Emperor's consent.[c]   But he had yet to learn what this obedience and these oaths were worth.   The Romans had eagerly joined in the expulsion of John; they soon began to regret him.   They were mortified to see their streets filled by a foreign soldiery, the habitual licence of their manners sternly repressed, their most cherished privilege, the right of choosing the universal bishop, grasped by the strong hand of a master who used it for purposes with which they did not sympathize.   In a fickle and turbulent people, disaffection quickly turned to rebellion.   One night, Otto's

Revolt of the Romans. troops being most of them dispersed in their quarters at a distance, the Romans rose in arms, blocked up the Tiber bridges, and fell furiously upon the Emperor and his creature the new Pope.   Superior valour and constancy triumphed over numbers, and the Romans were overthrown with terrible slaughter; yet this lesson did not prevent them from revolting a second time, after Otto's departure in pursuit of Adalbert.   John the Twelfth returned to the city, and when his pontifical career was speedily closed by the sword of an injured husband,[d] the people chose a new

[c] 'Cives fidelitatem repromittunt hoc addentes et firmiter iurantes nunquam se papam electuros aut ordinaturos praeter consensum atque electionem domini imperatoris Ottonis Caesaris Augusti filiique ipsius regis Ottonis.' — Liudprand, *Historia Ottonis*, c. 8.

[d] 'In timporibus adeo a dyabulo est percussus ut infra dierum octo spacium eodem sit in vulnere mortuus,' says Liudprand, c. 19, crediting with less

Pope in defiance of the Emperor and his nominee. Otto
again subdued and again forgave them, but when they rebelled for a third time, in A.D. 966, he resolved to shew them
what imperial supremacy meant. Thirteen leaders, among
them the twelve tribunes, were executed, the consuls
were banished, republican forms entirely suppressed,
the government of the city entrusted to the Pope as viceroy. He, too, must not presume on the sacredness of
his person to set up any claims to independence. Otto
regarded the pontiff as no more than the first of his subjects, the creature of his own will, the depositary of an
authority which must be exercised according to the discre-
tion of the sovereign. He obtained from his nominee, Leo
VIII, a confirmation of the veto on papal elections which
the citizens had yielded in A.D. 963 (and which it was
afterwards supposed that Hadrian I had granted to Charles)
in a decree which may yet be read among the documents
which constitute canon law.[e] The vigorous exercise of
such a power might be expected to reform as well as to
restrain the apostolic see ; and it was for this purpose, and
in noble honesty, that the Teutonic monarchs employed
it. But the fortunes of Otto in the city are a type of those
which his successors were destined to experience. Not-
withstanding their admitted rights and the momentary
enthusiasm with which they were greeted in Rome, not
all the efforts of Emperor after Emperor could gain any
firm hold on the capital they were so proud of. Visiting
it only once or twice in their reigns, they must be sup-

than his wonted craft the supposed author of John's death, who well might
have desired a long life for so useful a servant.

He adds — ' Sed eucharistiae viaticum, ipsius instinctu qui eumpercusserat,
non percepit.'

[e] *Corpus Iuris Canonici*, Dist. lxiii, ' *In synodo.*' A decree which is
probably substantially genuine, although the form in which we have it is evidently of later date.

ported among a fickle populace by a large army of strangers, which melted away with terrible rapidity under the sun of Italy amid the deadly hollows of the Campagna.[f]   Rome soon resumed her turbulent independence.

Otto's rule in Italy.

Causes partly the same prevented the Saxon princes from gaining a firm footing throughout Italy.   Since Charles the Bald had bartered away for the crown all that made it worth having, no Emperor had exercised effective authority there.   The *missi dominici* had ceased to traverse the country; the local governors had thrown off control, a crowd of petty potentates had established principalities by aggressions on their weaker neighbours.   Only in the dominions of great nobles, like the marquis of Tuscany and duke of Spoleto, and in some of the cities where the supremacy of the bishop was paving the way for a republican system, could traces of political order be found, or the arts of peace flourish.   Otto, who, though he came as a conqueror, ruled legitimately as Italian king, found his feudal vassals less amenable than in Germany.   While actually present he succeeded by progresses and edicts, and stern justice, in doing something to still the turmoil; on his departure Italy relapsed into that disorganization for which her natural features were not less answerable than the mixture of her races.   Yet it was at this era, when the confusion was wildest, that there appeared the first rudiments of an Italian nationality, based partly on geographical position, partly on the use of a common language and the slow growth of peculiar customs and modes of thought. But though already jealous of the Tedescan, Lombards and Tuscans were still very far from disputing his sway.   Pope, magnates, and cities bowed to Otto as king and Emperor; nor did he bethink himself of crushing while it was weak a sentiment whose developement threatened the existence of

f As to the fevers see Note X at end.

his empire. Holding Italy equally for his own with Germany, and ruling both on the same principles, he was content to keep it a separate kingdom, neither changing its institutions nor sending Saxons, as Charles had sent Franks, to represent his government.[g]

CHAP. IX.

The lofty claims which Otto acquired with the Roman crown urged him to resume the plans of foreign conquest which had lain neglected since the days of Charles : the growing vigour of the Teutonic people, now definitely separating themselves from surrounding races (this is the era when frontier countships such as the Marks of Brandenburg, Meissen, and Schleswig, were established), placed in his hands a force to execute those plans which his predecessors had wanted. In this, as in his other enterprises, the great Emperor was active, wise, successful. Retaining the southern half of Italy, and unwilling to confess the loss of Rome, the Eastern Emperors had not ceased to annoy her German masters by intrigue, and might now, under the vigorous leadership first of Nicephorus and then of the Armenian John Tzimiskes, hope again to menace them in arms. Policy, and the fascination which an ostentatiously legitimate court exercised over the Saxon stranger, made Otto, as Napoleon wooed Maria Louisa, seek for his heir the hand of the princess Theophano, daughter of the Emperor Romanus II. Bishop Liudprand's account of his embassy represents in an amusing manner the rival pretensions of the old and new Empires.[h] The Easterns, who fancied that with the name they preserved the character and rights of Rome, held it almost as absurd as it was wicked that a Frank should insult their prerogative by reigning in Italy as

Otto's foreign policy.

Towards Byzantium.

---

[g] There was a separate chancellor for Italy, as afterwards for the kingdom of Burgundy.

[h] Liudprand, *Legatio Constantinopolitana.*

Emperor. They refused him that title altogether; and
when the Pope had, in a letter addressed '*Imperatori Graecorum*,' asked Nicephorus Phocas, successor of Romanus II
and stepfather of Theophano, to gratify the wishes of the
Emperor of the Romans, the Eastern was furious. 'You
are no Romans,' said he, 'but wretched Lombards: what
means this insolent Pope? with Constantine all Rome
migrated hither.' The wily bishop appeased him by revil-
ing the citizens of Rome, while he insinuated that Constantinople had no right to take their name, and proceeded
to vindicate the Francia and Saxonia of his master.
'"Roman" is the most contemptuous name we can use
—it conveys the reproach of every vice, cowardice, falsehood, avarice. But what can be expected from the descendants of the fratricide Romulus? to his asylum were
gathered the offscourings of the nations: thence came
these κοσμοκράτορες.' Nicephorus among other demands
required the 'theme' or province of Rome as the price of
compliance;[1] his successor, and murderer, John Tzimiskes,
was more moderate, and Theophano became the bride of
Otto II.

Towards the   Holding the two capitals of Charles the Great, Otto
West Franks. might vindicate the suzerainty over the West Frankish
kingdom which it had been meant that the imperial title
should carry with it. Arnulf had asserted the claim by
making Eudes, the first king of the line which takes its
name from his grand-nephew Hugh Capet, receive the
crown as a feudatory: Henry the Fowler had been less
successful. Otto pursued the same course, intriguing
with the discontented nobles of the Carolingian Louis
d'Outremer, and receiving their fealty as Superior of
Roman Gaul. These pretensions, however, could have

[1] 'Sancti imperii nostri olim servos principes, Beneventanum scilicet,
tradat,' &c. — *Legatio*, c. 15. The epithet is worth noticing.

been made effective only by arms, and the feudal militia of the tenth century was no such instrument of conquest as the hosts of Clovis and Charles had been. The star of the Carolingian king upon the fortress-hill of Laon was paling before the rising greatness of the Parisian Capets: a Romano-Celtic nation had formed itself, distinct in tongue from the Franks, whom it was fast absorbing, and still less willing to submit to a Saxon stranger. The modern kingdom of France[j] may be said to date from the accession of Hugh Capet, A.D. 987, and the claims of the Roman Empire were never afterwards formally admitted.

Of that France, however, Aquitaine was virtually independent. Lotharingia and Burgundy did not belong to it at all. The former of these kingdoms had adhered to the West Frankish king, Charles the Simple, against the East Frankish Conrad: but now, as mostly German in blood and speech, threw itself into the arms of Otto, and was thenceforth (till the sixteenth and seventeenth centuries) an integral part of the Empire. Burgundy, a separate kingdom, had, by seeking from Charles the Fat a ratification of Boso's election, by admitting, in the person of Rudolf the first Transjurane king, the feudal superiority of Arnulf, acknowledged itself to be dependent on the German crown. Otto governed it for thirty years, nominally as the guardian of the young king Conrad (son of Rudolf II).

Lorraine and Burgundy.

Otto's conquests to the North and East approved him

---

[j] Liudprand calls the Eastern Franks 'Franci Teutonici' to distinguish them from the Romanized Franks of Gaul or 'Francigenae' as they were frequently called. The name 'Frank' seems even so early as the tenth century to have been used in the East as a general name for the Western peoples of Europe. Liudprand says that the Eastern Emperor included 'sub Francorum nomine tam Latinos quam Teutonicos.' Probably this use dates from the time of Charles.

a worthy successor of the first Emperor. He penetrated far into Jutland, annexed Schleswig, made Harold the Blue-toothed his vassal. The Slavic tribes were obliged to submit, to follow the German host in war, to allow the free preaching of the Gospel in their borders. The Hungarians he forced to forsake their nomad life, and relieved Europe from the fear of Asiatic invasions by strengthening the frontier of Austria. Over more distant

lands, Northern Spain and England, it was not possible to recover the commanding position of Charles. Henry, as head of the Saxon name, may have wished to unite its branches on both sides the sea,[k] and it was perhaps partly with this intent that he gained for Otto the hand of Edith, sister of the English king Athelstan the Victorious. But the claim of supremacy, if any there was, was repudiated by Edgar, when, exaggerating the lofty style assumed by some of his predecessors, he called himself 'Basileus and Imperator of Britain,' [1] thereby seeming to pretend to a sovereignty over all the nations of the island similar to that which the Roman Emperor claimed over the states of Christendom.

This restored Empire, which professed itself a continuation of the Carolingian, was in many respects different. It was less wide, including, if we reckon strictly, only Germany proper and two-thirds of Italy; or counting in

[k] Conring, *De Finibus Imperii.*

[1] Basileus was a favourite title of the English kings before the Conquest. Titles like this used in these early English charters prove, it need hardly be said, absolutely nothing as to the real existence of any rights or powers of the English king beyond his own borders. What they do prove (over and above the taste for florid rhetoric in the royal clerks) is the impression produced by the imperial style, and by the idea of the Emperor's throne as supported by the thrones of kings and other lesser potentates. See hereon Freeman, *Hist. of Norm. Conquest,* vol. i. ch. 3, § 4; who, however, draws from the use of such titles conclusions regarding the rights of the English kings over the whole of Britain which seem unwarranted.

subject but separate kingdoms, Burgundy, Bohemia and
Moravia, Poland, Denmark, perhaps Hungary. Its character was less ecclesiastical. Otto exalted indeed the spiritual potentates of his realm, and was earnest in spreading
Christianity among the heathen : he was master of the
Pope and Defender of the Holy Roman Church. But
religion held a less important place in his mind and
his administration : he made fewer wars for its sake, summoned no councils, and did not, like his predecessor, criti-
cise the discourses of bishops. It was also less Roman.
We do not know whether Otto associated with that name
anything more than the right to universal dominion and a
certain oversight of matters spiritual, nor how far he
believed himself to be treading in the steps of the earlier
Caesars. He could not speak Latin, though he tried in
middle life to learn it, he had few learned men around him,
he cannot have possessed the varied cultivation which had
been so fruitful in the mind of Charles. Moreover, the
conditions of his time were different, and did not permit
similar attempts at wide organization. The local potentates
would have submitted to no *missi dominici ;* separate laws
and jurisdictions would not have yielded to imperial capitularies ; the *placita* at which those laws were framed or
published would not have been crowded, as of yore, by
armed freemen. But what Otto could he did, and did it
to good purpose. Constantly traversing his dominions, he
introduced an order and prosperity before unknown, and left
everywhere the impress of an heroic character. Under
him the Germans became not only a united nation, but
were at once raised on a pinnacle among European peoples
as the imperial race, the possessors of Rome and Rome's
authority. The political connection with Italy, while stirring their spirit, brought with it a knowledge and culture
hitherto unknown, and gave the newly kindled energy an

object.   Germany became in her turn the instructress of the neighbouring tribes, who trembled at Otto's sceptre; Poland and Bohemia received from her their arts and their learning with their religion.   If the revived Romano-Germanic Empire was less splendid than the Empire of the West had been under Charles, it was, within narrower limits, firmer and more lasting, since based on national and social forces which the other had wanted.   It perpetuated the name, the language, the literature, such as it then was, of Rome; it extended her spiritual sway; it strove to represent that concentration for which men cried, and became a power to unite and civilize Europe.

Otto II,
A.D. 973–983.

Otto III,
A.D. 983–
1002.

The time of Otto the Great has required a fuller treatment, as the era of the Holy Empire's foundation : succeeding rulers may be more quickly dismissed.   Yet Otto III's reign cannot pass unnoticed : short, sad, full of bright promise never fulfilled.   His mother was the Eastern princess Theophano ; his perceptor the illustrious Gerbert of Aurillac (who had studied in the schools of Moorish Spain), archbishop, first of Rheims and afterwards of Ravenna : through the one he felt himself connected with the legitimacy of the Eastern Empire, and had imbibed its absolutist spirit ; by the other he had been reared in the dream of a renovated Rome, with her memories turned to realities.   To accomplish that renovation, who so fit as he who with the vigorous blood of the Teutonic conqueror inherited the venerable rights of Constantinople ?   It was his design, now that the solemn millennial era of the birth of Christ had arrived, to renew the majesty of the city and make her again the capital of a world-embracing Empire, victorious as Trajan's, despotic as Justinian's, holy as Constantine's.   His young and visionary mind was too much dazzled by the gorgeous fancies it created to see the world as it was — Germany rude,

His ideas.
Fascination
exercised
over him by
the name of
Rome.

Italy unquiet, Rome corrupt and faithless.   In A.D. 995, at CHAP. IX.
the age of fifteen, he took from his grandmother's hands
the reins of government, and entered Italy to receive his
crown, and quell the disorders of Rome.   There he put to
death the rebel Crescentius, in whom modern enthusiasm
has seen a patriotic republican, who, reviving the institutions of Alberic, had ruled as consul, or senator, sometimes
entitling himself Emperor.   The young monarch reclaimed,
perhaps extended, the privilege of Charles and Otto the
Great, by nominating successive pontiffs : first Bruno his
cousin (Gregory V), then Gerbert, whose papal name of
Sylvester II recalled significantly the ally of Constantine : *Pope*
Gerbert, to his contemporaries a marvel of science and *Sylvester II,*
learning, in later legend the magician who, at the price of *A.D. 1000.*
his own soul, purchased preferment from the Enemy, and
by him was at last carried off in the body.   With the substitution of these men for the profligate priests of Italy, began
that Teutonic reform of the Papacy which raised it from
the abyss of the tenth century to the point where Hildebrand found it.   The Emperors were working the ruin of
their power by their most disinterested acts.

With his tutor on Peter's chair to second or direct *Schemes of*
him, Otto laboured on his great project in a spirit almost *Otto III.*
mystic.   He had an intense religious belief in the Em- *Changes of*
peror's duties to the world — in his proclamations he *style and*
calls himself 'Servant of the Apostles,' 'Servant of Jesus *usage.*
Christ'[m] — together with the ambitious antiquarianism of
a fiery imagination, kindled by the memorials of the glory
and power he represented.   Even the wording of his laws

---

[m] In Pertz, *M. G. H.*, Diplomatum ii. part ii. n. 226: 'Otto servus apostolorum et deo favente Romanorum imperator Augustus.'   Ibid: n. 344: 'Otto
tercius Servus Iesu Christi et Romanorum imperator Augustus.'   These titles
become general after the beginning of 1000; there seems only one example
before (see n. 226).

witnesses to the strange mixture of notions that filled his
eager brain. 'We have ordained this,' says an edict, 'in
order that, the Church of God being freely and firmly
stablished, our Empire may be advanced and the crown of
our knighthood triumph; that the power of the Roman
people may be extended and the commonwealth be restored; so may we be found worthy after living righteously
in the tabernacle of this world, to fly away from the prison
of this life and reign most righteously with the Lord.' To
exclude the claims of the Eastern Court he used the title
'*Romanorum Imperator*' instead of the simple '*Imperator*'
of his predecessors. His seals bear a legend resembling
that used by Charles, *Renovatio* '*Imperii Romanorum*';
even the 'commonwealth,' despite the results that name
had produced under Alberic and Crescentius, was to be
re-established. He built a palace on the Aventine, then
the most healthy and beautiful quarter of the city; he
devised a regular administrative system of government for
his capital — naming a patrician, a prefect, and a body of
judges, who were commanded to recognize no law but the
Roman. The formula of their appointment has been preserved to us: in it the Emperor delivering to the judge
a copy of the code bids him 'with this code judge Rome
and the Leonine city and the whole world.' He introduced into the simple German court the ceremonious mag-
nificence of the East, not without giving offence to many
of his followers.[n] He asserted his prerogative by conferring the regal title upon the rulers of Hungary and Poland.
His father's wish to draw Italy and Germany more closely
together, he followed up by giving the chancellorship of
both countries to the same churchman, by maintaining a

---

[n] 'Imperator antiquam Romanorum consuetudinem iam ex magna parte
deletam suis cupiens renovare temporibus multa faciebat quae diversi diverse
sentiebant.' — Thietmar, *Chron.* bk. iv. c. 29 (Pertz, *M. G. H.* iii. p. 781).

strong force of Germans in Italy, and by taking his Italian
retinue with him through the Transalpine lands.   How far
these brilliant and wide-reaching plans were capable of
realization, had their author lived to attempt it, can be but
guessed at.   It is reasonable to suppose that whatever
power he might have gained in the South he would have
lost in the North.   Dwelling rarely in Germany, and in
sympathies more a Southern than a Teuton, he reined in
the fierce barons with no such tight hand as his grandfather had been wont to do; he displeased the Germans
by favouring the claim which the Pope advanced to control their prelates ; he neglected the schemes of northern
conquest ; he released the Polish monarch from the obligation of tribute, and relaxed the hold of Germany on the
Hungarians.   But all, save that those plans were his, is
now no more than conjecture, for Otto III, 'the wonder of
the world,' as his own generation called him, died childless
on the threshhold of manhood ; the victim, if we may trust
a story of the time, of the revenge of Stephania, the widow
of Crescentius, who ensnared him by her beauty, and slew
him by a lingering poison.   They carried him across the
Alps with laments whose echoes sound faintly from the
pages of monkish chroniclers, and buried him in the choir
of the basilica at Aachen some fifty paces from the tomb
of Charles beneath the central dome.   Two years had not
passed since, setting out on his last journey to Rome, he
had opened that tomb, had gazed on the great Emperor,
sitting on a marble throne, robed and crowned, with the
Gospel-book open before him ; and there, touching the
dead hand, unclasping from the neck its golden cross, had
taken as it were, an investiture of Empire from his Frankish forerunner.°   Short as was his life and few his acts,

° The details regarding the finding of the body of Charles, though given
by a contemporary annalist, have been recently discredited as inconsistent

Otto III is in one respect more memorable than any who went before or came after him. None save he desired to make the seven-hilled city again the seat of dominion, reducing Germany and Lombardy and Greece to their rightful place of subject provinces. No one else so forgot the present to live in the light of the ancient order; no other soul was so possessed by that fervid mysticism and that reverence for the glories of the past, whereon rested the idea of the mediaeval Empire.

The direct line of Otto the Great had now ended, and though the Franks might elect and the Saxons accept Henry II (called the Saint)[p] (great-grandson of Henry the Fowler and thus second cousin of Otto III), Italy was not bound by their acts. Neither the Empire nor the Lombard kingdom could yet be claimed as of right by the German king. Her princes placed Ardoin, marquis of Ivrea, on the vacant throne of Pavia, moved partly by the growing aversion to a Transalpine power, still more by the desire of impunity under a monarch feebler than any since Berengar. But the selfishness that had exalted Ardoin soon overthrew him. Ere long a party among the nobles, seconded by the Pope, invited Henry, who had already entered Italy in A.D. 1004; his strong army made opposition hopeless, and at Rome he received the imperial crown, A.D. 1014. The crowning there of three successive German kings, and the alliance of the second with an East Roman dynasty, had evidently strengthened the attraction

Italy independent.

Henry II Emperor, A.D. 1014-1024.

with Eginhard's statement that Charles was buried on the day of his death, and are open to other objections. But there are points in the account which seem unlikely to have been invented; and it is possible that the placing of the body in the tomb was only provisional, and that it was immediately afterwards embalmed and set in the position in which Otto III found it. — Cf. Hodgkin, *Italy and her Invaders*, vol. viii. p. 273.

[p] *Annales Quedlinb.*, ad ann. 1002, in Pertz, *M. G. H., Script.* iii. p. 78.

which the South had for the North. It is, perhaps, more
singular that the Transalpine kings should have clung so
pertinaciously to Italian sovereignty than that the Lombards should have so frequently attempted to recover their
independence. For the former had often little or no
hereditary claim, they were not secure in their seat at
home, they crossed a huge mountain barrier into a land of
treachery and hatred. But Rome's glittering lure was
irresistible, and the disunion of Italy promised an easy conquest. Surrounded by martial vassals, these Emperors were
generally for the moment supreme : once their pennons had
disappeared in the gorges of Tyrol, things reverted to their
former condition, and Tuscany was little more dependent
than France. In Southern Italy the viceroy of the *Southern*
Eastern Emperor ruled from Bari, and Rome was an out- *Italy.*
post instead of the centre of Teutonic power. A curious
evidence of the wavering politics of the time is furnished
by the Annals of Benevento, the Lombard town which on
the confines of the East Roman and West Roman realms
gave steady obedience to neither. They usually date by
and recognize the princes of Constantinople,q seldom men-
tioning the Franks, till the reign of Conrad II ; after him
the Western becomes *Imperator*, the Eastern, appearing
more rarely, is *Imperator Constantinopolitanus*. Assailed
by the Saracens, masters already of Sicily, these regions
seemed on the eve of being lost to Christendom, and
the Romans sometimes bethought themselves of return-

q *Annales Beneventani*, in Pertz, *M. G. H., Script.* iii. pp. 173 sq.; *e.g.* sub
anno 958 (p. 175). So an annalist at Salerno, writing at the end of the
tenth century, says that the true emperor is he who reigns at Constantinople
though 'the kings of the Gauls have now usurped the title.' 'Imperator
omnimodis non dici potest nisi qui regnum Romanum praeest, hoc est Con-
stantinopolitanum. Reges Gallorum nunc usurparunt sibi talem nomen, nam
antiquitus omnimodis sic non vocitati sunt.'—Chron. Salern. apud (Pertz,
M. G. H., Script. iii. p. 479).

ing under the sceptre of Constantinople. As the weakness of the East Roman monarchs in the South favoured the rise of the Apulian dominion which the Norman Robert Wiscard established (A.D. 1059–1077), so did the liberties of the Northern cities shoot up in the absence of the Germanic Emperors and the feuds of the territorial magnates. Milan, Pavia, Cremona, were only the foremost among many populous centres of industry, some of them already self-governing, all quickly absorbing or repelling the rural nobility, and not afraid to display by tumults their aversion to the Germans.

Conrad II,
A.D. 1024–
1039.

The reign of Conrad II (usually called the Salic), the first Emperor of the great Franconian line, is remarkable for the accession to the Empire of Burgundy, or, as it is after this time more often called, the kingdom of Arles.[r] Rudolf III, the last king, had proposed to bequeath it to Henry II, and the states were at length persuaded to consent to its reunion to the crown from which it had been separated, though to some extent dependent, since the death of Lothar I (son of Lewis the Pious). On Rudolf's death in 1032, Eudes, count of Champagne, endeavoured to seize it, and entered the North-western districts, from which he was dislodged by Conrad with some difficulty. Unlike Italy, it became an integral member of the Germanic realm : its prelates and nobles sat in imperial diets, and long retained the style and title of Princes of the Holy Empire. The central government was, however, seldom effective in these outlying territories, exposed always to the intrigues, finally to the aggressions, of Capetian France.

Henry III,
A.D. 1039–
1056.

Under Conrad's son Henry the Third the Empire attained the meridian of its power. At home Otto the Great's prerogative had not stood so high. The duchies, always

[r] See Appendix, Note A.

the chief source of disquietude, were allowed to remain
vacant or filled by the relatives of the monarch, who himself retained, contrary to usual practice, those of Franconia
and (for some years) Swabia.   Abbeys and sees lay virtually in his gift.   Intestine feuds were repressed by the
proclamation of a public peace.   Abroad, the feudal superiority over Hungary, which Henry II had gained by conferring the title of King with the hand of his sister Gisela,
was enforced by war, the country made almost a province,
and compelled to pay tribute.   In Rome no German sov- *His reform*
ereign had ever been so absolute.   A disgraceful contest *of the*
between three claimants of the papal chair had shocked *popedom.*
even the reckless apathy of Italy.[8]   Henry deposed them
all, and appointed their successor: he became hereditary
patrician, and wore constantly the green mantle and circlet
of gold which were the badges of that office, seeming, one
might think, to find in it some further authority than that
which the imperial name conferred.   A Roman synod
granted to Henry the right of nominating the supreme
pontiff; and the Roman priesthood, who had forfeited the
respect of the world even more by habitual simony than by
the flagrant corruption of their manners, were forced to
receive German after German as their bishop, at the bidding of a ruler so powerful, so severe, and so pious.   But
Henry's encroachments alarmed his own nobles no less
than the priesthood, and the reaction, which might have

---

[8] At a provincial synod held near Rheims in 991, Arnulf bishop of
Orleans had delivered a vehement condemnation of the conduct and pretensions of recent pontiffs, going so far as to declare the Pope to be Antichrist,
'sitting in the temple of God and setting himself forth as God' (2 Thess. ii.
4).   As Ranke remarks (*Weltgeschichte*, vii. p. 48), Arnulf and other opponents of papal claims were sadly hampered by the power ascribed to the
Pope in the Pseudo Isidorian decretals, which they did not know to be
forgeries.

been dangerous to himself, was fatal to his successor.[t]   A mere chance, as some may call it, determined the course of history.   The great Emperor died suddenly in A.D. 1056, and a child was left at the helm, while storms were gathering that might have demanded the wisest hand.

[t] The Abbey of Cluny was already the centre of a monastic movement in favour of the deliverance of the clergy from secular control.

CHAPTER X

STRUGGLE OF THE EMPIRE AND THE PAPACY

REFORMED by the Emperors and their Teutonic nominees, the Papacy had resumed in the middle of the eleventh century the ambitious schemes shadowed forth by Nicholas I, and which the degradation of the last age had only suspended. Under the guidance of her greatest mind, Hildebrand, the archdeacon of Rome, she now advanced to their completion, and proclaimed that war of the ecclesiastical power against the civil power in the person of the Emperor, which became the centre of the subsequent history of both. While the nature of the struggle cannot be understood without a glance at their previous connection, the vastness of the subject forbids an attempt to draw even its outlines, and restricts our view to those relations of Popedom and Empire which arise directly out of their respective positions as heads spiritual and temporal of the universal Christian state.

The eagerness of Christianity in the age immediately following her recognition as the religion favoured by the state to purchase by submission the support of the civil power, has been already remarked. The change from independence to supremacy was gradual. The tale we smile at, how Constantine, healed of his leprosy, granted the West to bishop Sylvester, and retired to Byzantium that no secular prince might interfere with the jurisdiction or profane the neighbourhood of Peter's chair, worked great effects through the belief it commanded for many centuries. Nay more, it had a sort of groundwork in fact.

Growth of the papal power.

Through the removal of the seat of government from the Tiber to the Bosphorus the Pope grew to be the greatest personage in the city, and in the prostration after Alarich's invasion he was seen to be so. Henceforth he alone was a permanent and effective, though still unacknowledged power, as truly superior to the senate and consuls in the revived municipal republic after the ninth century as Augustus and Tiberius had been to the faint continuance of their earlier prototypes. Pope Leo the First asserted the universal jurisdiction of his see,[a] and his persevering successors slowly enthralled Italy, Illyricum, Gaul, Spain, Africa, dexterously confounding their undoubted metropolitan and patriarchal rights with those of oecumenical bishop, in which they were finally merged. By his writings and the fame of his personal sanctity, by the conversion of England and the introduction of an impressive ritual, Gregory the Great did more than any other pontiff to advance Rome's ecclesiastical authority. Yet his tone to Maurice of Constantinople was deferential, to Phocas adulatory; his successors were not consecrated till confirmed by the Emperor or the Exarch; one of them was dragged in chains to the Bosphorus, and banished thence to Scythia. When the Image-breaking controversy and the intervention of Pipin weakened and ultimately broke the allegiance of the Popes to the East, the Franks, as patricians and Emperors, seemed to step into the position which Constantinople had lost.[b] At Charles's coronation says the Saxon poet,

> ' Et summus eundem
> Praesul adoravit, sicut mos debitus olim
> Principibus fuit antiquis.'

---

[a] 'Roma per sedem Beati Petri caput orbis effecta.' — See note g p. 31.

[b] 'Claves . . . vobis *ad regnum* dimisimus.' — Pope Gregory III to Charles Martel, in *Codex Carolinus,* ap. Muratori, *S. R. I.* iii. part ii. p. 76. Some, however, prefer to read 'ad rogum.'

Their relations were, however, no longer the same. If the Frank vaunted conquest, the priest spoke only of free gift. What Christendom saw was that Charles was crowned by the Pope's hands, and undertook as his principal duty the protection and advancement of the Holy Roman Church. The circumstances of Otto the Great's coronation gave an even more favourable opening to sacerdotal claims, for it was a Pope who summoned him to Rome and a Pope who received from him an oath of fidelity and aid, as it had been through the action of successive pontiffs that the fleeting Emperors of the preceding hundred years had each obtained the crown. In the conflict of three powers, the Emperor, the pontiff, and the people — represented by their senate and consuls, or by the demagogue of the hour — the most steady, prudent, and far-sighted was sure eventually to prevail. The Popedom had no minorities, as yet few disputed successions, few revolts within its own army — the host of churchmen through Europe. The conversion of Germany by the English Winfrith (St. Boniface), under its direct sanction, gave it a hold on the rising hierarchy of the greatest European state; the extension of the rule of Charles and Otto diffused in the same measure its emissaries and pretensions. The first disputes turned on the right of the prince to confirm the elected pontiff, which was afterwards supposed to have been granted by Hadrian I to Charles, in the decree quoted as '*Hadrianus Papa.*'[c] This '*ius eligendi et ordinandi summum pontificem,*' which Lewis I appears as abandoning by the '*Ego Ludovicus,*'[d] was claimed by the Carolingians whenever they felt themselves strong enough, and having fallen into desuetude in the troublous times of the Italian Emperors, was formally renewed to Otto

---

[c] *Corpus Iuris Canonici*, Dist. lxiii. c. 22.

[d] Dist. lxiii. c. 30. This decree is, however, probably spurious.

the Great by his nominee Leo VIII. We have seen it used, and used in the purest spirit, by Otto himself, by his grandson Otto III, last of all, and most autocratically, by Henry III. Along with it there had grown up a bold counter-assumption of the papal chair to be itself the source of the imperial dignity. In submitting to a fresh coronation by the Pope, Lewis the Pious tacitly admitted the invalidity of that previously performed by his father: Charles the Bald did not scout the arrogant declaration of John VIII,[e] that to him alone the Emperor owed his crown; and the council of Pavia,[f] when it chose that monarch king of Italy, repeated the assertion. Subsequent Popes knew better than to apply to the chiefs of Saxon and Franconian chivalry language which the feeble Neustrian had not resented; but the precedent remained, the weapon was only hid behind the pontifical robe to be flashed out with effect when the moment should come. There were also two other great steps which papal power had taken. By the invention or adoption of the False Decretals[g] had provided itself with a legal system suited to any emergency, and which gave it unlimited authority through the Christian world in causes spiritual and over persons ecclesiastical. Canonistical ingenuity found it easy in one way or another to make this include all causes and persons whatsoever: for crime is always, and wrong is

[e] 'Nos elegimus merito et approbavimus una cum annisu et voto patrum amplique senatus et gentis togatae,' &c., ap. Baron. *Ann. Eccl.*, ad ann. 876.

[f] 'Divina vos pietas B. principum apostolorum Petri et Pauli interventione per vicarium ipsorum dominum Ioannem summum pontificem . . . ad imperiale culmen S. Spiritus iudicio provexit.' — *Concil. Ticinense*, in Mur. *S. R. I.* ii. part i. p. 150.

[g] These decrees attributed to early Councils and Popes were forged, probably in Gaul, about the middle of the ninth century, and before the eleventh had become accepted as authentic. The collection which passed under the name of Isidore contains some genuine matter with a great deal more palpably invented.

often, sin, nor can aught be anywhere done which may
not affect the clergy. On the gifts of Pipin and Charles,
repeated and confirmed by Lewis I, Charles II, Otto I,
and Otto III, and now made to rest on the more venerable authority of the first Christian Emperor, it could
found claims to the sovereignty of Rome, Tuscany, and
all else that had belonged to the exarchate. Indefinite
in their terms, these grants were not meant by the
donors to convey full political authority over the districts
bestowed — that belonged to the head of the Empire —
but only, as in the case of other church estates, a sort of
perpetual usufruct, a beneficial enjoyment which did not
carry sovereignty, but might be deemed to carry a sort
of feudal lordship over the tenants who dwelt upon the
soil. They were, in fact, what we should call endow-
ments. Nor had the gifts been ever actually reduced into
possession : the Pope had been hitherto more frequently
the victim than the lord of the neighbouring barons. The
grants were, however, not denied, and might be made a
formidable engine of attack. Appealing to them, the Pope
could brand his opponents as unjust and impious; and
could summon nobles and cities to defend him as their
liege lord, just as, with no better original right, he subsequently invoked the help of the Norman conquerors of
Naples and Sicily.

The attitude of the Roman Church to the imperial
power at Henry the Third's death was externally respectful. The title of a German king to receive the crown
of the city was not seriously disputed and the Pope was
his lawful subject. Hitherto the initiative in reform had
come from the civil magistrate. But the secret of the
pontiff's strength lay in this : he, and he alone, could
confer the crown, and had therefore the right of imposing
conditions on its recipient. Frequent interregna, while

they had enabled the Pope to assume upon each occasion a more and more independent position, had prevented the power of the Transalpine sovereigns from taking firm root.   None of them could claim to reign by hereditary right : none could deny that the holy Church had before sought and might again seek a defender elsewhere.   And since the need of such defence had originated the 'transference of the Empire from the Greeks to the Franks,' since to render such defence was the Emperor's chief function, the Pope might surely hold it to be his duty as well as his right to see that the candidate was capable of fulfilling his task, to reject him if he neglected or misperformed it.

Hildebrandine reforms.

The first step was to remove a blemish in the constitution of the Church, by fixing a defined body to choose the supreme pontiff.   This Nicholas II did in A.D. 1059, under the counsel and impulse of the archdeacon Hildebrand.   His decree vested the election in the college of cardinals, while it contemplated the subsequent assent of the clergy and people of Rome and reserved the rights of Henry IV and more vaguely of his successors.[h]   Then the reforming spirit, kindled by the abuses and depravity of the last century, advanced apace.   Directed by Hildebrand, who after having exerted a predominant influence during two pontificates himself became Pope as Gregory the Seventh in A.D. 1073, it strove for two main objects — the enforcement of celibacy, especially on the secular clergy, who enjoyed in this respect considerable freedom ; and the extinction of simony.[i]   In the former, the Em-

[h] Even Hildebrand when elected recognized these rights.

It was at this time (A.D. 1059) that the same Pope, by investing the Norman Robert Wiscard with the title of duke of Apulia and Calabria as a fief of the Holy See, provided for his successors in the chair of Peter an ally whose help was to prove invaluable to them.

[i] The sin of Simon (Acts viii. 18–24) was deemed to include the employment of any corrupt means to obtain preferment to an ecclesiastical office.

perors and part of the laity were not unwilling to join:
the latter no one dared to defend in theory. But when
Gregory declared that it was sin for the ecclesiastic to
receive his benefice under conditions frcm a layman, and
so condemned the whole system of the feudal investitures
of land to the clergy, he aimed a deadly blow at the
authority of every secular ruler. Half of the land and
wealth of Germany was in the hands of bishops and
abbots, who would now be freed from the Emperor's
control to pass under that of the Pope. In such a state
of things government itself would be impossible.

Henry and Gregory already mistrusted each other: *Henry IV*
after this decree war was inevitable. The Pope cited his *and Gre-*
gory VII.
opponent to appear and be judged at Rome for his vices
and misgovernment. The Emperor [j] replied by convoking
a synod, which deposed and insulted Gregory. At once
the dauntless monk pronounced Henry excommunicate,
and fixed a day on which, if still unrepentant, he should
cease to reign. Supported by his own princes, the monarch might have defied a command backed by no external
force ; but the Saxons, never contented since the first
place had passed from their own dukes to the Franconians,
only waited the signal to burst into a new revolt, whilst
through all Germany the Emperor's tyranny and irregulari-
ties of life had sown the seeds of disaffection. Shunned,
betrayed, threatened, he rushed into what seemed the
only course left, and Canosa saw Europe's mightiest
prince, titular lord of the world, a suppliant before the
successor of the Apostle. Henry soon found that his
humiliation had not served him ; driven back into opposition, he defied Gregory anew, set up an anti-pope, overthrew the rival whom his rebellious subjects had raised,

j Strictly speaking, Henry was at this time only king of the Romans: he
was not crowned Emperor at Rome till 1084.

and maintained to the end of his sad and chequered life a power often depressed but never destroyed. Nevertheless had all other humiliation been spared, that one scene in the yard of the Countess Matilda's castle, an imperial penitent standing barefoot and woollen-frocked on the snow, till the priest who sat within should admit and absolve him, was enough to mark a decisive change, and inflict an irretrievable disgrace on the crown so abased.[k] Its wearer could no more, with the same lofty confidence, claim to be the highest power on earth, created by and answerable to God alone. Gregory had extorted the recognition of that absolute superiority of spiritual authority which he was wont to assert so sternly, proclaiming that to the Pope, as God's Vicar, all mankind are subject, and all rulers responsible, so that he, the giver of the crown, may also excommunicate and depose. And he discovered a simile which played a great part in subsequent controversy, a simile so happily suited to the modes of thought of the Middle Ages that no one dreamt of denying that it expressed the meaning of Scripture and the purpose of the Creator. Writing to William the Conqueror, king of England, he says:[1] "For as for the beauty of this world, that it may be at different seasons perceived by fleshly eyes, God hath disposed the Sun and the Moon, lights that outshine all others; so lest the creature whom His goodness hath formed after His own image in this world

[k] The castle of Canosa, of which only scanty ruins remain, stood on one of the northern outliers of the Apennines, some ten miles S.W. of Reggio (Modenese).

Lambert's account of the penitence, which he makes to last for three days, has recently been called in question: see Holder Egger, *Studien zu Lambert von Herzfeld* in *Neues Archiv der Gesellschaft für ältere deutsche Geschichtskunde* (vol. xix, 1894).

[1] Letter of Gregory VII to William I, A.D. 1080. — Jaffé, *Monumenta Gregoriana*, p. 419.

should be drawn astray into fatal dangers, He hath provided in the apostolic and royal dignities the means of ruling it through divers offices. . . . If I, therefore, am to answer for thee on the dreadful day of judgment before the just Judge who cannot lie, the creator of every creature, bethink thee whether I must not very diligently provide for thy salvation, and whether, for thine own safety, thou oughtest not without delay to obey me, that so thou mayest possess the land of the living.'

Gregory was not the inventor or first propounder of these doctrines; they had been before his day a part of mediaeval Christianity, interwoven with its most vital doctrines. Six centuries earlier Pope Gelasius I had implicitly stated them in a letter enjoining obedience on the Emperor Anastasius. They were held by many others in Gregory's day, and expressed with a more militant vehemence by his contemporary and friend Alfanus of Salerno.[m] But Gregory was the first who dared to apply them to the world as he found it. 'His was that rarest and grandest of gifts, an intellectual courage and power of imaginative belief which, when it has convinced itself of aught, accepts it fully with all its consequences, and shrinks not from acting at once upon it. A perilous gift, as the melancholy end of his own career proved, for men were found less ready than he had thought them to follow out with unswerving consistency like his the principles which all acknowledged. But it was the very suddenness and boldness of his policy that secured the ultimate triumph of his cause, awing men's minds and making that seem realized which had been till then a vague theory. His premises once admitted — and no one dreamt of denying them — the reasonings by which he established the superiority of spiritual to temporal jurisdiction were un-

[m] See as to Gelasius and Alfanus, and as to the view held by moderate churchmen, Note XI at end.

assailable. With his authority, in whose hands are the keys of heaven and hell, whose word can bestow eternal bliss or plunge in everlasting misery, no earthly potentate can compete or interfere. If his power extends into the infinite, how much more must he be supreme over things finite? It was thus that Gregory and his successors were wont to argue: the wonder is, not that they were obeyed, but that they were not obeyed more implicitly. In the second sentence of excommunication which Gregory passed upon Henry the Fourth are these words: —

'Come now, I beseech you, O most holy and blessed Fathers and Princes, Peter and Paul, that all the world may understand and know that if ye are able to bind and to loose in heaven, ye are likewise able on earth, according to the merits of each man, to give and to take away empires, kingdoms, princedoms, marquisates, duchies, countships, and the possessions of all men. For if ye judge spiritual things, what must we believe to be your power over worldly things? and if ye judge the angels who rule over all proud princes, what can ye not do to their slaves?'

Results of the struggle. Doctrines such as these do indeed strike equally at all temporal governments, nor were the Innocents and Bonifaces of later days slow to apply them so. On the Empire, however, the blow fell first and heaviest. As when Alarich entered Rome, the spell of ages was broken, Christendom saw its stateliest and most venerable institution dishonoured and helpless; allegiance was no longer undivided, for who could presume to fix in each case the limits of the civil and ecclesiastical jurisdictions? The potentates of Europe beheld in the Papacy a force which, if dangerous to themselves, could be made to repel the pretensions and baffle the designs of the strongest and haughtiest among them. Italy learned how to meet the Teutonic conqueror by gaining papal sanction for the leagues of her cities. The German princes, anxious to narrow the prerogative of their head, were the natural allies of his enemy, whose spiritual thunders, more terrible than their own lances, could enable them to depose an aspiring monarch, or extort from him any concessions they desired.   Their altered tone is marked by the promise they required from Rudolf of Swabia, whom, at the Pope's suggestion, they set up as a rival to Henry, that he would not endeavour to make the throne hereditary.

It is not possible here to dwell on the details of the great struggle of the Investitures, rich as it is in the interest of adventure and character, momentous as were its results for the future.   A word or two must suffice to describe the conclusion, not indeed of the whole drama, which was to extend over centuries, but of what may be called its first act.   Even that act lasted beyond the lives of the original performers.   Gregory the Seventh passed away at Salerno in A.D. 1085, exclaiming with his last breath, ' I have loved justice and hated iniquity, therefore I die in exile.'   Twenty-one years later Henry IV died, dethroned by an unnatural son whom the hatred of a relentless pontiff had raised in rebellion against him.   But that son, the Emperor Henry the Fifth, so far from conceding the points in dispute, proved an antagonist more ruthless and not less able than his father.   He claimed for his crown all the rights over ecclesiastics that his predecessors had ever enjoyed, and when at his coronation in Rome, A.D. 1111, Pope Paschal II refused to complete the rite until he should have yielded, Henry seized both Pope and cardinals and compelled them by a rigorous imprisonment to consent to a treaty which he dictated.   Once set free, the Pope, as was natural, disavowed his extorted concessions, and the struggle was protracted for ten years longer, until nearly half a century had elapsed from the first quarrel between Gregory VII and Henry IV.   The Concordat of Worms, concluded between Pope Calixtus II and Henry V, provided for the freedom of ecclesiastical elections and the renunciation by the Emperor of investiture by the ring and the crozier, but it left to him the right of investing the clergy with all temporalities by the sceptre, and the right to require from them (except those who held directly from the Pope) the performance of their duties as feudal vassals. This settlement was in form a compromise, designed to spare either party the humiliation of defeat. Yet the Papacy remained master of the field. The Emperor retained but one-half of those rights of investiture which had formerly been his. He could never resume the position of Henry III; his wishes or intrigues might influence the proceedings of a chapter, his oath bound him from open interference. He had entered the strife in the fullness of dignity; he came out of it with tarnished glory and shattered power. His wars had been hitherto carried on with foreign foes, or at worst with a single rebel noble; now his former ally was turned into his fiercest assailant, and had enlisted against him half his court, half the magnates of his realm. At any moment his sceptre might be shivered in his hand by the bolt of anathema, and a host of enemies spring up from every convent and cathedral.

Two other results of this great conflict ought not to pass unnoticed. The Emperor was alienated from the Church at the most unfortunate of all moments, the era
of the Crusades. To conduct a great religious war against the enemies of the faith, to head the church militant in her carnal as the Popes were accustomed to do in her spiritual strife, this was the very purpose for which an Emperor had been called into being; and it was indeed in these wars, more particularly in the first three of them, that the ideal of a Christian commonwealth, embodied in the theory of the mediaeval Empire, was

once for all and never again realized by the combined action of the great nations of Europe. Had such an opportunity fallen to the lot of Henry III, he might have used it to win back a supremacy such as had belonged to the first Carolingians. But Henry IV's proscription excluded him from all share in an enterprise which he must otherwise have led — nay more, committed it to the guidance of his foes. The religious feeling which the crusades evoked — a feeling which became the origin of the great orders of chivalry, and somewhat later of the two great orders of mendicant friars — turned against the power which resisted ecclesiastical claims, and was made to work the will of the Holy See, which had blessed and organized the project. A century and a half later the Pope did not scruple to preach a crusade against the Emperor himself.

Again, it was now that the first seeds were sown of that fear and hatred wherewith many among the German people never thenceforth ceased to regard the encroaching Romish court. Branded by the Church and forsaken by the nobles, Henry IV retained the affections of the burghers of Worms and Liége. It soon became the test of Teutonic patriotism to resist Italian priestcraft.

The changes in the internal constitution of Germany *Limitations* due to the long anarchy of Henry IV's reign are seen *of imperial* when the extent of the royal prerogative as it had *prerogative.* stood at the accession of Conrad II, the first Franconian Emperor, is compared with its state at Henry V's death. All fiefs are now hereditary, and when vacant can be granted afresh only by consent of the States; the jurisdiction of the crown is less wide; the idea is beginning to make progress that the most essential part of the Empire is not its supreme head but the totality of princes and barons. The greatest triumph of these feudal magnates is seen in the establishment of the elective principle, which when confirmed by the three free elections of Lothar II, Conrad III, and Frederick I, passes into an undoubted law. The Prince-Electors are mentioned in A.D. 1156 as a distinct and important body.[n] The bishops, too, whom the policy of Otto the Great and Henry II had raised, are now not less dangerous than the dukes, whose power it was hoped they would balance; possibly more dangerous, since protected by their sacred character and their allegiance to the Pope, while able at the same time to command the arms of their countless vassals. Nor were the two succeeding Emperors the men to retrieve those disasters. The Saxon Lothar the Second is the willing minion of the Pope; performs at his coronation a menial service unknown before, and takes a more stringent oath to defend the Holy See, that he may purchase its support against the Swabian party in his own dominions. Conrad the Third, the first Emperor of the great house of Hohenstaufen,[o] represents tendencies more anti-papal; but domestic troubles and an unfortunate crusade prevented him from effecting anything in Italy. He never even entered Rome to receive the crown.

Lothar II,
1125–1138.

Conrad III,
1138–1152.

[n] 'Gradum statim post Principes Electores.' — Frederick I's Privilege of Austria, in Pertz, *M. G. H., Legg.* ii. p. 101. As to the Electors, see chap. XIV, *post.*

[o] As to the castle of Hohenstaufen see Note XII at end.

CHAPTER XI

THE EMPERORS IN ITALY: FREDERICK BARBAROSSA

THE reign of Frederick the First, whom the Italians surnamed Barbarossa, is the most brilliant in the annals of the Empire. Its territory had been wider under Charles, its strength perhaps greater under Henry the Third, but it never appeared in such pervading vivid activity, never shone with such lustre of chivalry, as under the prince whom his countrymen have taken to be one of their national heroes, and who is still, as the half-mythic type of Teutonic character, honoured by picture and statue, in song and in legend, through the breadth of the German lands. The reverential fondness of his annalists and the whole tenour of his life go far to justify this admiration, and dispose us to believe that nobler motives were joined with personal ambition in urging him to assert so haughtily and carry out so harshly those imperial rights in which he had unbounded confidence. Under his guidance the Transalpine power made its greatest effort to subdue the two antagonists which then threatened and were fated in the end to destroy it — the Papacy and the spirit of municipal independence in Italy.

CHAP. XI.
Frederick I
(of Hohenstaufen),
1152–1189.

Even before Gregory VII's time it might have been predicted that two such potentates as the Emperor and the Pope, closely bound together, yet each with pretensions wide and undefined, must ere long come into

His relations to the Popedom.

collision. The boldness of that great pontiff in enforcing, the unflinching firmness of his successors in maintaining, the supremacy of clerical authority, inspired their supporters with a zeal and courage which more than compensated the advantages of the Emperor in defending rights he had long enjoyed. On both sides the hatred was soon very bitter. But even had men's passions permitted a reconciliation, it would have been found difficult to bring into harmony adverse principles, each theoretically irresistible, yet mutually destructive. As the spiritual power, in itself purer, since exercised over the soul and directed to the highest of all ends, eternal felicity, was entitled to the obedience of all, laymen as well as clergy; so the spiritual person, to whom, according to the view then universally accepted, there had been imparted by ordination a mysterious sanctity, could not without sin be subject to the lay magistrate, be installed by him in office, be judged in his court, and render to him any compulsory service. Yet it was no less true that civil government was indispensable to the peace and advancement of society; and while it continued to subsist, another jurisdiction could not be suffered to paralyze its workings, nor one-half of the people be altogether removed from its control. Thus the Emperor and the Pope were forced into hostility as champions of opposite systems, however fully each might admit the strength of his adversary's position, however bitterly he might bewail the violence of his own partisans. There had also arisen other causes of quarrel, less respectable but not less dangerous. The pontiff demanded and the monarch refused the lands which the Countess Matilda of Tuscany had bequeathed to the Holy See; Frederick claiming them as feudal suzerain, the Pope eager by their means to carry out those schemes

of temporal dominion which Constantine's donation CHAP. XI.
sanctioned, and Lothar's apparent renunciation of the
sovereignty of Rome had done much to encourage.
As feudal superior of the Norman kings of Naples and
Sicily, as protector of the towns and barons of North
Italy who feared the German yoke, the successor of Peter
wore already the air of an independent potentate.

No man was less likely than Frederick to submit to *Contest with*
these encroachments. He was a sort of imperialist Hilde- *Hadrian IV*
brand, strenuously proclaiming the immediate dependence
of his office on God's gift, and holding it every whit as
sacred as his rival's. On his first journey to Rome, he
refused to hold the Pope's stirrup,[a] as Lothar had done,
till Pope Hadrian the Fourth's threat that he would with-
hold the crown enforced compliance.[b] Complaints arising
not long after on some other ground, the Pope exhorted
Frederick by letter to shew himself worthy of the kindness of his mother the Roman Church, who had given him
the imperial crown, and would confer on him, if dutiful,
benefits still greater. This word benefits — *beneficia* —
understood in its usual legal sense of 'fief,' and taken in
connection with the picture set up at Rome to commemorate Lothar's homage, provoked angry shouts from the
nobles assembled in Diet at Besançon in Burgundy ; and
when the legate (afterwards Pope Alexander III) answered,

[a] A great deal of importance seems to have been attached to this symbolic
act of courtesy. See Art. I of the *Sachsenspiegel.* ' Deme pavese is ok gesat
to ridene to bescedener tiet up eneme blanken perde, unde de keiser sal ime
den stegerip halden dur de sadel nicht ne winde.'

[b] Hadrian IV (Nicholas Breakspear), the only Englishman who ever became Pope, born in poverty near St. Albans, had been a monk in the convent
to which he came begging alms, rose to be abbot, went to Rome on the
business of his house, and was made Cardinal by Eugenius III. He it was
who bestowed Ireland on the English king Henry II, all islands being within
the jurisdiction of the Holy See.

CHAP. XI.

'From whom, then, if not from our Lord the Pope, does your king hold the Empire?' his life was scarcely safe from their fury.   On this occasion Frederick's vigour and the remonstrances of the Transalpine prelates obliged Hadrian to explain away the obnoxious word, and remove the picture.   Soon after the quarrel was renewed by other causes, and came to centre itself round the Pope's demand that Rome should be left entirely to his government. Frederick, in reply, appeals to the civil law, and closes with the words, 'Since by the ordination of God I both am called and am Emperor of the Romans, in nothing but name shall I appear to be ruler if the control of the Roman city be wrested from my hands.'   That such a claim should need assertion marks the change since Henry III ; how much more that it could not be enforced.   Hadrian's tone rises into defiance; he mingles the threat of excommunication with references to the time when the Germans did not yet possess the Empire.   'What were the Franks till Pope Zacharias welcomed Pipin?   What is the Teutonic king now till consecrated at Rome by holy hands?   The chair of Peter has given and can withdraw its gifts.'

With Pope Alexander III.

The disputed papal election that followed Hadrian's death produced a second and more momentous conflict. Frederick, as head of Christendom, proposed to summon the bishops of Europe to a general council, over which he should preside, like Justinian or Heraclius.   Quoting the favourite text of the two swords, 'On earth,' he continues, 'God has placed no more than two powers : above there is but one God, so here one Pope and one Emperor. Divine Providence has specially appointed the Roman Empire as a remedy against continued schism.' [c]   The plan

[c] Letter to the German bishops in Rahewin; Bk. iv. ch. 5-6 (Pertz, *M. G. H.*, *Script.* xx. 476).

failed; and Frederick adopted the candidate whom his own faction had chosen, while the rival claimant, Alexander III, appealed, with a confidence which the issue justified, to the support of sound churchmen throughout Europe. The keen and long doubtful strife of twenty years that followed, while apparently a dispute between rival Popes, was in substance an effort by the secular monarch to recover his command of the priesthood, not less truly so than that contemporaneous conflict of the English Henry II and St. Thomas of Canterbury, with which it was frequently involved. Unsupported, not all Alexander's genius and resolution could have saved him : with the aid of the Lombard cities, whose league he had counselled and hallowed, and of the fevers of Rome, by which the conquering German host was suddenly annihilated, he won a triumph the more signal, that it was over a prince so wise and so pious as Frederick. At Venice, which, inaccessible by her position, maintained a sedulous neutrality, claiming to be independent of the Empire, yet seldom led into war by sympathy with the Popes, the two powers whose strife had roused all Europe were induced to meet by the mediation of the doge Sebastian Ziani. Three slabs of red marble in the porch of St. Mark's point out the spot where Frederick knelt in sudden awe, and the Pope with tears of joy raised him, and gave the kiss of peace. A later legend, to which poetry and painting have given an undeserved currency,[d] tells how the pontiff set his foot on the neck of the prostrate king, with the words, 'The young lion and the dragon shalt thou trample under feet.'[e] It needed not this exaggeration to enhance the significance of that scene, even more full of meaning for the future than it

[d] A picture in the great hall of the ducal palace (the Sala del Maggior Consiglio) represents the scene. See the description in Rogers's *Italy*.

[e] Psalm xci. 13.

was solemn and affecting to the Venetian crowd that thronged the church and the piazza. For it was the renunciation by the mightiest prince of his time of the project to which his life had been devoted: it was the abandonment by the secular power of a contest in which it had twice been vanquished, and which it could not renew under more favourable conditions.

Authority maintained so long against the successor of Peter would be far from indulgent to rebellious subjects. For it was in this light that the Lombard cities appeared to a monarch bent on reviving all the rights his predecessors had enjoyed: nay, all that the law of ancient Rome *Revival of the* gave her absolute ruler. It would be wrong to speak of a *study of the* rediscovery of the civil law. That system had never *civil law.* perished from Gaul and Italy, had been the groundwork of some codes or bodies of custom, and the substance, modified only by the changes in society, of many others. The Church excepted, no agent did so much to keep alive the memory of Roman institutions. The twelfth century now beheld the study cultivated with a surprising increase of knowledge and ardour, expended chiefly upon the extracts from the classical jurists contained in the Digest of the Emperor Justinian. First in Italy and the schools of the South, then in Paris and Oxford, they were expounded, commented on, extolled as the perfection of human wisdom, the sole, true, and eternal law. Vast as has been the labour and thought expended from that time to this in the elucidation of the civil law, it is hardly too much to say that in acuteness, in subtlety, in all the branches of legal science and art which can subsist without help from historical knowledge and the methods of historical criticism, these so-called Glossatores have been seldom equalled and never surpassed by their successors. The teachers of the canon law, who had not as yet become

the rivals of the civilian, and were accustomed to recur
to his books where their own were silent, spread through
Europe the fame and influence of the Roman jurisprudence; while its own professors were led both by their
feeling and their interest to give to all its maxims the
greatest weight and the fullest application. Men just
emerging from barbarism, with minds unaccustomed to
create and blindly submissive to authority, viewed written
texts with an awe to us incomprehensible. All that the
most submissive jurists of Rome had ever ascribed to
their monarchs was directly transferred to the Caesarean
majesty who inherited their name. He was 'Lord of
the world, absolute master of the lives and property of
all his subjects, that is, of all men; the sole fountain
of legislation, the embodiment of right and justice. These
doctrines, which the great Bolognese jurists, Bulgarus,
Martinus, Hugolinus, and others who surrounded Frederick, taught and applied, as matter of course, to a Teutonic,
a feudal king, were by the rest of the world not denied,
were accepted in fervent faith by his German and Italian
partisans. 'To the Emperor belongs the protection of the
whole world,' says bishop Otto of Freysing. 'The Emperor is a living law upon earth.'[f] To Frederick, at the
diet of Roncaglia, the archbishop of Milan speaks for the
assembled magnates of Lombardy: 'Do and ordain whatsoever thou wilt, thy will is law; as it is written, " Quicquid
principi placuit legis habet vigorem, cum populus ei et in
eum omne suum imperium et potestatem concesserit." '[g]
The Hohenstaufen himself was not slow to accept these
magnificent ascriptions of dignity, and though modestly
professing his wish to govern according to law rather than
override the law, was doubtless roused by them to a more

[f] 'Animata lex in terris,' document of 1230, in Pertz, *Legg*. ii. p. 277.
[g] Rahewin, iv. c. 4 (Pertz, *M. G. H., Script.* xx. 446).

*Frederick
in Italy.*

confident assertion of a prerogative so hallowed by age and by what seemed a divine ordinance.

That assertion was most loudly called for in Italy. The Emperors might appear to consider it a conquered country without privileges to be respected, for they did not summon its princes to the German diets, and over-awed its own assemblies at Pavia or Roncaglia by the Transalpine host that followed them. Its crown, too, was theirs whenever they crossed the Alps to claim it, while the elections on the banks of the Rhine might be adorned but could not be influenced by the presence of barons from the southern kingdom.[h] In practice, however, the imperial power stood lower in Italy than in Germany, for it had been from the first intermittent, depending on the personal vigour and present armed support of each in-vader. The theoretic sovereignty of the Emperor-king was nowise disputed: in the cities toll and tax were of right his: he could issue edicts at the Diet, and require the tenants in chief to appear with their vassals. But the revival of a control scarcely exercised since Henry IV's time was felt as an intolerable hardship by the great Lombard cities, proud of riches and population equal to that of the duchies of Germany or the kingdoms of the North, and accustomed for more than a century to a turbu-lent independence. For republican institutions and popu-lar freedom Frederick had little sympathy. At Rome the people, stirred by the fervour of Arnold of Brescia, had renewed, but with larger ideas, the attempt of Crescentius.[i] The city had thrown off the yoke of its bishop, and a com-monwealth under consuls and senate professed to emulate

[h] Frederick's election (at Frankfort) was made 'non sine quibusdam Italiae baronibus.'—Otto Fris. II. c. i (ibid. p. 391). But this was the exception.

[i] See as to Arnold's reforms *post*, chapter XVI.

the spirit while it renewed the forms of the primitive
republic. Its leaders had written to Conrad III,[k] asking
him to help them to restore the Empire to its position
under Constantine and Justinian; but the German, warned
by St. Bernard, had preferred the friendship of the Pope.
Filled with a vain conceit of their own importance, they
repeated their offers to Frederick when he sought the
crown from Hadrian the Fourth. A deputation, after
dwelling in highflown language on the dignity of the
Roman people, and their kindness in bestowing the sceptre
on him, a Swabian and a stranger, proceeded to demand a
largess ere he should enter the city. Frederick's anger
did not hear them to the end: 'Is this your Roman wisdom? Who are ye that usurp the name of Roman dignities? Your honours and your authority are yours no
longer; with us are consuls, senate, soldiers. It was not
you who chose us to be rulers, but Charles and Otto that
rescued you from the Greek and the Lombard, and conquered by their own might the imperial crown. That
Frankish might is still the same: wrench, if you can, the
club from Hercules. It is not for the people to give laws
to the prince, but to obey his command.'[1] This was
Frederick's version of the 'Translation of the Empire.'[m]

[k] 'Excellentissimo atque praeclaro urbis et orbis totius domino, Conrado,
Dei gratia Romano regi semper Augusto, S. P. Q. R. salutem et Romani
imperii felicem et inclitam gubernationem.' The letter winds up with the
following lines in which both the teachings of Arnold and the influence of the
Roman lawyers are recognizable. Cf. Otto Fris. I. c. 28 (ibid. pp. 366–367):

> 'Rex valeat, quidquid cupit obtineat, super hostes
> Imperium teneat, Romae sedeat, regat orbem
> Princeps terrarum, ceu fecit Iustinianus.
> Caesaris accipiat Caesar, quae sunt sua Praesul,
> Ut Christus iussit, Petro solvente tributum!'

[1] Otto Fris. II. c. 21 (ibid. p. 405).

[m] Later in his reign, Frederick condescended to negotiate with these
Roman magistrates against a hostile Pope, and entered into a sort of treaty
by which they were declared exempt from all jurisdiction but his own.

He who had been so stern to his own capital was not likely to deal more gently with the rebels of Milan and Tortona. In the contest by which Frederick is chiefly known to modern Italy, he is commonly painted as the foreign tyrant, the forerunner of the Austrian oppressor,[n] crushing under the hoofs of his cavalry the home of freedom and industry. Such a view is unjust to a great man and his cause. To the despot liberty is always licence; yet Frederick was the enforcer of admitted claims; the aggressions of Milan threatened her neighbours; the refusal, where no actual oppression was alleged, to admit his officers and allow his regalian rights, seemed a wanton breach of oaths and engagements, treason against God no less than himself.[o] Nevertheless our sympathy must go with the cities, in whose victory we recognize the triumph of freedom and civilization. Their resistance was at first probably a mere aversion to unused control, and to the enforcement of imposts less offensive in former days than now, and by long dereliction apparently obsolete.[p] Republican principles were not avowed, nor were sentiments of Italian nationality appealed to. But the progress of the conflict developed new motives and feelings, and gave the cities clearer notions of what they fought for. As the Emperor's antagonist, the Pope was their natural ally: he blessed their arms, and called on the barons of Romagna

[n] See the first note to Shelley's *Hellas.* Sismondi's history is largely answerable for this conception of Barbarossa's position.

[o] They say rebelliously, says Frederick, 'Nolumus hunc regnare super nos . . . at nos maluimus honestam mortem quam ut,' &c.— Letter in Pertz, *M. G. H., Legg.* ii. p. 116.

[p] 'De tributo Caesaris nemo cogitabat;
    Omnes erant Caesares, nemo censum dabat;
    Civitas Ambrosii, velut Troia, stabat,
    Deos parum, homines minus formidabat.'
Poems relating to the Emperor Frederick of Hohenstaufen, published by Grimm.

and Tuscany for aid; he made 'The Church' ere long
their watchword, and helped them to conclude that league
of mutual support by means whereof the party of the
Italian Guelfs was formed. Another cry, too, began to
be heard, hardly less inspiriting than the last, a cry that
had been silent for thirteen centuries, the cry of freedom
and municipal self-government—freedom little understood
and terribly abused, self-government which the cities who
claimed it for themselves refused to their subject allies,
yet both of them, through their power of stimulating effort
and quickening sympathy, as much nobler than the harsh
and repressive system of a feudal monarchy as the citizen
of republican Athens had risen above the slavish Asiatic
or the brutal Macedonian. Nor was the fact that Italians
were resisting a Transalpine invader without its effect.
There was as yet no distinct national feeling, for half
Lombardy, towns as well as rural nobles, fought under
Frederick; but events made the cause of liberty always
more clearly the cause of patriotism, and increased that
fear and hate of the Tedescan for which Italy has had
such bitter justification.

The Emperor was for a time successful: Tortona was *Temporary*
taken, Milan razed to the ground, and her name apparently *success of*
extinguished. Greater obstacles had been overcome, and *Frederick.*
a fuller authority was for the moment exercised than in
the days of Otto the Great or Henry the Third. The
glories of the first Frankish conqueror were triumphantly
recalled, and Frederick was compared by his admirers to
the hero whose canonization he had procured, and whom
he strove in all things to imitate.[q] 'He was esteemed,'
says one, 'second only to Charles in piety and justice.'
'We ordain this,' says a decree: 'Ut ad Caroli imitationem

[q] Charles the Great was canonized by Frederick's anti-pope in A.D. 1164
and confirmed afterwards by a Pope of undoubted title.

ius ecclesiarum statum reipublicae incolumem et legum integritatem per totum imperium nostrum servaremus.'[r] But the hold the name of Charles had on the minds of the people, and the way in which he had become, so to speak, an eponym of Empire, has better witnesses than grave documents. A rhyming poet sings :[s]—

'Quanta sit potentia vel laus Friderici
Cum sit patens omnibus, non est opus dici;
Qui rebelles lancea fodiens ultrici
Repraesentat Karolum dextera victrici.'

The Diet at Roncaglia was a chorus of gratulations over the re-establishment of order by the destruction of the dens of unruly burghers.

Victory of the Lombard League.

This fair sky was soon clouded. From her quenchless ashes uprose Milan; Cremona, forswearing old jealousies, helped to rebuild what she had destroyed, and the confederates, committed to what seemed an all but hopeless strife, clung faithfully together till on the field of Legnano the Empire's banner went down before the carroccio[t] of the free city. Times were changed since Aistulf and Desiderius had trembled at the distant tramp of the Frankish hosts. A new nation was arising, slowly reared through suffering into strength, now at last by heroic deeds conscious of itself. The power of Charles had over-leaped boundaries of nature and language that were too strong for his successor, and that grew henceforth ever firmer, till they made the Empire itself a delusive name. Frederick, though harsh in war, and now baulked of his most cherished hopes, could accept a state of things he had found it beyond his power to change: he signed

---

[r] *Acta Concil. Harzhem*, iii. p. 399.

[s] Poems relating to Frederick I, *ut supra*.

[t] The carroccio was a wagon with a flagstaff planted on it, which served the Lombards for a rallying-point in battle.

cheerfully and kept dutifully the peace of Constance,
which left him little but a titular supremacy over the
Lombard towns.

At home no Emperor since Henry III had been so *Frederick as*
much respected and so generally prosperous.   He had *German*
vast hereditary possessions, including, we are told, no less *king.*
than four hundred castles.   Uniting in his person the
Saxon and Swabian families, he healed on the northern
side of the Alps the long feud of Welf and Waiblingen :
his prelates were faithful to him, even against Rome : no
turbulent rebel disturbed the public peace.   Germany was
proud of a hero who maintained her dignity so well abroad,
and he crowned a glorious life with a happy death, leading the van of Christian chivalry against the Musulman.[u]
Frederick, the greatest of the Crusaders, as St. Louis is
the best, is among the noblest types of mediaeval character
in many of its shadows, in all its lights.

Legal in form, though in practice sometimes admitting
the exercise of an almost absolute authority, the government of Germany was, like that of other feudal kingdoms,
restrained chiefly by the difficulty of coercing refractory
vassals.   All depended on the monarch's character, and
one so vigorous and popular as Frederick could generally
lead the majority with him and overawe the rest.   A false
impression of the real strength of his prerogative might
be formed from the readiness with which he was obeyed,
for this was largely due to the tact which was happily
united with his firmness.   He repaired the finances of the
kingdom, controlled the dukes, introduced a more splendid
ceremonial, endeavoured to exalt the central power by
multiplying the nobles of the second rank, afterwards the
'college of princes,' and by trying to substitute the civil

[u] He was drowned in the river Kalykadnus in Cilicia — some say while
crossing it, others while bathing.

law and Lombard feudal code for the old Teutonic customs, different in every province. If not successful in this project, he fared better with another. Since Henry the Fowler's day towns had been growing up through Southern and Western Germany, especially where rivers offered facilities for trade. Cologne, Treves, Mainz, Worms, Speyer, Nürnberg, Ulm, Regensburg, Augsburg, were already considerable cities, not afraid to beard their lord or their bishop, and promising before long to counterbalance the power of the territorial oligarchy. Policy or instinct led Frederick to attach them to the throne, enfranchising many, granting, with municipal institutions, an independent jurisdiction, conferring various exemptions and privileges; while receiving in turn their good-will and loyal aid, in money always, in men when need came. His immediate successors trode in his steps, and thus there arose in the state a third order, the firmest bulwark, had it been rightly used, of imperial authority; an order whose members, the Free Cities, were through many ages the centres of German intellect and freedom, the only haven from the storms of civil war, the surest hope of future peace and union. In them national congresses used, in the dark days after 1815, to meet: from them aspiring spirits strove to diffuse those ideas of Germanic unity and free self-government, which they had done much to keep alive. Out of so many flourishing commonwealths, four only[x] were spared by foreign conquerors and faithless princes till the day came which made them again the members of a great and truly German state. To the

[x] Lübeck, Hamburg, Bremen, and Frankfort.

Of these Frankfort was annexed by Prussia in 1866, and her three surviving sisters have, by their entrance first into the North German confederation, and afterwards (1871) into the new German Empire, resigned a part of their independence.

primitive order of freemen, scarcely existing out of the
towns, except in Swabia and Switzerland, Frederick further commended himself by allowing them to be admitted
to knighthood, by restraining the licence of the nobles,
by imposing a public peace, by making justice in every
way more accessible and impartial.   To the southwest of
the green plain that girdles in the rock of Salzburg, the
gigantic mass of the Untersberg frowns over the road
which winds up a long defile to the glen and lake of
Berchtesgaden.   There, far up among its limestone crags,
in a spot scarcely accessible to human foot, the peasants
of the valley point out to the traveller the black mouth of
a cavern, and tell him that within the red-bearded Emperor
lies amid his knights in an enchanted sleep,[y] waiting the
hour when the ravens shall cease to hover round the peak,
and the pear-tree blossom in the valley, to descend with
his Crusaders and bring back to Germany the golden age
of peace and strength and unity.   Often in the evil days
that followed the fall of Frederick's house, often when
tyranny seemed unendurable and anarchy endless, men
thought on that cavern, and sighed for the day when the
long sleep of the just Emperor should be broken, and his
shield be hung aloft again as of old in the camp's midst, a
sign of help to the poor and the oppressed.

[y] The legend attaches itself also to a cave in the high and steep hill of the
Kyffhäuser in Thuringia (see Rückert's ballad, which begins ' Der alte Barbarossa, der Kaiser Friederich'). It is one which appears under various
forms in many countries. In its earlier form it seems to have related to
Frederick II, whose return to Germany was seriously hoped for as late as A.D.
1348 — a Swiss annalist writing then says that many people of different races
declared Frederick II would appear to reform the church whose corruptions
were generally deplored. In A.D. 1519 we find it told of Frederick I.

The Salzburg pear-tree could be seen till 1871

CHAPTER XII

IMPERIAL TITLES AND PRETENSIONS

THE era of the Hohenstaufen is perhaps the fittest point at which to turn aside from the narrative history of the Empire to speak shortly of the legal position which it professed to hold to the rest of Europe, as well as of certain duties and observances which throw a light upon the system it embodied. This is not indeed the era of its greatest power. That was already past. Nor is it conspicuously the era when its ideal dignity stood highest : for that remained scarcely impaired till three centuries had passed away. But it was under the Hohenstaufen, owing partly to the splendid abilities of the princes of that famous line, partly to the suddenly-gained ascendancy of the Roman law, that the actual power and the theoretical influence of the Empire most fully coincided. There can therefore be no better opportunity for noticing the titles and claims by which it announced itself the representative of Rome's universal dominion, and for collecting the various instances in which they were (either before or after Frederick's time) more or less admitted by the other states of Europe.

The territories over which Frederick would have declared his jurisdiction to extend may be classed under four heads : —

First, the German lands, in which, and in which alone, the Emperor was, up till the death of Frederick the Second (A.D. 1250), effective ruler.

Second, the non-German districts of the Holy Empire, where the Emperor was acknowledged as sole monarch, but in practice little regarded.

Third, certain outlying countries, owing allegiance to the Empire, but governed by kings of their own.

Fourth, the other states of Europe, whose rulers, while admitting the superior rank of the Emperor, were virtually independent of him.

Thus within the actual boundaries of the Holy Empire *Limits of the* were included only districts coming under the first and *Empire.* second of the above classes, *i.e.* Germany, Northern Italy, and the kingdom of Burgundy or Arles — that is to say, Provence, Dauphiné, the Free County of Burgundy (Franche Comté), and what is now Western Switzerland. Lorraine, Alsace, the rest of Switzerland and the Low Countries were of course parts of Germany. To the north-east, Bohemia and the Slavic principalities in Mecklenburg and Pomerania were as yet not integral parts of its body, but rather dependent outliers. Beyond the Mark of Brandenburg, from the Oder to the Vistula, dwelt pagan Lithuanians or Prussians,[a] free till the establishment among them of the Teutonic Knights, which took place with the approval of Frederick II in 1228–40.

Hungary had owed a doubtful allegiance since the days *Hungary.* of Otto I. Gregory VII had claimed it as a fief of the Holy See; Frederick wished to reduce it completely to subjection, but could not overcome the reluctance of his nobles. After Frederick II, by whom it was recovered from the Mongol hordes, no imperial claims were made for so many years that at last they became obsolete, and

---

[a] 'Pruzzi,' says the biographer of St. Adalbert, 'quorum Deus est venter et avaritia iuncta cum morte.' — Pertz, *M. G. H.*, *Scriptores*, iv. p. 593 (c. 27).

It is odd that this non-Teutonic people should have given their name to the great German kingdom of the present.

CHAP. XII.

Poland.

Denmark.

were confessed to be so by the Constitution of Augsburg, A.D. 1566.[b]

Under Duke Misico, Poland had submitted to Otto the Great, and continued, with occasional revolts, to obey the Empire, till the beginning of the Great Interregnum (as it is called) in 1254. Its duke was present at the election of Richard, A.D. 1257. Thereafter, in 1295, Duke Primislas had himself crowned king in token of emancipation (for the title of king which Otto III had granted to Boleslas I had become disused) and the country became independent, though some of its provinces were long afterwards reunited to the German state. Silesia, originally Polish, was attached to Bohemia by Charles IV, and so became part of the Empire; Posen and Galicia were seized by Prussia and Austria respectively, A.D. 1772.[c] Down to her partition in that year, the constitution of Poland remained in some points a copy of that which had existed in the German kingdom of the twelfth century.

Lewis the Pious had received the homage of the Danish king Harold, on his baptism at Mainz, A.D. 826; Otto the Great's victories over Harold Blue Tooth made the country subject, and added the Mark of Schleswig to the Empire: but the boundary soon receded to the Eyder, on whose banks might be seen the inscription, —

'Eidora Romani terminus imperii.'

[b] Conring, *De Finibus Imperii.* It is hardly necessary to observe that the connection of Hungary with the Hapsburgs is of comparatively recent origin, and of a purely dynastic nature. The position of the archdukes of Austria as kings of Hungary had nothing to do legally with the fact that many of them were also chosen Emperors, although practically their possession of the imperial crown had greatly aided them in grasping and retaining the thrones of Hungary and Bohemia.

[c] They however did not become incorporated with the Empire, being held by the houses of Hohenzollern and Hapsburg respectively as parts of their extra-imperial dominions.

King Peter[d] attended at the Diet held at Merseburg shortly after Frederick I's coronation, and received from the Emperor, who as suzerain had been required to decide a disputed question of succession to the Danish throne, his own crown; he did homage, and bore the sword before the Emperor. Since the Great Interregnum Denmark has been always free.

Otto the Great was the last Emperor whose suzerainty *France.* the West Frankish kings had admitted; nor were Henry VI and Otto IV successful in their attempts to enforce it. Boniface VIII, in his quarrel with Philip the Fair, offered the French throne, which he had pronounced vacant, to Albert I; but the wary Hapsburg declined the dangerous prize.[f] The superiority, however, which the Germans continued to assert, irritated Gallic pride, and led to more than one contest. Charles V of France gave the Emperor Charles IV black horses on which to ride into Paris, when the latter paid him a visit there, himself riding a white horse, because the custom of the Emperors had been, so says the chronicler, to enter their cities on a white charger. French jurists steadily insisted that their king held from God alone. Blondel denies the Empire any claim to the Roman name; and in A.D. 1648 the French envoys at Münster refused for some time to admit that precedence of the imperial envoys which no other European state disputed. Till recent times the title of the Archbishop of Treves, 'Archicancellarius per Galliam atque regnum Arelatense,' preserved the memory of an obsolete supremacy

[d] Letter of Frederick I to Otto of Freysing, prefixed to the latter's History, *M. G. H., Scriptores,* xx. p. 347. This king is also called Svend.

[f] In A.D. 1338 the Emperor Lewis IV, then allied to the English Edward III, adjudged to the latter Normandy, Aquitaine, and Anjou, and declared him entitled to the throne of France.

which the constant aggressions of France might seem to have reversed.

No reliance can be placed on the author who tells us that Sweden was granted by Frederick I to Waldemar the Dane; [g] the fact is improbable, and we do not hear that such pretensions were ever put forth before or after. Norway, too, seems to have been left untouched — the Emperors had no fleets — and Iceland, which had remained undiscovered [h] till long after the days of Charles the Great, was down to the year 1262 the only absolutely free Republic in the world. It is a curious illustration of mediaeval habits of thought that the envoys of the king of Norway, when seeking to persuade the Icelandic people to accept his supremacy, argued that monarchy was the form of government divinely ordained, and existed in every part of the European continent.

Nor does it appear that authority was ever exercised by any Emperor, after the first Carolingians, in Spain. Nevertheless the choice of Alfonso X by some of the German electors, in A.D. 1258, seems to imply that the Spanish kings were members of the Empire. And when, A.D. 1053, Ferdinand the Great of Castile had, in the pride of his victories over the Moors, assumed the title of 'Hispaniae Imperator,' the remonstrance of Henry III declared the rights of Rome over the Western provinces indelible, and the Spaniard, though protesting his independence, was forced to resign the usurped dignity.[i]

---

[g] Albertus Stadensis, *M. G. H., Script.* xi. p. 345, s. a. 1163.

[h] The Scots of Ireland, however, would seem to have occasionally visited it; and some few Irish hermits were found there by the first Norwegian colonists who landed in A.D. 874.

[i] There is an allusion to this in the poems of the Cid. Arthur Duck, *De Usu et Authoritate Iuris Civilis*, quotes the view of some among the older jurists, that Spain having been, so far as the Romans were concerned, a *res*

No act of sovereignty is recorded to have been done by any of the Emperors in England, though as heirs of Rome they might be thought to have better rights over it than over Poland or Denmark.[j] There was, however, a vague notion that the English, like other kingdoms, must depend on the Empire: a notion which appears in Conrad III's letter to John of Constantinople;[k] and which was countenanced by the submissive tone in which Frederick I was addressed by the Plantagenet Henry II.[l] English independence was still more compromised in the next reign, when Richard I, according to Hoveden, 'by the advice of his mother Eleanor stripped himself of the kingdom of England, and delivered it over to the Emperor as Lord of the World.' But as Richard was at the same time invested with the kingdom of Arles by Henry VI, his homage may have been for that fief only; and it was probably in that capacity that he voted (by his eight deputies), as a prince of the Empire, at the election of Frederick II. The case finds a parallel in the claims of England over the Scottish king, doubtful, to say the least, as regards the domestic realm of the latter, certain as

derelicta, recovered by the Spaniards themselves from the Moors, and thus acquired by *occupatio*, ought not to be subject to the Emperors.

[j] One of the greatest of English kings appears performing an act of courtesy to the Emperor which was probably construed into an acknowledgement of his own inferior position. Describing the Roman coronation of the Emperor Conrad II, Wippo (c. 16), *M. G. H., Script.* xi. p. 265, tells us, 'His ita peractis in duorum regum praesentia Ruodolfi regis Burgundiae et Chnutonis regis Anglorum divino officio finito imperator duorum regum medius ad cubiculum suum honorifice ductus est.'

[k] Letter in Otto Fris. i. c. 23 (*M. G. H., Script.* xx. p. 363): 'Francia et Hispania, Anglia Dania ceteraque regna . . . cum debita reverentia et obsequio nos frequentant.'

[l] Letter in Rahewin, iii. c. 7 (*M. G. H., Script.* xx. p. 419), says, 'Regnum nostrum vobis exponimus. . . . Vobis imperandi cedat auctoritas, nobis non deerit voluntas obsequendi.'

regards Cumbria, which he had long held from the Southern crown.[m]   But Germany had no Edward I.   Henry VI is said at his death to have released Richard from his submission[n] (this too may be compared with Richard's release to the Scottish king William the Lion), and Edward II declared the kingdom of England to be wholly free from all subjection to the Empire.[o]   Yet the notion survived: the Emperor Lewis the Bavarian, when he named Edward III his vicar in the great war between France and England, demanded, though in vain, that the English monarch should kiss his feet,[p] and the election of Edward as Emperor after the death of Lewis carried with it an implication that England was still in a certain sense a part of the Empire.   The Emperor Sigismund,[q] visiting Henry V at London, at the time of the meeting of the council of Constance, was met by the Duke of Gloucester, who, riding into the water to the ship where the Emperor sat, required

[m] 'Consilio Alianor matris suae, deposuit se de regno Angliae et tradidit illud imperatori (Henrico VI[to]) sicut universorum domino, et investivit eum inde per pilleum suum, sed imperator, sicut prolocutum est, statim reddidit ei in conspectu magnatum Alemanniae et Angliae, regnum Angliae praedictum tenendum de ipso pro quinque millibus librarum sterlingorum singulis annis de tributo solvendis, et investivit eum inde imperator per duplicem crucem de auro.   Sed idem imperator in morte sua de omnibus his et aliis conventionibus quietum clamavit ipsum Ricardum regem Angliae et heredes suos.' — Hoveden, *Chronicon*, ad ann. 1193, ed. Stubbs, Rolls Series, vol. iii. pp. 202–203. The alleged instances of homage by the Scots to the Saxon and early Norman kings are almost all complicated in some such way.   The Scottish kings had once held also the earldom of Huntingdon from the English crown, and some have supposed (but on no sufficient grounds) that homage was also done by them for Lothian.

[n] Hoveden, *ut supra.*

[o] 'Regnum Angliae ab omni subiectione imperiali esse liberrimum.' — Selden, *Titles of Honour*, part i. chap. ii.

[p] Edward refused upon the ground that he was '*rex inunctus.*'

[q] Sigismund had shortly before given great offence in France by dubbing knights.

him, at the sword's point, to declare that he did not come purposing to infringe on the king's authority in the realm of England.[r] One curious pretension of the imperial crown called forth many protests. It was declared by civilians and canonists that no notary public could have any standing, or attach any legality to the documents he drew or attested, unless he had received his diploma either from the Emperor or from the Pope. A strenuous denial of a doctrine so injurious was issued by the parliament of Scotland under James III.[s]

No Roman soldier ever trod the soil of Ireland, nor *Ireland.* did any mediaeval emperor ever exercise any authority there. But even in Ireland the influence of the imperial idea was felt. In that isle, before the Anglo-Norman invasion of the twelfth century, a chieftain or magnate whose wealth consisted in cattle, was accustomed to give them out among his dependants to be pastured; and thus the expression 'to receive stock' from any one came to denote the holding of a subordinate or vassal position, similar to that of the feudal tenant who receives land as a *beneficium* from his lord. Now the Brehon law, after shewing how the inferior princes may receive stock from the King of Erin — the Ard Righ or supreme king of the whole island (who, however, even when he existed, had little more than a titular authority) — goes on to say, 'When the King of Erin is without opposition (*i.e.* when he holds Dublin, Waterford, and Limerick, the three chief ports which

---

[r] Sigismund answered, 'Nihil se contra superioritatem regis praetexere.' Some have doubted the story.

[s] Selden, *Titles of Honour*, part i. chap. ii: 'Our Souverain Lord hes full jurisdiction and Free Empire within his Realme, that his Hienesse may make Notares and Tabelliones quahis instruments sall have full faith in all contracts and causes within the Realme.' Nevertheless, notaries in Scotland, as elsewhere, continued for a long time to style themselves 'Ego M. auctoritate imperiali (*or* papali) notarius.'

were often in the hands of Norsemen or Danes), he receives stock from the King of the Romans,' *i.e.* the Emperor. And one commentator (probably a cleric) adds that sometimes it is the Successor of Patrick (*i.e.* the Archbishop of Armagh) who gives stock to the King of Erin, thereby setting the Primate of Ireland in the position above the Emperor which the theory of high Papalists in continental Europe assigned to the Pope.[t]

Naples.   The kingdom of Naples and Sicily, although of course claimed as a part of the Empire, was under the Norman dynasty (A.D. 1060–1189) not merely independent, but the most dangerous enemy of the German power in Italy. Henry VI, the son and successor of Barbarossa, obtained possession of it by marrying Constance the heiress of the Norman kings. But both he and Frederick II treated it as a separate patrimonial state, instead of incorporating it with their more northerly dominions. After the death of Conradin, the last of the Hohenstaufen, it passed away to an Angevin, then to an Aragonese dynasty, continuing under both to maintain itself independent of the Empire, nor ever again, except under the Emperor Charles V, held by the occupant of the Germanic throne.

Venice.   One spot in Italy there was whose singular felicity of situation enabled her through long centuries of obscurity and weakness, slowly ripening into strength, to maintain her freedom unstained by any submission to the Frankish and German Emperors. Venice glories in deducing her origin from the fugitives who escaped from Aquileia when that city was destroyed by Attila: it is at least probable that her population received no sensible admixture of

[t] See *Senchus Mor.* ii. 225. My attention was called to this by Sir H. S. Maine: cf. his *Lectures on the Early History of Institutions*, p. 165. Ireland was the latest of Western Catholic countries to recognize the supremacy of the Chair of Peter ; she did not do so till after the Anglo-Norman conquest.

Teutonic settlers, and they continued during the ages of CHAP. XII.
Lombard and Frankish rule in Italy to regard the East
Roman sovereign as the representative of their ancient
masters.   Charles the Great acknowledged by treaty their
dependence on the East; and in the tenth century, when
summoned to submit to Otto II, they had said, 'We wish
to be the servants of the Emperors of the Romans' (the
Constantinopolitan).   Their fleet, joined with a force of
Frankish Crusaders, overthrew this very throne in A.D. 1204,
but the pretext of allegiance to the East had served its turn,
and had aided them in defying or evading the demands
of obedience made by the Teutonic princes.   Alone of all
the Italian republics, Venice never, down to her extinction
by France and Austria in A.D. 1797, recognized within
her bounds any secular Western authority save her own.

The kings of Cyprus and Armenia sent to Henry VI to *The East.*
confess themselves his vassals and ask his help.   Over
remote Eastern lands, where Frankish foot had never trode,
Frederick Barbarossa asserted the indestructible rights of
Rome, mistress of the world.   A letter to Saladin, amusing
from its absolute identification of his own Empire with
that which had sent Crassus to perish in Parthia, and had
blushed to see Mark Antony 'consulem nostrum' at the
feet of Cleopatra, is preserved by Hoveden : it bids the
Soldan withdraw at once from the dominions of Rome,
else will she, with her new Teutonic defenders, of whom a
pompous list follows, drive him from them with all her
ancient might.[u]

[u] It is not necessary to prove this letter to have been the composition of
Frederick or his ministers.   If it be (as it doubtless is) contemporary, it is
equally to the purpose as an evidence of the feelings and ideas of the age.
As its authenticity has been questioned, I may mention that it is to be found
not only in Hoveden, but also in the 'Itinerarium regis Ricardi,' in Ralph de
Diceto, and in the 'Chronicon Terrae Sanctae.'   See Dr. Stubbs' edition of
Hoveden, vol. ii. p. 356.

Unwilling as were the great kingdoms of Western Europe to admit the territorial supremacy of the Emperor, the proudest among them never refused, until the end of the Middle Ages, to recognize his precedence and address him in a tone of respectful deference. Very different was the attitude of the East Roman princes, who denied his claim to be an Emperor at all. The separate existence of the Eastern Church and Empire was always, as has been said above, a blemish in the title of the Teutonic sovereigns. But it was even more. It was a continuing protest against the whole system of an Empire Church of Christendom, centring in Rome, ruled by the successor of Peter and the successor of Augustus. Instead of the one Pope and one Emperor whom mediaeval theory presented as the sole earthly representatives of the invisible Head of the Church, the world saw itself distracted by the interminable feud of rivals, each of whom had much to allege on his behalf. It was easy for the Latins to call the Easterns schismatics and their Emperor an usurper, but practically it was impossible to dethrone him or reduce them to obedience — indeed the Teutonic sovereigns never made a serious claim to the provinces in which Greek was spoken — nor could the Eastern Church be treated, even in controversy, with the contempt that any Western schismatics would have incurred. But as the East Roman Empire is treated of in a separate chapter, it is sufficient here to indicate this one conspicuous exception to the general recognition of imperial supremacy.

*Dignities
and titles.*

Though Otto the Great and his successors had dropped all titles save the highest, they did not therefore endeavour to unite their several kingdoms, but continued to go through four distinct coronations at the four capitals of their Empire.[x] These are concisely given in the verses

[x] See Appendix, Note B.

of Godfrey of Viterbo, a notary of Frederick's house- CHAP. XII.
hold : [y] —

> 'Primus Aquisgrani locus est, post haec Arelati,
>   Inde Modoetiae regali sede locari
>   Post solet Italiae summa corona dari :
>   Caesar Romano cum vult diademate fungi
>   Debet apostolicis manibus reverenter inungi.'

By the crowning at Aachen, the old Frankish capital, the *The four crowns.*
monarch became 'king'; formerly 'king of the Franks,'
or 'king of the Eastern Franks'; now, since Henry II's
time, 'king of the Romans, always Augustus.' At Monza
(or, more rarely, at Milan) in later times, at Pavia in earlier
times, he became king of Italy, or of the Lombards; [z] at
Rome he received the double crown of the Roman Empire,
'double,' says Godfrey, as 'urbis et orbis' : —

> 'Hoc quicunque tenet, summus in orbe sedet;'

though others hold that, uniting the mitre to the crown,
it typifies spiritual as well as secular authority. The crown
of Burgundy or the kingdom of Arles, [a] first gained by
Conrad II, was a much less splendid matter, and carried
with it little effective power. Most Emperors never
assumed it at all, Frederick I not till late in life, when an
interval of leisure left him nothing better to do. These
four crowns [b] furnish matter of endless discussion to the

[y] Godefr. Viterb., *Pantheon, M. G. H., Script.* xxii. p. 221.

[z] It has been thought that the taking of the crown of Italy — it was pretty
regularly taken from Henry II's time, but whether by Otto II and Otto III is
less clear — was a recognition of the separate nationality of Italy. But the
fact that there had been a separate kingdom in Italy ever since Alboin's invasion made the crown seem to give some fuller, or more direct, rights to the
person who obtained it than he enjoyed simply as Emperor. Italy, though a
part of the Empire, had not been merged in Germany.

[a] See Appendix, Note A.

[b] Some, says Marquard Freher, add a fifth crown, of Germany (making
that of Aachen Frankish), supposed to belong to Regensburg.

old writers; they tell us that the Roman was golden, the German silver, the Italian iron, the metal corresponding to the dignity of each realm.[c] Others say that that of Aachen is iron, and the Italian silver, and give elaborate reasons why it should be so.[d] There seems to be no doubt that the allegory created the fact, and that all three crowns were of gold (or gilded silver), though in that of Italy there was and is inserted a piece of iron, a nail, it was believed, of the true Cross.

Meaning of the four coronations.

Why, it may well be asked, seeing that the Roman crown made the Emperor ruler of the whole habitable globe, was it thought necessary for him to add to it minor dignities which might be supposed to have been already included in this supreme one? The reason seems to be that the imperial office was conceived of as something different in kind from the regal, and as carrying with it not the immediate government of any particular kingdom, but a general suzerainty over and right of controlling all. Of this a pertinent illustration is afforded by an anecdote told of Frederick Barbarossa. Happening once to inquire of the famous jurists who surrounded him whether it was really true that he was 'lord of the world' (*dominus mundi*), one of them simply assented, another, Bulgarus, answered, 'Not as respects ownership' (*non quantum ad dominium*). In this dictum, which is evidently conform-

---

[c] 'Dy erste ist tho Aken: dar kronet men mit der Yseren Krone, so is he Konig over alle Dudesche Ryke. Dy andere tho Meylan, de is Sulvern, so is he Here der Walen. Dy drüdde is tho Rome ; dy is guldin, so is he Keyser over alle dy Werlt.' — Gloss to the *Sachsenspiegel*, quoted by Pfeffinger. Similarly Peter de Andlau.

[d] Cf. Gewoldus, *De Septemviratu imperii Romani*. One would expect some ingenious allegorizer to have discovered that the crown of Burgundy must be, and therefore is, of copper or bronze, making the series complete, like the four ages of men in Hesiod. But I have not been able to find any such.

able to the philosophical theory of the Empire, we have a pointed distinction drawn between feudal sovereignty, which supposes the prince original owner of the soil of his whole kingdom, and imperial sovereignty, which is irrespective of place and exercised not over things but over men, as God's rational creatures. But the Emperor, as has been said already, was also the East Frankish king, uniting in himself, to use the legal phrase, two wholly distinct 'persons,' and hence he might acquire more direct and practically useful rights over a portion of his dominions by being crowned king of that portion, just as a feudal monarch often came to be count of lordships whereof he was already feudal superior; or, to take a better illustration, just as a bishop may hold livings in his own diocese. That the Emperors, while continuing to be crowned at Milan and Aachen, did not in practice call themselves kings of the Lombards and of the Franks, was probably merely because these titles seemed insignificant compared to that of Roman Emperor.

In this supreme title, as has been said, all lesser honours were blent and lost, but custom or prejudice forbade the German king to assume it till actually crowned at Rome by the Pope.[e] Matters of phrase and title are never unimportant, least of all in an age not only uncritical but also superstitiously attached to forms and precedents : and this restriction had the most important consequences. The reverence for Rome as the ancient seat of power, and the

'Emperor' not assumed till the Roman coronation.

---

[e] Hence the numbers attached to the names of the Emperors are often different in German and Italian writers, the latter reckoning neither Henry the Fowler nor Conrad I. So Henry III (of Germany) calls himself 'Imperator Henricus Secundus'; and all distinguish the years of their *regnum* from those of their *imperium*. Cardinal Baronius insists on calling Henry V Henry III, not recognizing Henry IV's coronation, because it was performed by an antipope.

sense of the close relation between the temporal and the spiritual sovereign, created an association which soon became indissoluble between the office and title of Emperor, and the crowning in the City by the Pope.[f] 'Rome,' says the biographer of St. Adalbert, 'seeing that she both is and is called the head of the world and the mistress of cities, is alone able to give to kings imperial power, and since she cherishes in her bosom the body of the Prince of the Apostles, she ought of right to appoint the Prince of the whole earth.'[g] The crown was therefore too sacred to be conferred by any one but the supreme Pontiff, or in any city less august than the ancient capital. Had it become hereditary in any family, Lothar I's, for instance, or Otto's, this feeling might have worn off; as it was, each successive transfer to a new family or dynasty, to Guido, to Otto I, to Henry II, to Conrad the Salic, strengthened it. The force of custom, tradition, precedent, is immense, when checked neither by written rules nor by free discussion. What sheer assertion will do is shewn by the success of a forgery so gross as the Pseudo-Isidorian decretals, accepted at first because it occurred to no one, nor was it obviously any one's interest, to contest their genuineness, accepted afterwards, when their tendency was perceived, because they had by this time found general currency, recognized ultimately as valid because they had passed into authorized collections. No arguments are needed to discredit the alleged decree of Pope

Origin and results of this practice.

[f] For Sir H. S. Maine's conjecture that Charlemagne took the title of Roman Emperor because he wished to be something more than King of the Franks — 'the Chieftain who would no longer call himself King of the tribe must claim to be Emperor of the World' (*Ancient Law*, p. 105) — I have been unable to find any evidence.

[g] Life of St. Adalbert (written at Rome early in the eleventh century probably by a brother of the monastery of SS. Boniface and Alexius) in Pertz, *M. G. H.*, *Script.* iv. p. 590 (c. 21).

Benedict VIII,[h] which forbade the German prince to take the name or office of Emperor till approved and consecrated by the Pontiff, but a doctrine so favourable to papal pretensions was sure not to want advocacy ; Hadrian IV proclaims it in the broadest terms, and through the efforts of the clergy and the spell of reverence in the Teutonic princes, it passed into an unquestioned belief.[i] That none ventured to use the title till the Pope conferred it, made it seem to depend on his will, enabled him to exact conditions from every candidate, and gave colour to his pretended suzerainty. Since by feudal theory every honour and estate is held from some superior, and since the divine commission has been without doubt issued directly to the Pope, must not the whole earth be his fief, and he the lord paramount, to whom even the Emperor is a vassal ? This argument, which drew plausibility from the rivalry between the Emperor and other monarchs, as compared with the undisputed[j] authority of the Pope, was a favourite with the

[h] Given by Rudolphus Glaber, *M. G. H., Script.*, on p. 59 (bk. i. c. 5). It is on the face of it an impudent forgery : 'Ne quisquam audacter Romani Imperii sceptrum praepostere gestare princeps appetat neve Imperator dici aut esse valeat nisi quem Papa Romanus morum probitate aptum elegerit, eique commiserit insigne imperiale.'

[i] The *Sachsenspiegel* says, Election by the Germans gives the person chosen the right to be crowned; consecration by the bishops gives him the power and title of king; consecration by the Pope gives him the power and title of Emperor. 'Die düdeschen solen durch recht den koning kiesen. Svenne die gewiet wert von den bischopen die dar to gesat sin, so uppe den stul to Aken kumt, so hevet he koninglike walt unde koningliken namen. Svenne yn die paues wiet, so heute he des rikes gewalt unde keiserliken namen.'

So a poem of Frederick I's time (see Note XVII at end) says,

    'Mos fuit ut Romam tendant sumantque coronam
    Teutonici reges; nec habet magnum ullus eorum
    Imperii nomen, donec a praesule summo
    Sumpserit oblatum manibus diadema sacratis.'

[j] The denial of the supreme jurisdiction of Peter's chair by the Eastern

high sacerdotal party : first distinctly advanced by Hadrian IV, when he set up the picture [k] representing the homage of Lothar II, which had so irritated the followers of Barbarossa, though it had already been hinted at in Gregory VII's gift of the crown to Rudolf of Swabia, with the line —

'Petra dedit Petro, Petrus diadema Rudolfo.'[1]

Nor was it only by putting him at the Pontiff's mercy that this dependence of the imperial name on a coronation in the city injured the German sovereign.[m] With strange inconsistency it was not pretended that the Emperor's rights were any narrower before he received the rite : he could summon synods, confirm papal elections, exercise jurisdiction over the citizens : his right to receive the crown itself was not, at least till the days of Gregory VII,

churches affected very slightly the belief of Latin Christendom, just as the existence of a rival Emperor at Constantinople with at least as good a legal title as the Teutonic Caesar, was readily forgotten or ignored in Germany and Italy.

[k] Odious especially for the inscription, —

'Rex venit ante fores nullo prius urbis honore;
Post homo fit Papae, sumit quo dante coronam.'

Another version of the first line is, —

'Rex stetit ante fores iurans prius urbis honores.'

Cf. *M. G. H., Script.* xx. p. 422 (Rahewin, iii. 10).

[1] 'The Rock (*i.e.* Christ) gave the crown to Peter, and Peter (*i.e.* the Pope) to Rudolf.'

[m] Mediaeval history is full of instances of the superstitious veneration attached to the rite of coronation (made by the Church almost a sacrament), and to the special places where or even utensils and emblematic objects with which it was performed. Every one knows the importance in France of Rheims and its sacred *ampulla*, brought down from heaven by a dove. So the Scottish king must be crowned at Scone, an old seat of Pictish royalty — Robert Bruce risked a great deal to receive his crown there. So no Hungarian coronation was valid unless made with the crown of St. Stephen; the possession whereof is still accounted so valuable by the Austrian court.

Great importance seems to have been attached to the imperial globe (Reichsapfel) which the Pope delivered to the Emperor at his coronation.

seriously denied. No one thought of contesting the claim
of the German nation to the Empire, or the authority of
the German electors, strangers though they were, to give
Rome and Italy a master. The republican followers of
Arnold of Brescia might murmur, but they could not dispute the truth of the proud lines in which the poet who
sang the glories of Barbarossa[n] describes the result of the
conquest of Charles the Great : —

> 'Ex quo Romanum nostra virtute redemptum
> Hostibus expulsis, ad nos iustissimus ordo
> Transtulit imperium, Romani gloria regni
> Nos penes est. Quemcunque sibi Germania regem
> Praeficit, hunc dives summisso vertice Roma
> Suscipit, et verso Tiberim regit ordine Rhenus.'

But the real strength of the Teutonic kingdom was
wasted in the pursuit of a glittering toy : once at least
in his reign each Emperor undertook a long and dangerous expedition, and dissipated in a costly and ever to
be repeated strife the forces that might have achieved
conquest elsewhere, or made him feared and obeyed at
home.

At this epoch appears another title, of which more must
be said. To the accustomed 'Roman Empire' Frederick I
adds the epithet of 'Holy.' Of its earlier origin, under
Conrad II (the Salic), which some have supposed,[o] there
is no documentary trace.[p] So far as is known it occurs

The title 'Holy Empire.'

---

[n] Whether the poem which used to pass under the name of Gunther Ligurinus be contemporary or the work of some later scholar is for the present
purpose indifferent. The better opinion now seems to be that the poem
belongs to the age of Frederick, and that 'Ligurinus' is its title.

[o] Zedler, *Universal-Lexicon*, s. v. *Reich*.

[p] It does not occur before Frederick I's time in any of the documents
printed in Pertz's collection; and this is the date which Boeclerus also
assigns in his treatise, *De Sacro Imperio Romano*, vindicating the terms 'sacrum' and 'Romanum' against the aspersions of Blondel.

first in the summons or circular letter issued by Frederick in A.D. 1157, requiring the magnates of the Empire to give him their aid in his expedition against the recalcitrant cities of Lombardy: 'Quia urbis et orbis gubernacula tenemus iuxta diversos eventus rerum et successiones temporum sacro imperio et divae reipublicae consulere debemus,' where the second phrase is a synonym repeating the idea of the first. It occurs also afterwards in other documents of his reign, as for example in a letter to the East Roman Emperor Isaac Angelus. Used occasionally by Henry VI and Frederick II, it is more frequent under their successors, William, Richard, Rudolf, till after Charles IV's time it becomes habitual, and during the last few centuries the familiar description in current speech of the Germanic State.[s]

The adoption of the title did not mark or coincide with any constitutional or political change, for the Empire, as has already been shewn, was in its wider form essentially and substantially the creation of Charles, in its narrower form, as practically consisting of Germany and Northern Italy (of course also with a vague unenforceable claim to universal sovereignty), the creation of Otto the Great. Nor are its original meaning and the motives which led Frederick and his first successors to employ it, altogether clear. Some have regarded it as a perpetuation of the court style of Rome and Constantinople which attached sanctity to the person of the monarch: thus David Blondel, contending for the honour of France, calls it a mere epithet of the Emperor, applied by confusion to his government.[t]

[q] Pertz, *Constitutiones et Acta Publica*, vol. i. p. 224.

[r] Ibid. iv. p. 99.

[s] Readers of Goethe's *Faust* will remember the student's song:
'Das liebe heil'ge Römische Reich,
Wie hält's nur noch zusammen?'

[t] Blondellus, *Adv. Chiffletium*. Most of these theories are stated by

Others saw in it a religious meaning, referring to Daniel's prophecy, or to the fact that the Empire was contemporary with Christianity, or to Christ's birth under it.[u]   Strong churchmen derived it from the dependence of the imperial crown on the Pope.   There were not wanting those who maintained that it meant nothing more than great or splendid.   There need not, however, be any great doubt as to its true sense and purport.   The ascription of sacredness to the person, the palace, the letters, and so forth, of the sovereign, so common in the later ages of ancient Rome, had been partly retained in the German court. Liudprand calls Otto 'imperator sanctissimus.'[x]   Still this sanctity, which the Easterns above all others lavished on their princes, is something personal, is nothing more than the divinity that in all countries doth hedge a king.   Far more intimate and peculiar was the relation of the revived Roman Empire to the Church and religion.   As has been said already, it was neither more nor less than the Visible Church, seen on its secular side, the Christian society organized as a state under a form divinely appointed, and therefore the name 'Holy Roman Empire' was the needful and rightful counterpart to that of 'Holy Catholic Church.'[y]   Such had long been the belief, and so the title

Boeclerus.   Jordanes (*Chronica*) says, 'Sacri imperii quod non est dubium sancti Spiritus ordinatione, secundum qualitatem ipsam et exigentiam meritorum humanorum disponi.'

[u] Marquard Freher's notes to Peter de Andlau, book i. chap. vii.

[x] So in the song on the capture of the Emperor Lewis II by Adalgisus of Benevento, we find the words, 'Ludhuicum comprenderunt sancto pio Augusto.' (Quoted by Gregorovius, *Geschichte der Stadt Rom im Mittelalter*, iii. p. 185; Eng. trans. iii. 169.)

[y] In the older churches of Germany one sometimes finds the tomb of a cardinal with the familiar inscription, 'S. R. E. Card. Presb. (or Diac.)' (Sanctae Romanae Ecclesiae Cardinalis Presbyter), and hard by the tomb of an elector with 'S. R. I. Princ. Elect.' (Sacri Romani Imperii Princeps Elector). The correspondence of the descriptions expresses the exact corre-

might have had its origin as far back as the tenth or ninth century, might even have emanated from Charles himself. Alcuin in one of his letters uses the phrase 'imperium Christianum.' But there was a further reason for its introduction under the second Hohenstaufen, immediately after his contest with Pope Hadrian IV. Ever since Hildebrand had claimed for the priesthood exclusive sanctity and supreme jurisdiction, extreme papalists had been wont to speak of the civil power as being, compared with that of their own chief, merely secular and earthly. It may be conjectured that to meet this reproach, no less injurious than insulting, Frederick or his advisers began to use in public documents the expression 'Holy Empire'; thereby wishing to assert the divine institution and religious duties of his office. Previous Emperors had called themselves 'Catholici,' 'Christiani,' 'ecclesiae defensores';[z] now their State itself is consecrated an earthly theocracy. 'Romanum imperium . . . ad remedium tam perniciosi morbi (*sc.* schismatis) divina providit clementia,'[a] writes Frederick to the English Henry II. The theory was one which the best and strongest Emperors had most striven to carry out; it continued to be zealously upheld long after it had ceased to be practicable. In the proclamations of mediaeval kings there is a constant dwelling on their divine commission. Power in an age of violence sought to justify while it enforced its commands, to make brute force less brutal by appeals to a higher sanction. This is seen nowhere more than in the style of the German sovereigns: they delight in the phrases 'maiestas sacrosancta,'[b] 'impe-

spondence of the positions, spiritual and temporal, as conceived of in the fourteenth and fifteenth centuries.

[z] Goldast, *Constitutiones.*

[a] Pertz, *M. G. H., Legg.* ii. p. 119.

[b] 'Apostolic majesty' was the proper title of the king of Hungary. The Austrian court has recently revived it.

rator divina ordinante providentia,' 'divina pietate,' 'per misericordiam Dei'; many of which were preserved till, like those used now by other European kings, like our own 'Defender of the Faith,' they had become at last more grotesque than solemn. The freethinking Emperor Joseph II, at the end of the eighteenth century, was 'Advocate of the Christian Church,' 'Vicar of Christ,' 'Imperial head of the faithful,' 'Leader of the Christian army,' 'Protector of Palestine, of general councils, of the Catholic faith.' [c]

The title, if it added little to the power, yet certainly seems to have increased the dignity of the Empire, and by consequence the jealousy of other states, of France especially. This did not, however, go so far as to prevent its recognition by the Popes and the French kings,[d] and after the sixteenth century it would have been a breach of diplomatic courtesy to omit it. Nor have imitations been wanting: witness such phrases as 'Holy Russia,' and such titles as 'Most Christian king (France),' 'Catholic king (Spain),' 'Defender of the Faith (England).'

[c] Moser, *Römische Kayser.*

[d] Urban IV used the title in 1259; Francis I (of France) calls the Empire 'sacrosanctum.'

CHAPTER XIII

FALL OF THE HOHENSTAUFEN: RENEWED STRIFE OF PAPACY AND EMPIRE

IN the three preceding chapters the Holy Empire has been described in what is not only the most brilliant but the most momentous period of its history; the period of its rivalry with the Popedom for the chief place in Christendom. For it was mainly through their relations with the spiritual power, by their friendship and protection at first, no less than by their subsequent hostility, that the Teutonic Emperors influenced the developement of European politics. The reform of the Roman Church which went on during the reigns of Otto I and his successors down to Henry III, and which was chiefly due to the efforts of those monarchs, was the true beginning of the grand period of the Middle Ages, the first of that long series of movements, changes, and creations in the ecclesiastical system of Europe which was, so to speak, the master current of history, secular as well as religious, during the centuries which followed. The first result of Henry the Third's purification of the Papacy was seen in the attempt of Gregory the Seventh to subject all jurisdiction to that of his own chair, and in the long struggle of the Investitures, which brought out into clear light the opposing pretensions of the temporal and spiritual powers. Although destined in the end to bear far other fruit, the immediate effect of this struggle was to evoke in all classes an intense religious feeling; and, in opening up

new fields of ambition to the hierarchy, to stimulate
wonderfully their capacity for political organization.   It was
this impulse that gave birth to the Crusades, and that
enabled the Popes, stepping forth as the rightful leaders
of a religious war, to bend it to serve their own ends : it
was thus too that they struck the alliance — strange as
such an alliance seems now — with the rebellious cities of
Lombardy, and proclaimed themselves the protectors of
municipal freedom.   But the third and crowning triumph
of the Holy See was reserved for the thirteenth century.
In the foundation of the two great orders of ecclesiastical
knighthood, the all-powerful all-pervading Dominicans
and Franciscans, the religious fervour of the Middle Ages
culminated : in the overthrow of the only power which
could pretend to vie with her in antiquity, in sanctity, in
universality, the Papacy saw herself exalted to rule alone
over the kings of the earth.   Of that overthrow, following
with terrible suddenness on the days of strength and
glory which we have just been witnessing, this chapter has
now to speak.

It happened strangely enough that just while their *Henry VI,*
ruin was preparing, the house of Swabia gained over *1190–1197.*
their ecclesiastical foes what seemed likely to prove an
advantage of the first moment.   The son and successor
of Frederick Barbarossa was Henry VI, a man who had
inherited all his father's severity with none of his father's
generosity.   By his marriage with Constance, the heiress
of the Norman kings, he had become master of Naples
and Sicily.   Emboldened by the possession of what had
been hitherto the stronghold of his predecessors' bitterest
enemies, and able to threaten the Pope from south as
well as north, Henry conceived a scheme which might
have wonderfully changed the history of Germany and
Italy.   He proposed to the Teutonic magnates to lighten

their burdens by uniting these newly-acquired countries to the Empire, to turn their feudal lands into allodial, and to make no further demands for money on the clergy, on condition that they should pronounce the crown hereditary in his family. Results of the highest importance would have followed this change, which Henry advocated by setting forth the perils of interregna, and which he doubtless meant to be but part of an entirely new system of polity. Already so strong in Germany, and with an absolute command of their new kingdom, the Hohenstaufen might have dispensed with the renounced feudal services, and built up a firm centralized system, like that which was already beginning to develope itself in France. First, however, the Saxon princes, then some ecclesiastics headed by Conrad archbishop of Mainz, opposed the scheme; the pontiff withdrew his consent, and Henry had to content himself with getting his infant son Frederick the Second chosen king of the Romans. On Henry's untimely death the election was set aside, and the contest which followed between Otto of Brunswick (son of the Saxon duke Henry the Lion and of Matilda sister of Richard Cœur de Lion)

Philip, 1198- and Philip of Hohenstaufen (brother of Henry the Sixth)
1208. gave the Popedom, now guided by the genius of Innocent the Third, an opportunity of extending its sway at the

Innocent III expense of its antagonist. The Pope moved heaven and
and Otto IV. earth on behalf of Otto, whose family had been the constant rivals of the Hohenstaufen, and who was himself willing to promise all that Innocent required ; but Philip's personal merits and the vast possessions of his house gave him while he lived the ascendancy in Germany. His death by the hand of an assassin, while it seemed to vindicate the Pope's choice, left the Swabian party without a head, and the papal favourite was soon recognized over the whole Empire. But Otto IV became less submissive as he

felt his throne more secure. Though he was a Welf by
birth, he had no sooner received the imperial crown at
Rome, than he retracted the engagements he had made,
and proceeded to reclaim both the territories that had belonged to the Countess Matilda and the rights he had but
just forsworn. The Roman Church at last deposed and excommunicated her ungrateful son, and Innocent rejoiced in
a second successful assertion of pontifical supremacy, when
Otto was dethroned by the youthful Frederick the Second,
whom a tragic irony sent into the field of politics as the
champion of the Holy See, whose hatred was to embitter
his life and extinguish his house.

Upon the events of that terrific strife, for which Emperor and Pope girded themselves up once more, upon the
narrative of Frederick the Second's career, with its romantic adventures, its sad picture of marvellous powers lost on
an age not ripe for them, blasted as by a curse in the
moment of victory, it is not necessary, were it even possible, here to enlarge. That conflict did indeed determine
the fortunes of the German kingdom no less than of the
republics of Italy, but it was upon Italian ground that it
was fought out and it is to Italian history that its details
belong. So too of Frederick himself. Out of the long
array of the Germanic successors of Charles, he is, with
Otto III, the only one who comes before us with a genius
and a frame of character that are not those of a Northern
or a Teuton.[a] There dwelt in him, it is true, all the
energy and knightly valour of his father Henry and his

---

[a] I quote from the *Liber Augustalis* printed among Petrarch's works the
following curious description of Frederick : ' Fuit armorum strenuus, linguarum
peritus, rigorosus, luxuriosus, epicurus, nihil curans vel credens nisi temporale :
fuit malleus Romanae ecclesiae.'

As Otto III had been called ' mirabilia mundi,' so Frederick II is spoken
of in his own time as ' stupor mundi et immutator mirabilis.' (So Matth.
Paris.)

grandfather Frederick I. But along with these, and changing their direction, were other gifts, inherited perhaps
from his half Norman, half Italian mother and fostered
by his education in Sicily, where Musulman and Byzantine
influences were still potent,[b] a love of luxury and beauty,
an intellect refined, subtle, philosophical. Through the
mist of calumny and legend it is but dimly that the truth
of the man can be discerned, and the outlines that appear
serve to quicken rather than appease the curiosity with
which we regard one of the most extraordinary personages
in history. A sensualist, yet also a warrior and a politician ; a profound lawgiver and an impassioned poet ; in his
youth fired by crusading fervour, in later life persecuting
heretics while himself accused of blasphemy and unbelief ;
of winning manners and ardently beloved by his followers,
but with the stain of more than one cruel deed upon his
name, he was the marvel of his own generation, and succeeding ages looked back with awe, not unmingled with
pity, upon the inscrutable figure of the last Emperor who
had braved all the terrors of the Church and died beneath
her ban, the last who had ruled from the sands of the
ocean to the shores of the Ionian sea. But while they
pitied they condemned. The undying hatred of the Papacy threw round his memory a lurid light ; him and him
alone of all the imperial line, Dante, the worshipper of the
Empire, must perforce deliver to the flames of hell.[c]

Struggle of Frederick with the Papacy.   Placed as the Empire was, it was scarcely possible for
its head not to be involved in war with the constantly
aggressive Popedom — aggressive in its claims of territo-

---

[b] The remains of Frederick's palace castle, now sadly neglected, may be
seen at Brancaccio, about two miles SSE. of Palermo, his favourite residence.
His body lies in a porphyry sarcophagus in the cathedral, where also his father
Henry VI is buried.

[c] 'Quà entro è lo secondo Federico.' — *Inferno*, canto x.

rial dominion in Italy as well as of ecclesiastical jurisdiction throughout the world.   But it was Frederick's peculiar misfortune to have given the Popes a hold over him which they well knew how to use.   In a moment of youthful enthusiasm he had taken the cross from the hands of an eloquent monk, and his delay to fulfil the vow was branded as impious neglect.   Excommunicated by Gregory IX for not going to Palestine, he went, and was excommunicated for going : having concluded an advantageous peace, he sailed for Italy, and was a third time excommunicated for returning.   To Pope Gregory he was at last after a fashion reconciled, but with the accession of Innocent IV the flame burst out afresh.   The struggle filled and embittered the rest of Frederick's life.   It continued through the reign of his son Conrad IV, and proved fatal to his grandson Conradin, last scion of the great Swabian house.

The special pretexts which kindled the strife need not be enumerated : the real causes were always the same, and could only be removed by the submission of one or other combatant.   Chief among them was Frederick's possession of South Italy and Sicily.   Now were seen the fruits which the first Frederick had stored up for his house when he gained for Henry his son the hand of the Norman heiress. Apulia and Sicily had been for some two hundred years recognized as a fief of the Holy See, and the Pope, who felt himself in danger while encircled by the powers of his rival, was determined to use his feudal right to the full and make it the means of extinguishing imperial authority throughout Italy.   But although the strife had arisen out of territorial disputes, it soon assumed a religious character, it reopened every ancient fountain of hatred, and passed into a contest between the civil and the spiritual potentate. The time was one of intellectual upheaval and unrest : heresies were rife : the air was full of new doctrines.   To

CHAP. XIII. this troubled or rebellious spirit Frederick, himself perhaps influenced by Muslim speculation, and certainly no dutiful son of the Church, made his appeal. The claim of the Papacy to control the secular power was met by a counter-claim on the Emperor's part to exercise ecclesiastical authority — it would almost seem to create a new imperial Church of which he should be the head. Strange tales were told of his own beliefs and purposes. Some said that he sought to establish a new and better religion, that he deemed himself to be, like the Fatimite Sultans of Egypt, a sort of emanation from the divinity, and received nothing less than adoration from his followers. Others denounced him as an unbeliever who rejected the priesthood because they could no longer work miracles, who placed Moses and Christ beside Mohammed as impostors, who refused to admit as true anything that could not be proved from facts by human reason. Whatever ground these charges may have had, they inflamed the minds of men, and passion grew hotter than it had ever been in the days of Henry IV and Hildebrand, of Barbarossa and Alexander III. The Popes saw in Frederick the most dangerous of their enemies, because he struck at the root of their claims and sought to divert from them the allegiance of Christendom. They branded him as an apostate : they asserted that the Empire had been given to the Germans as a fief to be held from the Apostolic See, and declared that the power of Peter, symbolized by the two keys, was secular as well as spiritual. The Emperor appealed to law, to the indelible rights of Caesar; he claimed the right of reforming the Church against the will of the hierarchy,[d] compared him-

---

[d] Frederick is reported to have said : 'Si principes imperii institutioni meae assentirent, ego utique multo meliorem modum credendi et vivendi cunctis nationibus ordinare vellem.' — *Chron. Sanpetr. Erfurt.* (quoted by Huillard Bréholles, *Historia Diplom. Frederici II,*[di] Introd. DXV). Not only

self to Elijah rooting out the prophets of Baal, and denounced his foe as the Antichrist of the New Testament, since it was God's representative on earth whom he was resisting. The one scoffed at anathema, upbraided the avarice of the Church, and treated her soldiery, the friars, with a severity not seldom ferocious. The other solemnly deposed a rebellious and heretical prince, offered the imperial crown to Robert of France, to the heir of Denmark, to Hakon the Norse king,[e] succeeded at last in raising up rivals in Henry of Thuringia and William of Holland. Frederick died in the midst of his strife, A.D. 1250, and his son Conrad IV (associated with him in the Empire since 1237) survived him only four years. Germany was by this time a prey to anarchy, for Conrad had been occupied with efforts to save Italy. Manfred, an illegitimate son of Frederick II, maintained the contest there till his defeat and death near Benevento in 1266; and with Conrad or Conradin, son of Conrad IV, a gallant boy of fifteen who had crossed the Alps to assert his rights to Sicily (which the Pope had bestowed on Charles of Anjou), the house of Hohenstaufen ended.

Though this long struggle was a continuation of that which began nearly two centuries before under Henry IV,

by his partizans but in his own letters Jesi, his birthplace, is referred to as Bethlehem, while Pier delle Vigne, his minister, is spoken of as the Peter of the new Church, ' Petrus in cuius petra fundatur imperialis ecclesia et Augustalis animus roboratur in coena cum discipulis' (Huillard Bréholles, *ut supra*, DXIII). This may be the origin of Dante's reference to Piero as holding ' both the keys of the heart of Frederick ' (*Inf.* xiii. 58).

The wizard Michael the Scot, whose lean ghost Dante found in Malebolge (*Inf.* xx. 115), was astrologer to Frederick II and translated for him some works of Aristotle.

e Hakon, one of the greatest of the kings of Norway, and the one whose diplomacy succeeded in obtaining the submission of Iceland, refused, saying that he would fight against the enemies of the Church, but not against those of the Pope.

yet in this latest phase it is not so much the Teutonic Emperor who is attacked as the Sicilian king, the unbeliever and friend of Mohammedans, the hereditary enemy of the Church, the assailant of Lombard independence, whose success must leave the Papacy defenceless. And as it was from the Sicilian kingdom that the strife had chiefly sprung, so was the possession of the Sicilian kingdom a source as much of weakness as of strength, for it distracted Frederick's forces and put him in the false position of a liegeman resisting his lawful suzerain. Truly, as the Greek proverb says, the gifts of foes are no gifts, and bring no profit with them. The Norman kings were more terrible in their death than in their life : they had sometimes baffled the Teutonic Emperor; their heritage destroyed him.

Conrad IV,
1250–1254.
With Frederick fell the Empire. From the ruin that overwhelmed the greatest of its houses it emerged, living indeed, and destined to a long life, but so shattered, crippled, and degraded, that it could never more be to Europe and to Germany what it once had been. In the last act of the tragedy were joined the enemy who had now blighted its strength and the rival who was destined to insult its weakness and at last blot out its name.
A.D. 1268.
The murder, after his defeat at Tagliacozzo, of Frederick's grandson Conradin — a hero whose youth and whose chivalry might have moved the pity of any other foe — was approved, if not suggested, by Pope Clement; it was wrought by the minions of Charles of Anjou.

Italy lost to
the Empire.
The Lombard league had successfully resisted Frederick's armies and the more dangerous Ghibeline nobles : their strong walls and swarming population made defeats in the open field hardly felt; and now that South Italy had passed away from a German line — first to an Angevin, afterwards to an Aragonese dynasty — it was plain

that the peninsula was irretrievably lost to the Emperors.
Why, however, should they not still be strong beyond the
Alps? was their position worse than that of England
when Normandy and Aquitaine no longer obeyed a Plantagenet? The force that had enabled them to rule so
widely would be all the greater in a narrower sphere.

So indeed it might once have been, but now it was *Decline of*
too late. The German kingdom broke down beneath the *imperial*
weight of the Roman Empire. To be universal sovereign *power in*
Germany.
Germany had sacrificed her own political unity and the
vigour of her national monarchy. The necessity under
which projects in Italy and disputes with the Pope laid
each Emperor of purchasing by concessions the support
of his own princes, the ease with which in his absence the
magnates could usurp, the difficulty which the monarch
returning found in resuming the privileges of his crown,
the temptation to revolt and set up pretenders to the
throne which the Holy See held out — these were the
causes whose steady action laid the foundation of that
territorial independence which rose into a stable fabric at
the era of the Great Interregnum. Frederick II had by *The Great*
two Pragmatic Sanctions, A.D. 1220 and 1232, formally *Interregnum.*
granted rights, already beginning to be rooted in custom,
which were wide enough to give the bishops and nobles
practical sovereignty in their own towns and territories,
except when the Emperor should be present; and thus
his direct jurisdiction became restricted to his narrowed
domain, and to the cities immediately dependent on the
crown. With so much less to do, an Emperor became
altogether a less necessary personage; and hence the
seven magnates of the realm, now by law or custom virtually sole electors, were in no haste to fill up the place of
Conrad IV, whom the supporters of his father Frederick
had acknowledged. William of Holland was in the field,

Double election of Richard of England and Alfonso of Castile.

State of Germany during the Interregnum.

but resisted by the Swabian party: on his death, in 1256, a new election was called for, and at last set on foot. The archbishop of Cologne advised his brethren to choose some one rich enough to support the dignity, not strong enough to be feared by the electors: both requisites met in the Plantagenet Richard, earl of Cornwall, brother of the English Henry III. He received three, eventually four votes, came to Germany, and was crowned at Aachen. But three of the electors, finding that the sums he had paid to them were smaller than those received by others, seceded in disgust, and chose Alfonso X of Castile,[f] who, shrewder than his competitor, continued to watch the stars at Toledo, enjoying the splendours of his title while troubling himself about it no further than to issue now and then a proclamation.[g] Meantime the condition of Germany was frightful. The new Didius Julianus, the chosen of princes baser than the praetorians whom they copied, had neither the character nor the outward power and resources to make himself respected. Every floodgate of anarchy was opened: prelates and barons extended their domains by war: robber-knights infested the highways and the rivers: the misery of the weak, the tyranny and violence of the strong, were such as had not been seen for centuries. Things were worse than they had ever been under the Saxon and Franconian Emperors; for the petty nobles who had then been in some measure controlled by their dukes, were now, after the extinction of several of the great houses, left without any feudal superior. Only in the cities were shelter or peace to be found. Those of the Rhine had already leagued themselves for mutual

---

[f] Surnamed, from his scientific tastes, 'the Wise.'

[g] The Interregnum is by some reckoned as the two years before Richard's election; by others as the whole period from the death of Frederick II or that of his son Conrad IV till Rudolf's accession in 1273.

defence, and maintained a struggle in the interests of
commerce and order against universal brigandage.   At
last, when Richard had been some time dead, it was felt
that such things could not go on for ever : with no public
law, and no courts of justice, an Emperor, the embodiment
of legal government, was the only resource.   The Pope
himself, having now sufficiently improved the weakness of
his enemy, found the disorganization of Germany beginning to tell upon his revenues, and threatened that if the
electors did not appoint an Emperor, he would.   Thus
urged, they chose, in A.D. 1273, Rudolf, count of Hapsburg, founder of the house of Austria.[h]

CHAP. XIII.

*Death of
Richard,
A.D. 1271.*

*Rudolph of
Hapsburg,
1273-1292.*

From this point there begins a new era.   We have seen
the Roman Empire revived in A.D. 800, by a prince whose
vast dominions gave ground to his claim of universal monarchy ; again erected in A.D. 962, on the narrower but
firmer basis of the German kingdom.   We have seen Otto
the Great and his successors during the three following
centuries, a line of monarchs of unrivalled vigour and
abilities, strain every nerve to make good the pretensions
of their office against the rebels in Italy and the ecclesi-

*Change in
the position
of the Em-
pire.*

[h] 'Electores imperii ad indictum et mandatum domini papae apud Franch-
enfurte super electione convenientes, comitem Rudolfum . . . in regem ele-
gerunt.' — Ann. S. Rudb. Salisb. ad ann. (Pertz, *M. G. H.* ix). Rudolf,
though only a count, had considerable possessions, was a man of force, and
had won fame and popularity.   He had been faithful to Frederick II and
Conrad IV, and had accompanied Conradin into Italy.   Hapsburg (Habichts-
burg, 'Hawk's Burgh') is a castle (built about A.D. 1020) in the Aargau on
the banks of the Aar, and near the line of railway from Olten to Zürich, from
a point on which a glimpse of its ruins may be had.   'Within the ancient
walls of Vindonissa,' says Gibbon, 'the castle of Hapsburg, the abbey of
Königsfelden, and the town of Brugg have successively arisen.   The philosophic traveller may compare the monuments of Roman conquests, of feudal or
Austrian tyranny, of monkish superstition, and of industrious freedom.   If he
be truly a philosopher, he will applaud the merit and happiness of his own
time.'

astical power.   These efforts had now failed signally and hopelessly.   Each successive Emperor had entered the strife with resources scantier than his predecessors, each had been more decisively vanquished by the Pope, the Lombard cities, and the German princes.   The Holy Roman Empire might, and, so far as its practical utility was concerned, ought now to have been suffered to expire ; nor could it have ended more worthily than with the last of the Hohenstaufen.   That it did not so expire, but lived on six hundred years more, till it became a piece of antiquarianism hardly more venerable than ridiculous — till, as Voltaire said, it was neither Holy nor Roman nor an Empire — was owing partly indeed to the belief, still unshaken, that it was a necessary part of the world's order, yet chiefly to its connection, which was by this time indissoluble, with the German kingdom.   The Germans had confounded the two characters of their sovereign so long, and had grown so fond of the style and pretensions of a dignity whose possession appeared to exalt them above the other peoples of Europe, that it was now too late for them to separate the local from the universal monarch.   If a German king was to be maintained at all, he must be Roman Emperor ; and a German king there must still be.   Deeply, nay, mortally wounded as the event proved his power to have been by the disasters of the Empire to which it had been linked, the time was by no means come for its extinction.   In the unsettled state of society, and the conflict of innumerable petty potentates, no force save feudalism was able to hold society together ; and its efficacy for that purpose depended, as the anarchy of the recent Interregnum shewed, upon the presence of the recognized feudal head.

That head, however, was no longer what he had been. The relative position of Germany and France was now

exactly the reverse of that which they had occupied two
centuries earlier.   Rudolf was as conspicuously a weaker *Decline of*
sovereign than Philip III of France, as the Franconian *the regal*
power in
Emperor Henry III had been stronger than the Capetian *Germany as*
Philip I.   In every other state of Europe the tendency *compared*
with France
of events had been to centralize the administration and *and Eng-*
increase the power of the monarch, even in England not *land.*
to diminish it : in Germany alone had political union become weaker, and the independence of the princes more
confirmed.   The causes of this change are not far to seek.
They all resolve themselves into this one, that the German king attempted too much at once.   The rulers of
France, where manners were less rude than in the other
Transalpine lands, and where the Third Estate rose into
importance more quickly, had reduced one by one the
great feudatories by whom the first Capetians had been
scarcely recognized.   The English kings had annexed
Wales, Cumbria, and part of Ireland, had retained a prerogative great if not uncontrolled, and exercised no doubtful sway through every corner of their country.   Both
had won their successes by the concentration on that
single object of their whole personal activity, and by the
skilful use of every device whereby their feudal rights,
personal, judicial, and legislative, could be applied to fetter
the vassal.   Meantime the German monarch, whose utmost
efforts it would have needed to tame his fierce nobles and
maintain order through wide territories occupied by races
unlike in dialect and customs, had been struggling with
the Lombard cities and the Normans of South Italy, and
had been for full two centuries the object of the unrelent-
ing enmity of the Roman pontiff.   And in this latter contest, by which more than by any other the fate of the
Empire was decided, he fought under disadvantages far
greater than his brethren in England and France.   William

the Conqueror had defied Hildebrand, William Rufus had resisted Anselm; but the Emperors Henry the Fourth and Frederick the First had to cope with prelates who were Hildebrand and Anselm in one; the spiritual heads of Christendom as well as the primates of their special realm, the Empire. And thus, while the ecclesiastics of Germany were a body more formidable from their possessions than those of any other European country, and enjoyed far larger privileges, the Emperor could not, or could with far less effect, win them over by invoking against the Pope that national feeling which made the cry of Gallican liberties so welcome even to the clergy of France.

Relations of the Papacy and the Empire. After repeated defeats, each more crushing than the last, the imperial power, so far from being able to look down on the papal, could not even maintain itself on an equal footing. Against no pontiff since Gregory VII had the monarch's right to name or confirm a Pope, undisputed in the days of the Ottos and of Henry III, been made good. It was the turn of the Emperor to repel a similar claim of the Holy See to the function of reviewing his own election, examining into his merits, and rejecting him if unsound, that is to say, impatient of priestly tyranny. A letter of Innocent III, who was the first to make this demand in terms, was inserted by Gregory IX in his digest of the Canon Law, the inexhaustible armoury of the churchman, and continued to be quoted thence by every canonist till the end of the sixteenth century.[1] It was not difficult to find grounds on which to base such a doctrine. Gregory VII deduced it with characteristic boldness from the power of the keys, and the superiority over all other dignities which must needs appertain to the

---

[1] *Corpus Iuris Canonici*, Decr. Greg. i. 6, cap. 34, *Venarabilem:* 'Ius et authoritas examinandi personam electam in regem et promovendam ad imperium ad nos spectat, qui eum inungimus, consecramus et coronamus.'

Pope as arbiter of eternal weal or woe.   Others took their
stand on the analogy of clerical ordination, and urged that
since the Pope in consecrating the Emperor gave him a
title to the obedience of all Christian men, he must have
himself the right of approving or rejecting the candidate
according to his merits.   Others again, appealing to the
Old Testament, shewed how Samuel discarded Saul and
anointed David in his room,[j] and argued that the Pope now
must have powers at least equal to those of the Hebrew
prophets.   But the ascendancy of the doctrine dates from
the time of Pope Innocent III, whose ingenuity discovered
for it an historical basis.   It was by the Apostolic See, he
declared, that the Empire was taken away from the Greeks
and given to the Germans in the person of Charles,[k] and
the authority which Leo then exercised as God's representative must abide thenceforth and for ever in his successors,
who can therefore at any time recall the gift, and bestow
it on a person or a nation more worthy than its present
holders.   This is the famous theory of the Translation of
the Empire, which plays so large a part in controversy
down to the seventeenth century,[l] a theory with plausibility

[j] Lewis II, not presaging the future, uses this parallel in his letter (before
referred to) to the East Roman Emperor Basil: 'Nam Francorum principes
primo reges, deinde vero imperatores, dicti sunt ii dumtaxat qui a Romano
pontifice ad hoc oleo sancto perfusi sunt. . . . Porro si calumpniaris
Romanum pontificem, quod gesserit, poteris calumpniari et Samuel, quod
spreto Saule, quem ipse unxerat, David in regem ungere non renuerit.'

[k] 'Illis principibus,' writes Innocent, 'ius et potestatem eligendi regem
[Romanorum] in imperatorem postmodum promovendum recognoscimus, ad
quos de iure ac antiqua consuetudine noscitur pertinere, praesertim quum ad
eos ius et potestas huiusmodi ab apostolica sede pervenerit, quae Romanum
imperium in persona magnifici Caroli a Graecis transtulit in Germanos.' —
Decr. Greg., *ut supra*, *Venerabilem*.

[l] Its influence, however, as Döllinger (*Das Kaiserthum Karls des Grossen
und seiner Nachfolger*) remarks, first became great when this letter, some
forty or fifty years after Innocent wrote it, was inserted in the digest of the
Canon Law. Döllinger gives an interesting account of the course of theory

enough to make it generally successful, yet one which to an impartial eye appears far removed from the truth of the facts.[m] Leo III did not suppose, any more than did Charles himself, that it was by his sole pontifical authority that the crown was given to the Frank; nor do we find such a notion put forward by any of his successors down to the twelfth century.[n] Gregory VII in particular, in a remarkable letter dilating on his prerogative, appeals to the substitution by papal interference of Pipin for the last Merovingian king, and even goes back to cite the case of Theodosius humbling himself before St. Ambrose, but says never a word about this 'Translatio,' excellently as it would have served his purpose.[o]

Sound or unsound, however, these arguments did their work, for they were urged skilfully and boldly, and none denied that it was by the Pope alone that the crown could be lawfully imposed. In some instances the rights claimed were actually made good. Thus Innocent III withstood Philip and overthrew Otto IV; thus another haughty priest commanded the electors to choose the Landgrave of Thuringia (A.D. 1246), and was by some of them obeyed; thus Gregory X compelled the recognition of Rudolf, who subsequently (A.D. 1279) admitted

upon this subject, and of the various misconceptions and perversions (in writers of the twelfth and three following centuries) of the events connected with the breach between the Popes and the East Roman Emperors, and the consequent transference of the Empire to the Germans.

[m] See chapter V, *ante*.

[n] Pope Leo IX had, however, in 1054 claimed for his see rights over the Empire, based upon the Donation of Constantine, which would have covered the power to transfer the crown. Cf. his letter to Michael, Patriarch of Constantinople, in Migne, vol. cxliii. Ep. C. pp. 744 sqq.

[o] Upon this so-called 'Translation of the Empire,' many books remain to us: many more have probably perished. A good although far from impartial summary of the controversy may be found in Vagedes, *De Ludibriis Aulae Romanae in transferendo Imperio Romano.*

in a letter to Pope Nicholas III that the Germans owed the imperial crown to the Papacy. His son Albert I, anxious for the support of Boniface VIII against the German archbishops, made a similarly humiliating acknowledgement of the alleged right of transfer.

These admissions were, however, virtually recalled and the rights of the Empire strenuously asserted in the long and bitter conflict maintained against four successive Popes by the Emperor Lewis the Fourth. At the death of Henry VII, Pope Clement V, a Frenchman by birth, who had transferred his seat from turbulent Rome to Avignon,[p] claimed for himself the Vicariate of the vacant Empire and claimed also a general supremacy over the imperial crown. His successor, Pope John XXII, while reasserting his claim to the Vicariate,[q] summoned Lewis and his rival Frederick of Austria, both of whom had obtained some electoral votes, to submit their pretensions

[p] Avignon was not yet in the territory of France: it lay within the bounds of the kingdom of Arles. But the French power was nearer than that of the Emperor; and pontiffs, many of them French by extraction, sympathized with princes of their own race.

[q] 'Vacante imperio Romano, cum in illo ad saecularem iudicem nequeat haberi recursus, ad summum pontificem, cui in persona B. Petri terreni simul et coelestis imperii iura Deus ipse commisit, imperii praedicti iurisdictio regimen et dispositio devolvitur.' — Bull *Si fratrum* (of John XXII, in A.D. 1316), in *Bullar. Rom.* So again: 'Attendentes quod Imperii Romani regimen cura et administratio tempore quo illud vacare contingit ad nos pertinet, sicut dignoscitur pertinere.' Boniface VIII, refusing to recognize Albert I because he was ugly and one-eyed ('est homo monoculus et vultu sordido, non potest esse Imperator'), and had taken a wife from the serpent brood of Frederick II ('de sanguine viperali Friderici'), had some fifteen years before declared himself Vicar of the Empire.

In the ninth century, before these pretensions had been dreamt of, Pope John VIII dated his documents during vacancies of the imperial throne, 'imperatore domino nostro Iesu Christo,' a form not uncommon in the Middle Ages. So in a vacancy of the Popedom documents were sometimes dated 'Petro pontificante.'

to his decision, and when Lewis refused, his resentment, accentuated by the Emperor's opposition to his schemes for strengthening himself in Italy by stirring up enemies against the Ghibeline chiefs there, led him to form the plan of ejecting Lewis from the throne and transferring it to the French king Charles IV. John accordingly required the Emperor to resign the crown and shew himself obedient to the Holy See, without whose approval, it was insisted, no election was valid. Lewis protested and appealed to a General Council, but was promptly excommunicated, and his subjects declared to be released from their allegiance. Having by this time overthrown his rival Frederick, and finding that national feeling had been roused in Germany by the arrogance of the Pope, Lewis took courage, obtained a legal opinion in his favour from the University of Bologna, enlisted in his service a host of Franciscan friars who were embarked in a furious quarrel of their own with the Pope, and obtained the powerful aid of two of the greatest among mediaeval thinkers, the Paduan Marsilius[r] and the English Franciscan William of Ockham. These men became his confidential advisers, and wrote pamphlets long enough to be called treatises on his behalf against the Pope. Stimulated by the counsels of Marsilius and John of Jandun, another bold spirit from the University of Paris, Lewis marched upon Rome and made friends with the Roman people, who thereupon summoned Pope John to return to his see, and on his refusal chose Lewis as their Senator. Extruding the Pope's ally king Robert of Naples they named Sciarra Colonna Prefect of the City, and authorized him and three other syndics to

perform the coronation. This accordingly took place. After the Emperor had, by a startling departure from pre-

---

[r] As to Marsilius, see Note XIII at end. Ockham's contentions are most fully set forth in a book he wrote much later, entitled *Octo Quaestiones*.

cedent, received the crown from lay hands, he was consecrated by bishops whom the Pope had excommunicated.[a]
Thereupon Lewis (who had appointed Marsilius papal
vicar in the City) and the Romans proceeded in a solemn
parliament to depose Pope John (by the name of Jacques
of Cahors) for heresy and treason, and as a 'Destroyer
of Peace.'[t] A Franciscan friar was chosen Pope in
his place and crowned with the tiara by the hands of the
Emperor.

These revolutionary proceedings, which could hardly
have been attempted but for the absence of John XXII
at Avignon and the disgust excited by his arrogance and
greed,[u] are doubly surprising as being carried through by
a man whom his subsequent conduct shews to have been
weak and vacillating. But it was rather to the weakness
than to the strength of Lewis that they were due. He
was in the hands of three strong men, one of them,
Castruccio Castracani, lord of Lucca, a brilliant and unscrupulous Ghibeline leader, the other two, Marsilius and
John of Jandun, uncompromising theorists, prepared to
strike at the cardinal doctrines on which papal authority

[a] An annalist observes: 'Fuere qui dubitarent an invito pontifice haec rite
agerentur: caeterum Populus Romanus e contra contendebat suas esse partes
imperium conferre, Pontificis autem consecrare, iisdem auspiciis Carolum
enim magnum tunc demum coronatum esse postquam Populus Romanus eum
imperare iussisset.' — *Nicol. Burgund.*, ad ann. 1328 (quoted by Gregorovius,
History of Rome in the Middle Ages).

[t] This phrase suggests the hand of Marsilius, whose gigantic pamphlet on
behalf of the Emperor was entitled *Defensor Pacis*.

[u] How far this disgust had gone among religious men even fifty years
earlier is shewn by the language of the Franciscan St. Bonaventura, who
does not object to the view that Rome is the harlot of the Apocalypse
who makes drunk princes and people, seeing that in Rome ecclesiastical posts
are bought and sold; there the rulers of the Church meet, despising God and
serving lust, belonging to Satan and plundering the treasure of Christ (quoted
by Friedberg, *Die mittelalterlichen Lehren über das Verhältniss von Staat
und Kirche*). Cf. Dante, *Purg.* xxxii. 109.

rested. Nor is it only as the boldest assertion of the rights of the Empire that the action of Lewis in Rome is memorable. It was also the one instance in which the Romans gave effect to their cherished doctrine that the transference of the imperial crown to Charles the Great had been their doing, the one instance in which the Teutonic power, allying itself with the Roman people, used their pretensions to be the fountain of legal right not only to supersede the Pope in his function of crowning the German king, but also to restore to them the function of choosing their own pastor, who in becoming bishop of Rome becomes also bishop of the whole world. To this point had the union of the ancient Roman law with the Aristotelian doctrines of the State brought the fiery scholastic champions of the secular power, who once and once only during the Middle Ages found an opportunity for putting their theories into practice.

As it was the extravagant pretensions of Boniface VIII and John XXII that had caused this reaction against their office, so the extreme measures taken by Lewis provoked in turn a reaction against himself. The Romans were fickle, as was their wont : Castruccio, obliged to return to Tuscany, and alienated from the Emperor, died soon afterwards, as did Sciarra Colonna. Lewis was forced to abandon Rome, and in 1329 the Romans solemnly abjured both Lewis and their antipope, who next year flung himself at John's feet. Meanwhile the Emperor, having lost his hold on Italy, sought after his return to Germany to propitiate the Pope. John, haughty and inexorable, insisted on absolute submission.[x] His successor,

---

[x] He also required, though in vain, the punishment of Marsilius and John of Jandun, whom he called two beasts from hell ('duas bestias de abysso Sathanae ').

Benedict XII, influenced by France, was less peremptory
but no more compliant; and Clement VI (1344–52)
renewed the excommunication and required Lewis to
admit that the Empire was a fief of the Holy See. The
German Estates, however, shewing more spirit than the
Emperor himself, in two Diets held at Frankfort in 1338
and 1339, solemnly enounced and embodied in a Pragmatic Sanction the declaration that the Empire is held
from God alone, and that the sovereign, once duly chosen
by the electors, needs no confirmation or approval by
the Pope.[y] The electors in their famous conference held
at Rhense in 1338 made a like declaration.

The writings of Ockham and Marsilius seem to have
had considerable influence on opinion; and the book
of Marsilius, entitled *Defensor Pacis*, is indeed one of
the most remarkable treatises that remain to us from
the Middle Ages. In holding that the ultimate source
of power is in the people, Marsilius does not stand
alone, for this position, sanctioned by the well-known
doctrine of the old Roman law that the supreme authority of the Emperor springs from a delegation to him
by the people of their inherent powers,[z] is to be found
in other mediaeval publicists. But he goes further,
maintaining that the Church does not consist in any
special sense of the clergy, but of all Christians; that
a General Council stands above the Pope, that it ought
to consist of laymen as well as of clerics, that persons
of different religious opinions ought to be all equal before

---

[y] 'Imperialis dignitas et potestas est immediate a solo Deo; et de iure
imperii et consuetudine antiquitus approbata postquam aliquis eligitur in imperatorem sive regem ab electoribus imperii concorditer, vel maiori parte
eorumdem statim ex sola electione est rex verus et imperator censendus . . .
nec Papae sive sedis apostolicae aut alicuius alterius approbatione indiget.'—
Apud Goldast, *Constitut. Imp.* i. 336.

[z] *Digest* i. 4. 1; *Inst.* i. 2. 6.

the law, and that the priesthood have no right to judge, much less to punish, heresy, since each man is answerable for his speculative opinions to the judgement of Christ only. Marsilius denies to the clergy the right to hold property (except what is needed to support life), as also any immunities or privileges outside their purely spiritual sphere of action, declares that Christ did not come on earth to establish any worldly power (*regnum meum non est de hoc mundo*), that the Pope ought not to have any such power, — the power of the keys does not imply it, for God alone can remit sins, — that the distinction of bishops and priests has no basis in the New Testament. He argues that St. Peter had no pre-eminence over the other apostles, that it is doubtful whether he was ever bishop of Rome, or even came to Rome at all, and that such authority as the Pope enjoys is due solely to the fact that Rome had been the old imperial city. No wonder that Pope Clement VI observed, after perusing the *Defensor Pacis*, 'Never have I read a worse heretic.'

These doctrines struck at the root not merely of the particular claim made by John XXII, but of the whole sacerdotal system of the Middle Ages. Their enunciation coincided with the most extreme assertion of high Papalist doctrine ever made. Agostino Trionfo's book on the Power of the Pope, dedicated to John XXII as the book of Marsilius had been to Lewis IV, claims for the Holy See absolute power over all secular sovereigns in all matters, temporal as well as spiritual. There is no appeal from him even to God, much less to a council, for his judgement is God's. He may conceivably lapse into heresy, and, if so, he ceases *ipso facto* to be Pope, because spiritual life resides in faith, without which he is spiritually dead, as a corpse is not a man. But he is bound by no law except the Divine. He

stands higher than the angels, and may receive the same
sort of adoration as is rendered to the Blessed Virgin
and the Saints. He can at his pleasure depose an
Emperor, appoint another, withdraw their functions from
the electors, cancel any law issued by an Emperor or
king, because he represents God upon earth with the
plenitude of God's authority.[a]

In these propositions laid down by Trionfo, with the
hearty approval of the Papal Curia, ecclesiastical pretensions may be deemed to have reached their high-
water mark; and it presently appeared that the tide was
beginning to turn. As the view which placed the Vicar
of God little below God Himself came rather too late, for
it went further than the opinion of Europe was now
disposed to follow, so on the other hand the book of
Marsilius came too early to have its full effect. Two
centuries were to pass before the soil was ready to
receive the seed which this precursor of Luther and
Zwingli had sown.[b] During those two centuries the Popes
steadily declined in reputation and authority. Some of

[a] Papalists used to quote the text, 'All power is given me in heaven and
on earth,' as proof of the temporal authority of the Pope, for Christ's power
was Peter's, and Peter's passed to his successors.

[b] A reason why the assaults of Marsilius and Ockham, as indeed of earlier
impugners of the claims of the Papacy, did not make a deeper impression may
perhaps be found in the fact that there was one doctrine, that relating to the
Eucharist, which they did not dispute. Sacerdotalism stood deep-rooted in
sacramentalism, and it was the denial of the dogma of the Real Presence that
in the sixteenth century undermined the foundation whereon the power of
the priesthood and Peter's see rested.

Upon the struggle of Lewis IV and the Popes, see besides Gregorovius
(*History of Rome in the Middle Ages*), Friedberg, *Die mittelalterlichen Lehren
über das Verhältniss von Staat und Kirche* (1874), and Riezler, *Die liter-
arischen Widersacher der Päpste zur Zeit Ludwig des Baiers* (1874), both of
whom deal fully with Marsilius and Ockham. Some excellent observations
may also be found in Mr. R. L. Poole's *Illustrations of the History of Mediaeval Thought* (1884), chaps. viii and ix.

their moral sway over men's minds was lost while they dwelt at Avignon under the shadow of France. Still more was lost in the Great Schism which divided the Church for more than a generation (A.D. 1378–1417); [e] and most of all was lost by the avarice and extortion — a cause of irritation to the clergy almost as much as to the laity — of which not a few pontiffs were guilty during this long period. After the middle of the fifteenth century the Popes, by this time firmly re-established in Rome, became more occupied with the building up of a temporal dominion in Italy than with the assertion of their authority over emperors and kings. So far indeed as the Emperor was concerned, they had the less need to trouble him, because Charles the Fourth had (A.D. 1355) abandoned to the Pope those territorial rights over Rome and Italy for which his predecessors had fought. No succeeding Emperor tried to make them good. The great Council of Constance, in which Western Christendom assembled under the auspices of the Emperor Sigismund, deposed two rival Popes, and obtained the resignation of a third, offered an opportunity which a man with the vigour and loftiness of Henry the Third might have seized to recover the influence of the imperial office and to use it for the benefit of the Church. But Sigismund was no Henry the Third; nor did any one after him essay the perhaps impossible task of correcting the abuses of ecclesiastical power. The Hapsburg Frederick the Third, timid and superstitious, abased himself before the Romish Court; and the long line of his Austrian successors has generally adhered to the alliance then struck.

[e] That this Schism did not shake the authority of the Pope even more seriously shews how firm was the hold which the idea of the unity of Christendom in Church and State had upon the mediaeval mind.

CHAPTER XIV

THE GERMANIC CONSTITUTION : THE SEVEN ELECTORS

THE reign of Frederick the Second was not less fatal to
the domestic power of the German king than to the European supremacy of the Emperor. His two Pragmatic
Sanctions had conferred rights that made the feudal aristocracy almost independent, and the long anarchy of the
Interregnum had enabled them not only to use but to extend and fortify their power. Rudolf of Hapsburg had
striven, not wholly in vain, to coerce their insolence, but
the contest for the crown between his son Albert and
Adolf Count of Nassau which followed his death, the
short and troubled reign of Albert himself, the absence
of Henry the Seventh in Italy, the civil war of Lewis of
Bavaria and Frederick duke of Austria, rival claimants of
the imperial throne, the difficulties in which Lewis, the successful competitor, found himself involved with a succession of Popes — all these circumstances tended more and
more to narrow the influence of the crown and complete the
emancipation of the turbulent nobles. They now became
virtually supreme in their own domains, enjoying full jurisdiction (certain appeals excepted), the right of legislation,
privileges of coining money, of levying tolls and taxes:
some had scarcely even a feudal bond to remind them of
their allegiance. The numbers of the nobility who held
directly of the crown had increased prodigiously by the
extinction of the dukedoms of Franconia and Swabia, and
the reduction in area of that of Saxony : along the Rhine

CHAP. XIV.

*Territorial
Sovereignty
of the Princes.*

Adolf,
1292–1298.

Albert I,
1298–1308.

Henry VII,
1308–1314.

Lewis IV,
1314–1347.

the lord of a single tower was often almost an independent prince. The petty tyrants whose boast it was that they owed fealty only to God and the Emperor shewed themselves in practice equally regardless of both powers. Preeminent were the three great houses of Austria, Bavaria, and Luxemburg, this last having acquired Bohemia, A.D. 1309. Next came the electors, already considered collectively more important than the Emperor, and forming for themselves considerable principalities. Brandenburg and the Rhenish Palatinate are strong states before the end of this period; Bohemia and the three archbishoprics almost from its beginning.

The chief object of the magnates was to keep the monarch in his present state of helplessness. The Hohenstaufen had been strong by their hereditary dominions as well as by their imperial authority: Frederick I is said to have been lord of four hundred castles. Unfortunately the Emperors who followed that great house had not similar patrimonial possessions; and indeed Rudolf was chosen because his private resources were too slender to make him an object of disquiet. Till the expense which the crown entailed had begun to prove ruinous to its wearer, the electors preferred to confer it on some petty prince, such as were Rudolf and Adolf of Nassau and Günther of Schwartzburg, seeking when they could to keep it from settling in one family. They bound the newly elected monarch to respect all their present immunities, including those which they had just extorted as the price of their votes; they checked all his attempts to recover lost lands or rights: they ventured at last (in 1399) to depose their anointed head, Wenzel, king of Bohemia, whose dissipated life and neglect of his duties certainly justified their displeasure. Thus fettered, the Emperor sought only to make the most of his short tenure, using his position to

aggrandize his family and raise money by the sale of crown
estates and privileges. His individual action and personal
relation to the subject was replaced by a merely legal and
formal one : he represented order and legitimate ownership, and so far was still necessary to the political system. But imperial progresses through the country were
abandoned : unlike his predecessors, who, when they assumed the sceptre, had turned from the administration of
their own domains to the service of the nation, he lived
mostly in his own states, sometimes beyond the Empire's
frontier.

How thoroughly the national character of the office was
gone is shewn by the repeated attempts to bestow it on
foreign or half-foreign potentates, who could not fill the
place of a German king of the good old vigorous type.
Not to speak of Richard and Alfonso, the French Charles
Count of Valois was proposed against Henry VII,[a] and
Edward III of England actually elected against Charles
IV (the English parliament forbade him to accept). Sigismund, though he belonged to the house of Luxemburg,
was, when chosen, a Hungarian king with interests primarily Hungarian ; and George Podiebrad who was elected
against Frederick III ruled over a Bohemia which felt
itself more Slavonic than Germanic. The Emperor's only
hope would have been in the support of the cities. During
the thirteenth and fourteenth centuries they had increased
wonderfully in population, wealth, and boldness : the
Hanseatic confederacy was the mightiest power of the
North, and cowed the Scandinavian kings : the towns of
Swabia and the Rhine formed great commercial leagues,
maintained regular wars against the counter-associations
of the nobility, and seemed at one time, by an alliance with

CHAP. XIV.
*Policy of the
Emperors.*

*Power of the
cities.*

[a] As to Peter Du Bois' scheme for securing power in Italy to the kings of
France, see Note XIV at end.

CHAP. XIV.   the already virtually independent Switzers,[b] on the point
of turning West Germany into a federation of free municipalities.   Feudalism, however, was still too strong; the
cavalry of the nobles was irresistible in the field, and the
thoughtless Wenzel, who might have helped and used them,
let slip a golden opportunity of repairing the losses of two
centuries.   After all, the Empire was perhaps past redemp-
tion, for one fatal ailment paralyzed all its efforts.   The
Financial   Empire was poor.   The constructive abilities of Frederick I
distress.   and his grandson, which ought to have been applied, as was
the constructive talent of the English Henry II, to the establishment of an immediate financial control by the crown,
and the introduction of some scheme of direct taxation,
were distracted by their enterprises in Italy; and neither
from princes, from ecclesiastics, nor from cities was any
adequate royal revenue secured.   The crown lands, which
had suffered heavily under Frederick II, were further
usurped during the confusion that followed; till at last,
through the reckless prodigality of sovereigns who sought
only their immediate interest, little was left of the vast
and fertile domains along the Rhine from which the Saxon
and Franconian Emperors had drawn the chief part of their
revenue.   Regalian rights, the second fiscal resource, had
fared no better.   Tolls, customs, mines, rights of coining,
of harbouring Jews, and so forth, were either seized or
granted away: even the advowsons of churches had been
sold or mortgaged; and the imperial treasury depended
mainly on an inglorious traffic in honours and exemptions.
Things were so bad under Rudolf that the electors refused
to make his son Albert king of the Romans, declaring that,
while Rudolf lived, the public revenue which with difficulty

----

[b] The first League of the three Forest Cantons was formed in 1308.
Others were added by degrees: and the number of eight was completed by
the accession of Bern in 1353.

supported one monarch, could much less maintain two at the same time.[c] Sigismund told his Diet, 'Nihil esse imperio spoliatius, nihil egentius, adeo ut qui sibi ex Germaniae principibus successurus esset, qui praeter patrimonium nihil aliud habuerit, apud eum non imperium sed potius servitium sit futurum.' Patritius, the secretary of Frederick III, declared that the revenues of the Empire scarcely covered the expenses of its ambassadors.[d] Poverty such as these expressions point to, a poverty which became greater after each election, not only involved the failure of the attempts which were sometimes made to recover usurped rights,[e] but put every project of reform within or war without at the mercy of a jealous Diet. The three orders of which that Diet consisted, electors, princes, and cities,[f] were each of them bent on its own interests and mutually hostile ; their niggardly grants did no more than keep the Empire from dying of inanition.

The changes thus briefly described were in progress when Charles the Fourth, king of Bohemia, son of that blind king John of Bohemia who fell at Cressy, and grandson of the Emperor Henry VII, found himself settled

Charles IV (A.D. 1347–1378), and his electoral constitution.

[c] Quoted by Moser, *Römische Kayser*, from *Chron. Hirsaug.*: 'Regni vires temporum iniuria nimium contritae vix uni alendo regi sufficerent, tantum abesse ut sumptus in nutriendos duos reges ferre queant.' So at Rupert's death, under whom the mischief had increased greatly, most bishops were, we are told, better off than the Emperor.

[d] 'Proventus Imperii ita minimi sunt ut legationibus vix suppetant.' — Quoted by Moser. In 1495, Maximilian told his Diet 'Das römische Reich sei jetziger Zeit ein grosser Last und falle davon kleiner Beth' (the Empire is a heavy burden, with little gain therefrom) ; and Granvella, Charles V's minister, said at the Diet of Speyer: 'The Emperor has, for the support of his dignity, not a hazel-nut's worth of profit from the Empire.'

[e] Albert I tried in vain to wrest the tolls of the Rhine from the grasp of the Rhenish electors.

[f] The cities did not, however, definitely establish their right to appear as an Estate or College in the Diet until A.D. 1489.

upon the throne which he had, as a candidate favoured by the Pope, disputed for some years with Lewis IV. His skilful and consistent policy aimed at settling what he perhaps despaired of reforming, and the famous instrument which, under the name of the Golden Bull, became the corner-stone of the Germanic constitution, confessed and legalized the independence of the electors and the powerlessness of the crown. The most conspicuous defect of the existing system was the uncertainty of the elections, followed as they usually were by a civil war. It was this which Charles set himself to redress.

German kingdom not originally elective.

The kingdoms founded on the ruins of the Roman Empire by the Teutonic invaders presented in their original form a rude combination of the elective with the hereditary principle. One family in each tribe had, as the offspring of the gods, an indefeasible claim to rule, but from among the members of such a family the warriors were free to choose the bravest or the most popular as king.[g] That the German crown came to be purely elective, while in France, Castile, Aragon, England, and most other European states, the principle of strict hereditary succession established itself, was due to the failure of heirs male in three successive dynasties; to the restless ambition of the nobles, who, since they were not, like the French, strong enough to disregard the royal power, did their best to weaken it; to the intrigues of the churchmen, zealous for a method of appointment prescribed by their own law and observed in capitular elections; to the wish of the Popes to gain an opening for their own influence and make effective the veto which they claimed; above all, to the conception of the imperial office as one too holy to be, in

[g] The Aethelings of the line of Cerdic, among the West Saxons, the Swedish Ynglings, the Bavarian Agilolfings, may thus be compared with the Achaemenids of Persia or the heroic houses of early Greece.

the same manner as the regal, transmissible by descent. CHAP. XIV.
Had the German, like other feudal kingdoms, remained
merely local, feudal, and national, it would without doubt
have ended by becoming a hereditary monarchy. Transformed as it was by the Roman Empire, this could not be.
The headship of the human race being, like the Papacy,
the common inheritance of all mankind, could not be confined to a single family, nor pass like a private estate by
the ordinary rules of succession.

The right to choose the war-chief belonged, in the earliest *Electoral*
ages, to the whole body of freemen. Their suffrage, which *body in primi-*
must have been very irregularly exercised, became by de- *tive times.*
grees vested in their leaders, but the assent of the multitude, although ensured already, was needed to complete
the ceremony. It was thus that Henry the Fowler, and
Henry the Saint, and Conrad II were chosen.[h] Though
even tradition might have commemorated what extant
records place beyond a doubt, it was commonly believed,
till the end of the sixteenth century, that the elective constitution had been established, and the privilege of voting
confined to seven persons, by a decree of Gregory V and
Otto III, which a famous jurist describes as ' lex a pontifice
de imperatorum comitiis lata, ne ius eligendi penes populum Romanum in posterum esset.'[i] St. Thomas says,

[h] Wippo, describing the election of Conrad the Franconian, says, ' Inter
confinia Moguntiae et Wormatiae dum convenissent cuncti primates et, ut ita
dicam, vires et viscera regni,' cii ; *M. G. H., Script.*, xi. 257. So Bruno says
that Henry IV 'regnum . . . electione communi suscepit': *M. G. H., Script.*
v. p. 330. So Amandus, secretary of Frederick Barbarossa, in describing his
election, says : ' Multi illustres heroes ex Lombardia, Tuscia, Ianuensi et aliis
Italiae dominiis, ac maior et potior pars principum in Transalpino regno.'—
Quoted by Mur. *Antiq.* Diss. iii. vol. i. p. 94. And see many other authorities to the same effect, collected by Pfeffinger, *Vitriarius illustratus.*

[i] Alciatus, *De Formula Romani Imperii.* He adds that the Gauls and
Italians were incensed at the preference shewn to Germany. So too Landolfo
Colonna, *De Translatione Imperii Romani.*

'Election ceased from the times of Charles the Great to those of Otto III, when Pope Gregory V established that of the seven princes, which will last as long as the holy Roman Church, who ranks above all other powers, shall have judged expedient for Christ's faithful people.'[j] Since it tended to exalt the papal power, this fiction was accepted, no doubt honestly accepted, and spread abroad by the clergy. And indeed, like so many other fictions, it had a sort of foundation in fact. The premature death without an heir of Otto III, the fourth of a line of monarchs among whom son had regularly succeeded to father, threw back the crown into the gift of the nation, and was no doubt one of the chief causes why it did not in the end become hereditary.[k]

Thus under the Saxon and Franconian sovereigns, the throne was theoretically elective, the assent of the chiefs and their followers being required, though little more likely to be refused than it was to an English or a French king; practically hereditary, since both of these dynasties succeeded in occupying it for four generations, the father procuring the son's election during his own lifetime. So it might well have continued had the German king been a merely national king like his brethren in France and England. But, under the operation of the influences already described, the territorial aristocracy, sometimes aided by the Pope, were able to turn the developement of the ancient constitution into a new channel, so that the German kingdom became in point of law incontestably elective, and so con-

[j] Quoted by Gewoldus, *De Septemviratu Sacri Imperii Romani,* himself a strenuous advocate of Gregory's decree, though he lived in the comparatively critical days of Ferdinand II. As late as A.D. 1648 we find Pope Innocent X maintaining that the sacred number *Seven* of the electors was 'apostolica auctoritate olim praefinitus.' — Bull *Zelo Domus* in *Bullar. Roman.*

[k] Sometimes we hear of a decree made by Pope Sergius IV and his cardinals (of course equally fabulous with Otto's). So John Villani, iv. 2.

tinued ever thereafter. The precise steps by which this came to pass, and the nature of the proceedings at an election, have been matter for long and tangled controversy. Some points remain doubtful, because the original authorities are curt or vague in their accounts, especially as respects the procedure at those uncontested elections in which a reigning Emperor secured the choice of his son during his own lifetime.[1] Without attempting to discuss these points, a few general propositions may be stated as probably true.[m]

In the process of choosing a German king to be afterwards raised to the dignity of Roman Emperor, three stages may be distinguished.

The first stage is that of the deliberations and negotiations of the magnates which issue in the selection of one from among several candidates. For this process there would seem to have been, down till the middle of the thirteenth century, no rules formally prescribed and observed. There was no recognized method of voting, nor does the right of voting appear to be confined to any specified persons. Things were in practice determined not by a majority of votes, but by the personal, official, and territorial weight and power of those who took part.

---

[1] As early as 1152 we read, 'Id iuris Romani Imperii apex habere dicitur ut non per sanguinis propaginem sed per principum electionem reges creentur.' — Otto of Freysing, Book II. c. 1.   Gulielmus Brito, writing not much later, says —

> 'Est etenim talis dynastia Theutonicorum
> Ut nullus regnet super illos, ni prius illum
> Eligat unanimis cleri populique voluntas.'

— *M. G. H., Script.* xxvi. p. 334.

[m] There is a considerable literature on the early electoral system. Among more recent writers, reference may be made to Waitz, *Deutsche Verfassungsgeschichte;* Maurenbrecher, *Geschichte der deutschen Königswahlen;* Linder, *Die deutschen Königswahlen*, 1893, and *Der Hergang bei den deutschen Königswahlen*, 1899, Schröder, *Lehrbuch der deutschen Rechtsgeschichte.*

The number of the nobles whom custom admitted to join might be greater or less, but in fact the influence of the leading princes, ecclesiastical and secular, prevailed. Sometimes these magnates were allowed, or took it upon themselves, to make a preliminary selection, from all those who might be considered candidates for the throne, either of a certain small number, or of one only, to be thereupon presented to the nobles generally as the man fittest to be chosen. As early as 1156 this preliminary and informal selection, which took place at the election of Conrad II in 1024, of Lothar II in 1125, and of Frederick I in 1152, had obtained the name of Praetaxation; and in the persons who exercised it we may find the germ of the electoral college of later times.[n]

The second stage of the process consisted in the solemn declaration by the princes, usually in the order of their official status or rank, of their choice of a particular person as king. This was the formal *Electio* in the strict sense of the word, and this custom required to be unanimous. In it certain magnates, three ecclesiastical and three or four secular, secured the right of delivering their voice first: and this prerogative voice would seem to have set them in a position of special authority which led to their being ultimately recognized as the persons exclusively entitled to elect. They were doubtless those, or the chief among those, who occasionally exercised the function of praetaxation. Here legal theory may have helped to settle what custom had left vague. It is first in the famous law book called the *Saxon Mirror* (*Sachsenspiegel*) compiled by

---

[n] In the case of a papal election, a two-thirds majority was required (as it is in a convention of the Democratic party in the United States for the selection of a Presidential candidate). But an unanimous choice seems to have been originally required in Germany, and the need for it was first expressly negatived by the electors in their solemn gathering at Rhense in A.D. 1338.

Eike von Reppgau about A.D. 1230, that six princes (of whom more anon) are named as enjoying a special right. They are said to be 'first in the choice,' the first to make that formal expression of acceptance which technically constituted the election.[o]

The last part of the process was the approval of the counts and other minor nobles,[p] completed by that acclamation of the multitude which preserved the tradition of choice by the nation as a whole, but which gradually lost its importance under the preponderating influence of the great ecclesiastical and secular potentates. As we find, down at least till the middle of the twelfth century, no legal line drawn between those who were and those who were not entitled to vote — indeed, so far as law went, it might be said that all nobles and knights were entitled to some sort of voice — there was evidently a wide door open for disputes, and when an election was disputed, no means except war existed for settling it (Pope Innocent III and his successors claimed, but the Germans denied, a right of interference).[q] Contests there were, and contests would have been more frequent had there not been a strong tendency to prefer the heir of the preceding sovereign, and had not the crown been often secured by a reigning Emperor for his son. A sense of the danger involved in this absence of fixed rules probably contributed to make

[o] This second stage was formally the effective and binding act, the election (*Kur*) in a strict sense, though in fact it was only the ratification and formal announcement of a selection already made. Where there was no real contest, as where an Emperor procured by the exercise of his influence with the princes severally the election of his son, it became the whole election.

[p] The term *laudatio*, a declaration of consent with a pledge of loyalty, is used to describe sometimes this acceptance by the larger body, sometimes both of what have been here distinguished as the second and third parts of the process of election.

[q] See the Bull *Venerabilem*, already quoted, of Pope Innocent III.

the nation more and more disposed to recognize a special right of choice as vested in the few great potentates who towered above the other princes.

Comparing the electoral constitution of the Empire at the death of the last Saxon Emperor in A.D. 1024, and at the death of the last Hohenstaufen in 1254, we see that two great changes had passed upon it. It had become a fundamental doctrine that the Germanic (and imperial) throne, unlike the thrones of other countries, was purely elective. So clearly did the princes perceive this to be the keystone of their freedom that the influence and the liberal offers of Henry VI [r] failed to induce them to surrender their privilege. And at the same time that practice of preliminary selection, and that right of being the first to deliver a formal elective voice, which have been already referred to, had ripened into a practically exclusive privilege of election. As this privilege became vested in a small body, the assent of the rest of the nobility began to be assumed as virtually given or certain to be given, so that after a time it passed not only out of use, but almost out of memory. Even in 1198 Pope Innocent III speaks of 'princes specially entitled to choose the Roman king.[s] On the double choice of Richard and Alfonso, A.D. 1257, the substantial question was as to the majority of votes in the electoral college:[t] neither then nor afterwards was there any practical recognition of the rights of the other princes, counts, and barons, important as their voices had been three centuries earlier.

The origin of that college is a matter somewhat intricate

[r] See pp. 205–206, *supra*.

[s] 'Principes ad quos principaliter spectat regis Romani electio.'

[t] The electors who chose Richard do indeed in their report to Pope Urban IV say that they acted after deliberating with other magnates, and by their common consent, but they assert that by custom the election belongs to certain princes, seven in number.

and obscure.   At the election of Frederick I in A.D. 1152,
certain princes led and decided the choice of the nation,
and at the election of Philip in 1198 the preponderant
influence of a few is again apparent.[u]   But we do not
yet find anything to indicate that a legal right as distinguished from a practically admitted preëminence had
become vested in any particular persons.[x]   First in
the *Sachsenspiegel* do we find six named as specially,
one can hardly say exclusively, entitled, viz. the three
Rhenish archbishops — the Count Palatine of the Rhine,
the duke of the Saxons, and the Margrave of Brandenburg.
Other authorities of the time recognize a seventh, the king
of Bohemia, whom the *Sachsenspiegel* rejects as not being
German.   Then in A.D. 1263 a letter of Pope Urban IV
declares (adopting the view stated by the friends of
Richard of Cornwall, and by that time generally accepted
in Germany), that by immemorial custom the right of
choosing the Roman king belongs to seven persons, the
seven who had just divided their votes on Richard and
Alfonso of Castile.   Of these seven, the three archbishops
of Mainz, Treves, and Cologne, pastors of the oldest and
richest sees, represented the German Church and had
always borne a leading part in elections.   The other four
ought, according to the ancient constitution, to have been
the dukes of the four nations, Franks, Swabians, Saxons,
Bavarians, to whom had also belonged the four great
offices of the imperial household.   But of these dukedoms
the two first named were now extinct, and their place and

[u] The English Richard of Hoveden, writing of this election, which happened in his lifetime, singles out four princes as chief electors, viz. the archbishops of Mainz and Cologne, the duke of Saxony, and the Count Palatine
of the Rhine (ad ann. 1198).

[x] There was no authority which would have been recognized as legally
competent to confer a special right.   Such constitution as the Empire had
rested upon custom only.

power in the State, as well as the household offices they had held, had descended upon two principalities of more recent origin, those, namely, of the Palatinate of the Rhine and the Margraviate of Brandenburg. The Saxon duke, though with greatly narrowed dominions, retained his leading place and his office of arch-marshal, and the claim of his Bavarian compeer would have been equally indisputable had it not so happened that both he and the Palsgrave of the Rhine were members of the great house of Wittelsbach. This house had acquired the dukedom of Bavaria in 1180 and the Palatinate, which represented the vote of the extinct dukedom of Lorraine, in 1214; but as both dignities were united in one person, no difficulty arose until the death of Duke Otto the Illustrious in 1253. When his sons shared his dominions, Lewis becoming Palsgrave, and Henry Duke of Bavaria, nothing was settled as to the vote and other rights of an elector, and before long both sons claimed these, and both with apparently reasonable grounds. The number Seven was now, however, beginning to be recognized as sacred : the king of Bohemia[y] would not relinquish the place to which he laid claim as cupbearer; and the other electors were unwilling to see two votes enjoyed by one family. Thus a contest, which more than once nearly led to war, arose between the rival lines of Wittelsbach, and between the Bavarian line (whose title was thought the weaker of the two) and the king of Bohemia. Rudolf I, who in 1289 pronounced in favour of

---

[y] The claim of the king of Bohemia seems to have been made technically in respect of his office of cupbearer, practically because he was the equal in power and rank of any of the other electors. It was disputed partly on the ground that his kingdom was not properly German. 'Rex Bohemiae qui pincerna est non eligit quia non est Teutonicus' (Albert. Stad. A.D. 1240, following the phrase of the *Sachsenspiegel*, 'Die schenke des rikes die koning von behemen, die ne heuet nenen kore, umme dat he nicht düdesch nis').— *M. G. H., Script.* xi. p. 367.

Bohemia, and Lewis IV, who directed that the vote should be exercised by the two lines alternately, in vain attempted to settle it, nor was it laid to rest until the issuing and confirming, at the Diets of Nürnberg and Metz in 1356, of Charles IV's Golden Bull.   This instrument, thenceforth *Golden Bull* regarded as a fundamental law of the Empire, after finally *of Charles IV*, assigning the disputed vote and office of cupbearer to A.D. 1356. Bohemia (of which Charles was then king) proceeds to lay down a variety of rules for the conduct of imperial elections.   Frankfort is fixed as the place of election, as a tradition dating from East Frankish days preserved the feeling that both election and coronation ought to take place on Frankish soil ; the archbishop of Mainz is named convener of the electoral college ; to Bohemia is given the first, to the Count Palatine the second place among the secular electors.   A majority of votes was in all cases to be decisive.   As to each electorate there was attached a great office, it was supposed as early as the time of the *Sachsenspiegel* that this was the title by which the vote was possessed ; though in truth the office and the right of election had both the same source, for the great offices naturally belonged to the greatest of the imperial feudatories.   The three prelates were archchancellors of Germany, Gaul and Burgundy, and Italy respectively : Bohemia cupbearer, the Palsgrave seneschal, Saxony marshal, and Brandenburg chamberlain.[z]

---

[z] The names and offices of the seven are concisely given in these lines, which appear in the treatise of Marsilius of Padua, *De Translatione Imperii Romani*, c. xi (printed in Goldast, *Monarchia Imperii*, ii. p. 153) : —

'Moguntinensis, Trevirensis, Coloniensis,
Quilibet imperii sit Cancellarius horum;
Et Palatinus dapifer, Dux portitor ensis,
Marchio praepositus camerae, pincerna Bohemus,
Hi statuunt dominum cunctis per saecula summum.'

It is worth while to place beside this the first stanza of Schiller's ballad,

These arrangements, under which disputed elections became far less frequent, remained undisturbed till the breaking out of the Thirty Years' War, when the Emperor Ferdinand II by an unwarranted stretch of prerogative deprived (in 1621) the Palsgrave Frederick (king of Bohemia and husband of Elizabeth, the daughter of James I of England) of his electoral vote, and transferred it (1623) to his own partisan, Maximilian of Bavaria. At the peace of Westphalia the mediaeval mysticism which revered the number Seven had become out of date, so the Palsgrave *Eighth electorate.* was reinstated as eighth elector, Bavaria retaining her vote and rank, but with a provision that if the Bavarian branch of the house of Wittelsbach should come to an end, the Palsgrave should step into its place, which accordingly happened on the extinction of the Bavarian line in 1777. The sacred number having been once broken through, less scruple was felt in making further changes. *Ninth electorate.* In A.D. 1692, the Emperor Leopold I conferred a ninth electorate on the house of Brunswick-Lüneburg, which was then in possession of the duchy of Hanover and succeeded to the throne of Great Britain in 1714; and, in

Der Graf von Hapsburg, in which the coronation feast of Rudolf is described:—

'Zu Aachen in seiner Kaiserpracht,
    Im alterthümlichen Saale,
Sass König Rudolphs heilige Macht
    Beim festlichen Krönungsmahle.
Die Speisen trug der Pfalzgraf des Rheins,
Es schenkte der Böhme des perlenden Weins,
    Und alle die Wähler, die sieben,
Wie der Sterne Chor um die Sonne sich stellt,
Umstanden geschäftig den Herrscher der Welt,
    Die Würde des Amtes zu üben.'

It is a poetical licence, however (as Schiller himself admits), to bring the Bohemian there, for King Ottocar was far away at home, mortified at his own rejection, and already meditating war.

A.D. 1708, the assent of the Diet thereto was obtained. It was in this way that English kings came again to vote, as Richard the First had voted five centuries before, at the election of a Roman Emperor.

It is not a little curious that the only potentate who continued down to our own days to entitle himself Elector should be one who never actually joined in electing an Emperor, having been under the arrangements of the old Empire a simple Landgrave.[a] In A.D. 1803, Napoleon, among other sweeping changes in the Germanic constitution, procured the extinction of the electorates of Cologne and Treves, annexing their territories to France, and gave the title of Elector, as the highest after that of king, to the Duke of Würtemberg, the Margrave of Baden, the Landgrave of Hessen-Cassel, and the Archbishop of Salzburg.[b] Three years afterwards the Empire itself ended, and the title became meaningless.

As the Germanic Empire is the most conspicuous example of a monarchy not hereditary that the modern world has seen, we may pause for a moment to consider what light its history throws upon the character of elective monarchy in general, a contrivance which has always had attractions for a certain class of political theorists.

[a] The electoral prince (Kurfürst) of Hessen-Cassel. His retention of the title had this advantage, that it enabled the Germans readily to distinguish electoral Hesse (Kur-Hessen) from the Grand Duchy (Hessen-Darmstadt) and the landgraviate (Hessen-Homburg). This last relic of the electoral system passed away in 1866, when the Elector of Hessen was dethroned, and his territories (to the satisfaction of the inhabitants, whom he had worried by a long course of petty tyrannies) annexed to the Prussian kingdom, along with Hanover, Nassau, and the free city of Frankfort.

[b] France having annexed the whole left bank of the Rhine, the archiepiscopal chair of Mainz was transferred to Regensburg. It was now the only spiritual electorate, for the archbishopric of Salzburg had been secularized for the benefit of the archduke Ferdinand of Austria, in order to compensate him for the loss of Tuscany.

Objects of an elective monarchy : how far attained in Germany.

Choice of the fittest.

First let it be observed how difficult, one might almost say impossible, it was found to maintain in practice the elective principle. In point of law, the imperial throne was from the tenth century to the nineteenth absolutely open to any orthodox Christian candidate. But as a matter of fact, the competition was confined to a few powerful families, and there was always a strong tendency for the crown to become hereditary in some one of these. Thus the Franconian Emperors held it from A.D. 1024 till 1125, the Hohenstaufen, themselves the heirs of the Franconians, for more than a century (1138–1254 with an interruption of fifteen years); the house of Luxemburg enjoyed it during four (though not continuous) reigns, and when in the fifteenth century it fell into the tenacious grasp of the Hapsburgs, they managed to retain it thenceforth (with but one trifling interruption) till it vanished out of nature altogether. Therefore the chief benefit which the scheme of elective sovereignty seems to promise, that of putting the fittest man in the highest place, was but seldom attained, and attained even then rather by good fortune than by design. Yet it is to be noted that every monarch from Henry the Fowler down to Charles IV, a space of four centuries, was a man of character and energy, who spent himself freely in the service of the State. Germany had no such ruler as England suffered from in John, or Edward II, or Richard II; nor was the average of capacity so high among the kings of France.

Restraint of the sovereign.

No similar objection can be brought against the second ground on which an elective system has sometimes been advocated, its operation in moderating the power of the crown, for this was attained in the fullest and most ruinous measure. We are reminded of the man in the fable, who opened a sluice to water his garden, and saw his house swept away by the furious torrent. The power of the crown was not moderated but destroyed. Each successful candidate was forced to purchase his title by the sacrifice of rights which had belonged to his predecessors, and must repeat the same shameful policy later in his reign to procure the election of his son. Feeling at the same time that his family could not make sure of keeping the throne, he treated it as a life-tenant is apt to treat his estate, seeking only to make out of it the largest present profit. And the electors, aware of the strength of their position, presumed upon it and abused it to assert an independence such as the nobles of other countries could never have aspired to.

Modern political speculation supposes the method of appointing a ruler by the votes of his subjects, as opposed to the system of hereditary succession, to be an assertion by the people of their own will as the ultimate fountain of authority, an acknowledgement by the prince that he is no more than their minister and deputy. To the theory of the Holy Empire nothing could be more repugnant. This will best appear when the aspect of the system of election at different epochs in its history is compared with the corresponding changes in the composition of the electoral body which have been described as in progress from the ninth to the fourteenth century. In very early days, the tribe chose a ruler, who was, though he usually belonged to the most noble family, little more than the first among his peers, with a power circumscribed by the will of his subjects. In the tenth and eleventh centuries, the right of choice had passed into the hands of the magnates, and the people were only asked to assent. In the same measure had the relation of prince and subject taken a new aspect. We must not expect to find, in such rude times, a clear apprehension of the technical quality of the elective process, and the throne had indeed become for a season so

Recognition of the popular will.

nearly hereditary that the election was often a mere matter of form. But it seems to have been regarded, not as a delegation of authority by the nobles and people, with a power of resumption implied, but rather as their subjection of themselves to the monarch who enjoys, as of his own right, a wide and ill-defined prerogative. In yet later times, when, as has been shewn above, the assembly of the chieftains and the applauding shout of the host had been superseded by the secret conclave of the seven electoral princes, the strict legal view of election became fully established, and no one was supposed to have any title to the crown except what a majority of votes might confer upon him. Meantime, however, the conception of the imperial office itself had been thoroughly permeated by religious ideas ; and the fact that the sovereign did not, like other princes, reign by hereditary right, but by the choice of certain persons, was supposed to be an enhancement

Conception of the electoral function. and consecration of his dignity. The electors, to draw what may seem a subtle, but is nevertheless a real distinction, selected, but did not create. They only named the person who was to receive what it was not theirs to give. God, say the mediaeval writers, not deigning to interfere visibly in the affairs of this world, has willed that these seven princes of Germany should discharge the function which once belonged to the senate and people of Rome, that of choosing His earthly viceroy in matters temporal. But it is immediately from Himself that the authority of this viceroy comes, and men can have towards him no relation except that of obedience. It was in this period, therefore, when the Emperor was in practice the mere nominee of the electors, that the belief in his divine right stood highest, to the exclusion either of the mutual responsibility of feudalism, or of any practically enforcible responsibility to the people.

Peace and order appeared to be promoted by the institutions of Charles IV, which removed one fruitful cause of civil war.   But these seven electoral princes acquired, with their extended privileges, a marked and dangerous predominance in Germany.   They had once already, in their famous meeting at Rhense[c] in 1338, acted as an independent body, repudiating in the name of the nation the extravagant claims of the Pope, and declaring that it was by their election alone that the Emperor acquired his rights.   The position which they had then assumed, in a heartily patriotic spirit, was now legalized and made permanent.   They became a separate order in the State, and were to enjoy full regalian rights in their territories.[d] Causes were not to be evoked from their courts, save when justice should have been denied: their consent was necessary to all public acts of consequence.   They claimed, as the choosers of the sovereign, to be the representatives of the ancient Roman Senate: and, since in the Middle Ages every institution must have its religious side, the persons of these senators were held to be sacred,

[c] See p. 225.   Rhense is a hamlet on the left bank of the Rhine, some four or five miles above Coblentz.   A little way north of it, and on the very shore, between the stream and the railway, stands, half hidden by walnut trees, the so-called Königsstuhl, a modern restoration of the building erected by Charles IV in 1376 for the meetings of the electors, who from long time past had been wont to assemble here.   It was the point where the territories of the four Rhenish electors touched one another.   Here several imperial elections were made: the last, Rupert's, in 1400.

[d] Goethe, whose imagination was wonderfully attracted by the splendours of the old Empire, has given in the second part of *Faust* a sort of fancy sketch of the origin of the great offices and the territorial independence of the German princes.   Two lines express concisely the fiscal rights granted by the Emperor to the electors : —

'Dann Steuer, Zins und Beed', Lehn und Geleit und Zoll,

Berg-, Salz- und Münz-regal euch angehören soll.'

Maximilian said of Charles IV : 'Carolo quarto pestilentior pestis nunquam alias contigit Germaniae.'

and the seven mystic luminaries of the Holy Empire, typified by the seven lamps of the Apocalypse, soon gained
much of the Emperor's hold on popular reverence, as well
as that actual power which he lacked.   To Charles, who
viewed the German Empire much as Rudolf had viewed
the Roman, this result came not unforeseen.   For him,
the old dreams of world dominion had become as remote
and obsolete as the dream of recovering Jerusalem.   With
few scruples, and little sense of what the honour of his
crown required, he was an astute and thoroughly practical
politician.   Nothing of the old chivalric spirit of his grandfather Henry appears in his character or his conduct.   He
saw in his office a means of serving personal ends, and
to them, while appearing to exalt by elaborate ceremonies its ideal dignity, he deliberately sacrificed what real
strength was left.   The object which he sought steadily
through life was the prosperity of the Bohemian kingdom,
and the advancement of his own house.   In the Golden
Bull, whose seal bears the legend —

'Roma caput mundi regit orbis frena rotundi' ^e —

there is not a word of Rome or of Italy.   To Germany
he was indirectly a benefactor, by the foundation of the
University of Prague,[f] the mother of all her schools:
otherwise her bane.   He legalized anarchy, and called it a
constitution.   The sums expended in obtaining the ratification of the Golden Bull, in procuring the election of his
son Wenzel, in aggrandizing Bohemia at the expense of
Germany, had been amassed by keeping a market in which
honours and exemptions, with what lands the crown retained, were put up openly to be bid for.   In Italy the

[e] This line is said to be as old as the time of Otto III.

[f] The University of Prague was founded in A.D. 1347, on the model of the
University of Paris, where Charles had himself studied.   After it came Vienna
(1365), Erfurt (1379), Heidelberg (1385–1386).

Ghibelines saw, with shame and rage, their chief hasten to Rome with a scanty retinue, and return from it as swiftly, at the mandate of an Avignonese Pope, leaving the city the very day on which he had been crowned, halting on his route only to traffic away the last rights of his Empire. The Guelf might cease to hate a power he could now despise.

Thus, alike at home and abroad, the German king had become practically powerless by the loss of his feudal privileges, and saw the authority that had once been his parcelled out among a crowd of rapacious nobles. Meantime how had it fared with the rights which he claimed by virtue of the imperial crown?

CHAPTER XV

THE EMPIRE AS AN INTERNATIONAL POWER

CHAP. XV.

Theory of the Roman Empire in the fourteenth and fifteenth centuries.

THAT the Roman Empire survived the seemingly mortal wound it had received at the era of the Great Interregnum, and continued to put forth pretensions which no one was likely to make good where the Hohenstaufen had failed, has been attributed to its identification with the German kingdom, in which some life was still left. But this was far from being the only cause which saved it from extinction. It had not ceased to be upheld in the fourteenth and fifteenth centuries by the same singular theory which had in the ninth and tenth been strong enough to re-establish it in the West. The character of that theory was indeed somewhat changed, for if not positively less religious, it was less exclusively so. In the days of Charles and Otto, the Empire, in so far as it was anything more than a tradition from times gone by, rested upon the belief that with the Visible Church there must be coextensive a single Christian state under one head and governor. But now that the Emperor's headship had been repudiated by the Pope, and his interference in matters of religion denounced as a repetition of the sin of Uzziah; now that the memory of mutual injuries had kindled an unquenchable hatred between the champions of the ecclesiastical and those of the civil power, it was natural that the latter, while they urged, fervently as ever, the divine sanction given to the imperial office, should at the same time be led to seek some further basis whereon to establish its claims. What that basis was, and how Chap. XV. they were guided to it, will best appear when a word or two has been said on the nature of the change that had passed on Europe in the course of the three preceding centuries, and the progress of the human mind during the same period.

Such has been the accumulated wealth of literature, and so rapid the advances of science among us since the close of the Middle Ages, that it is not now possible by any effort fully to enter into the feelings with which the relics of antiquity were regarded by those who saw in them their only possession. It is indeed true that modern art and literature and philosophy have been produced by the working of new minds upon old materials: that in thought, as in nature, we see no new creation. But with us the old has been transformed and overlaid by the new till its origin is forgotten: to them ancient books were the only standard of taste, the only vehicle of truth, the only stimulus to reflection. Hence it was that the most learned man was in those days esteemed the greatest: hence the creative energy of an age was exactly proportioned to its knowledge of and its reverence for the written monuments of those that had gone before. For until they can look forward, men must look back: till they should have reached the level of the old civilization, the nations of mediaeval Europe must continue to live upon its memories. Over them, as over us, the common dream of all mankind had power; but to them, as to the ancient world, that golden age which seems now to glimmer on the horizon of the future was shrouded in the clouds of the past. It is to the fifteenth and sixteenth centuries that we are accustomed to assign that new birth of the human spirit — if it ought not rather to be called a renewal of its strength and quickening of its sluggish life —

with which the modern time begins. And the date is well chosen, for it was then first that the transcendently powerful influence of Greek literature began to work upon the world. But it must not be forgotten that for a long time previous there had been in progress a great revival of learning, and still more of zeal for learning, which being caused by and directed towards the literature and institutions of Rome, might fitly be called the Roman or Latin Renaissance. The twelfth century saw this revival begin with that eager study of the legislation of Justinian, whose influence on the doctrines of imperial prerogative has been noticed already. The thirteenth witnessed the rapid spread of the scholastic philosophy, a body of systems most alien, both in subject and in method, to anything that had arisen among the ancients, yet one to whose developement Greek metaphysics and the theology of the Latin fathers had largely contributed, and the spirit of whose reasonings was far more free than the presumed orthodoxy of its conclusions suffered to appear. In the thirteenth and fourteenth centuries there arose in Italy the first great masters of painting and song; and the literature of the new languages, springing into the fulness of life in the *Divina Commedia*, adorned not long after by the names of Petrarch and Chaucer, assumed at once its place as a great and ever-growing power in the affairs of men.

Now, along with the literary revival, partly caused by, partly causing it, there had been also a wonderful stirring and uprising in the mind of Europe. The yoke of church authority still pressed heavily on the souls of men; yet some had been found to shake it off, and many more murmured in secret. The tendency was one which shewed itself in various and sometimes apparently opposite directions. The revolt of the Albigenses, the spread of the Cathari and other so-called heretics, the excitement created by the writings of Wiclif and Huss, witnessed to the fearlessness wherewith it could assail the dominant theology. It was present, however skilfully disguised, among those scholastic doctors who busied themselves with proving by natural reason the dogmas of the Church: for the power which can forge fetters can also break them. It took a form more dangerous because of a more direct application to facts, in the attacks, so often repeated from Arnold of Brescia downwards, upon the wealth and corruptions of the clergy, and above all of the papal court. For the agitation was not merely speculative. *Influence of* There was beginning to be a direct and rational interest *thought upon the arrange-* in life, a power of applying thought to practical ends, *ments of* which had not been seen before. Man's life among his *society.* fellows was no longer a mere wild beast struggle; man's soul no more, as it had been, the victim of ungoverned passion, whether it was awed by supernatural terrors or captivated by examples of surpassing holiness. Manners were still rude, and governments unsettled; but society was learning to organize itself upon fixed principles; to recognize, however faintly, the value of order, industry, equality; to adapt means to ends, and conceive of the common good as the proper end of its own existence. In a word, Politics had begun to exist, and with them there had appeared the first of a class of persons whom friends and enemies may both, though with different meanings, call ideal politicians; men who, however various have been the doctrines they have held, however impracticable many of the plans they have advanced, have been nevertheless alike in their devotion to the highest interests of humanity, and have frequently been derided as theorists in their own age to be honoured as the prophets and teachers of the next.

CHAP. XV.

*Separation of
the peoples of
Europe into
hostile king-
doms : conse-
quent need of
an interna-
tional power.*

Now it was towards the Roman Empire that the hopes and sympathies of these political speculators as well as of the jurists and poets of the fourteenth and fifteenth centuries were constantly directed. The cause may be gathered from the circumstances of the time. The most remarkable event in the history of the last three hundred years had been the formation of nationalities, each distinguished by a peculiar language and character, and by steadily increasing differences of habits and institutions. And as upon this national basis there had been in most cases established strong monarchies, Europe was broken up into disconnected bodies, and the cherished scheme of a united Christian state appeared less likely than ever to be realized. Nor was this all. Sometimes through race-antagonism, more often by the jealousy and ambition of their sovereigns, these countries were constantly involved in war with one another, violating on a larger scale, and with scarcely less destructive results than in time past, the peace of the religious community ; while each of them was at the same time torn within by frequent insurrections, and desolated by long and bloody civil wars. The new nationalities were too fully formed to allow the hope that by their extinction a remedy might be applied to these evils. They had grown up in spite of the Empire and the Church, and were not likely to yield in their strength what they had won in their weakness. But it still appeared possible to soften, if not to overcome, their antagonism. What might not be looked for from the erection of a presiding power common to all Europe, a power which, while it should oversee the internal concerns of each country, not dethroning the king, but treating him as an hereditary viceroy, should be more especially charged to prevent strife between kingdoms, and to maintain the public order of Europe by being not only the fountain of international law, but also the judge in its causes and the enforcer of its sentences?

To such a position had the Popes aspired. They were indeed excellently fitted for it by the respect which the sacredness of their office commanded; by their control of the tremendous weapons of excommunication and interdict; above all, by their exemption, as the heads of an order which belonged to no one nation, from those narrowing influences of place, or blood, or personal interest, which it would be their chiefest duty to resist in others. And there had been pontiffs whose fearlessness and justice were worthy of their exalted office, and whose intervention was gratefully remembered by those who found no other helpers. Nevertheless, judging the Papacy by its conduct as a whole, it had been tried and found wanting. Even when its throne stood firmest and its purposes were most pure, one motive had always biassed its decisions — a partiality to the most submissive. During the greater part of the fourteenth century it was at Avignon the willing tool of the French kings; in the pursuit of a temporal principality it had mingled in and been contaminated by the unhallowed politics of Italy; its supreme council, the college of cardinals, was distracted by the intrigues of two bitterly hostile factions. And while the power of the Popes had declined steadily, though silently, since the days of Boniface the Eighth, the arrogance of the great prelates and the vices of the inferior clergy had provoked throughout Western Christendom a reaction against the pretensions of all sacerdotal authority. As there is no theory at first sight more attractive than that which entrusts all government to a supreme spiritual power, which, knowing what is best for man, shall lead him to his true good by appealing to the highest principles of his nature, so there is no disappointment more bitter than that of those who find that the holiest office may be polluted by the lusts and passions of its holder ; that craft and hypocrisy lead while fanaticism follows ; that here too, as in so much else, the corruption of the best is worst. Some such disappointment there was in Europe now, and with it a certain disposition to look with favour on the secular power : a wish to escape from the unhealthy atmosphere of clerical despotism to the rule of positive law, harsher, it might be, yet surely less corrupting. Espousing the cause of the Roman Empire as the chief opponent of priestly claims, this tendency found it, with shrunken territory and diminished resources, fitter in some respects for the office of an international judge and mediator than it had been as a great national power. For though far less widely active, it was losing that local character which was fast gathering round the Papacy. With feudal rights no longer enforcible, and removed, except in his patrimonial lands, from direct contact with the subject, the Emperor was not, as heretofore, conspicuously a German and a feudal king, and occupied an ideal position less marred by the incongruous accidents of birth and training, of national and dynastic interests.

Duties attributed to the Empire.   To that position three cardinal duties were attached. He who held it must typify spiritual unity, must preserve peace, must be a fountain of that by which alone among imperfect men peace is preserved and restored, law and justice. The first of these three objects was sought not only on religious grounds, but also from that longing for a wider brotherhood of humanity towards which, ever since the barrier between Jew and Gentile, Greek and barbarian, was broken down, the aspirations of the higher minds of the world have been constantly directed. Placed in the midst of Europe, the Emperor was to bind its races into, one body, reminding them of their common faith, their common blood, their common interest in each other's welfare. And he was therefore above all things, claiming indeed to be upon earth the representative of the Prince of Peace, bound to listen to complaints, and to redress the injuries inflicted by sovereigns or peoples upon each other; to punish offenders against the public order of Christendom; to maintain through the world, looking down as from a serene height upon the schemes and quarrels of meaner potentates, that supreme good without which neither arts nor letters, nor the gentler virtues of life, can rise and flourish. The mediaeval Empire was in its essence what its modern imitators have sometimes professed themselves: the Empire was Peace: the oldest and noblest title of its head was 'Imperator pacificus.'[a] And that he might be the peacemaker, he must be the expounder of justice and the author of its concrete embodiment, positive law; chief legislator and supreme judge of appeal, like his predecessor

[a] The archbishop of Mentz addresses Conrad II on his election thus: 'Deus quum a te multa requirat tum hoc potissimum desiderat ut facias iudicium et iustitiam et pacem patriae quae respicit ad te, ut sis defensor ecclesiarum et clericorum, tutor viduarum et orphanorum.' — Wippo, Vita Chuonradi, c. 3 (*M. G. H.*, *Script.* xi. p. 260). So Pope Urban IV writes to Richard: 'Ut Imperii Romani fastigium et eius culmen praesidens specialis advocati et defensoris praecipui circa ecclesiam gerat officium et . . . inimicis consternatis eiusdem in pacis pulchritudine sedeat populus Christianus et requie opulenta quiescat.' — Raynald. *Ann. Eccl.*, ad ann. 1263.

Compare also the 'Edictum de crimine laesae maiestatis' issued by Henry VII in Italy: 'Ad reprimenda multorum facinora qui ruptis totius debitae fidelitatis habenis adversus Romanum imperium, in cuius tranquillitate totius orbis regularitas requiescit, hostili animo armati conentur nedum humana, verum etiam divina praecepta, quibus iubetur quod omnis anima Romanorum principi sit subiecta, scelestissimis facinoribus et rebellionibus demoliri,' &c. — Pertz, *M. G. H.*, *Legg.* ii. p. 544.

See also a curious passage in the Life of St. Adalbert, describing the beginning of the reign at Rome of the Emperor Otto III, and his cousin and nominee Pope Gregory V: 'Laetantur cum primatibus minores civitatis: cum afflicto paupere exultant agmina viduarum, quia novus imperator dat iura populis; dat iura novus papa' (*M. G. H.*, *Script.* iv. p. 591).

the compiler of the *Corpus Iuris*, the one and only source
of all legitimate authority. In this sense, as governor
and administrator, not as owner, is he, in the words of the
jurists, Lord of the world [b]; not that its soil belongs to him
in the same sense in which the soil of France or England
belongs to their respective kings: he is the steward of
Him who has received the nations for His inheritance and
the uttermost parts of the earth for His possession. It is,
therefore, by him alone that the idea of pure right, acquired
not by force but by legitimate devolution from those whom
God Himself had set up, is visibly expressed upon earth.
To find an external and positive basis for that idea is a
problem which it has at all times been more easy to evade
than to solve, and one peculiarly distressing to those who
could neither explain the phenomena of society by reducing it to its original principles, nor inquire historically
Divine right how its existing arrangements had grown up. Hence the
of the attempt to represent human government as an emanation
Emperor. from divine: a view from which all the similar but less
logically consistent doctrines of divine right that have prevailed in later times are borrowed.

From the struggle of the Investitures onwards there had
been much debate as to the source of civil authority. One
theory sought it in the Visible Church. Christ had committed power to Peter: Peter had transmitted it to his
successors: it was from those successors that the Emperor
must obtain it. The other theory based itself on history
and on law. God's providence had conferred the rule of
the world upon the Roman people; and the Roman people
had delegated their power to Augustus and his successors,
for had it not been written, 'Populus ei (*sc.* Principi Romano) et in eum omne suum imperium et protestatem
concessit'? [c] Nor did this view fail to reinforce itself by

[b] See p. 194, *ante*.　　　[c] *Inst. Iust.* i. 2. 6 ; cf. *Dig.* i. 4. 1.

the appeal to the passages of Scripture which enjoin obedience to the powers that be, because they are ordained of
God.[d] Some thinkers conceived the delegation by the
people to the Emperor to have been final and irrevocable.
Some held it compatible with a fresh action by the people,
and pointed out that when the Empire was transferred
from the Easterns to the Franks by the election of Charles
the Great, Rome (or the West generally) had resumed its
ancient rights, and the Pope did no more than act as the
spokesman of the people. Some, again, went so far as to
argue that an Emperor who palpably transgressed the Law
of Nature — it was agreed that both Emperor and Pope
were subject to the Law of Nature, which was practically
the Law of God — might be deposed by his subjects. An
avowed heretic, for instance, could not demand obedience ;
indeed, an heretical or, let us say, anti-Christian Emperor
like Julian would be a contradiction in terms. It was even
held by some that not only the right of election, but also
supreme legislative power, remained always in the people,
though no one could say how the people were to exercise
it, for there were no organs for popular legislation. A further and indeed an insoluble question was : Who were the
people ? The followers of Arnold of Brescia saw in the
inhabitants of Rome the same *populus Romanus* which had
of old exerted universal dominion. But such a claim was
too bold even for the Middle Ages, and the better accepted
view understood by ʻthe peopleʼ either the whole of the
Emperor's actual subjects (*totus populus imperio Romano
subiectus* [e]), or all Christians, or mankind as a whole,[f]

[d] See esp. Romans xiii. 1–5 ; 1 Peter ii. 13–15.

[e] Lupold of Bebenburg, *De Iure Regni et Imperii Romani*, cc. 12 and 17;
and so William of Ockham, *Octo Quaestiones.*

[f] Cf. Ockham, *Octo Quaestiones* (quoted by Gierke, *Iohannes Althusius*),
p. 85, note 30.

i.e. all nations, acting, as Ockham suggests, by a majority. Widely as opinions differed upon these matters there was on two points a general agreement. Power originally belonged to the people, and was conferred by them upon the Emperor. Even St. Thomas of Aquinum recognizes this, though some later writers held that Christ when He came took all power to Himself and bestowed it upon Peter. This doctrine of popular sovereignty, partly founded on the *Politics* of Aristotle, embodied ideas that belonged to Greek republican theory as well as traditions that had descended from Roman republican law. It contained, in germ,[g] the principles of the English, American, and French revolutions : it is one of the most curious links between the ancient and the modern world. The other point touched the nature of the power which the Emperor exercised. Being exercised under direct responsibility to God that power came from God, though it had come through the gift of the people. It was all the more conformable to divine and natural law because it did not pass by descent, but was conferred by electors who, like the cardinals when choosing a Pope, were only instruments in the hand of God, their function having been entrusted to them by God and the people.[h] Being thus derived from the Law of God and of Nature, the rights of the Emperor are eternal

[g] See on this subject Gierke, *ut supra*, chap. iii.

[h] 'Populus Romanus habet potestatem eligendi imperatorem per ipsum ius divinum et naturale . . . unde electores qui communi consensu omnium Alemannorum et aliorum qui imperatori subiecti erant tempore Henrici II constituti sunt, radicalem vim habent ab ipso omnium consensu, qui sibi naturali iure imperatorem constituere poterant.' — Nicholas of Cues (afterwards Cardinal), *De Concordantia Catholica*, iii. c. 4, ap. Schard. *Syntagma*, p. 360.

The views of the anti-Papal writers in and after the time of Lewis IV are usually tinged by their wish to find a remedy for the evils of papal autocracy in a General Council which it would be the function of the Emperor to convoke. Their eyes are fixed quite as much on the needs of the Church herself as on the constitutional rights of the Empire against the Papacy.

and imprescriptible. They exist irrespective of their actual exercise, and no voluntary abandonment, not even an express grant, can impair them. Pope Boniface the Eighth[1] reminds the king of France, and imperialist lawyers till the seventeenth century repeated the claim, that he, like other princes, is of right and must ever remain subject to the Roman Emperor. And the sovereigns of Europe long continued to address the Emperor in language, and yield to him a precedence, which admitted the inferiority of their own position.[j]

It is easy to see how it was to the Roman Emperor, and to him only, that the international duties and privileges above mentioned could be attributed. Being Roman, he was of no nation, and therefore fittest to judge between contending states, and appease the animosities of race. His was the imperial tongue of Rome, not only the vehicle of religion and law, but also, since no other was understood everywhere in Europe, the necessary medium of diplomatic

Roman Empire, why an international power.

[1] 'Vicarius Iesu Christi et successor Petri transtulit potestatem imperii a Graecis in Germanos ut ipsi Germani . . . possint eligere regem Romanorum qui est promovendus in Imperatorem et monarcham omnium regum et principum terrenorum. Nec insurgat superbia Gallicorum quae dicat quod non recognoscit superiorem: mentiuntur, quia de iure sunt et esse debent sub rege Romanorum et Imperatore.' — Speech of Boniface VIII, April 30, 1303 (Pfeffinger, *Corp. iur. publ.* i. 377). It is curious to compare with this the words addressed nearly five centuries earlier by Pope John VIII to Lewis, king of Bavaria: 'Si sumpseritis Romanum imperium, omnia regna vobis subiecta existent.' — Jaffé, *Reg. Pont.* p. 281.

[j] So Alfonso, king of Naples, writes to Frederick III: 'Nos reges omnes debemus reverentiam Imperatori, tanquam summo regi, qui est Caput et Dux regum.' — Quoted by Pfeffinger, i. 379. And Francis I (of France), speaking of a proposed combined expedition against the Turks, says, 'Caesari nihilominus principem ea in expeditione locum non gravarer ex officio cedere.' — Marquard Freher, *Script. rer. Germ.* iii. 425. For a long time no European sovereign save the Emperor ventured to use the title of 'Majesty.' The imperial chancery conceded it in 1633 to the kings of England and Sweden; in 1641 to the king of France. Zedler, *Universal Lexicon, s. v.* Majestät.

intercourse. As there was no Church but the Holy Roman Church, and he its temporal head, it was by him that the communion of the saints in its outward form and on its secular side was represented, and to his keeping that the sanctity of peace must be entrusted. As direct heir of those who from Julius to Justinian had shaped the legal principles generally recognized through Europe,[k] he was, so to speak, legality personified (*animata lex in terris*); the only sovereign on earth who, being possessed of power by an unimpeachable title, could by his grant confer upon others rights equally valid. And as he claimed to perpetuate the greatest political system the world had known, a system which still moves the wonder of those who see before their eyes empires as much wider than the Roman as they are less symmetrical, and whose vast and complex machinery far surpassed anything the fourteenth century possessed or could hope to establish, it was not strange that he and his government (assuming them to receive the obedience to which they were entitled) should be taken as the ideal of a perfect monarch and a perfect state.

There was in this theory nothing that was absurd, though much that was impracticable. The ideas on which it rested are still unapproached in grandeur and simplicity, still as far in advance of the average thought of Europe, and as unlikely to find men or nations fit to apply them, as when they were promulgated five hundred years ago. The practical evil which the establishment of such a universal monarchy was intended to meet, that of wars and hardly less ruinous preparations for war between the states of Europe, remains what it was then. The remedy

---

[k] With the progress of society and the growth of commerce the local customs were, through the greater part of Western and Central Europe, beginning either to give way to or to be remodelled and supplemented by the Civil Law.

which mediaeval theory proposed has been in some
measure applied by the construction and reception of the
rules we call international law; the greater difficulty of
erecting a tribunal which can decide with the power of
enforcing its decisions, remains unsolved.[1]

Of the many applications and illustrations of these
doctrines which mediaeval documents furnish, it will
suffice to adduce two or three. No imperial privilege was
prized more highly than the power of creating kings, for
there was none which raised the Emperor so much above the
rulers of the various nations. In this, as in other international concerns, the Pope soon began to claim a jurisdiction,
at first concurrent, then separate and independent. But
the older and more consistent view assigned it, as flowing
from the possession of supreme secular authority, to the
Emperor; and it was from him that the rulers of Burgundy,
Bohemia, Hungary, apparently Poland also, received the
regal title.[m] The prerogative was his in the same manner
in which that of conferring titles is still held to belong to
the sovereign in every modern kingdom. And so when
Charles the Bold, last duke of French Burgundy, proposed

Illustrations

Right of creating kings.

[1] The recently created Hague Tribunal can render decisions in cases submitted to it, but cannot enforce its judgements.

[m] Thus we are told of the Emperor Charles the Bald, that he confirmed the
election of Boso, king of Burgundy and Provence, 'Dedit Bosoni Provinciam
(*sc.* Carolus Calvus), et corona in vertice capitis imposita, eum regem appel-
lari iussit, ut more priscorum imperatorum regibus videretur dominari.' —
Regin. *Chron.*, ad ann. 877 (*M. G. H., Script.* i. p. 589). This statement is
in fact incorrect, but it evidences the views of the time. Frederick II made
his son Enzio (that famous Enzio whose romantic history every one who has
seen Bologna will remember) king of Sardinia, and also erected the duchy
of Austria into a kingdom, although for some reason the title seems never
to have been used; and Lewis IV gave to Humbert of Dauphiné the title
of king of Vienne, A.D. 1336. Otto III is said to have conferred the title
of king on Boleslas of Poland, and when the Elector Frederick of Brandenburg sought to make himself king of Prussia in A.D. 1700, he was obliged to
obtain the Emperor's consent.

to turn his wide and populous dominions into a kingdom, it was from Frederick III that he sought permission to do so. The Emperor, however, was greedy and suspicious, the duke uncompliant; and when Frederick found that terms could not be arranged between them, he stole away suddenly, and left Charles to carry back, with ill-concealed mortification, the crown and sceptre which he had brought ready-made to the place of interview.[n]

Chivalry.   In the same manner, as representing what was common to and valid throughout all Europe, nobility, and more particularly knighthood, centred in the Empire. The great Orders of Chivalry were international institutions, whose members, having consecrated themselves a military priesthood, had no longer any country of their own, and could therefore be subject to no one save the Emperor and the Pope. For knighthood was constructed on the analogy of priesthood, and knights were conceived as being to the world in its secular aspect exactly what priests, and more especially the monastic orders, were to it in its religious aspect: to the one body was given the sword of the flesh, to the other the sword of the spirit; each was universal, each had its autocratic head.[o] Singularly, too, were these

[n] The duke of Lithuania is said to have treated with Sigismund for the bestowal on him of the title of king. — Cf. Pfeffinger, *Corp. Iur. Publ.* i. 424.

Henry VIII of England when he rebelled against the Pope called himself king of Ireland (his predecessors had used only the title 'Dominus Hiberniae') without asking the Emperor's permission, in order to shew that he repudiated the temporal as well as the spiritual dominion of Rome. The Act 24 Hen. VIII, cap. 12 (Statute of Appeals) is said to be designed 'to keep the imperiall crown of this realm from the anoyaunce as well of the See of Rome as from the auctoritie of other foreyne potentates attempting the diminution or violacion thereof.' These 'other foreyne potentates' are probably the Emperors.

[o] It is probably for this reason that the *Ordo Romanus* directs the Emperor and Empress to be crowned (in St. Peter's) at the altar of St. Maurice, the patron saint of knighthood.

notions brought into harmony with the feudal polity. Caesar was lord paramount of the world : its countries great fiefs, whose kings were his tenants in chief, the suitors of his court, owing to him homage, fealty, and military service against the infidel.

One illustration more of the way in which the Empire was held to be something of and for all mankind cannot be omitted. Although from the practical union of the imperial with the German throne none but Germans were latterly chosen to fill it,[p] it remained in point of law absolutely free from all restrictions of country or birth. In an age of the most intense aristocratic exclusiveness, the highest office in the world was the only secular one open to all Christians. The old writers, after debating at length the qualifications that are or may be desirable in an Emperor, and relating how in pagan times Gauls and Spaniards, Moors and Pannonians, were thought worthy of the purple, decide that two things, and no more, are required of the candidate for Empire : he must be free-born, and he must be orthodox.[q]

Persons eligible as Emperors.

It is not altogether easy to estimate the respective influence exerted by each of the three revivals which I have attempted to distinguish. The spirit of the ancient world

The Empire and the New Learning.

[p] See especially Gerlach Buxtorff, *Dissertatio ad Auream Bullam;* and Augustinus Stenchus, *De Imperio Romano;* quoted by Marquard Freher. It was keenly debated, while Charles V and Francis I (of France) were rival candidates, whether any one but a German was eligible. By birth Charles was either a Spaniard or a Fleming; but this difficulty his partisans avoided by holding that he had been, according to the civil law, *in potestate* of Maximilian his grandfather. However, to say nothing of the Guidos and Berengars of earlier days, the examples of Richard and Alfonso are conclusive as to the eligibility of others than Germans. Edward III of England was, as has been said, actually elected; Henry VIII of England was a candidate. And attempts were frequently made to elect the kings of France. — Cf. Pfeffinger, *Vitriarius illustratus*, pp. 69 sqq.

[q] See Note XV at end.

by which the men who led these movements fancied themselves animated, was in truth a pagan, or at least a strongly secular spirit, in many respects inconsistent with the associations which had now gathered round the imperial office. And this hostility did not fail to shew itself when at the beginning of the sixteenth century, in the fulness of the Renaissance, a direct and for the time irresistible sway was exercised by the art and literature of Greece, when the mythology of Euripides and Ovid supplanted that which had fired the imagination of Dante and peopled the visions of St. Francis; when men forsook the image of the saint in the cathedral for the statue of the nymph in the garden; when the uncouth jargon of scholastic theology was equally distasteful to the scholars who formed their style upon Cicero and to the philosophers who drew their inspiration from Plato. That meanwhile the admirers of antiquity did ally themselves with the defenders of the Empire, was due partly indeed to the false notions that were entertained regarding the early Caesars, yet still more to the common hostility of both schools to the Papacy. It was as successor of Old Rome, and by virtue of her traditions, that the Holy See had established so wide a dominion; yet no sooner did Arnold of Brescia and his followers begin to claim liberty in the name of the ancient constitution of the Roman city, than they found in the Popes their bitterest foes, and turned for help to the secular monarch against the clergy. With similar aversion did the Papal Curia view the revived study of the ancient jurisprudence, so soon as it became, in the hands of the school of Bologna and afterwards of the jurists of France, a power able to assert its independence and resist ecclesiastical pretensions. In the ninth century, Pope Nicholas the First had himself judged in the famous case of Teutberga, wife of Lothar, according to the civil law: in the thirteenth, his successors [r] forbade its study, and the canonists strove to expel it from Europe.[s] And as the current of educated opinion among the laity was beginning, however imperceptibly at first, to set against sacerdotal tyranny, it followed that the Empire would find sympathy in any effort it could make to regain its lost position. Thus the Emperors became, or might have become had they seen the greatness of the opportunity and been strong enough to improve it, the exponents and guides of the political movement, the pioneers, in secular matters at least, of the Reformation. But the revival came too late to arrest, if not to adorn, the decline of their office. The growth of a national sentiment in the several countries of Europe, which had already gone too far to be arrested, and was urged on by forces far stronger than the theories of Catholic unity which opposed it, imprinted on the resistance to papal usurpation, and even on the instincts of political freedom, that form of narrowly local patriotism which they long retained and have not yet wholly lost. It can hardly be said that upon any occasion, except the gathering of the Council of Constance by Sigismund, did the Emperor appear filling a truly international place. For the most part he exerted in the politics of Europe an influence little greater than that of other princes. In actual resources he stood below the kings of France and England, far below his vassals the Visconti of Milan.[t] Yet this helplessness, such was men's

The doctrine of the Empire's rights and functions never carried out in fact.

[r] Honorius II in 1229 forbade it to be studied or taught in the University of Paris. Innocent IV published some years later a still more sweeping prohibition.

[s] See Savigny, *Geschichte des römischen Rechts im Mittelalter*, vol. iii. pp. 81, 341-347.

[t] Gian Galeazzo Visconti overcame Rupert in 1401. Charles the Bold of Burgundy was a potentate incomparably stronger than the Emperor Frederick III from whom he sought the regal title.

faith or their timidity, and such their unwillingness to make prejudice bend to facts, did not prevent his dignity from being extolled in the most sonorous language by writers whose imaginations were enthralled by the halo of traditional glory which surrounded him.

We are thus brought back to ask, What was the connection between imperialism and the literary revival?

Attitude of the men of letters.

To moderns who think of the Roman Empire as the heathen persecuting power, it is strange to find it depicted as the model of a Christian commonwealth. It may seem stranger still that the study of antiquity should have made men advocates of arbitrary power. Democratic Athens, oligarchic Rome, suggest to us Pericles and Brutus : the moderns who have striven to apply the spirit of antiquity to politics have been men like Algernon Sidney, and Vergniaud, and Shelley. The explanation is the same in both cases.[u] The ancient world was known to the earlier Middle Ages by tradition, freshest for what was latest, and by the authors of the old Empire. Both presented to them the picture of a mighty despotism and a civilization brilliant far beyond their own. Writings of the fourth and fifth centuries, unfamiliar to us, were to them authorities as high as Livy or Tacitus ; yet Virgil and Horace too had sung the praises of the first and wisest of the Emperors. To the enthusiasts of poetry and law, Rome meant universal monarchy ;[x] to those of religion, her name called up the undimmed radiance of the Church under Sylvester and Constantine. Petrarch, the apostle of the dawning Renaissance, is excited by the least attempt to revive even the shadow of imperial greatness : as he had hailed Cola di Rienzo, he welcomes Charles IV into Italy, and execrates his departure. The following passage is

Petrarch.

[u] Cf. Sismondi, *Républiques italiennes*, iv. chap. xxvii.
[x] As to Justinian, see Dante, *Paradiso*, canto vi.

taken from his letter to the Roman people asking them to receive back Rienzo :—'When was there ever such peace, such tranquillity, such justice, such honour paid to virtue, such rewards distributed to the good and punishments to the bad, when was ever the state so wisely guided, as in the time when the world had obtained one head, and that head Rome; the very time wherein God deigned to be born of a virgin and dwell upon earth. To every single body there has been given a head; the whole world therefore also, which is called by the poet a great body, ought to be content with one temporal head. For every two-headed animal is monstrous; how much more horrible and hideous a portent must be a creature with a thousand different heads, biting and fighting against one another! If, however, it is necessary that there be more heads than one, it is nevertheless evident that there ought to be one to restrain all and preside over all, that so the peace of the whole body may abide unshaken. Assuredly both in heaven and in earth the sovereignty of one has always been best.'

His passion for the heroism of Roman conquest and the ordered peace to which it brought the world, is the centre of Dante's political hopes: he is no more a Ghibeline embittered by exile, but a patriot whose fervid imagination sees a nation arise regenerate at the touch of its rightful lord. Italy, the spoil of so many Teutonic conquerors, is the garden of the Empire which Henry is to redeem: Rome the mourning widow, whom Albert is denounced for neglecting.[y] Passing through Purgatory, the poet sees Rudolf of Hapsburg seated gloomily apart, mourn-

---

[y] 'Vieni a veder la tua Roma, che piagne
    Vedova, sola, e dì e notte chiama:
    "Cesare mio, perchè non m' accompagne?"'
            Purgatorio, canto vi. 112.

ing his sin in that he left unhealed the wounds of Italy.[z] In the deepest pit of Hell's ninth circle lies Lucifer, huge, three-headed; in each mouth a sinner whom he crunches between his teeth, in one mouth Iscariot the traitor to Christ, in the others the two traitors to the first Emperor of Rome, Brutus and Cassius.[a] To multiply illustrations from other parts of the poem would be an endless task; for the idea is ever present in Dante's mind, and displays itself in a hundred unexpected forms.[b] Virgil himself is selected to be the guide of the pilgrim through hell and Purgatory, not so much as being the great poet of antiquity, as because he 'was born under Julius and lived beneath the good Augustus,' because he was divinely charged to sing of the Empire's earliest and brightest glories. Strange, that the shame of one age should be the glory of another. For Virgil's melancholy panegyrics upon the destroyer of the republic are no more like Dante's appeals to the coming saviour of Italy than is Caesar Octavianus to Henry count of Luxemburg.

Attitude of the Jurists. The visionary zeal of the man of letters was seconded by the more sober devotion of the lawyer. Conqueror, theologian, and jurist, Justinian is a hero greater than either Julius or Constantine, for his enduring work bears him witness. Absolutism was the civilian's creed:[c] the phrases 'legibus solutus,' 'lex regia,' whatever else tended in the same direction, were taken to express the prerogative of him whose official style of Augustus, as well as the vernacular name of 'Kaiser,' designated the legitimate

---

[z] *Purgatorio*, canto vii. 94.   [a] *Inferno*, canto xxxiv. 52.

[b] See especially the long passage on the Roman Eagle in *Parad.* xviii, xix, and xx.

[c] Not that the doctors of the civil law were necessarily political partisans of the Emperors. Savigny says that there were on the contrary more Guelfs than Ghibelines among the jurists of Bologna. — *Geschichte des röm. Rechts im Mittelalter*, vol. iii. p. 80.

successor of the compiler of the *Corpus Iuris*. Since it
was upon this legitimacy that his claim to be the fountain
of law rested, no pains were spared to seek out and
observe every custom and precedent by which Old Rome
seemed to be connected with her representative.

Of the many instances that might be collected, it would
be tedious to enumerate more than a few. The offices
of the imperial household, instituted by Constantine the
Great, were attached to the noblest families of Germany.
The Emperor and Empress, before their coronation at
Rome, were lodged in the chambers called those of
Augustus and Livia;[d] a bare sword was borne before
them by the praetorian prefect; their processions were
adorned by the standards — eagles, wolves, and dragons,
which had figured in the train of Hadrian or Theodosius.[e]
The constant title of the Emperor himself, according to
the style introduced by Probus, was 'semper Augustus,'
or 'perpetuus Augustus,' which erring etymology translated
'at all times increaser of the Empire.'[f] Edicts issued by
a Franconian or Swabian sovereign were inserted as
Novels[g] in the *Corpus Iuris*, in the latest editions of
which custom still allows them a place. The *pontificatus
maximus* of his pagan predecessors was supposed to be
preserved by the admission of each Emperor as a canon
of St. Peter's at Rome and St. Mary's at Aachen.[h] Some-

Imitations of Old Rome.

[d] Cf. Palgrave, *Normandy and England*, vol. ii (of Otto and Adelheid).
The *Ordo Romanus* talks of a 'Camera Iuliae' in the Lateran palace, reserved
for the Empress.

[e] See notes to *Chron. Casin.* in Muratori, *S. R. I.* iv. 515.

[f] 'Zu aller Zeiten Mehrer des Reichs.'

[g] *Novellae Constitutiones.*

[h] Marquard Freher, *Scr. Rer. Germ.* iii. The question whether the seven
electors vote as *singuli* or as a *collegium*, is solved by shewing that they have
stepped into the place of the senate and people of Rome, whose duty it was
to choose the Emperor, though (it is naïvely added) the soldiers sometimes
usurped it. — Peter de Andlau, *De Imperio Romano.*

times we even find him talking of his consulship.[1] Annalists usually number the place of each sovereign from
Augustus downwards.[j] The notion of an uninterrupted
succession, which moves the stranger's wondering smile
as he sees ranged round the magnificent Golden Hall of
Augsburg the portraits of the Caesars, laurelled, helmeted,
and periwigged, from Julius the conqueror of Gaul to
Joseph the partitioner of Poland, was to those generations not an article of faith only because its denial was
inconceivable.

*Reverence for
ancient forms
and phrases
in the Middle
Ages.*
And all this historical antiquarianism, as one might call
it, which gathers round the Empire, is but one instance,
though the most striking, of that eager wish to cling to
the old forms, use the old phrases, and preserve the old
institutions to which the annals of mediaeval Europe bear
witness. It appears even in trivial expressions, as when
a monkish chronicler says of evil bishops deposed, *Tribu
moti sunt*, or talks of the 'senate and people of the
Franks,' when he means a council of chiefs surrounded
by a crowd of half-naked warriors. A certain continuity
of institutions there had really been. One may say, for
instance, that the mediaeval trade-guilds, though often
traceable to a different source, represented the old
collegia, and that villenage was not unconnected with the
system of *coloni* under the later Empire. But the men
of the Middle Ages were not thinking of such cases when
they reproduced the old phrases in drawing up edicts
and charters on Roman precedents. They imitated for

[i] Thus Charles, in a capitulary added to a revised edition of the Lombard
law issued in A.D. 801, says, 'Anno consulatus nostri primo.' — *M. G. H.*, *Legg.*
i. p. 83. So Otto III calls himself 'Consul Senatus populique Romani.'

[j] Francis II, the last Emperor, was one hundred and twentieth (or one
hundred and twenty-second) from Augustus. Some chroniclers call Otto the
Great Otto II, counting in Salvius Otho, the successor of Galba.

the love of imitating, and liked to fancy themselves to be Chap. XV
the heirs of an old order which had never quite vanished.
Even in remote Britain, the Teutonic invaders used after a
time Roman ensigns, and stamped their coins with Roman
devices; called themselves 'Basileis' and 'Augusti.' Especially did the cities perpetuate Rome through her most
lasting boon to the conquered, municipal self-government;
those of later origin emulating in their adherence to
antique style others which, like Nismes and Cologne,
Zürich and Augsburg, could trace back their institutions
to the *coloniae* and *municipia* of the first centuries. On
the walls and gates of hoary Nürnberg the traveller still
sees emblazoned the imperial eagle, with the words
'Senatus populusque Norimbergensis,' and is borne in
thought from the quiet provincial town of to-day to the
stirring republic of the fourteenth century: thence to the
Forum and the Capitol of her greater prototype.[k] For, in
truth, through all that period which we call the Dark and
Middle Ages, men's minds were possessed by the belief
that all things continued as they were from the beginning,
that no chasm never to be recrossed lay between them
and that ancient world to which they had not ceased to
look back. We who are centuries removed can see that
there had passed a great and wonderful change upon
thought, and art, and literature, and politics, and society
itself: a change whose best illustration is to be found in
the process whereby there arose out of the primitive
basilica the Romanesque cathedral, and from it in turn
the endless varieties of Gothic. But so gradual was the

---

[k] Nürnberg herself was not of Roman foundation. But this makes the
imitation all the more curious. [She is no longer (1904) a quiet town as
when the lines in the text were written forty years ago.] The fashion even
passed from the cities to rural communities like some of the Swiss cantons,
e.g. 'Senatus populusque Uronensis.'

change that each generation felt it passing over them no more than a man feels that perpetual transformation by which his body is renewed from year to year; while the few who had learning enough to study antiquity through its contemporary records were prevented, by the utter want of criticism and of what we call historical feeling, from seeing how prodigious was the contrast between themselves and those whom they admired. There is nothing more modern than the critical spirit which fastens upon the differences between the minds of men in one age and in another; which endeavours to make each age its own interpreter, and judge what it did or produced by a relative standard. Such a spirit was, before the last two or three centuries, foreign to art as well as to philosophy and history. The converse and the parallel of the fashion of calling mediaeval offices by Roman names, and supposing them therefore the same, is to be found in those old German pictures of the siege of Carthage or the battle between Porus and Alexander, where in the foreground two armies of knights, mailed and mounted, are charging each other like Crusaders, lance in rest, while behind, through the smoke of cannon, loom out the Gothic spires and towers of the beleaguered city. And thus, when we remember that the notion of progress and developement, and of change as the necessary condition thereof, was unwelcome or unknown in mediaeval times, we may better understand, though we do not cease to wonder, how men, never doubting that the political system of antiquity had descended to them, modified indeed, yet in essence the same, should have believed that the Frank, the Saxon, and the Swabian ruled all Europe by a right which seems to us not less fantastic than the fabled charter whereby Alexander the Great bequeathed his empire to the Slavonic race for the love of Roxolana.

It is a part of that perpetual contradiction of which the history of the Middle Ages is full, that this belief was often quite out of relation to actual facts. The more abjectly helpless the Emperor becomes, so much the more sonorous is the language in which the dignity of his crown is extolled. His power, we are told, is eternal, the provinces having resumed their allegiance after the barbarian irruptions;[1] it is incapable of diminution or injury: exemptions and grants by him, so far as they tend to limit his own prerogative, are invalid:[m] all Christendom is still of right subject to him, though it may contumaciously refuse obedience.[n] The sovereigns of Europe are solemnly warned that they are resisting the power ordained of God.[o] No laws can bind the Emperor, though he may choose to live according to them: no court can judge him, though

[1] Aeneas Sylvius Piccolomini (afterwards Pope Pius II), an acute versatile and somewhat cynical politician, in his book *De Ortu et Authoritate Imperii Romani*.

[m] Thus some civilians held Constantine's Donation null; and the canonists, though originally clear as to its legality, came to doubt whether the Emperor had any right to make it for the opposite reason, viz. that it was needless, because the Pope possessed already what it purported to convey.

[n] 'Et idem dico de istis aliis regibus et principibus, qui negant se esse subditos regi Romanorum, ut rex Franciae, Angliae, et similes. Si enim fatentur ipsum esse Dominum universalem, licet ab illo universali domino se subtrahant ex privilegio vel ex praescriptione vel consimili, non ergo desunt esse cives Romani, per ea quae dicta sunt. Et per hoc omnes gentes quae obediunt S. matri ecclesiae sunt de populo Romano. Et forte si quis diceret dominum Imperatorem non esse dominum et monarcham totius orbis, esset haereticus, quia diceret contra determinationem ecclesiae et textum S. evangelii, dum dicit, "Exivit edictum a Caesare Augusto ut describeretur universus orbis." Ita et recognovit Christus Imperatorem ut dominum.'— Bartolus, *Commentary on the Pandects*, xlviii. i. 24; *De Captivis et postliminio reversis.*

[o] Peter de Andlau, *multis locis* (see esp. cap. viii), and other writings of the time. Cf. Dante's letter to Henry VII: (Ep. vii) 'Romanorum potestas nec metis Italiae nec tricornis Europae margine coarctatur. Nam etsi vim passa in angustum gubernacula sua contraxit undique, tamen de inviolabili

he may condescend to be sued in his own : none may presume to arraign the conduct or question the motives of him who is answerable only to God. So writes Aeneas Sylvius while Frederick the Third, chased from his capital by the Hungarians, is wandering from convent to convent, an imperial beggar; while the princes, whom his subserviency to the Pope has driven into rebellion, are offering the imperial crown to Podiebrad the Bohemian king.[p]

Henry VII,
A.D. 1308–
1313.

But the career of Henry the Seventh in Italy is the most remarkable illustration of the Emperor's position : and imperialistic doctrines are set forth most strikingly in the treatise which the greatest spirit of the age wrote to herald or commemorate the advent of that hero, the *De Monarchia* of Dante.[q] Rudolf, Adolf of Nassau, Albert of Hapsburg, none of them crossed the Alps or attempted to aid the Italian Ghibelines who battled in the name of their throne. Concerned only to restore order and aggrandize his house, and thinking apparently that nothing more was to be made of the imperial crown, Rudolf was content never to receive it, and purchased the Pope's goodwill by surrendering his jurisdiction in the capital, and his claims over the bequest of the Countess Matilda. Henry the Luxemburger ventured on a bolder course ; urged perhaps

iure fluctus Amphitritis attingens vix ab inutili unda Oceani se circumcingi dignatur. Scriptum est enim

"Nascetur pulchra Troianus origine Caesar,
Imperium Oceano, famam qui terminet astris." '

So Fr. Zoannetus, as late as the sixteenth century, declares it to be a mortal sin to resist the Empire, as the power ordained of God.

[p] Cf. Gerlach Buxtorff, *Dissertatio ad Auream Bullam.*

[q] Boccaccio says that the *De Monarchia* was written in the view of Henry's expedition; and he has been generally followed. Though Witte holds that Dante wrote it before his exile, the balance of argument seems to be decidedly in favour of the older view which assigns it to a later date, possibly 1311 or 1312. See Toynbee, *Dante Studies*, p. 302. Dante sees in Paradise the place, marked by a crown, reserved for Henry VII (*Par.* xxx. 134–138).

only by his lofty and chivalrous spirit, perhaps in despair at effecting anything with his slender resources against the princes of Germany. Crossing from his Burgundian dominions with a scanty following of knights, and descending from the Cenis upon Turin, he found his prerogative as high in men's belief after sixty years of neglect as it had stood under the last Hohenstaufen. The cities of Lombardy opened their gates ; Milan decreed a vast subsidy ; Guelf and Ghibeline exiles alike were restored, and imperial vicars appointed everywhere. Supported by the Avignonese pontiff, Clement V, who dreaded the restless ambition of his French neighbour, king Philip the Fair, Henry had the interdict of the Church as well as the ban of the Empire at his command. But the illusion of success vanished as soon as men, recovering from their first impression, began to be again governed by their ordinary passions and interests, and not by an imaginative reverence for the glories of the past. Tumults and revolts broke out in Lombardy ; at Rome the king of Naples held St. Peter's, and the coronation, performed by the Pope's legates, must take place in the half-ruined basilica of St. John Lateran, on the southern bank of the Tiber.[r] The hostility of the Guelfic league, headed by the Florentines, Guelfs even against the Pope, obliged Henry to depart from his impartial and republican policy, and to purchase the aid of the Ghibeline chiefs by granting them the government of cities. Meantime the Pope himself, under pressure from France, had become unfriendly, and was throwing difficulties in his path. With few troops, and *Death of* encompassed by enemies, the heroic Emperor sustained *Henry VII.* an unequal struggle for a year longer, till, A.D. 1313, he sank beneath the fevers of the deadly Tuscan summer. His German followers believed, nor has history wholly

---

[r] The church, half destroyed by fire in A.D. 1308, was not yet rebuilt.

CHAP. XV.

*Later Em-
perors in
Italy.*

*Dante's feel-
ings and
theories.*

*The 'De
Monarchia.*

rejected the tale, that poison was given him by a Domini-can monk, in sacramental wine.

Others after him descended from the Alps, and Lewis IV even vindicated, during a few troubled months, the rights of his crown in Rome.[s] But the rest came, either like Rupert and Sigismund, at the behest of a faction, which found them useful tools for a time, then flung them away in scorn; or like Charles the Fourth and Frederick the Third, as the docile creatures of a French or Italian pon-tiff. With Henry the Seventh ends the history of the Empire in Italy, and Dante's book is an epitaph instead of a prophecy. A sketch of its argument will convey a notion of the feelings with which the noblest Ghibelines fought, as well as of the spirit in which the Middle Ages were accustomed to handle such subjects.

Weary of the endless strife of princes and cities, of the factions which within every city strove against each other, seeing municipal freedom, the only mitigation of turbu-lence, vanish with the rise of domestic tyrants, Dante raises a passionate cry for some power to still the tempest, not to quench liberty or supersede local self-government, but to correct and moderate them, to restore unity and peace to hapless Italy. His reasoning is throughout closely syllogistic: he is alternately the jurist, the theo-logian, the scholastic metaphysician: the poet of the *Divina Commedia* is betrayed only by the compressed energy of diction, by his clear vision of the unseen, rarely by a glowing metaphor.

Monarchy is first proved to be the true and rightful form of government.[t] Men's objects are best attained during universal peace: this is possible only under a

[s] See above, chapter XIII.

[t] This was the argument of the Norwegian envoys at the Icelandic Althing in 1262: see chapter XII, p. 186, *ante.*

monarch. And as he is the image of the divine unity, so man is through him made one, and brought most near to God. There must, in every system of forces, be a 'primum mobile'; to be perfect, every organization must have a centre, into which all is gathered, by which all is controlled.[u] Justice is best secured by a supreme arbiter of disputes, himself untempted by ambition, since his dominion is already bounded only by ocean. Man is best and happiest when he is most free; to be free is to exist for one's own sake. To this noblest end does the monarch and he alone guide us; other forms of government are perverted,[x] and exist for the benefit of some class; he seeks the good of all alike, being to that very end appointed.[y]

Abstract arguments are then confirmed from history. Since the world began there has been but one period of perfect peace, and but one of perfect monarchy, that, namely, which existed at our Lord's birth, under the sceptre of Augustus. Since then the heathen have raged, and the kings of the earth have stood up; they have set themselves against their Lord, and His anointed the Roman prince.[z] The universal dominion, the need for which has been thus established, is then proved to belong to the Romans. Justice is the will of God, a will to exalt Rome shewn through her whole history.[a] Her virtues

[u] Suggesting the celestial hierarchies of Dionysius the Areopagite.

[x] Quoting Aristotle's *Politics*.

[y] 'Non enim cives propter consules nec gens propter regem, sed e converso consules propter cives, rex propter gentem.' (Bk. i. ch. 12.)

[z] 'Reges et principes in hoc unico concordantes, ut adversentur Domino suo et uncto suo Romano Principi,' having quoted 'Quare fremuerunt gentes'; Psalm II. (Bk. ii. ch. 1.)

[a] Especially in the opportune death of Alexander the Great, which delivered Italy from the danger of a Macedonian conquest.

In his *Convito* (iv. 5) Dante argues for the divine choice of Rome from the fact that Aeneas came from Troy to Italy to found it at the very time when king David, the progenitor of Christ's mother, was born.

deserved honour : Virgil is quoted to prove those of Aeneas, who by descent and marriage was the heir of the three continents : of Asia through Assaracus and Creusa ; of Africa by Electra (daughter of Atlas and mother of Dardanus) and by Dido (!) ; of Europe by Dardanus and by Lavinia. God's favour was approved in the fall of the shields to Numa, in the miraculous deliverance of the capital from the Gauls, in the hailstorm after Cannae. Justice is also the advantage of the State : that advantage was the constant object of the virtuous Cincinnatus, and the other heroes of the republic. They conquered the world for its own good, and therefore justly, as Cicero attests ;[b] so that their sway was not so much the command as the protection of the whole earth. Nature herself, the fountain of all right, had, by their geographical position and by the gift of a genius so vigorous, marked them out for universal dominion : —

> ' Excudent alii spirantia mollius aera,
> Credo equidem : vivos ducent de marmore vultus ;
> Orabunt causas melius, coelique meatus
> Describent radio, et surgentia sidera dicent :
> Tu regere imperio populos, Romane, memento ;
> Hae tibi erunt artes ; pacisque imponere morem,
> Parcere subiectis, et debellare superbos.'

Finally, the right of war asserted, Christ's birth, and death under Pilate, ratified their government.[c] For Christian doctrine requires that the procurator should have been a lawful judge,[d] which he was not unless Tiberius was a

[b] Cic. *De Off.* ii. 8. 'Ita ut illud patrocinium orbis terrarum potius quam imperium poterat nominari.'

[c] Dante goes so far as to speak of the Kingdom of Heaven under the name of Rome, and of Christ as Roman. Beatrice says to him : —

> ' Sarai meco senza fine cive
> Di quella Roma onde Cristo è Romano.'

[d] 'Si Romanum imperium de iure non fuit, peccatum Adae in Christo non fuit punitum. . . . Et supra totum humanum genus Tiberius, cuius vicarius

lawful Emperor. Else Adam's sin and that of his race was not duly punished in the person of the Saviour.

The relations of the imperial and papal power are then examined, and the passages of Scripture (tradition being rejected), to which the advocates of the Papacy appeal, are elaborately explained away. The argument from the sun and moon [e] does not hold, since both lights existed before man's creation, and at a time when, as still sinless, he needed no controlling powers. Else *accidentia* would have preceded *propria* in creation. The moon, too, does not receive her being nor all her light from the sun, but so much only as makes her more effective. So there is no reason why the temporal should not be aided in a corresponding measure by the spiritual authority. This difficult text disposed of, others fall more easily; Levi and Judah, Samuel and Saul, the incense and gold offered by the Magi; [f] the two swords, the power of binding and loosing given to Peter. Constantine's Donation was illegal: no single Emperor or Pope can disturb the everlasting foundations of their respective thrones: the one had no right to bestow, nor the other to receive, such a gift. In giving the imperial crown to Charles the Great, Leo the Third exceeded his powers: '*usurpatio iuris non facit ius.*' It is alleged that all things of one kind are reducible to one individual, and so all men to the Pope. But Emperor and Pope differ in kind, and so far as they are men, are reducible only to God, on whom the Empire

---

erat Pilatus, iurisdictionem non habuisset nisi Romanum imperium de iure fuisset. Hinc est quod Herodes, quamvis ignorans quid faceret, sicut et Caiaphas, quum verum dixit de coelesti decreto, Christum Pilato remisit ad iudicandum.' (Bk. ii. ch. 13.)

[e] See Note XVI at end.

[f] Typifying the spiritual and temporal powers. Dante meets this by distinguishing the homage paid to Christ from that which His Vicar can rightfully demand.

immediately depends; for it existed before Peter's see, and was recognized by Paul when he appealed to Caesar. The temporal power of the Papacy can have been given neither by natural law nor divine ordinance, nor universal consent: nay, it is against its own Form and Essence, the life of Christ, who said, 'My kingdom is not of this world.'

Man's nature is twofold, corruptible and incorruptible: he has therefore two ends, active virtue on earth, and the enjoyment of the sight of God hereafter; the one to be attained by practice conformed to the precepts of philosophy, the other by the theological virtues. Hence two guides are needed, the Pontiff and the Emperor, the latter of *The 'De* whom, in order that he may direct mankind in accordance *Monarchia':* with the teachings of philosophy to temporal blessedness, *conclusion.* must preserve universal peace in the world. Thus are the two powers equally ordained of God, and the Emperor, though supreme in all that pertains to the secular world, is in some things dependent on the Pontiff, since earthly happiness is subordinate to eternal. 'Let Caesar, therefore, shew towards Peter the reverence wherewith a firstborn son honours his father, that, being illumined by the light of his paternal favour, he may the more excellently shine forth upon the whole world, to the rule of which he has been appointed by Him alone who is of all things, both spiritual and temporal, the King and Governor.' So ends the treatise.

Dante's arguments are not stranger than his omissions. No suspicion is breathed against the genuineness of Constantine's Donation; no proof is adduced, for no doubt is felt, that the Empire of Henry the Seventh is the legitimate continuation of that which had been swayed by Augustus and Justinian. Yet Henry was a German, sprung from Rome's barbarian foes, the elect of those who had neither part nor share in Italy and her capital.

CHAPTER XVI

THE CITY OF ROME IN THE MIDDLE AGES

'IT is related,' says Sozomen in the ninth book of his Ecclesiastical History, 'that when Alarich was hastening against Rome, a holy monk of Italy admonished him to spare the city, and not to make himself the cause of such fearful ills. But Alarich answered, "It is not of my own will that I do this; there is One who forces me on, and will not let me rest, bidding me spoil Rome."' [a]

Towards the close of the tenth century the Bohemian Woytech, famous in after legend as St. Adalbert, forsook his bishopric of Prague to journey into Italy, and settled himself in the Roman monastery of Sant' Alessio. After some few years passed there in religious solitude, he was summoned back to resume the duties of his see, and laboured for awhile among his half-savage countrymen. Soon, however, the old longing came over him: he resought his cell upon the brow of the Aventine, and there, wandering among the ancient shrines, and taking on himself the menial offices of the convent, he abode happily for a space. At length the reproaches of his metropolitan, the archbishop of Mainz, and the express commands of Pope Gregory the Fifth, drove him back over the Alps, and he set off in the train of Otto the Third, lamenting, says his biographer, that he should no more enjoy his beloved quiet in the mother of martyrs, the home of the Apostles, golden

---

[a] *Hist. Eccl.* l. ix. c. 6 τὸν δὲ φάναι, ὡς οὐχ ἐκὼν τάδε ἐπιχειρεῖ, ἀλλά τις συνεχῶς ἐνοχλῶν αὐτὸν βιάζεται, καὶ ἐπιτάττει τὴν Ῥώμην πορθεῖν.

Rome. A few months later he died a martyr among the pagan Lithuanians of the Baltic.[b]

Nearly four hundred years later, and nine hundred after the time of Alarich, Francis Petrarch writes thus to his friend John Colonna : —

'Thinkest thou not that I long to see that city to which there has never been any like nor ever shall be ; which even an enemy called a city of kings ; of whose people it hath been written, "Great is the valour of the Roman people, great and terrible their name" ; concerning whose unexampled glory and incomparable empire, which was, and is, and is to be, divine prophets have sung ; where are the tombs of the apostles and martyrs and the bodies of so many thousands of the saints of Christ ? ' [c]

It was the same irresistible impulse that drew the warrior, the monk, and the scholar towards the mystical city which was to mediaeval Europe more than Delphi had been to the Greek or Mecca to the Islamite, the Jerusalem of Christianity, the city which had once ruled the earth, and now ruled the world of disembodied spirits.[d] For there was then, as there is now, something in Rome to

[b] See the two Lives of St. Adalbert in Pertz, *M. G. H.* iv, evidently compiled soon after his death.

[c] Another letter of Petrarch's to John Colonna, written immediately after his arrival in the city, runs thus : — ' In praesens nihil est quod inchoare ausim, miraculo rerum tantarum et stuporis mole obrutus . . . praesentia vero, mirum dictu, nihil imminuit sed auxit omnia : vere maior fuit Roma maioresque sunt reliquiae quam rebar : iam non orbem ab hac urbe domitum sed tam sero domitum miror. Vale' (*Epp. Fam.* ii. 14). The *reliquiae* have been sadly reduced since Petrarch wrote, but the stranger still feels after his first day in Rome that the city is more wonderful than he expected.

[d] The idea of the continuance of the sway of Rome under a new character is one which mediaeval writers delight to illustrate. In Appendix, Note C, there is quoted as a specimen a poem upon Rome, by Hildebert (bishop of Le Mans, and afterwards archbishop of Tours), written in the beginning of the twelfth century.

attract men of every class. The devout pilgrim came to pray at the shrine of the Prince of the Apostles, too happy if he could carry back to his monastery in the forests of Saxony or by the bleak Atlantic shore the bone of some holy martyr; the lover of learning and poetry dreamed of Virgil and Cicero among the shattered columns of the Forum; the Teutonic kings, in spite of pestilence, treachery and seditions, came with their hosts to seek in the ancient capital of the world the fountain of temporal dominion. She was more glorious in her decay and desolation than the stateliest seats of modern power. Nor has the spell yet wholly lost its power. To half the Christian nations Rome has remained the metropolis of religion, to all the metropolis of art. In her streets, and hers alone among the cities of the world, may every form of human speech be heard.

But while men thought thus of Rome, what was Rome herself?

The modern traveller, after his first few days in Rome, when he has looked out upon the Campagna from the summit of St. Peter's, paced the chilly corridors of the Vatican, and mused under the echoing dome of the Pantheon, when he has passed in review the monuments of regal and republican and papal Rome, begins to seek for some relics of the twelve hundred years that lie between Constantine and Pope Julius the Second. 'Where,' he asks, 'is the Rome of the Middle Ages, the Rome of Alberic and Hildebrand and Rienzo? the Rome which dug the graves of so many Teutonic hosts; whither the pilgrims flocked; whence came the commands at which kings bowed? Where are the memorials of the brightest age of Christian architecture, the age which reared Cologne and Rheims and Westminster, which gave to Italy the cathedrals of Tuscany and the wave-washed palaces of Venice?'

To this question there is no answer. Rome, the mother of the arts, has scarcely a building to commemorate those times, for to her they were times of turmoil and misery, times in which the shame of the present was embittered by recollections of a brighter past. Nevertheless a minute scrutiny may still discover, hidden in dark corners or disguised under an unbecoming modern dress, much that carries us back to the mediaeval town, and helps us to realize its social and political condition. Therefore a brief notice of the state of Rome during the Middle Ages, with especial reference to those monuments which the visitor may still examine for himself, may have its use, and is no unfitting pendant to an account of the institution which drew from the City its name and its magnificent pretensions. Moreover, as will appear more fully in the sequel, the history of the Roman people is an instructive illustration of the influence of the ideas upon which the Empire itself rested, as well in their weakness as in their strength.[e]

It is not from her capture by Alarich, nor even from the more destructive ravages of the Vandal Gaiserich, that the material and social ruin of Rome must be dated, but rather from the repeated sieges which she sustained during the war of Justinian against the Ostrogoths.[f] This

---

[e] The history of the City has been written by Ferdinand Gregorovius in his *Geschichte der Stadt Rom im Mittelalter*, of which there exists an English translation. [Since this chapter was written, in 1865, much has been done to unveil by excavation the antiquities of early imperial Rome, but little (except the church of S. Maria Antica) which throws light on the mediaeval city has been discovered.]

[f] The great siege in which Belisarius defended the city against Witigis is fully and vividly described by Procopius, *Bell. Goth.* bks. i. and ii.

After capturing the city in A.D. 546, Totila, who had at first intended to destroy it utterly, turned out the inhabitants, and Rome stood empty for more than a month. See Procop., *Goth.* iii. 22 (ἐν Ῥώμῃ ἄνθρωπον οὐδένα ἐάσας, ἀλλ' ἐρῆμον αὐτὴν τὸ παράπαν ἀπολιπών); and cf. Hodgkin, *Italy and her Invaders*, bk. v. ch. 20.

struggle, however, long and exhausting as it was, would not have proved so fatal had the previous condition of the city been sound and healthy. Her wealth and population in the middle of the fifth century were probably little inferior to what they had been in the most prosperous days of the imperial government. But this wealth was entirely gathered into the hands of a small and luxurious aristocracy. The crowd that filled her streets was composed partly of poor and idle freemen, unaccustomed to arms and long since deprived of political rights; partly of a far more numerous herd of slaves, gathered from all parts of the world, and morally even lower than their masters. There was no middle class, and no effective municipal administration, for although the senate and consuls with many of the lesser magistracies continued to exist, they had for centuries enjoyed little power, and were nowise fitted to lead and rule the people. Hence it was that when the long Gothic war and the subsequent inroads of the Lombards had reduced the great families to beggary, the old framework of society dissolved and could not be replaced. In a State rotten to the core there was no vital force left for reconstruction. The ancient forms of political activity had been too long dead to be recalled to life: the people wanted the moral force to produce new ones, and all the authority that could be said to exist in the midst of anarchy tended to centre itself in the chief of the new religious society.

So far Rome's condition was like that of the other great towns of Italy and Gaul. But in two points her case differed from theirs, and to these the difference of her after fortunes may be traced. Her bishop had at hand no temporal potentate to overshadow his dignity or check his ambition, for the vicar of the Eastern court lived far away at Ravenna, and seldom interfered except

CHAP. XVI.
Causes of the rapid decay of the City.

Peculiarities in the position of Rome.

to ratify a papal election or punish a more than commonly outrageous sedition. Her population received an all but imperceptible infusion of that Teutonic blood and those Teutonic customs by whose stern discipline the inhabitants of Northern Italy were in the end renovated. Everywhere the old institutions had perished of decay: in Rome the social and economic conditions were such that it was only out of the ecclesiastical system that new institutions could arise. Her condition was therefore the most pitiable in which a community can find itself, one of ceaseless struggle without purpose or progress. The citizens were divided into three orders: the military class, including what was left of the ancient aristocracy; the clergy, a host of priests, monks, and nuns, attached to the countless churches and convents; and the people, or *plebs*, as they are called, a poverty-stricken rabble without trade, without industry, with little municipal organization to bind them together. Of these two latter classes the Pope was the natural leader; the first was divided into factions headed by some three or four of the great families, whose quarrels kept the town in incessant bloodshed. The internal history of Rome from the eighth to the twelfth century is an obscure and tedious record of the contests of these factions with each other, and of the aristocracy as a whole with the slowly-growing power of the Church.

Her condition in the ninth and tenth centuries.

The revolt of the Romans from the Image-breaking Emperors in the East, followed as it was by the reception of the Franks as patricians and Emperors, is an event of the first importance in the history of Italy and of the Popedom. In the domestic constitution of Rome it made little change. With the instinct of a profound genius Charles the Great saw that Rome, though it might be ostensibly the capital, could not be the seat of government for his dominions. He continued to reside in Germany, and did not even fit up as a palace any one of the group of dwellings that stood, some of them still comparatively unscathed, upon the Palatine. For a time the awe of his power, the presence of his *missus* or lieutenant, and the occasional visits of his successors Lothar and Lewis II to the city, repressed her internal disorders. But after the death of the prince last named, and still more after the dissolution of the Carolingian Empire itself, Rome relapsed into a state of profligacy and barbarism to which, even in that age, Europe supplied no parallel, a barbarism which had inherited the vices of civilization without its virtues. The papal office in particular seemed to have lost its religious character, as many of its occupants had lost all claim to moral purity. For more than a century the chief priest of Christendom was no more than a tool of some ferocious faction among the nobles. Criminal means had raised him to the throne; violence, sometimes going the length of mutilation or murder, deprived him of it. The marvel is, a marvel in which papal historians have not unnaturally discovered a miracle, that after sinking so low, the Papacy should ever have risen again. Its rescue and exaltation to the pinnacle of glory was accomplished not by the Romans but by the efforts of the Transalpine Church, aiding and prompting the Saxon and Franconian Emperors. Yet even the religious reform did not abate intestine turmoil, and it was not till the twelfth century that a new spirit began to work in politics, which ennobled if it could not heal the sufferings of the Roman people.

Ever since the days of Alberic [g] their pride had revolted against the haughty behaviour of the Teutonic Emperors. From still earlier times they had been jealous of sacerdotal authority, and now watched with alarm the rapid extension of its influence. The events of the twelfth cen-

Growth of a republican feeling: hostility to the Popes.

[g] See chapter VI, *supra.*

tury gave these feelings a definite direction.   It was the time of the struggle of the Investitures, in which Gregory VII and his disciples had been striving to draw power over the things of this world as well as over those of the next into their grasp.   It was the era of the revived study of Roman law, by which alone the extravagant pretensions of the decretalists could be resisted.   The Lombard and Tuscan towns had become flourishing republics, independent of their bishops, and at open war with their Emperor. Municipal self-government already existed at Rome in some rude form, but now its recent developement in other parts of Italy, and especially in the North, naturally told upon the imperial city and vivified its old traditions. *Arnold of Brescia in Rome, 1146-1155.* While all these things were stirring the minds of the Romans, Arnold of Brescia came preaching religious reform, denouncing the simoniacal practices and corrupt life of the clergy, not indeed, like some others of the so-called schismatics of his time, rejecting a sacerdotal order, but proclaiming that confession ought to be made not to it, but by Christians to one another,[h] that the sinfulness of a priest destroyed the value of the sacraments he administered, that spiritual persons ought to be confined to spiritual duties and neither to possess worldly goods nor exercise secular authority.[i]   On the minds of the Romans such teaching fell like the spark upon dry grass.   They threw off the yoke of the Pope, against which the *Comune di Roma* had often struggled; they drove out the imperial prefect, reconstituted the senate and what they called the

[h] A contemporary poem (see Note XVII at end) says: —

'Non debere illis populum delicta fateri

Sed magis alterutrum, nec eorum sumere sacra.'

[i] Arnold's denunciations of the corruptions in the Church were probably no stronger than those of his contemporary St. Bernard, but the latter condemned Arnold's doctrines while admiring the austerity of his life.   So the poem: 'Vir nimis austerus duraeque per omnia vitae.'

equestrian order (apparently an organization of the minor CHAP. XVI.
nobles), appointed consuls, struck their own coins, and professed to treat the Germanic Emperors as their nominees,
whose authority, though admitted as legitimate, was in
their view derived from the Roman people. To have successfully imitated the republican constitution of the cities
of Northern Italy would have been much, but with this
they were not content. Knowing in a vague ignorant way
that there had been a Roman republic before there was a
Roman Empire, they fed their vanity with visions of a
renewal of all their ancient forms, and saw in fancy their
senate and people sitting again upon the Seven Hills and
ruling over the kings of the earth. Stepping, as it were,
into the arena where Pope and Emperor were contending
for the headship of the world, they rejected the one as a
priest, and declaring the other to be only their creature,
they claimed as theirs the true and lawful inheritance of
the world-dominion which their ancestors had won. Antiquity was in one sense on their side, and to us now it
seems less strange that the Roman people should aspire
to rule the earth than that a German barbarian should
rule it in their name. But practically the scheme was
absurd, and could not maintain itself against any serious
opposition. As a modern historian aptly expresses it,
'they were setting up ruins:' they might as well have
tried to raise a stately temple out of the broken columns
that strewed their Forum. The reverence which the men
of the Middle Ages felt for Rome was given altogether to
the name and to the place, and nowise to the people.
Their armed force was insignificant: so far from holding
Italy in subjection, they could scarcely maintain themselves
against the hostility of Tusculum.

Yet it might have been worth the while of the Germanic
Emperors to have made the Romans their allies, and bridled

by their help the temporal ambition of the Popes. Over-
tures were addressed to Conrad the Third in 1146 — he
refused to receive the envoys or to answer the letter —
and again in 1151. Another opportunity arose when
Frederick the First approached Rome in 1155 at the head
of a great army.[j] But the Swabian repelled in the most
contumelious fashion the envoys of the senate. Even
while he dreaded and resisted, he always respected the
Vicar of Christ: towards the Romans he felt the contempt
of a feudal king for burghers, and of the Lord of the World
for a petty knot of rebels. Pope Hadrian the Fourth,
whose insight found no heresy more dangerous than one
which threatened the authority of the clergy, had, by the
terrible weapon of interdict and with the support of the
greater nobles, driven Arnold of Brescia out of Rome; and
when the fugitive found protection, near Viterbo, from one
of the counts of the district, the Pope required Frederick
to seize him. The Emperor was at that moment seeking to
induce the Pope to crown him, so Arnold was taken, tried
by the prefect of the city, hanged, his body burned, and
his ashes cast into the Tiber, lest the people should treasure them up as relics.[k] His constancy in the presence of
death, his refusal to recant, the calm dignity of his silent confession and prayer, softened the executioners, while it moved
the beholders to tears; and the Emperor himself regretted
too late his hasty compliance with the Pope's demand.[l]

Arnold is a remarkable figure, not only because he
sought to reinvigorate the civic life of Rome but also
because his is one of the earliest and clearest of the voices

[j] *Supra*, p. 175.

[k] This treatment of the dead was not unusual in the Middle Ages. The
remains of John Wiclif were disinterred from the chancel of his church at
Lutterworth nearly forty years after his death and thrown into a stream called
the Swift, which runs past the village.

[l] See Note XVII at end.

that were raised from time to time throughout the Middle Ages against the fatal secularization of the Church by wealth and temporal authority. The Church he desired was a church of apostolic poverty. He was an idealist, who taught, says his contemporary John of Salisbury, 'things most consonant to the law of Christians, and most remote from actual life.'[m] Though a disciple of Abelard, he is less a dialectician than a theologian, perhaps less a theologian than a practical reformer, appealing to the words of Scripture, and seeking to bring back the primitive simplicity of the early days of Christianity. He is a forerunner in one sense of Dante, in another of Marsilius of Padua, one may even say, of the reformers of the sixteenth century. And, though the attempt to revive against the Pope the long obsolete powers of the Roman people may now seem fanciful, it must be remembered that the rights of the laity against the sacerdotal order and its head had, in the world as it then stood, no institution whereto they could attach themselves, no means whereby to make themselves respected, except the Emperor — whom the Romans sought to win — and the organization, under the Emperor, of a municipal republic. Arnold was hopelessly overmatched. Material force was against him; and the main stream of opinion was still running strongly in the channel into which Gregory VII had directed the hierarchical doctrine of his time. Nor did that stream slacken till the beginning of the fourteenth century. But it is the mark of a hero to be willing to face desperate odds : and those who in the end of the fifteenth century saw the papal court sunk in corruption, in worldliness, and indeed in a sort of paganism, might well deem that the Catholic Church would have fared better if the principles of Arnold had prevailed.

CHAP. XVI.

Significance of Arnold's career.

[m] 'Dicebat quae Christianorum legi concordant plurimum et a vita quam plurimum dissonant.'

CHAP. XVI.

The martyrdom of their Lombard leader did not quench the hopes of his Roman followers. The republican constitution continued to exist, and rose from time to time, during the weakness or the absence of the pontiff, into a brief and fitful activity.[n] It was indeed recognized by the Popes themselves. They used to receive the title and authority of Senator for life, and in particular, in A.D. 1337, Benedict XII gratefully accepted from the people the offices of Senator and Captain, Syndic and Defensor of the Republic.[o] Once awakened, the idea, seductive at once to the imagination of the scholar and the vanity of the Roman citizen, could not wholly disappear, least of all while the Popes were absent at Avignon, and two centuries after Arnold's time it found a more brilliant though less disinterested exponent in the tribune Nicholas Rienzo.[p]

Career of the tribune Cola di Rienzo.

The career of this singular personage is misunderstood by those who suppose him to have been possessed of profound political insight, a republican on modern principles. He was indeed, despite his overweening conceit and what seems to us his charlatanry, both a patriot and a man of genius, in temperament a poet, filled with soaring ideas. But those ideas, although dressed out in gaudier colours by his lively fancy, were after all only the old ones, memories of the long-faded glories of the heathen republic, and a series of scornful contrasts levelled at her present oppressors, both of them shewing no vista of future greatness

---

[n] The series of papal coins is interrupted (with one or two slight exceptions) from A.D. 984 (not long after the time of Alberic) to A.D. 1304. In their place we meet with various coins struck by the municipal authorities, some of which bear on the obverse the head of the Apostle Peter, with the legend 'Roman. Pricipe' : on the reverse the head of the Apostle Paul, legend, Senat. Popul. Q. R. Gregorovius, *ut supra.*

[o] Gregorovius, bk. xi. ch. 4.

[p] Rienzo seems to be a corruption of the name Laurence. The tribune calls himself in his Latin letters, 'Nicolaus Laurentii.'

except through the revival of those ancient names to which CHAP. XVI, there were no things to correspond.

It will be remembered that in A.D. 1327 the Emperor Lewis IV had, in his conflict with Pope John XXII, suddenly embraced and turned to account the claims of the city. Against the hostility of the Church he set the will of the Roman people. Acting under their decree Sciarra Colonna and his three fellow Syndics crowned the Bavarian, following, as was alleged, the precedent of A.D. 800, when Charles the Great had received the Empire as the gift of the Romans. If Cola di Rienzo, then a youth of fourteen, witnessed the coronation, this recognition of the rights of Rome may well have sunk deep into his mind. Some seventeen years later, being then a notary in the A.D. 1344. Pope's service, he began a strange campaign addressed to the eyes no less than to the ears of the multitude, in which he displayed allegorical pictures, and delivered harangues upon those ancient rights of Senate and People which he was seeking to bring back into effective action, taking as his text, on one famous occasion, an inscription recording the statute by which the *imperium* had been conferred upon Vespasian.q In A.D. 1347 he effected with the aid of *His revo-* some conspirators, and with the consent of the Papal Vicar, *lution.* a sort of bloodless revolution, obtained a decree by which he was placed at the head of the executive government as Tribune, effected a number of reforms, and bridled the excesses of the nobility. He then despatched letters to all the chief cities of Italy inviting them to send repre-

q This inscription on a brazen tablet may still be seen in the Capitol. Boniface VIII had hidden it away. Cola says, 'Tabula magna erea erat literis antiquis insignita quam Bonifacius Papa VIII in odium Imperii occultavit et de ea quoddam altare construxit, a tergo litteris occultatis.' (Document in Papencordt's *Cola di Rienzo*.) It has now become a precious historical authority for the constitutional history of the old Empire.

sentatives to a great assembly to be held at Rome. Some of them complied, and many more received the invitation respectfully, for there was a general desire to be rid of intestine strife and to recall the Pope from Avignon to Rome. In a gathering of jurists, and again in a Roman Parliament, Cola solemnly declared Rome to be the Head of the World, and (it is said) revoked all the gifts, concessions, and privileges which had been conferred by previous rulers, from Constantine downwards, upon the Holy See and the Germanic Electors.[r] Somewhat later, repeating this declaration, he conferred the Roman citizenship upon all the cities of Italy, proclaiming them to be free, asserted for the city and people of Rome and for Italy the rights of the Empire and the function of choosing the Emperor, and cited the seven Electors and all others in Germany to appear before him and defend such rights as they claimed. Even the rival Emperors Lewis IV and Charles king of Bohemia (who had been chosen against Lewis in A.D. 1346) were included in this citation. The Romans applauded, but these latest assumptions, coupled with the whimsical antics into which Cola's vanity had betrayed him, were too much for the public opinion of Italy, and far too much for the Pope. Clement VI denounced the Tribune as a heretic, and bade the Vicar depose him : the nobles gathered their forces against Rome, Cola quailed and fled ; and when, after years of exile among the Apennines, and of captivity first in Bohemia (whither he had gone to win the favour of Charles IV),

Attempt to unite Italy under Rome.

[r] Whether, however, he intended to annul all the gifts to the Holy See has been doubted; a contemporary says he does not think the revocation 'extendat se ad dominium Papae sed ad electores et Alamanniae imperatores credo quod se extendat et opinio omnium Romanorum est.' — Cochetus, *ap.* Papencordt, *ut supra*, Doc. 9.

So Petrarch, in a letter to the Roman people, calls Rome 'totius magnificentiae humanae supremum domicilium.' — (*Epist.* sine tit. iii.)

and afterwards at Avignon, he was sent back to Rome by CHAP. XVI. Pope Innocent VI under the wing of Cardinal Albornoz, A.D. 1354. he perished after a brief spell of authority, torn to pieces by the fierce and fickle populace. Cola, with some learn- *Cola's* ing, and a passionate love of antiquity, possessed dazzling *character and ideas.* eloquence and histrionic power. But he had no grasp of actualities, no sense of what was possible, no faculty for prompt decision, and what was no less fatal, he lacked both military skill and physical courage. In his later career he was by turns a Ghibeline and a Guelf, equally willing to bid for the favour of the Emperor and for the support of the Pope. His appeals were made, not to demo-cratic principles but to antiquity, to the unquenched faith in the name of Rome, to that nascent spirit of Italian nationality which resented the intrusion of the foreigner. The idea of an Italy united with Rome for its capital is the only one of his dreams which proved, after five cen-turies, to be ultimately realizable; but his career did nothing to bring it nearer. He is memorable not as a creator of new ideas, but as one of the last and most fanci-ful exponent of those old ideas which were destined soon thereafter to fade and vanish away, as the moon's light dies out under the brightening dawn. This dawn, how-ever, was as yet scarcely visible. Men's minds still lay under the old spell. The acts and plans of the Tribune, though they astonished his contemporaries by their bold-ness, do not seem to have been deemed either so strange or so utterly unpractical as they appear to us to-day. In the breasts of men like Petrarch, who loved Rome even more than they distrusted her people, the enthusiasm of Cola found a sympathetic echo: others scorned and de-nounced him as an upstart, a demagogue, possibly a heretic, certainly a rebel. But both friends and enemies seem to

[*] See Note XVIII at end of volume.

have comprehended and regarded as natural his feelings
and designs, which were altogether those of his age.
Being, however, a mere matter of imagination, not of
reason, having no anchor, so to speak, in realities, no true
relation to the world as it then stood, these schemes of
republican revival were as transient and unstable as they
were quick of growth and gay of colour.   As the authority
of the Popes became consolidated, and free municipalities
disappeared elsewhere throughout Italy, the dream of a
renovated Rome at length withered up and fell and died.
Its last struggle was made in the conspiracy of Stephen
A.D. 1453. Porcaro, in the time of Pope Nicholas the Fifth ; and from
that time onward there was no question of the supremacy
of the bishop within his holy city.

It is never without a certain regret that we watch the
disappearance of a belief, however illusive, around which
the love and reverence of mankind once clung.   But this
illusion need be the less regretted in that it had only
the feeblest influence for good on the state of mediaeval
Causes of the Rome.   During the three centuries that lie between
failure of the Arnold of Brescia and Porcaro, the disorders of Rome
struggle for were hardly less violent than they had been in the Dark
independence. Ages, and to all appearance worse than those of any
other European city.   There was a want not only of
fixed authority, but of those elements of social stability
which the other cities of Italy possessed.   In the greater
republics of Lombardy and Tuscany the bulk of the population were artizans, hard-working orderly people; while
above them stood a prosperous middle class, engaged
mostly in commerce, and having in their system of trade-
guilds an organization both firm and flexible.   It was by
foreign trade that Genoa, Venice, and Pisa became great,
as it was the wealth acquired by manufacturing industry
that enabled Milan and Florence to overcome and incor-

porate the territorial aristocracies which surrounded them.

Rome possessed neither source of riches. She was ill-placed for trade; having no market she produced no goods to be disposed of, and the unhealthiness which long neglect had brought upon her Campagna made its fertility unavailable. Already she stood as she stood down to our own time, lonely and isolated, a desert at her very gates. As there was no industry, so there was *Internal* nothing that deserved to be called a citizen class. The *condition of the city.* people were a mere rabble, prompt to follow the dema- *The people.* gogue who flattered their vanity, prompter still to desert him in the hour of danger. Superstition was with them a matter of national pride, but they lived too near sacred things to feel much reverence for them: they ill-treated the Pope and fleeced the pilgrims who crowded to their shrines: they were probably the only community in Europe that sent no recruit to the armies of the Cross. Priests, monks, and all the nondescript hangers-on of an ecclesiastical court formed a large part of the population; while of the rest many were supported in a state of half-mendicancy by the countless religious foundations, them-selves enriched by the gifts or the plunder of Latin Christendom. The noble families were numerous, turbu- *The nobility.* lent, ferocious; they were surrounded by bands of unruly retainers, and waged a constant war against each other from their castles in the adjoining country or in the streets of the city itself. Had things been left to take their natural course, one of these families, the Colonna, for instance, or the Orsini, would probably have ended by overcoming its rivals, and have established, as was the case in the republics of Lombardy, Romagna, and Tuscany, a 'signoria' or local tyranny, like those which had once prevailed in the cities of Greece. But the *The bishop.*

presence of the sacerdotal power, as it had hindered the growth of feudalism, stood also in the way of such a developement as this, and in so far aggravated the confusion of the city. Although the Pope did not till the fifteenth century establish his title as legitimate sovereign, he was by far the most considerable person in Rome, and the only one whose authority had both a permanent and an official character. But the reign of each pontiff was short; he had no military force, he was frequently — and from 1305 till 1378 continuously — absent from his see. He was, moreover, very often a member of one of the great families, and, as such, no better than a faction leader at home, while venerated by the rest of Europe as the Universal Priest.

The Emperor. The person who should have been to Rome what the national king was to the cities of France, or England, or Germany, was the Emperor. But he was like one of those wandering hero-spectres in the *Odyssey* who draw from a draught of blood a momentary vitality, and then relapse into shadowy feebleness. When he came with an army, and the streets of Rome were filled with slaughter, he secured a few days or weeks of power. At other times his phantom authority did little more than furnish a pretext to the Colonna and other Ghibeline chieftains for their opposition to the papal party. Even his abstract rights were matter of controversy. The Popes, whose predecessors had been content to govern as the lieutenants of Charles and Otto, now maintained that Rome as a spiritual city could not be subject to any temporal jurisdiction, and that she was therefore not really a part of the Emperor's dominions, though at the same time his capital. Not only, it was urged, had Constantine yielded up Rome to Sylvester and his successors, Lothar the Saxon had at his coronation formally renounced his sovereignty by doing homage to the pontiff and receiving

the crown as his vassal.   The Popes felt then as they
feel now, that their dignity and influence would suffer if
they should even appear to admit in their place of residence the jurisdiction of a civil potentate, and although
they could not secure their own authority, they were at
least able to exclude any other.   Hence it was that they
were so uneasy whenever an Emperor came to them to
be crowned, that they raised up difficulties in his path,
and endeavoured to be rid of him as soon as possible.
And here something must be said of the programme, as *Visits of the*
one may call it, of these imperial visits to Rome, and of *Emperors to*
the marks of their presence which the Germans left be- *Rome.*
hind them, remembering always that after the time of
Frederick the Second it was rather the exception than
the rule for an Emperor to be crowned in his capital at all.

The traveller who to-day enters Rome by the railway
from the north, slips in before he is aware, is huddled into
a vehicle at the terminus, and set down at his hotel in the
middle of the modern town before he has caught a glimpse
of the city from a distance.   Fifty years ago when he came
overland from Tuscany along the bleak road that passes
near Veii and crosses the Milvian bridge, he had indeed
from the slopes of the Ciminian range a splendid prospect
of the sea-like Campagna, girdled in by glittering hills, but
of the city he saw no sign, save the pinnacle of St. Peter's,
until he was within the walls.   Far otherwise was it in the
Middle Ages.   Then travellers of every grade, from the *Their*
humble pilgrim to the new-made archbishop who came in *approach.*
the pomp of a lengthy train to receive from the Pope the
pallium of his office, approached from the north or north-
east side ; following a track along the hilly ground on the
Tuscan side of the Tiber until they halted on the brow of
Monte Mario—the Mount of Joy[t]—and saw the city of

[t] The Germans called this hill, which is one of the highest in or near

CHAP. XVI.

their solemnities lie spread before them, from the great pile of the Lateran far away upon the Coelian hill, to the basilica of St. Peter's at their feet. They saw it not, as now, a sea of billowy cupolas, but a mass of low, red-roofed houses, varied by tall brick towers, and at rarer intervals by masses of ancient ruin, then larger far than now; while over all rose those two monuments of the best of the heathen Emperors, monuments that still look down, serenely changeless, on the armies of new nations and the festivals of a new religion — the columns of Marcus Aurelius and Trajan.

Their entrance.

From Monte Mario the Teutonic host descended, when they had paid their orisons, into the Neronian field, the piece of flat land that lies outside the gate of St. Angelo.ᵘ Here it was the custom for the elders of the Romans to meet the elected Emperor, present their charters for confirmation, and receive his oath to preserve their good customs.ˣ Then a procession was formed: the priests and monks, who had come out with hymns to greet the Emperor, led the way; the knights and soldiers of Rome, such as they were, came next; then the monarch, followed by a long array of Transalpine chivalry. Passing into the city they advanced to St. Peter's, where the Pope, surrounded by his clergy, stood on the great staircase of the basilica to welcome and bless the Roman king. On the

Rome, conspicuous from a beautiful group of stone-pines and cypresses upon its brow, Mons Gaudii; the origin of the Italian name, Monte Mario, is not known, unless it be, as some think, a corruption of Mons Malus.

There is now a fortification on the top which makes the best point of view less accessible than it used to be.

It was on this hill that Otto the Third hanged Crescentius and his followers.

ᵘ This Campus Neronianus — the name is as old as the sixth century: see Procop. *Goth.* i. 19 — has since 1885 been largely covered by the houses of the new quarter of Rome called Prati di Castello.

ˣ See the *Ordo Romanus* in Muratori's third Dissertation in the *Antiquitates Italiae medii aevi.*

next day came the coronation, with ceremonies too elaborate for description,[y] ceremonies which, we may well believe, were seldom duly completed. Far more usual were
other rites, of which the book of ritual makes no mention,
unless they are to be counted among the 'good customs'
of the Romans'; the clang of war-bells, the battle-cry of
German and Italian combatants. The Pope, when he *Hostility of*
could not keep the Emperor from entering Rome, re- *Pope and*
quired him to leave the bulk of his host without the walls, *Germans.*
and if foiled in this, sought safety in raising up plots and
seditions against his too powerful friend. The Roman
people, on the other hand, violent as they often were
against the Pope, had nevertheless a sort of national pride
in him. Very different were their feelings towards the
Teutonic chieftain, who came from a far land to receive
in their city, yet without thanking them for it, the ensign
of a power which the prowess of their forefathers had won.
Bereft of their ancient right to choose the universal bishop,
they clung all the more desperately to the belief that it
was they who chose the universal prince ; and were mortified afresh when each successive sovereign contemptu-
ously scouted their claims, and paraded before their eyes
his rude barbarian cavalry. Thus it was that a Roman
sedition was the usual accompaniment of a Roman coronation. The three revolts against Otto the Great have been
already described. His grandson Otto the Third, in spite
of his passionate fondness for the city, was met by the
same faithlessness and hatred, and departed at last in

[y] Great stress was laid on one part of the procedure, — the holding by the
Emperor of the Pope's stirrup for him to mount, and the leading of his palfrey for some distance. Frederick Barbarossa's omission of this mark of
respect when Pope Hadrian IV met him on his way to Rome, had nearly
caused a breach between the two potentates, Hadrian absolutely refusing the
kiss of peace until Frederick should have gone through the form, which he
was at last forced to do in the presence of the army: 'fortiter streugam tenuit.'

despair at the failure of his attempts at conciliation.[z]   A century afterwards Henry the Fifth's coronation produced violent tumults, occasioned by his seizing the Pope and cardinals in St. Peter's, and keeping them prisoners till they submitted to his terms.   Remembering this, Pope Hadrian the Fourth would fain have forced the troops of Frederick Barbarossa to remain without the walls, but the rapidity of their movements disconcerted his plans and anticipated the resistance of the Roman populace.   Having established himself in the Leonine city,[a] Frederick barricaded the bridge over the Tiber under the fortress of St. Angelo, and was duly crowned in St. Peter's.   But the rite was scarcely finished when the Romans, who had assembled in arms on the Capitol, dashed over the bridge, fell upon the Germans, and were with difficulty repulsed by the personal efforts of the Emperor.   Into the city, whose narrow streets and thick-set strongholds made advance dangerous, he did not venture to pursue them, nor was he at any period of his reign able to make himself master of the whole of it.   Finding themselves similarly baffled, his successors at last accepted their position, and were content to take the crown on the Pope's conditions and depart without further question.

[z] A remarkable speech of expostulation made by Otto III to the Roman people (after one of their revolts) from the tower of his house on the Aventine has been preserved to us.   It begins thus: 'Vosne estis mei Romani? Propter vos quidem meam patriam, propinquos quoque reliqui; amore vestro Saxones et cunctos Theotiscos, sanguinem meum, proieci; vos in remotas partes imperii nostri adduxi, quo patres vestri cum orbem ditione premerent numquam pedem posuerunt; scilicet ut nomen vestrum et gloriam ad fines usque dilatarem; vos filios adoptavi: vos cunctis praetuli.' — *Vita S. Bernwardi ;* in Pertz, *M. G. H.* t. iv.

(It is from this form 'Theotiscus' that the Italian 'Tedesco' seems to have been derived.)

[a] The Leonine city, so called from Pope Leo IV, lay between the Vatican and St. Peter's and the river.

Coming so seldom and remaining for so short a time, it is not wonderful that the Teutonic Emperors should, in the seven centuries from Charles the Great to Charles the Fifth, have left fewer marks of their presence in Rome than Titus or Hadrian alone has done; fewer and less considerable even than those which tradition attributes to Servius Tullius and the elder Tarquin. Those monuments which do exist are just sufficient to make the absence of all others more conspicuous. The most important dates from the time of Otto the Third, the only Emperor who attempted to make Rome his permanent residence. Of the palace, possibly nothing more than a tower, which he built on the Aventine, no trace has been discovered; but the church, founded by him to receive the ashes of his friend the martyred St. Adalbert, may still be seen upon the island in the Tiber. In it there stands, in front of the high altar, an ancient marble font which shews upon one side a figure of St. Adalbert, and on another side one of the Emperor himself, both executed in the rude style of the eleventh century. Having received from Benevento relics supposed to be those of Bartholomew the Apostle,[b] it became dedicated to that saint, and is at present the church of San Bartolommeo in Isola, whose quaintly picturesque bell-tower of red brick, now grey with extreme age, looks out from among the orange-trees of a convent garden over the swift-eddying yellow waters of the Tiber.

Otto the Second, son of Otto the Great, died at Rome, and lies buried in the crypt of St. Peter's, the only Emperor who has found a resting-place among the graves of the Popes.[c] His tomb is not far from that of his nephew Pope Gregory the Fifth: it is a plain one of roughly chis-

CHAP. XVI.
Memorials of the Germanic Emperors in Rome.

Of Otto the Third.

Of Otto the Second.

---

[b] It would seem that Otto was deceived, and that in reality they are the bones of St. Paulinus of Nola.

[c] As to the burial-places of the Emperors, see Note XIX at end.

CHAP. XVI.

elled marble. The lid of the superb porphyry sarcophagus in which he lay for a time now serves as the great font of St. Peter's, and may be seen in the baptismal chapel on the left of the entrance of the church, not far from the monument to the last of the English Stuarts. Last of all must be mentioned a curious relic of the Emperor Frederick the Second, the prince whom of all others one would least expect to see honoured in the city of his foes. It is an inscription in the palace of the Conservators upon the Capitoline hill, built into the wall of the great staircase, and relates the victory of Frederick's army over the Milanese, and the capture of the carroccio[d] of the rebel city, which he sends as a trophy to his faithful Romans. These are all or nearly all the traces of her Teutonic lords that Rome has preserved till now. Pictures indeed there are in abundance, from the mosaic of the Scala Santa at the Lateran[e] and the curious frescoes in the church of Santi Quattro Incoronati,[f] down to the paintings of the Sistine antechapel and the Stanze of Raphael in the Vatican, where the triumphs of the Popedom over all its foes are set forth with matchless art and equally matchless unveracity. But these are mostly long subsequent to the events they describe, and these all the world knows.

Of Frederick the Second.

Associations of the highest interest would have attached to the churches in which the imperial coronation was per-

[d] See note [t], p. 178.

[e] See p. 116.

[f] These highly curious frescoes are in the chapel of St. Sylvester attached to the very ancient church of Quattro Santi on the Coelian hill, and are supposed to have been executed in the time of Pope Innocent III, possibly reproducing more ancient pictures which had disappeared. They represent scenes in the life of the Saint, more particularly the making of the famous donation to him by Constantine, who submissively holds the bridle of his palfrey. See p. 169. The picture was evidently executed under the influence of the claim advanced by Hadrian IV.

formed — a ceremony which, whether we regard the dignity of the performers or the splendour of the adjuncts, was probably the most imposing that Europe has known. But old St. Peter's disappeared in the end of the fifteenth century, not long after the last Roman coronation, that of Frederick the Third, while the basilica of St. John Lateran, in which Lothar the Saxon and Henry the Seventh were crowned, damaged by time and by fire and an earthquake in the fourteenth century, has been so wofully modernized that we can hardly figure it to ourselves as the same building.[g]

Causes of the want of mediaeval monuments in Rome.

Bearing in mind what was the social condition of Rome during the Middle Ages, it becomes easier to understand the architectural barrenness which at first excites the visitor's surprise. Rome had no temporal sovereign, and there were therefore only two classes who could build at all, the nobles and the clergy. Of these, the former had seldom the wealth, and never the taste, which would have enabled them to construct palaces graceful as the Venetian or massively grand as the Florentine and Genoese. Moreover, the constant practice of war within the city made defence the first object of a house, beauty and convenience the second. Down to the middle of the fifteenth century, fortresses rather than mansions were what the great families needed. The nobility, therefore, either adapted ancient edifices to their purpose or built out of their materials those huge square towers of brick, a few of which still frown over the narrow streets in the older parts of Rome. We may judge of their number

Barbarism of the aristocracy.

[g] The last imperial coronation, that of Charles the Fifth, took place in the church of St. Petronius at Bologna, Pope Clement VII being unwilling to receive Charles in Rome. It is a grand church, but the choir, where the ceremony took place, has been 'restored' out of recognition since Charles's time.

from the statement that the senator Brancaleone levelled one hundred and forty of them, as Frederick I had in his time destroyed a good many. With perhaps no more than one exception, that of the so-called House of Rienzo, a building obviously older by at least two centuries than the Tribune's time, these towers are the only domestic edifices in the city erected before the middle of the fifteenth century. The vast palaces to which strangers now flock for the sake of the picture galleries they contain, have been most of them constructed in the sixteenth or seventeenth centuries, a few even later. Among the earliest is that Palazzo Cenci,[h] whose gloomy low-browed arch so powerfully affected the imagination of Shelley.

Why more was not done by the clergy. It was no want of wealth that hampered the architectural efforts of the clergy, for large revenues flowed in upon them from every corner of Christendom. A good deal was actually spent upon the erection or repairs of churches and convents, although with a less liberal hand than that of such great Transalpine prelates as Hugh of Lincoln or Conrad of Cologne. But the Popes always needed money for their projects of ambition, and in times when disorder and corruption were at their height the work of building stopped altogether. Thus it was that after the time of the Carolingians scarcely a church was erected, though some were repaired and enlarged, until the beginning of the twelfth century, when the reforms of Hildebrand had breathed new zeal into the priesthood. The Babylonish captivity of Avignon, as it was called, with the Great Schism of the West that followed upon it, was the cause

A.D. 1308–1377.
A.D. 1378–1417.

[h] The name of Cenci is a very old one at Rome: it is supposed to be an abbreviation of Crescentius. We hear in the eleventh century of a certain Cencius, who on one occasion made Gregory VII prisoner. The Palazzo Venezia at the southern end of the present Corso is also of early date.

of a second similar intermission, which lasted nearly a
century and a half.

At every time, however, even when his work went on *Tendency of*
most briskly, the labours of the Roman architect took the *the Roman*
builders to
direction of restoring and readorning old churches rather *adhere to*
than of erecting new ones.   While the Transalpine coun- *the ancient*
manner.
tries, except in a few favoured spots, such as Provence and
part of the Rhineland, remained during several ages with
few and rudely built stone churches, Rome possessed, as
the inheritance of the earlier Christian centuries, a profusion of houses of worship, some of them still unsurpassed in splendour, and far more than adequate to the
needs of her diminished population.   In repairing these
from time to time, the original form and style of work
were, down to the days of the Renaissance, in most cases
preserved, while in constructing new churches, the abundance of models, beautiful in themselves and hallowed as
well by antiquity as by religious feeling, enthralled the
invention of the workman, bound him down to be at best
a faithful imitator, and forbade him to deviate at pleasure
from the old-established manner.   Thus it befell that while
his brethren throughout the rest of Europe were passing
by successive steps from the old Roman and Byzantine
styles to Romanesque, and from Romanesque to Pointed,
the Roman architect scarcely departed from the plan and
arrangements of the primitive basilica.   This is one chief
reason why there is so little of Gothic work in Rome, so
little even of Romanesque like that of Pisa.   What there *Absence of*
is appears chiefly in the pointed window, more rarely in *Gothic in*
Rome.
the arch, seldom or never in spire or tower or column.
Only one of the existing churches of Rome is Gothic
throughout, and that, the Dominican church of Sta. Maria
sopra Minerva, was built by foreign monks.   In some of
the other churches, and especially in the cloisters of the

convents, instances may be observed of the same style: in others slight traces, by accident or design almost obliterated.[i]

Destruction and altera- tion of the old buildings:

The mention of obliteration suggests a third cause of the comparative want of mediaeval buildings in the city — the constant depredations and changes of which she has been the subject. Ever since the time of Constantine Rome has been a city of destruction, and Christians have vied with pagans, citizens with enemies, in urging on the

By invaders. fatal work. Her siege and capture by the Norman Robert Wiscard,[j] the ally of Hildebrand against Henry the Fourth, was far more ruinous than the attacks of the Goths or Vandals, and itself yields in atrocity to the sack of Rome in A.D. 1527 by the soldiers of the Catholic king and most

By the Romans of the Middle Ages. pious Emperor Charles the Fifth.[k] Since the days of the first barbarian invasions the Romans have gone on building with materials taken from the ancient temples, theatres, law-courts, baths, and villas, stripping them of their gorgeous casings of marble, pulling down their walls for the sake of the blocks of travertine, setting up their own hovels on the top or in the midst of these majestic piles. Thus it has been with the memorials of paganism: a somewhat different cause has contributed to the disappearance of the

---

[i] See Note XX at end.

[j] A good deal of the mischief done by Robert Wiscard, from which the parts of the city lying beyond the Coliseum towards the river and St. John Lateran never recovered, is attributed to the Saracenic troops in his service. Saracen pirates are said to have once before sacked Rome. Gaiserich was not a heathen, but he was a furious Arian, which, as far as respect to the churches of the orthodox went, was nearly the same thing. The seven-branched candlestick and other vessels of the Second Temple, which Titus had brought from Jerusalem to Rome, are said to have been carried off by the Vandals and lost on the voyage to Africa.

[k] We are told that one cause of the ferocity of the German part of the army of Charles was their anger at the ruinous condition of the imperial palace.

mediaeval churches. What pillage, or fanaticism, or the

wanton lust of destruction did in the one case, the osten-
tatious zeal of modern times has done in the other. The
era of the final establishment of the Popes as temporal
sovereigns of the city is also that of the supremacy of the
Renaissance style in architecture. After the time of
Nicholas the Fifth, the pontiff against whom, it will be
remembered, the spirit of municipal freedom made its
last struggle in the conspiracy of Porcaro, everything was
built in the neo-classic style, and the prevailing enthusiasm
for the antique produced a corresponding dislike to everything mediaeval, a dislike conspicuous in men like Julius
the Second and Leo the Tenth, from whom the grandeur
of modern Rome may be said to begin. Not long after
their time the great religious movement of the sixteenth
century, while triumphing in the north of Europe, was in
the south met and overcome by a counter-reformation in
the bosom of the old church herself, and the construction
or restoration of ecclesiastical buildings became again the
passion of the devout.[1] No employment, whether it be
called a pleasure or a duty, could have been better suited
to the court and aristocracy of Rome. They were indolent;
wealthy, and fond of displaying their wealth; full of good
taste, and anxious, especially when advancing years had
chased away youth's pleasures, to be full of good works
also. Popes and cardinals and the heads of the great
families vied with one another in building new churches
and restoring or enlarging those they found till little of
the old was left; raising over them huge cupolas, substituting massive pilasters for the single-shafted columns,
adorning the interior with a profusion of rare marbles, of

---

[1] Under the influence, partly of this anti-pagan spirit, partly of his own
restless vanity, partly of a passion to be doing something, Pope Sixtus the
Fifth destroyed or spoiled not a few monuments of antiquity.

carving and gilding, of frescoes and altar-pieces by the best masters of the sixteenth and seventeenth centuries. None but a bigoted mediaevalist can refuse to acknowledge the warmth of tone, the repose, the stateliness, of the churches of modern Rome; but even in the midst of admiration the sated eye turns away from the wealth of ponderous ornament, and longs for the clear pure colour, the simple yet grand proportions, that give a charm to the buildings of an earlier age.

Existing relics of the Dark and Middle Ages. Few of the ancient churches have escaped untouched; many have been altogether rebuilt. There are also some, however, in which the modernizers of the sixteenth and subsequent centuries have spared two features of the old structure, its rounded apse or tribune and its bell-tower. The interior of the concave tribune is usually covered *The mosaics.* with mosaics, exceedingly interesting, both from the ideas they express and as the only monuments of pictorial art that remain to us from the Dark Ages.[m] To speak of them, however, as they deserve to be spoken of, would involve a digression for which there is no space here. The campanile or bell-tower is a quaint little square brick tower, of no great height, usually standing detached from the church, and having in its topmost, sometimes also in its other upper stories, several arcade windows, divided by tiny marble pillars.[m] What with these campaniles, then far more numerous than they are now, and with the huge brick fortresses of the nobles, towers must have held in the landscape of the mediaeval city very much the part which domes do now. Although less imposing, they were probably more picturesque, the rather as in the earlier part of the Middle Ages the houses and churches, which are now mostly crowded together on the flat of the Campus Martius, were scattered over the heights and slopes of the

[m] See Note XXI at end.

Coelian, Aventine, and Esquiline hills, regions which were deserted after the ruin wrought by Robert Wiscard, and which remained almost unbuilt upon till the recent growth of the city has (since 1870) begun to cover the Esquiline and part of the Coelian with houses.[n] Modern Rome lies chiefly on the opposite or north-eastern and north-western sides of the Capitol, and the change from the old to the new site of the city was not completed until the sixteenth century. The Rome of Frederick Barbarossa and Arnold of Brescia lay mostly round the Capitol and between the Capitol and the Tiber; it included the old suburb of Trastevere, but not the region near St. Peter's, which constituted the (then still separate) Leonine city. In A.D. 1536, in anticipation of the entry of Charles the Fifth, the rebuilding of the Capitol (afterwards carried on by Michael Angelo) was begun upon foundations said to have been laid by the first Tarquin; and the palace of the Senator, the greatest municipal edifice of Rome, which had hitherto looked towards the Forum and the Coliseum, was made to front in the direction of St. Peter's and the modern town, which had then already begun to spread out over the old Campus Martius and the slopes of the Quirinal.

The Rome of to-day is no more like the city of Rienzo than she is to the city of Trajan; just as the Roman church of the twentieth century differs profoundly, complete as her historical continuity may appear, from the church of Hildebrand. But among all their changes, both church and city have kept themselves wonderfully free from the intrusion of foreign, or at least of Teutonic, *Changed aspect of the city of Rome.*

[n] The Palatine hill seems to have been then, as it is for the most part now, a waste of stupendous ruins. In the great imperial palace upon its northern and eastern sides an official of the Eastern court had his residence in the beginning of the eighth century. In the time of Charles the Great, some seventy years later, this palace was no longer habitable.

CHAP. XVI.

Analogy between her architecture and her civil and ecclesiastical constitution.

elements, and have faithfully preserved at all times something of an old Roman character. Latin Christianity inherited from the imperial system of old that firmly knit yet flexible organization, which was one of the grand secrets of its power. The great men whom mediaeval Rome gave to or trained up for the Papacy were, like their predecessors of the ancient world, administrators, legislators, statesmen; seldom enthusiasts themselves, but perfectly understanding how to use and guide the enthusiasm of others — of the French and German crusaders, of such men as Francis of Assisi and Dominic and Ignatius. Between Catholicism in Italy and Catholicism in Germany or England there was always, as there is still, a perceptible difference. So also, if the analogy be not too fanciful,

Preservation of an antique character in both.

was it with Rome the city. Socially she seemed always drifting towards feudalism; yet she never fell into its grasp. Materially, her architecture was at one time considerably influenced by Pointed forms, yet Gothic never became, as in the rest of Europe, the dominant style. It approached Rome late, and departed from her early, so that we scarcely notice its presence, and seem to pass almost without a break from the old Romanesque° to the new Graeco-Roman of the Renaissance. Thus regarded, the history of the city, both in her political fortunes and in her buildings, is seen to be intimately connected with that of the Holy Empire itself. The Empire in its title and its pretensions expressed the idea of the permanence of the institutions of the ancient world; Rome the city had, in externals at least, carefully preserved their traditions: the names of her magistracies, the character of her buildings, all spoke of antiquity, and gave it a strange and shadowy life in the midst of new races and new forms of faith.

Based on the feeling of the unity of mankind, the Empire

° Such as we see it in the later and lesser churches of basilica form.

was a perpetuation of the Roman dominion into which the

old nationalities had been absorbed, with the addition of the Christian element which had created a new nationality that was also universal. By the extension of her citizenship to all her subjects heathen Rome had become the common home, and, figuratively, even the local dwelling-place of the civilized races of man. By the theology of the time Christian Rome had been made the mystical type of humanity, the one flock of the faithful scattered over the whole earth, the holy city whither, as to the temple on Moriah, all the Israel of God should come up to worship. She was not merely an image of the mighty world, she was the mighty world itself in miniature. The pastor of her local church is also the universal bishop ; the seven suffragan bishops who consecrate him are overseers of petty sees in Ostia, Antium, and the like, towns lying close round Rome ; the cardinal priests and deacons who join these seven in electing him derive their title to be princes of the Church, the supreme spiritual council of the Christian world, from the incumbency of a parochial cure within the precincts of the city. Similarly, her ruler, the Emperor, is ruler of mankind ; he is deemed to be chosen by the acclamations of her people : [p] he must be duly crowned in one of her basilicas. She is, like Jerusalem of old, the mother of us all.

There is yet another way in which the record of the

---

[p] The appearance on the stage of the seven Germanic electors was a result of the confusion of the German kingdom with the Roman Empire, and in strictness they ought to have had nothing to do with the Roman crown at all. The right to bestow it could only — on principle — belong to some Roman authority, and those who felt the difficulty were driven to suppose a formal cession of their privilege by the Roman people to the seven electors. See p. 235, *supra;* and cf. Matthew Villani (iv. 77), 'Il popolo Romano, non da se, ma la chiesa per lui, concedette la elezione degli Imperadori a sette principi della Magna.'

domestic contests of Rome throws light upon the history of the Empire. From the eleventh century to the fifteenth her citizens did not cease to demand in the name of the old republic their freedom from the tyranny of the nobles and the Pope, and their right to rule over the world at large. These efforts — selfish and fantastic we may call them, yet men like Petrarch did not disdain to them their sympathy — issued from the same theories and were directed to the same ends as those which inspired Otto the Third and Frederick Barbarossa and Dante himself. They witness to the same incapacity to form any ideal for the future except a revival of the past ; the same belief that one universal state is both desirable and possible, but possible only through the means of Rome : the same refusal to admit that a right which has once existed can ever be extinguished. In the days of the Renaissance these notions were passing silently away : the succeeding century brought with it misfortunes that broke the spirit of the nation. Italy was the battlefield of Europe : her wealth became the prey of a rapacious soldiery : Florence, the noblest of her republics, was conquered by an unfeeling Emperor, and handed over to a despot as a pledge of amity to a selfish Medicean Pope. When the hope of independence had been lost, the people turned away from politics to live for art and literature, and found, before many generations had passed, how little such devotion could compensate for the departure of a national spirit, and of the activity of civic life. A century after the golden days of Ariosto and Raphael, Italian literature had become frigid and affected, while Italian art was dying of mannerism.

Extinction of the Florentine republic, A.D. 1530.

At length, after long ages of sloth, the stagnant waters were troubled. The Romans, who had lived in listless contentment under the paternal sway of the Popes, received new ideas from the advent of the revolutionary armies of

France, and found the papal system, since its re-establishment in 1815 as an ecclesiastical bureaucracy, less tolerable *Feelings of*
than it had been of yore. When the rest of Italy had been *the modern*
Italians
delivered from the rule of Hapsburgs and Bourbons, the *towards*
name of Rome became again a rallying-cry for the patriots *Rome.*
of Italy, but in a sense most unlike the old one. The contemporaries of Arnold and Rienzo desired freedom as a
step to universal domination : their descendants, inspired
by national patriotism as well as by civic pride, more wisely
sought to be the capital of the Italian kingdom. Dante
prayed for a monarchy of the world, a reign of peace and
Christian brotherhood : those who, five centuries later,
invoked his name as the earliest prophet of their creed strove
after an idea that never crossed his mind — the gathering
of all Italians into a national state. Yet this he and they
had in common, — they and he alike desired to exclude
the Papacy from the sphere of secular government.

One who watched the long struggle of the Italians to
make Rome the free capital of a united nation, from the
days of the Mazzinian triumvirate of 1849 to the happier
day when the army of Victor Emmanuel passed through
the Porta Pia, may be permitted to recall the sentiments
of that time, now grown dim to the new generation.

Dull common-sense politicians in other countries did
not then understand this passion for Rome as a capital,
and used to lecture the Italians on their flightiness. The
Italian patriots did not themselves argue or pretend that
the banks of the Tiber were a suitable site for a capital.
They admitted, in the days before 1870 to which I am
referring, that Rome was lonely, unhealthy, and in a bad
strategical position ; that she had no particular facilities
for trade ; that her people were less thrifty and industrious
than the Tuscans or the Piedmontese. Nevertheless all
Italy cried with one voice for Rome, believing that her

CHAP. XVI. national life could never thrill with a strong and steady pulsation till the ancient capital had become the nation's heart. They felt that it was owing to Rome — Rome pagan as well as Christian — that they had once played so grand a part in the drama of European history, and that the recollections of those glorious days had done much to create the passion for national unity. This enthusiasm for a famous name was substantially the same feeling as that which created and hallowed the Holy Empire of the Middle Ages. The events which on both sides of the Atlantic befell during the momentous forty years between 1830 and 1870 proved that men were not then, any more than they had ever been before, chiefly governed by calculations of material profit and loss. Sentiments, fancies, theories, retained their power; the spirit of poetry had not wholly passed away from politics. Strange, therefore, as seems to us the worship paid to the name of mediaeval Rome by those who saw the sins and the misery of her people, it can hardly have been an intenser feeling than was the imaginative reverence wherewith the patriots of Italy during those years of struggle looked on the city whence, as from a fountain, all the streams of their national life had sprung, and in which, as in an ocean, they were all again to mingle.

CHAPTER XVII

THE EAST ROMAN EMPIRE

DURING the Middle Ages, Western statesmen and churchmen, Western thinkers and writers, took little note of the Eastern Empire which stubbornly held its ground at Constantinople down to A.D. 1453. Its claim to represent the ancient dominion of Rome was practically ignored. Its splendid efforts in the defence of civilization against the fierce tribes of the North, and the still more formidable Musulmans of the East, received slight recognition, and scarcely any support. Even in later times the part played by the people and rulers of New Rome was inadequately appreciated, and it is only in our own days that history has begun to atone for this long neglect.[a]

The two imperial lines, which the revolt of Italy and the coronation of Charles the Great in A.D. 800 substituted for the one Roman Emperor whom Christian doctrine had required and continued to require, were, after that fateful year, always rivals and usually unfriendly rivals.

[a] Gibbon does much less than justice to them : and the first modern historian who set them in a fuller and fairer light was the late Mr. Finlay. Le Beau, in his *Histoire du Bas-Empire*, gave a *résumé* of East Roman history useful in its day, and among more recent works of value are those of Karl Hopf (in Ersch and Gruber, vols. 85 and 86), and of Hertzberg (*Geschichte der Byzantiner*), with the excellent *History of the Later Roman Empire* of J. B. Bury.

A full bibliography will be found in the learned and luminous *Geschichte der byzantinischen Litteratur* of K. Krumbacher, which is itself of great service for a comprehension of Byzantine history generally.

But their direct relations either of negotiation or of armed hostility were infrequent.   Each went its own way.   Each had foes of its own to confront.   Each affected the other much less than might have been expected, when it is remembered that each maintained its claim to be the heir of Rome, and to perpetuate the political and religious traditions of the early Christian Emperors.   Yet few as the points of contact were, the history of the East Roman is a necessary complement to that of the West Roman Empire, for the course of events in each throws an instructive light upon the course of events in the other. As the divergences are worth noting, so too are the resemblances.   Both Empires rested upon the memories of Rome.   Both stood in a peculiar relation to the Christian Church.   Both had to deal with the instreaming races of the North.   But these conditions of life told differently upon the one and upon the other, and gave a different direction to their respective fortunes.

To sketch, even in outline, the long and chequered and romantic history of the Eastern Empire would be altogether outside the scope of this book.   But from among the salient features that mark its annals I may single out for comment a few which specially serve to illustrate the parallel or divergent history of the West.

Slight effect on the East Roman Empire of the coronation of Charles the Great.

It has already been remarked (see p. 26 and p. 62, *supra*) that neither the extinction of the line of Emperors who reigned in the West down to A.D. 476, nor the establishment of a second imperial line at Old Rome by the coronation of Charles the Great in A.D. 800, was an event of critical significance in the history of the East Roman realm.   By the event of A.D. 476 the Eastern monarch became the sole legal representative of Roman claims, claims still admitted in theory, to the lordship of the whole Western world.   But the only practical result of this nominally enlarged authority was to induce, fifty years afterwards, Justinian's reconquest of North Africa, Sicily, Sardinia, and Italy, territories which added nothing to the effective strength of the Empire, and which were successively lost, Africa in the seventh, Sicily and Sardinia in the ninth, Italy partly in the eighth and partly in the eleventh century. By the event of A.D. 800 the right to represent Rome, carrying with it the headship of the whole Christian commonwealth, was withdrawn from the Eastern line, so far as the Roman Church and the Franks could withdraw it, so that such titular sovereignty, by this time shadowy, as still remained to the Roman Emperor over the world at large, became henceforth vested in those Western potentates, first Frankish, then Italian, ultimately German, who could obtain it from the hands of the Pope, or (in later days) by the election of the German princes. But this effort to transfer the claim to universal monarchy did not affect the legal rights of the Eastern sovereign in the countries which actually obeyed him, and affected but slightly the position he held towards the states that bordered on his own. Though he had lost Rome he continued to hold Southern Italy; nor did any of his nearer provinces in Thrace, or Greece, or Asia shew any signs of turning to his new Teutonic rivals. To the Westerns (other than the Southern Italians) he was already merely a name; so none of their peoples or cities, except Venice, thought of cleaving to him. To the Easterns he had been, and still remained, not only the national monarch of whom they were proud, but the legitimate heir of Old Rome; for the coronation of Charles in which the Pope, the citizens of Old Rome, and the Franks had joined, was in their eyes an outrageous usurpation. Thus the Eastern Empire was, for practical purposes, no more weakened by the incoming of Charles, and afterwards of

Otto the Great, than it had been strengthened by the disappearance of Romulus Augustulus in A.D. 476. We may therefore cast our glance over its history as a whole, covering a thousand years from the accession of Arcadius in A.D. 395 — the point at which the real political separation of East and West begins — to the taking of Constantinople by Mohammed the Second in A.D. 1453.

Constant struggles of the Eastern Empire: A long history! longer than that of any European monarchy, or indeed of any monarchy save those of China and Japan; and a history which amazes us by the power of recovery and rejuvenescence which this singular state displays. From the time of Justinian onwards, it had to support, against formidable enemies on either side, a veritable and unending struggle for life, longer and more perilous than the struggle which in earlier days Rome had for centuries maintained against the Samnites, against Carthage, and against the Italian allies.

against the Northern barbarians, On the north swarms of fierce savages poured down in succession upon it from the wilds of Scythia. First, about the beginning of the sixth century, came various Slavonic tribes. Then the Avars, established along the Theiss and *A.D. 619 and 626.* the Middle Danube, began a long series of desolating raids, and twice appeared before Constantinople. Then, early in the seventh century, the Bulgarians, a Finnish people, moved out of their old seats on the Volga and the Kama, occupied the region which now bears their name, laid waste and ultimately settled in the adjoining parts of Thrace (where they became blent with, and adopted the speech of the Slavic tribes), and threatened Constantinople itself. Further to the north-east, the Petchenegs, also a Finnic or Tatar race, having established themselves in the steppes of the Dnieper and the Don, frequently attacked the frontiers; and somewhat later, the Russians (perhaps led by chieftains of Scandinavian stock), descending the

Dnieper in their light boats and crossing the Euxine, were twice repelled with difficulty from the walls of the capital. Of all these enemies the Bulgarians were the most dangerous because the nearest. The Emperor Basil II reduced them in the tenth century to nominal subjection, but they regained their freedom within less than a century, and continued to threaten the Empire until they fell before the rising power of the Ottoman Turks. While the greater part of Thrace had thus been overspread by the Bulgarians, the North-west provinces had passed to the Slavs, the power of whose leading kingdom culminated in the reign of the Servian Tsar Stephen Dushan in the thirteenth century. Thus, speaking broadly, it may be said that, from the middle of the sixth century onwards, the Empire was constantly at war with these Northern barbarians, and often seemed on the point of succumbing to their attacks.

Meantime it had to resist still more terrible foes advancing from the south. The first wave of Arab invasion tore away Syria and Egypt, rolled over Asia Minor, and carried a Musulman host to the shores of the Bosphorus (A.D. 673). After many long and fierce struggles the whole of Asia Minor was recovered, and in the end of the tenth and beginning of the eleventh century even Northern Syria (except Tyre and Damascus) and Armenia were reconquered by John Tzimiskes and Basil II. But in the middle of the eleventh the rise of the Seljukian Turks drove back the Romans from Syria, and by degrees forced them out of the eastern and central parts of Asia Minor. Armenia was lost for ever, and in the thirteenth century only a strip of country along the Black Sea and the Sea of Marmora remained to Christianity. The ruin of Central and Southern Asia Minor, in earlier ages one of the most flourishing and populous regions of the world, dates from

against the Musulman Arabs and Turks.

Battle of Manzikert, A.D. 1071.

CHAP. XVII. the devastating border wars in which Turks and Romans alternately harried it.

Attack of the Crusaders, A.D. 1204. Yet neither the Bulgarians, nor the Arabs, nor the Seljukian sultans inflicted so deadly a blow on the Empire as did those from whom enmity ought least of all to have been expected. The Normans, after winning South Italy, attacked the Eastern Roman territories in Epirus, and were with difficulty repelled by Manual Comnenus. In A.D. 1204 a powerful fleet of Latin Christians, French, German, and Venetian, setting out on the Fourth Crusade, turned aside from the professed aim of their expedition, besieged and took Constantinople, and set up a short-lived *Latin Em-* line of Latin Emperors there. From this catastrophe *perors,* A.D. the Empire never really recovered. After the fall of the Latin dynasty a vigorous prince of East Roman stock and Orthodox faith, already reigning at Nicaea, regained the throne, and his successors, ruling mere fragments of the old territory in Europe and Asia, held the throne till the Ottoman Turks, by that time masters of the whole of its dominions on the European continent, captured the city in 1453.

The record of these constant wars against two sets of enemies is a splendid record, for, sometimes on one side and sometimes on the other, the fortunes of the East Romans seemed often desperate. The admiration which their resistance excites becomes even greater when we reflect that the Empire had no natural frontiers easily defensible in war, and that it was frequently troubled by the struggles of rival aspirants for the crown. The causes of the strength it shewed for defence, and the source of the vitality which enabled it so often to recover from wounds apparently deadly, deserve to be examined.

High among those causes is to be placed the perpetuation of the name and traditions of the ancient Roman

CHAP. XVII.

*Causes of
the long
resistance
of the
Eastern
Empire.*

*Traditions
of Rome.*

power. The thought that they were Romans, the heirs and representatives of the great ruling race which had brought the whole world under its sway, was the life-spring of this strangely mixed people, in whose veins there flowed scarcely any Italian blood, and very few of whom could speak the Roman tongue. The Western peoples called them Greeks, as modern Europe has been wont to do. But as they were not Greeks in race, for the descendants of the Greek colonies on the Aegean and the Propontis can have contributed but a slight infusion of Greek blood, so neither, though their art and letters were Hellenistic, did they shew many of the distinctive qualities which had marked the Greeks of the classical ages. Still less were they Romans by stock or by character, though they called themselves, and were called throughout the East, by that title, perpetuated in the names Roum and Roumelia given to their territories, and the name Romaic used to describe their language. But the old name and the old institutions, changed indeed in the course of ages, but changed by no sudden break, gave them a sense of superiority over all other peoples, a pride and self-confidence which supported them in many a dark hour. This made them a nation, and indeed a nation which, though local diversities and local forms of speech survived, was for defensive purposes closely welded together. Though we hear of many insurrections in the capital, many contests for the crown between rival claimants, there is scarcely ever a racial or provincial revolt, seldom any attempt of a magnate to set himself up as ruler of an independent realm. The Empire stood one and indivisible against all its foes. This sentiment of an imperial nationality, no longer universal, but national in the strictest sense, because bound into one not only by political ties, but also by those of language, ideas, and manners,[b] became further intensified by the existence of one great centre of population. Constantinople gave strength to the Empire, through its incomparable position, all but impregnable to attack. It was an admirable centre for naval operations, since it touched both the Mediterranean and the Euxine, and could use the sea for expeditions to the distant points that were threatened. It was also a wonderful reservoir of national energy. Though the East Roman armies were mainly composed of the barbarian or semi-barbarian subjects who dwelt in the frontier provinces, the teeming population and the riches of the city intensified the spirit and pride of the whole people, and gave the Empire a heart whose pulsations were felt to the furthest extremities. In the tenth century, before the rise of the great Italian republics, Constantinople stood practically alone in the Christian world as a centre of commerce, wealth, and splendour, with a thousand inhabitants for every hundred that could be found in Old Rome or in the largest cities of Germany or Gaul.[c]

And Constantinople was also the centre of a well ordered administration such as existed nowhere else in the world. That highly organized civil service which ancient Rome had built up from the days of Julius Caesar to those of Diocletian had been preserved in full efficiency down into the twelfth century, in the end of and after which the signs of decay became more evident.[d] It powerfully contributed to hold the provinces together, to provide the government, always pressed by costly wars, with a revenue,

[b] Although many dissimilarities continued to subsist in the outlying provinces, and even in the highlands of Greece.

[c] The Norse Sagas call it Micklegarth (the Great City).

[d] By that time maritime commerce had largely passed into the hands of the Italian cities, especially Genoa, industry had begun to decline, and the rural population were impoverished. The border wars and raids of the twelfth and thirteenth centuries desolated Asia Minor, which has never recovered.

and to maintain the public order and public confidence which enable industry and commerce to flourish. One may almost say that, as Constantinople was the heart, so the civil service supplied the nerves and sinews of the monarchy. In this respect the East Roman Empire stood contrasted with its Romano-Germanic sister. Charles the Great attempted to govern his wide dominions by imperial officers sent forth to carry out his orders and correct and control the action of the local magnates. But he had nothing that could be called an administrative system. Neither had Otto the Great or his Saxon, Franconian, or Swabian successors. The only permanent organization their realm possessed was the intricate and cumbrous machinery of feudalism, hardly better fitted for war than it was for advancement in the arts of peaceful life. And none of the Teutonic monarchs had a city which could be called in any true sense a capital. Least of all did they find such a centre in Rome, the most disaffected spot in their dominions.

As an efficient civil administration helped to maintain the internal prosperity of the Empire, and enabled it to bear the cost of war, so the excellence of its military arrangements gave it strength for defence. The army was skilfully organized and carefully drilled: it had a system of scientific tactics: it drew recruits from outside the Empire as well as from the more warlike of the races that dwelt within. The fleet, efficiently appointed and trained, remained for a long time, perhaps down to the twelfth century, superior to any hostile navy it had to encounter. And the Easterns had at their disposal an extremely important implement of warfare in that mysterious 'Romaic' or 'Greek' Fire or 'Sea Fire' invented by Kallinikus in the seventh century—a liquid which they cast upon the vessels of an enemy, and which burnt or exploded where it fell. It often secured to them a victory, or covered them in retreat.[e]

Despotic government of the Empire.

The East Roman monarchy was a pure despotism. After the accession of Claudius Caesar, the third successor of Augustus, no one seems ever to have thought either of restoring the shattered republican constitution or of creating any monarchical constitution whatever, that is to say, any set of institutions designed to associate the people with the conduct of government, or to determine the succession to the throne, or to limit the authority of its occupant. In the ancient world monarchy had come to mean autocracy. For more than a thousand years the very idea of a regular constitution, in the Greek sense or old Roman sense, as well as in that mediaeval sense which re-emerged with the rise of the Italian republics in the twelfth century, seemed to have utterly vanished. It was assumed that the Emperor must be an irresponsible ruler. It was left to chance to determine who should be Emperor. A body called the Senate continued to exist, as it continued to exist at Old Rome, and it submissively recognized the person who had already made himself master of the city. But the crown was the price of the strongest. No body of persons had an effective legal right to choose its wearer. A palace intrigue, the favour of a queen, a rising in the streets, the caprice of an army returning from the field, threw it into the hands of some aspirant perhaps hitherto unknown : and he became at once a sort of God upon earth, sometimes entitled 'Equal to the Apostles,'[f] approached with slavish prostrations, sole legislator and

[e] See Bury, *History of Later Roman Empire*, vol. ii. p. 319, for a receipt for the making of it given by Marcus Graecus in the tenth century. Some of the ingredients of one kind of it are those of gunpowder ; but it does not seem to have been used to hurl projectiles.

[f] Ἰσαπόστολος, a title first applied to Constantine the Great. As to the coronations of the Emperors, see Note XXI at end.

supreme judge, virtual master of the lives and property of all his subjects. The crimes by which he might have risen did not diminish the sanctity which his person received from the office. Despotism was of course tempered, as it must always be, by various environing influences, by the sentiment of the Church, by public opinion, sometimes expressing itself in sedition or insurrection, by the views and interests of the noble families of the capital, and (in later days) of the great land-holders in the rural districts. But these factors acted practically, not through any legal channels. Thus the Eastern Empire has only a dynastic, an ecclesiastical, and a military history. It has no constitutional history. The Teutonic Empire, which, though an *Absence of* autocracy in theory, was never a despotism in fact, had in *any regular* all its phases some sort of constitution, and what might be *constitution.* called a kind of political life. At several moments it became the theatre for a conflict of great principles. But the Eastern Empire had no political life whatever. In it no strife of principles arose. It was always substantially the same institution, which no one thought of changing — a monarchy not only above law but in so far outside law as that law had nothing to do with determining the person on whom it descended. In a state constantly at war this concentration of power in one hand had some advantages; just as the absence of regular rules of succession had the merit of giving to energy and ambition opportunities for displacing the incapable. Men of force came more readily to the top than they do in hereditary monarchies. There was of course a tendency for the throne to become settled in a family, for an Emperor usually tried to secure the succession for his son or some other relative either by publicly destining him for power, or by associating him as co-Emperor during his own life. Sometimes a woman of character was able to bestow the crown on successive husbands,

CHAP. XVII. who got in this way (perhaps by the aid of murder) a sort of title by affinity.   But when the vigour of a reigning stock began to die out, the stock usually disappeared, and an upstart adventurer set up a new dynasty.   Several times such a bold and strenuous man became the deliverer of the Empire from its foes.   Heraclius, Leo the Isaurian, Basil the First, and the founder of the Comnenian line, were all men of conspicuous force and capacity.   The advent of each marked a renewal of the aggressive power of the State.

Association of the imperial government with the Orthodox Church.   But of all the causes which prolonged the existence of the Eastern Empire the most potent was its association, one might say its identification, with the Orthodox Church. Religion had for a time been in the East a disruptive force. The theological controversies of the fifth and sixth centuries had contributed to bring about the loss of Egypt and Syria to the Musulmans in the seventh century, for the Monophysites of those regions, hostile to the doctrine settled by the Council of Chalcedon, which was then dominant at Constantinople, offered only a feeble resistance to the invader.   So in later days the diffusion of the so-called heresies of the Bogomiles or Paulicians weakened the loyalty of the North-western provinces.   But the Orthodox faith, once it had been defined and determined by the first six Councils, fixed itself deep in the people of the capital and of the districts which formed the solid nucleus of the Empire, and presently grew into a bond of incalculable strength.   Side by side with the pride in the Roman name, it created a national feeling far more intense than the sentiment of common subjection to a world-embracing power which had sprung up and become a unifying force under the Antonines and their successors.   Some historians of the eighteenth century thought that Christianity hastened the fall of the Roman Empire.   Rather may it

be said that Christianity saved the Roman Empire.   As it
was the sense of one faith binding men into one commonwealth of the faithful that kept alive the imperial idea in
the West, and enabled Charles and Otto to set up the ancient image on a new Teutonic pedestal, so it was the sense
that they were the people chosen of God and Christ to
defend that faith, a sense constantly stimulated by strife
with heathen on the north and Musulmans on the south,
that gave hope, courage, and unity to the East Romans all
through the Dark and Middle Ages.[g] Well would it have
been for them if in the last fatal years and months they
could have so far abated their devotion to the minutiae of
the Orthodox creed and to the claims of their own spiritual chief as to have bought by prompter, franker, and
fuller concessions the help of the Pope and of Latin arms.[h]

When we pass to consider the points in which the
Eastern Empire may profitably be compared with that of
its Western sister, three will be found to deserve special
examination: the relations of each power to the Northern invaders, its relations to the Church, its relations to
the traditions and institutions of ancient Rome.

As from the fourth century onwards it was the mission   *Relations of*
and the glory of the Latin Church to convert and civilize   *the Empire*
the invading races of the North who descended upon the   *and the*
                                                             Church to the
Western provinces,[i] so too did the Eastern Church and   *barbarians*
                                                             of the North.

[g] This is of course more true of the people of the capital and the more
civilized central districts of the Empire than of the outlying parts, in some of
which a sort of heathenism survived for some time, while ancient semi-heathen
superstitions and usages survived still longer.

[h] The Council which sat first at Ferrara and then at Florence did in A.D.
1439 effect a sort of union of the Eastern and Western churches; but the
action of the Eastern Emperor and his prelates in yielding on most of the
points was disapproved by a large part of his people, and caused bitter dissensions at Constantinople.

[i] The Germans eastward of the Rhine were, however, largely converted by
Scottish missionaries from Ireland, such as St. Columban and St. Gall, who

Empire, when they found, somewhat later, swarms of Slav and Bulgarian heathen settling on their borders, begin after a time to impart their culture to these formidable neighbours. Both divisions of the Christian world had the same task: both in a manner fulfilled it. Yet there are striking differences. The West had to deal chiefly with Teutonic peoples, most of them already partially Christianized (though many were at first Arians), and most of them well advanced beyond mere barbarism. Much of its work was done before the revolt of North Italy in the eighth century severed East and West. The East received the attacks of Slavonic and Finnish tribes, all heathen, all rude and fierce, and therewithal, if not inferior in natural intelligence, yet in a far lower stage of culture. When, in the fifth and sixth centuries, the Goths, Vandals, Burgundians, Franks, and Lombards settled in the Roman provinces the imperial power was dying. These intruding settlers scarcely deemed themselves its enemies; and most of them soon began to cherish such of its institutions as survived, and to bow themselves to the teachings of the Latin Church.[1] They became easily blent with the Roman provincials. The Franks who stood out as the leading race presently became the defenders of the Popedom, took up the traditions of the old Empire, accepted the transference of its crown to their own sovereign, and kept it thenceforth in Teutonic hands. The Roman sceptre became their sceptre, and there remained no sense of antagonism between the children of the conquered and those of the conquerors. But in the East, though the Slavs who settled in Macedonia,

acted independently of Rome, as well as by Anglo-Saxon missionaries such as St. Boniface, who went with papal approval.

[1] As to certain exceptions, *e.g.* in the case of the Lombards, see above, chapter III.

Illyria, and Greece during the seventh and eighth centuries CHAP. XVII.
became Graecized and subjects, if somewhat unruly subjects, of the Emperor, the later Slavonic intruders, and
still more the Finnish Bulgarians, came as savage pagan
plunderers, destroyed such Roman civilization as they
found and were thenceforth (with a few intervals of peace)
deadly enemies. The Empire maintained a continual
conflict with them. They were ultimately converted (the *Conversion*
Bulgarians in A.D. 864, the Servians about the same time), *of the Bul-*
and with their new faith they received the use of letters, *garians*
the rudiments of law, and a certain measure of culture. *and Serbs.*
Somewhat later, the same change passed upon the Russians, who, standing further away, came into less close
and frequent contact with the East Romans, a contact
sometimes of alliance and sometimes of warfare. Constantinople became to all these peoples the metropolis
of religion and civilization, and the colour which their
religion then received is still evident in all the churches
of Eastern Europe. The peculiar spirit of Byzantine
Christianity may be discerned to-day as well in the attitude
of the Church of Russia to the Tsar as in the attitude of
the Russian and Hellenic peoples to their clergy. But all
these Danubian and trans-Danubian races, Serbs, Bulgars,
Roumanians, and Russians, remained outside the circle
of imperial traditions. They never imbibed the Roman
spirit, never became absorbed into the secular civilization
which New Rome had preserved. Still less did they so *The bar-*
mingle with its population as to give to the East Roman *barians*
realm that new life, that rich and varied developement of *never taken*
into the
letters, thought, and art, which in Italy issued from the *Empire.*
mingling of the Teutonic and Italic elements. There
were occasional marriage alliances between the royal
houses of these nations and the imperial houses. Not
a few of the best generals of the Empire and some of its

CHAP. XVII. ablest sovereigns were of Slavonic, as still more were of Armenian blood. The pride of Constantinople might have refused to accept a barbarian king as Roman Emperor. Yet had it been possible for Simeon the mighty Bulgarian Tsar of the tenth century, himself, like the Gothic Theodorich, educated at Constantinople, or for Vladimir the Great who ruled the Russians eighty years later, to be crowned in St. Sophia as Charles had been crowned in St. Peter's, the Eastern Empire might have widened its foundation, and have received an accession of strength sufficient to enable it to repel the Latin Crusaders in 1204 and to hold Asia Minor against the Seljukian Sultans. Simeon did indeed take the title of Basileus, and did obtain from Pope Nicholas I a grant of the imperial crown, as the price of his adhesion to the Latin Church: but nothing came of this brief alliance. Or, again, had the men of the Eastern Empire been strong enough to conquer, to incorporate and to assimilate the Balkanic peoples, such an infusion of new blood might have given it a fresh and long enduring life. That events took a different course, that the Empire, the Serbs, and the Bulgarians weakened one another by incessant strife, that the destroying Ottomans were thus, and by the apathy of Western Europe, permitted to overspread these vast provinces, and hold them in cruel bondage for many centuries, may well be deemed to be, like the extinction of the Ostrogothic race in Italy, one of the great and unredeemed catastrophes of history. Driven within ever narrowing limits, with a population that had now become slender and impoverished, the Eastern Empire perished. The peoples to the North — Bulgarians, Serbs of Servia and Bosnia, and Roumanians, crushed beneath the Ottoman yoke, were left far behind in the march of European civilization. Only within the last seventy or

eighty years have they begun to add that new culture
which the West has bestowed to the scanty relics of
what they learned from Byzantium seven hundred years
before.

The Church was the mainstay as well of the Eastern
as of the Western Empire. In the latter it recalled the
imperial title to life : in the former it kept that title
alive through many troublous centuries. But here the
resemblance ends. In the West, the Latin Church found
itself free to grow and develope without interference from
the secular power. No Emperor after Constantine dwelt
in Rome, and from A.D. 476 to A.D. 800 there was no
Emperor at all in Italy.[k] The bishop of the imperial city
had the field to himself. Even when strong men like
Charles and Otto bore the sceptre, the head of the State
was too distant and crossed the Alps too rarely to be able
to impose a permanent restraint on the head of the Church.
But in the East the Church sprang up under the shadow
of the Empire, and remained thereafter, both ecclesiasti-
cally and spiritually, a stunted growth. In the days
of Justinian, a high spirited African prelate remarked
that the Greek bishops, having wealthy churches,
were afraid to oppose the Emperor. Justinian, arro-
gating to himself the virtual control of the Church, kept
the Patriarch of Constantinople bitted and bridled :
and although the archbishop of the imperial city was
always a personage to be reckoned with, capable of
exerting a potent influence in ecclesiastical quarrels,
and sometimes even in contests for the throne, he never

Relations of Church and Empire in the East and in the West.

[k] The Emperor Constans II paid a brief visit in A.D. 663 ; he was disgusted
with Constantinople, but found Rome no more agreeable, and spent his last
years at Syracuse. Heraclius, when (A.D. 617) he thought of removing the
seat of power from Constantinople, had meant to fix it not at Rome but at
Carthage.

disputed the civil supremacy of the Emperor, never, as did his brother at Old Rome, attempted to claim the right of selecting or deposing the successor of Constantine. Even when the loss of Syria and Egypt had practically removed from him the rivalry of the three ancient patriarchates of Jerusalem, Alexandria, and Antioch, the ecclesiastical head of the Eastern hierarchy could not pretend to the authority that belonged to the Latin Patriarch, who held the keys of the Kingdom of Heaven.[1] In his chair of Constantinople no apostle had sat: of none of his predecessors had the fateful words been spoken, 'Thou art Peter, and upon this rock will I build my Church.'

Inferior position of the Eastern Patriarch.

After the days of Pope Gregory VII, the Church of Rome was at least the equal, and sometimes almost the mistress, of the Empire. The Eastern Church was always the handmaid of the Eastern State.[m] The Teutonic Emperor was the shadow of the Pope, cast on the secular world. The Eastern Patriarch was the shadow of the Emperor, cast on the spiritual world. A truly National Church she was, and as a National Church she gave immense cohesion and vitality to the East Roman realm. She was less arrogant, less corrupted by wealth, perhaps less penetrated by political worldliness than the Western Church had in the thirteenth century become. The Emperors also gained by escaping those long and bitter struggles with the ecclesiastical power which lasted in the West from the

[1] The claims of the Roman See are fully set forth in an interesting and characteristic letter of Pope Leo IX to the Eastern Emperor, which may be read in Mansi, *Concil.* vol. xix. col. 635.

[m] Cp. Liudprand, *Legatio Constantinopolitana*, c. 63. The bishop of Leucas assured Liudprand that his church had to pay the Emperor 100 aurei every year, and all the other churches more or less according to their means. 'Quod quam iniquum sit,' says Liudprand, 'patris nostri Ioseph acta demonstrant': for when he taxed Egypt in the time of famine he left the land of the priests free.

middle of the eleventh to the middle of the fourteenth century. But the East Roman nation, both as a secular and a religious community, suffered by the subjection into which the Church had been brought. Its spirit was roused by no great conflict of principles like that which stirred and stimulated the thoughts and feelings of Italians and Germans, of Frenchmen and Englishmen, in the days of the mediaeval Popes, and which, never completely closed, found its later expression in the movement for religious reform which rent the Christian community in the sixteenth century. It had not the glorious exuberance of emotional as well as intellectual life which illumines the annals of the Western Church from the eleventh to the sixteenth century. It could show no such names as those of St. Anselm, Peter Abelard, St. Thomas Aquinas, St. Francis, William of Ockham, John Wiclif, Gerson, Savonarola, Erasmus, Luther, Ignatius Loyola, Zwingli, Calvin. That the Orthodox Church of the East, whose fold contains more than a hundred millions of men, is to-day in all the countries that adhere to it, in Russia and Roumania, in Bulgaria, Servia, and Greece, so much less of an intellectual and spiritual factor in the life of the people than are the various branches of the Western Church, whether the Roman Catholic branch or the countless forms of Protestantism, is largely due to the heavy hand which the Eastern monarchs laid upon their Patriarch and their bishops.

Other causes no doubt there were for the decadence of Eastern Christianity. As in the mediaeval West the teachings of the Gospel and its appeal to the individual soul were overlaid, sometimes even obscured, by the conception of a Visible Church within which alone salvation can be found, because it is only by her ministers that the sacraments can be dispensed, so in the East the passionate theological controversies regarding the Trinity and

Character of Eastern Christianity.

the Incarnation which had filled the minds of laity as well as clergy, from the fourth to the seventh century, led to the exaltation of doctrinal orthodoxy as the central and vital element in the Christian life. The Eastern Church no doubt also valued itself upon its catholicity, as the Western Church valued itself upon its orthodoxy. But just as the sense of membership in one great body organized under one Vicar of God upon earth is the characteristic note of the one, so the full acceptance in the exactly right sense of all the dogmas enunciated by the Church is specially and pre-eminently distinctive of the other. This fettering of the mind by the decrees of ancient Councils, this concentration of attention on abstract and sometimes scarcely comprehensible propositions, is doubtless accountable not only for a deficient sense of the duty of the Church to enforce morality in conduct (a point better cared for in the Latin Church), but also for much of the glacial torpor which the history of Eastern Christianity sets before us. But the control of the civil power and the nationalizing of religion until religion seems to become a sort of ceremonial function of the State have also been paralyzing influences. Thus the Eastern rulers failed even more conspicuously than the Catholic West failed, and than Protestant kingdoms have also failed, to solve the problem of maintaining a religious community in dependence on, or in legal connection with, the civil government without at the same time injuring its spiritual freedom, and rendering it less responsive to the changing currents of thought and feeling among its members.

Respective claims of the two Empires to represent Rome.

The enquiry which of the two rival imperial lines had, after A.D. 800, the better title to represent ancient Rome is one fitter to occupy the minds of controversialists in the tenth century than to be debated in the twentieth :

nor is there much use in asking which of the two had preserved a more genuinely Roman character, for both States had, like all human institutions, whether ecclesiastical or civil, undergone changes which made them essentially different from the majestic predecessor whose name they bore. To us both seem almost equally unlike the heathen Empire, for both were Christian, and while the one was feudal the other had taken an Oriental colour. But it is worth while to examine the view which each took of itself, and the sense in which each deemed itself to represent the rights and the glories of the ancient World Power ; for, however strange may seem to us the ideas that inspired the Teutonic and the Byzantine princes respectively, those ideas were potent factors in history.

The two lines were always rivals, since neither would or could admit the title of the other to the great inheritance. This made them enemies, and their enmity was intensified by the antagonism of what we may call, from the languages they used in worship, the Greek and Latin Churches. Disputes on points of doctrine and on points of ecclesiastical precedence had arisen in the sixth and seventh centuries. The mutual aversion of the Churches, embittered by the quarrel over the use of images in worship, was prolonged, after that source of strife had vanished, by the refusal of the Patriarchs at Constantinople to admit the supremacy of the chair of Peter, till in the ninth, and more definitely in the middle of the eleventh century, aversion passed into the schism which finally severed the two communions, that fatal schism, without which neither would the Crusaders of A.D. 1204 have attacked a Christian capital, nor would that capital, in its last hour of dire necessity two and a half centuries later, have been abandoned by the Western nations. Other causes for the alienation of the two Churches there were, but the chief one was a point of doctrine which, though subtle theologians may draw a chain of inferences from it, was and remains beyond the reach of ordinary human intelligence, the question whether the Holy Spirit proceeds from the Father and the Son or from the Father alone.

Pretensions of each imperial line. Each of the rival lines had much to allege on its behalf. The Easterns traced, from Constantine downwards, an unbroken succession of monarchs always reigning in the same city, preserving, along with the Roman name, the titles and ceremonies, the supremacy in ecclesiastical affairs, and the civil institutions which had existed in the days of the first Christian Emperor. No breach of continuity affected their title. In Eastern eyes the coronation of Charles the Great was an act of unholy rebellion: his successors barbarian intruders, ignorant of the laws and usages of the ancient State, and with no claim to be deemed Romans except that which the favour of an arrogant pontiff might confer. Standing all by themselves, a bright spot of civilization in a barbarian world, with wild Bulgarians to the north and Muslim sons of the desert to the south, they formed an extravagant conceit of their own importance, and plumed themselves all the more upon the incomparable lustre of their crown. Seldom, and only when sore need drove them to courtesy, did they recognize the titles used by the Frankish and German sovereigns. Basil the Macedonian reproached the Western Emperor Lewis the Second with presuming to use the name of Basileus ; to which the Frank retorted that he was as much an Emperor as Basil, but that anyhow *Basileus* was only the Greek for 'king,' and need not mean 'Emperor' at all. Nicephorus Phocas refused to call Otto the Great anything but 'King of the Lombards':[n] Conrad III was

---

[n] Liutprand, *Legatio Constantinopolitana.* Nicephorus says, 'Vis maius scandalum quam quod se imperatorem vocat' (cap. xxv).

addressed by Kalo-Joannes as 'amice imperii mei Rex': [o]
Isaac Angelus, more insolently, styled Frederick the First
'chief prince of Alemannia.' [p] The great Hohenstaufen,
half resentful, half contemptuous, told the Eastern envoys
that he was Romanorum Imperator, and bade their master
call himself 'Romaniorum,' from the Thracian province of
Romania. Once, at least, an Eastern sovereign attempted
to extrude his Teutonic competitor from the lordship of
the world. When Frederick the First was engaged in his
struggle with Pope Alexander the Third and the cities of
Lombardy, Manuel Comnenus, the most valiant and most
aspiring of his line, while attempting to reconquer Southern Italy from the Norman kings, gave his support to the
rebellious Lombards, helped the Milanese to rebuild their
walls, sought to win over the nobles of Rome, and invited
the Pope to deprive Frederick of the imperial crown and
restore it to himself as the rightful claimant. The wary
pontiff, however, though the request was accompanied by
a promise to secure the reunion of the Eastern and Western Churches, as well as by large gifts of money, could not
see his way to so revolutionary a step as a reversal of that
'Translation of the Empire,' which had been effected by
his predecessor three centuries and a half before. 'These
things,' he said, 'are too high for me and too complicated.' [q]
He was wise. The chasm that divided the East from the
West was already too wide to be thus bridged.

Against that legitimacy and continuity on which the *Strength of the Western position:*
East Romans relied, the Western monarchs had two things
to set. With them was the City. With them was the *Rome and*
Chair of the Apostle. The chroniclers who describe the *the Pope.*
coronation of Charles justly dwell upon the fact that 'he
held Rome, the mother of Empire, where the Caesars had

[o] Otto of Freysing, i. c. 30.   [p] See Note XXII at end.
[q] See *Vita Alexandri III*, ap. Muratori, *S. R. T.* iii. i. 460, col. ii. B–E.

always been wont to sit,' and that it was the successor of Peter who placed the crown upon his brow.[r] Rome and the Catholic Church, these were the two pillars of Empire: and with these the Germans and Italians were so well content that they scarcely felt the rival pretensions of Constantinople to be a flaw in the title of their Emperor. The Eastern Church was no doubt then, as she is now, a thorn in the side of the Papacy. But the Pope was the last person who could, in his quarrels with the Teutonic sovereigns, use the Eastern claim in any argument against them, because to have treated Constantinople as the equal of Rome would have been to lower his own see to the level of Constantinople, as well as to question the validity of the transference effected by Pope Leo III. Neither, however, did any other antagonists of the Teutonic Emperors — as for instance the writers who in the fourteenth and fifteenth centuries maintained the independence of the crown of France — lay stress upon the existence of an Empire in the East as evidence against the claim of the

Slight knowledge of the East in the West. Germanic sovereign to oecumenical supremacy. The truth seems to be that the Western World, from the ninth century onwards, knew and cared comparatively little about the East. The intellectual and social unity of Europe was in those days maintained by the clergy and especially, after the middle of the thirteenth century, by the friars: and the clergy seldom passed outside the bounds of Latin Christendom. By land there was little intercourse, except when a crusading host passed through, for rude Slavonic tribes lay between, and such sea trade as went on between Italy and Constantinople — after the eleventh century it was chiefly in the hands of the Pisans, the Genoese, and the Venetians — did little to establish relations in the sphere of thought and literature, how little may be judged

[r] See chap. V, *supra.*

from the paucity of Greek MSS. in Western Europe. Even Dante could not read Greek and never saw a Greek copy of the Homeric poems.[a] Thus the mass of the people scarcely remembered the existence of the Eastern Christians: and of those who did, the most part thought of them as Samaritans who refused to worship at Jerusalem, perverse rebels against the authority of the Apostolic See, who were little better than heretics or infidels. And although the few ecclesiastics of superior knowledge and insight could not treat the pretensions of communities which had been among the first to embrace Christianity, and had preserved so many of its ancient forms, with the scorn that was felt for Western sectaries, although the Roman Church has never questioned the validity of Eastern orders, nor deemed those who stand within the Eastern fold to be outside the bounds of covenanted salvation, still these leaders of opinion were so preoccupied by the established theory of the identity of the Roman Church and the Roman Empire, and so convinced of the right of Peter to choose whom he would as the temporal guardian of his flock, that they could not apprehend the weak points in their own position or the strength of their opponents'. Enthralled by the majesty of their own theory, a theory which existed outside the sphere of fact, they were not disturbed by a fact inconsistent with it.

They lived in a sort of cloudland, where the real truths seemed to be those grand ideas that shone upon them like stars through an encircling mist. Their preoccupation

[a] Nearly forty years after Dante's death Petrarch succeeded in procuring a MS. of the *Iliad* and *Odyssey*, and some years later Boccaccio, who had obtained another MS., had it literally translated into Latin and sent it to Petrarch. These are the first we hear of in Italy. See Paget Toynbee, *Dante Studies and Researches*, p. 205. However, Robert Grosseteste, bishop of Lincoln, knew Greek, and his famous contemporary, Roger Bacon, appears to have composed a Greek Grammar.

with the conception of a universal Christian commonwealth was a part of that imaginative vision and mystic sense which ennoble the Middle Ages, and which make it delightful and refreshing to turn back to those times from the garish day of a world ruled by the methods of physical science and the methods of historical criticism. This power it was which enabled them to bequeath to us so much on which our imagination still feeds, so much splendid poetry, so much myth and fancy and legend, matter fit for poetry, on which the creative genius of later centuries has worked.

The East Romans less disposed to idealize their Emperor.

The West was full of imaginative minds, not in Italy, Provence, and Germany only, but as far as remote Erin and still remoter Iceland. But the East Romans were not imaginative. They were a practical people, with their eyes fixed on the actual. Superstitious they were, and full of a reverence for the past which often ran into a fantastic antiquarianism. But they were neither poetical nor mythopoeic. Their Emperor was a living and familiar personage. He was, like the kings of other countries, king over a nation, the ruler of a realm which, once universal, had been narrowed to a nation, with a national language and a national character. He was indeed a far more resplendent sort of king than were the kings of the barbarians, being the successor of the Caesars of old, with a never abandoned claim to be the first of all potentates. But he was so essential to their particular state, so firmly rooted in all its traditions, that neither the disobedience of the Roman city nor the hostility of the Roman pontiff affected their confidence in his right and their right to represent the Roman dominion. The rivalry of the West had no doubt cost them Italy, and it detracted from their importance in the eyes of other nations. It was an odious fact, like the existence of the Bulgarians, who had robbed them

of Thrace, and the existence of the Hagarenes,[t] who had
robbed them of Syria.   But it never shook their self-confidence, and their sense of immeasureable superiority to the
barbarians of Central and Western Europe.   Even Latin
had become to them what it had been to the Athenians
ten centuries before, a barbarian language.

This difference of attitude illustrates the contrast be- *Contrast of*
tween the people of the Western and those of the Eastern *the East and*
Empire in the sphere of thought and letters. *the West as*
respects
The Holy Empire, except in so far as it was united with *literature*
the German kingdom, was a dream, a sublime conception, *and*
half theology and half poetry, of the unity of mankind, *thought.*
who are themselves the children of God, as realized in one
Church, which is also a State, and in one State, which is
also a Church.   The East Roman Empire was a reality, a
tangible fact in an actual world, drawing neither strength
nor beauty from any theory, and not appearing to need
any theory to support it.   Why was this so?   Why did
not the same group of ideas which had kept alive the
memory of Rome in the West down to the days of Charles
the Great, and which in the eleventh, twelfth, and thirteenth centuries developed those ideas into that ordered
form which they held in men's minds in the time of Dante
—why did not these ideas fill and sway men's minds in the
East also, and find due expression in their literature and
their art?   Why did not the Ideal array the Actual in
those gorgeous hues which the great Westerns lavished
on their two heads of Christendom, the Sun and the Moon
of their ethereal firmament?

One reason may have been because the Emperor had *Why did the*
in the East always been a tangible and permanent fact. *East theorize*
The Easterns were reverent, and they were not less super- *so little*
regarding
the Empire?

[t] This was the name by which they usually called their Saracen or Arab
enemies.

stitious than the Westerns. Superstition goes with a profound belief in forms and ceremonies. But the constant presence of the successor of Constantine made him an object not so fit to be idealized as the Emperor of tradition had become in the West, and dispensed with the need for a philosophic theory.[u] The autocrat of Constantinople required no doctrinal scheme to buttress his power: the Western did require it just because he was less able to stand by his own strength. So perhaps we may find another reason in the fact that the East had not in its capital a mystic Mother of Empire, such as was Old Rome, filled with the bones of martyrs, and had not, as its chief pastor, the Universal Bishop, the living representative on earth of the Divine Word in heaven. The Patriarch of Constantinople was only a primate, standing not greatly above other bishops. Constantinople was, moreover, an artificial creation, the work of one Emperor, suddenly raised into a capital out of a town previously famous only for its admirable site. It had neither the immemorial renown nor the hallowed associations of the elder city on the Tiber.

Yet perhaps we must seek a still deeper cause. The East was not steeped, as was the West, in the idea of a Church organized and administered like a State. Italy, which had stamped her type of practical intellect upon the whole Latin West, had achieved in earlier days two great things: she had created an Administration and a Law fitted for a world. The Hellenistic East, not Greek in the old classical sense, as we are too apt to assume, but a mix-

---

[u] It must be admitted that the Popes of the (later) ninth and tenth centuries were a reality in Rome and a reality not fit for idealization. But it was the Catholic world at a distance that idealized their office: it was the Teutonic Emperors that effected the great reformation which begins at the end of the tenth century.

ture of Hellenic and Asiatic elements, had shewn no gift
for the creation of institutions, but had applied an amazing
speculative and dialectic faculty to the abstract problems
of theology. After the extinction of imperial rule in the
West, the Latin Church, still permeated by the practical
instincts of Rome, went on developing an ecclesiastical
organization, modelled upon the civil administration which
had perished, till her efforts culminated in the mediaeval
hierarchy and the system of Canon Law. She could not
think of the Christian people except in the form of a body
of worshippers organized under a government, and a government with an autocratic head. Thus she created the
Pope; and the Pope (as we have seen [x]) re-created the
Emperor. But to the Eastern Christians, occupied as
they had been with determining the nature of God and
of Christ, the Christian people appeared in the form of
a body of worshippers professing exactly the same lifegiving
dogmas. Doctrine, not organization, came first in their
minds. As their civil administration had never been
shattered, they had less need, even if they had possessed
the capacity, to build up an ecclesiastical system like that
of the West; nor would the secular power have permitted
them to do so. Hence they did not turn their Patriarch
into a Pope: and hence there was no Pope to create an
Emperor in his own image. Herein may lie an explanation of the seeming paradox that the Eastern monarch,
with far greater practical authority in ecclesiastical affairs
than his Western rivals exercised, except perhaps in the
days of Charles and again of Henry the Third, had not
that ideal position in the world of politics, morals, and
religion — three things which were virtually the same
to these mediaeval thinkers — which Christian theory assigned to the Emperor in the West.

[x] See chapter VII, *ante.*

Let us note one more difference, affecting the conception of the imperial office, between the temper and mind of East and of West.

The intellect of the East Romans had ceased to be creative. Whether it was that they had not experienced that renewal of vital forces which the intermixture of Northern blood gave to the Italians, or that they lacked the freshness of vision and susceptibility to impressions which a new set of social conditions create, or that they were too much isolated, too little stirred by peaceful intercourse with other peoples (for their contact with their neighbours was almost always hostile), or whether they were oppressed by the stores of knowledge which had come down to them from the ancient world — whatever be the cause, they seemed to want intellectual initiative and that kind of constructive faculty which depends on imagination. Their talent and their industry — and there was plenty both of talent and of industry — ran to the piling up of knowledge, the recording of facts, the investigation of minute points in theology or in archaeology.[y] The West had creative power without learning: the East had learning without creative power. This is perhaps the reason why the Eastern Empire lost, and may never regain, its hold upon the interest of mankind. Standing apart and unfriended, it has a splendid record of stubborn resistance to formidable enemies on every side, and of a patriotism which the bitterest internal discords never extinguished. Its annals are full of striking incidents and brilliant personalities. But these personalities, brilliant by their energy and their adventures, seldom touch the deepest springs of interest, for they are not associated with great principles,

[y] There was a great deal of literary activity at Constantinople, and it was not confined, as it practically was in the West, to clerics ; laymen who were men of affairs wrote and wrote well.

nor does any literary or artistic genius, rising to greatness among his fellow countrymen, cast his rays upon them. After Justinian's days, the East Roman Empire produced, and has left us, little in the higher forms of art and nothing in institutions. It added nothing to the common store of thought and beauty in literature. It produced no speculative philosophy like that of the great Western schoolmen, no romantic figures in whom the gifts of thought and of action were united, like Bernard of Clairvaux and Arnold of Brescia, and least of all any poetry like that of mediaeval Provence and Italy.

Yet it has been a mighty factor in history, for it stemmed for centuries the tide of Asiatic invasion, and it kept alive a Church which has helped to create and maintain an intense national feeling among the largest and most swiftly growing of modern European peoples. The Russians, who are as much a religious as a political community, carry with them over the vast spaces of Northern and Central Asia the traditions of an Empire conterminous with a Church, an Empire which is at once the offspring and the guardian of the Orthodox Faith.

CHAPTER XVIII

THE RENAISSANCE: CHANGE IN THE CHARACTER OF THE EMPIRE

CHAP.
XVIII.

Wenzel,
A.D. 1378–
1400.
Rupert,
1400–1410.
Sigismund,
1410–1438.
*Council of
Constance,*
1414–1418.

IN Frederick the Third's reign the Empire sank to its lowest point. It had shot forth a fitful gleam under Sigismund, who in convoking and helping to guide the Council of Constance had revived one of the highest functions of his predecessors. The precedents of the first great oecumenical councils, and especially of the Council of Nicaea, had established the principle that it belonged to the Emperor, even more properly than to the Pope, to convoke ecclesiastical assemblies from the whole Christian world. The tenet commended itself to the reforming party in the Church, headed by John Gerson, chancellor of the University of Paris, whose aim it was, while making no changes in matters of faith, to correct the abuses which had grown up in discipline and government, and limit the power of the Popes by exalting the authority of General Councils, to whom it was now sought to ascribe an immunity from error superior to that, whatever it might be, which resided in the successor of Peter. And although it was only the sacerdotal body, not the whole Christian people, who were thus made the exponents of the universal religious consciousness, the doctrine was nevertheless a foreshadowing of the larger claims which were soon to follow. The existence of the Holy Empire and the existence of General Councils were, as has been already remarked, essential parts of one and the same theory,[a] and it was therefore more than a coincidence that the last occasion on which the whole of Latin Christendom met to deliberate and act as a single commonwealth,[b] was also the last on which that commonwealth's lawful temporal head appeared in the exercise of his international functions. Never afterwards was he, in the eyes of Europe, anything more than a German monarch.

CHAP. XVIII.

It might seem doubtful whether he would long remain a monarch at all. When Sigismund died leaving no male heir the electors chose as Emperor his son-in-law Albert of Hapsburg, who had just been made king of Hungary. Albert was a man of ability and character, who might have done something to restore the power of the crown. But he died after two years : and his successor Frederick duke of Styria, a Hapsburg of the younger line, had neither the energy nor the courage which the conditions of the moment required. So when in A.D. 1493 the long and calamitous reign of Frederick ended, it was impossible for the princes to see with unconcern the condition into which their selfishness and turbulence had brought the Empire. The time was indeed critical. Hitherto the Germans had been protected rather by the weakness of their enemies than by their own strength. From France there had been little to fear while the English menaced her on one side and the Burgundian dukes on the other; from England still less while she was torn by the strife of York and Lancaster. But now throughout Western Europe the power

Albert II, 1438–1440. Frederick III, 1440–1493.

Weakness of Germany as compared with the other states of Europe.

---

[a] It is not without interest to observe that the Council of Basel (A.D. 1431–1443) showed signs of reciprocating imperial care by claiming those very rights over the Empire to which the Popes were accustomed to pretend.

[b] The Councils of Basel and Florence were not recognized from first to last by all Europe, as was the Council of Constance. When the Assembly of Trent met (A.D. 1545), the great religious schism had already made a general council, in the true sense of the word, impossible.

of the feudal oligarchies was broken ; and its chief countries were being, by the establishment of fixed rules of
succession and the absorption of the smaller into the larger
principalities, rapidly built up into compact and aggressive
military monarchies. Thus Spain became a great state by
the union of Castile and Aragon, and the conquest of the
Moors of Granada. Thus in England there arose the
popular despotism of the Tudors. France had in the first
half of the fifteenth century been desolated by intestine
feuds, and for a time prostrate at the feet of England.
Now, enlarged and consolidated under Lewis the Eleventh
and his successors, she began to acquire that predominant
influence on the politics of Europe which her commanding
geographical position, the martial spirit of her people, and
the restless ambition of her rulers, secured to her during
several centuries. Meantime there had appeared in the
far East a foe still more terrible. The capture of
Constantinople gave the Turks a firm hold on Europe,
and inspired them with the hope of effecting in the
fifteenth century what Abderrahman and his Spanish
Saracens had so nearly effected in the eighth — of establishing the faith of Islam through all the provinces that
obeyed the Western as well as the Eastern Caesars. The
navies of the Ottoman sultans swept the Mediterranean ;
their well appointed armies pierced Hungary and threatened
Vienna.

*Loss of im-
perial
territories.*

Nor was it only that formidable enemies had arisen
without : the frontiers of Germany herself were exposed
by the loss of those adjoining territories which had
formerly owned allegiance to the Emperors. Poland,
once tributary, had shaken off the yoke at the Great
Interregnum, and had recently wrested West Prussia from
the Teutonic knights, and compelled their Grand Master
to swear allegiance in respect of East Prussia, which they

still retained.   Bohemia, where German culture had struck
deeper roots, remained a member of the Empire; but the
privileges she had obtained from Charles the Fourth, and
the subsequent acquisition of Silesia and Moravia, made
her virtually independent.   The restless Hungarians
avenged their former vassalage to Germany by frequent
inroads on her eastern border.

Imperial power in Italy ended with the life of Frederick *Italy.*
the Second, for the ill starred expeditions of Henry the
Seventh and Lewis the Fourth gave it only a brief and
fleeting revival.   Rupert did indeed cross the Alps, but it
was as the hireling of Florence; Frederick the Third received the Lombard as well as the imperial crown, but it
no longer conveyed the slightest power.   In the beginning
of the fourteenth century Dante still hopes the renovation
of his country from the action of the Teutonic Emperors.
A little later Matthew Villani sees clearly that they do
not and cannot reign to any purpose south of the Alps.[c]
Nevertheless the phantom of imperial authority lingers
on for a time.   It is put forward by the Ghibeline tyrants
of the cities to justify their attacks on their Guelfic neighbours : even resolute republicans like the Florentines do
not yet venture altogether to reject it, however unwilling
to permit its exercise.   Before the middle of the fifteenth
century, the names of Guelf and Ghibeline had ceased to

[c] 'E però venendo gl' imperadori della Magna col supremo titolo, e volendo
col senno e colla forza della Magna reggere gli Italiani, non lo fanno e non
lo possono fare.' — M. Villani, iv. 77.

Matthew Villani's etymology of the two great faction names of Italy is
worth quoting, as a fair sample of the skill of mediaevals in such matters : —
'La Italia tutta è divisa mistamente in due parti, l' una che seguita ne' fatti
del mondo la santa chiesa — e questi son dinominati Guelfi; cioè, guardatori
di fè.   E l' altra parte seguitano lo 'mperio o fedele o enfedele che sia delle
cose del mondo a santa chiesa.   E chiamansi Ghibellini, quasi guida belli;
cioè, guidatori di battaglie.'

have any sense or meaning; the Pope was no longer the protector nor the Emperor the assailant of municipal freedom, for municipal freedom itself had wellnigh disappeared. But the old war-cries of the Church and the Empire were still repeated as they had been three centuries before, and the rival principles that had once enlisted the noblest spirits of Italy on one or other side had sunk into a pretext for wars of aggrandizement or of a hatred now become traditional. That which had been remarked long before in Greece was seen to be true here; the spirit of faction outlived the cause of faction, and became itself the new and prolific source of a useless and endless strife.

After Frederick the Third no Emperor was crowned in Rome, and almost the only trace of that connection between Germany and Italy, to maintain which so much had been risked and lost, was to be found in the obstinate belief of the later Hapsburg Emperors, that their own claims, though often purely dynastic and personal, could be strengthened by an appeal to the imperial rights of their predecessors. Because Frederick Barbarossa had overawed Lombardy with a Transalpine host they fancied themselves the better entitled to demand duchies for themselves and their relatives, and to entangle the Empire in wars wherein no interest but their own was involved.

Burgundy.   The kingdom of Burgundy or Arles, if it had never added much strength to the Empire, had been useful as an outwork against France. And thus its loss — Dauphiné passing over, partly in A.D. 1350, finally in 1457, Provence in 1486 — proved a serious calamity, for it brought the French nearer to Switzerland, and opened to them a tempting passage into Italy. The Emperors did not for a time expressly renounce their suzerainty over these lands, but if it was hard to enforce a feudal claim over a rebellious landgrave in Germany, how much harder to control a vassal who was also the mightiest king in Europe.

On the north-west frontier, the fall in A.D. 1477 of the CHAP.
great principality which the dukes of French Burgundy XVIII.
were building up was seen with pleasure by the Rhine-
landers whom Charles the Bold, the last duke, had incessantly alarmed.   The duchy of Burgundy, a part of its
territories, fell to the king of France as feudal suzerain ;
other parts, including the Netherlands, passed to the house
of Hapsburg by the marriage of Mary, daughter of Duke
Charles, to Maximilian son of Frederick the Third and
afterwards Emperor.   The effect of its fall was to leave
France and Germany directly confronting each other, and
it was soon seen that the balance of strength lay on the
side of the less numerous but better organized and more
active nation.

Switzerland, too, could no longer be considered a part of *Switzerland.*
the Germanic realm.   The revolt of the Forest Cantons,
in A.D. 1313, was against the oppressions practised in the
name of Albert count of Hapsburg, rather than against
the legitimate authority of Albert the Emperor.   But
although several subsequent sovereigns, and among them
conspicuously Henry the Seventh and Sigismund, favoured
the Swiss liberties, yet while the antipathy between the
Confederates and the territorial nobility gave a peculiar
direction to their policy, the accession of new cantons to
their body, and their brilliant success against Charles the
Bold in A.D. 1477, made them proud of a separate national
existence, and not unwilling to cast themselves loose from
the stranded hulk of the Empire.   Maximilian tried to
conquer them, but after a furious struggle, in which the
valleys of Western Tyrol were repeatedly laid waste by
the peasants of the Engadin, he was forced to give way,
and in A.D. 1500 recognized them by treaty as practically
independent.   Not, however, till the peace of Westphalia,
in A.D. 1648, was the Swiss Confederation in the eye of

public law a sovereign state, and even after that date some of the towns continued to stamp their coins with the double eagle of the Empire, as some of the North Italian cities also did in days when the power of the Emperor had become merely a memory.

*Internal
weakness.*

If these losses of territory were serious, far more serious was the plight in which Germany herself lay. The country had now become not so much an Empire as an aggregate of very many small states, governed by princes who would neither remain at peace with each other nor combine against a foreign enemy, under the nominal presidency of an Emperor who had little lawful authority, and could not exert what he had.[d] The electors had for a time acted together as a body claiming to exert control over imperial affairs; and their Union (*Kurfürstenverein*), formed at Bingen in A.D. 1424, imposed stringent conditions on the newly elected Emperor Albert II in 1438. But dissensions presently arose between them; and the Diet or National Assembly was by its constitution and its cumbrous methods of procedure unfit to introduce reforms or to weld the component principalities into a united realm.

There was another cause, besides those palpable and obvious ones already enumerated, to which this state of things must be ascribed. That cause is to be found in the theory which regarded the Empire as an international power, supreme among Christian states. From the day when Otto the Great was crowned at Rome, the characters of German king and Roman Emperor were united in one person, and it has been shewn how that union tended

---

[d] 'Nam quamvis Imperatorem et regem et dominum vestrum esse fateamini, precario tamen ille imperare videtur: nulla ei potentia est; tantum ei paretis quantum vultis, vultis autem minimum.' — Aeneas Sylvius to the princes of Germany, quoted by Hippolytus a Lapide, *De Ratione Status in Imperic Romano Germanico.*

more and more to become a fusion. If the two offices, in
their nature and origin so dissimilar, had been held by
different persons, the Roman Empire would most probably
have soon disappeared, while the German kingdom grew
into a robust national monarchy. The connection of the
two gave a longer life to the one and a feebler life to the
other, while at the same time it transformed both. So long
as Germany was only one of the countries that bowed beneath their sceptre it was possible for the Emperors, though
we need not suppose they troubled themselves with specu-
lations on the matter, to distinguish their imperial authority,
as international and more than half religious, from their
royal, which was, or was meant to be, national and feudal.
But when within the narrowed bounds of Germany these
international functions had ceased to have any meaning,
when the rulers of England, Spain, France, Denmark, Hungary, Poland, Italy, Burgundy, had in succession repudiated
imperial control, and the Lord of the World found himself
obeyed by none but his own people, he would not sink
from being Lord of the World into a simple Teutonic king,
but continued to play in the more contracted theatre the
part which had belonged to him in the wider. Thus did
Germany instead of Europe become the sphere of his international jurisdiction ; and her electors and princes,
originally mere vassals, no greater than a count of Champagne in France, or an earl of Chester in England, stepped
into the place which it had been meant that the several
monarchs of Christendom should fill. If the effective
power of their head had been in the sixteenth century
what it was in the eleventh, the additional dignity so assigned to these magnates might have signified very little.
But coming in to confirm and justify the liberties already
won, the new theory of their relation to the sovereign had
a great though at the time scarcely perceptible influence in

CHAP.
XVIII.

*Influence of
the theory of
the Empire
as an inter-
national
power upon
the Germanic
constitution.*

changing the Germanic Empire, as we may now begin to call it, from a state into a sort of confederation or body of states, united indeed for some of the purposes of government, but separate and independent for others more important. Thus, and that in its ecclesiastical as well as its civil organization, Germany became a miniature of Christendom.[e] The Pope, though he retained the wider sway which his rival had lost, was in an especial manner the head of the German clergy, as the Emperor was of the laity: the three Rhenish prelates sat in the supreme college beside the four temporal electors: the nobility of prince-bishops and abbots was as essential a part of the constitution and as influential in the deliberations of the Diet as were the dukes, counts, and margraves of the Empire. The world-embracing Christian state was to have been governed by a hierarchy of spiritual pastors, whose graduated ranks of authority should exactly correspond with those of the temporal magistrates, who were to be, like them, endowed with worldly wealth and power, and to enjoy a jurisdiction co-ordinate although distinct. This system, which it was in vain attempted to establish in Europe during the eleventh and twelfth centuries, was in its main features that which prevailed in the Germanic Empire from the fourteenth century onwards. And conformably to the analogy which may be traced between the position of the archdukes of Austria in Germany after the fifteenth century, and the place which the four Saxon and the two first Franconian Emperors had once held in Europe, both being recognized as titular leaders in all that concerned the common interest, in the one case of the Christian, in the other of the whole German people, while neither of them had

Position of the Emperor in Germany compared with that of his predecessors in Europe.

[e] See Aegidi, *Der Fürstenrath nach dem Luneviller Frieden;* a book which throws more light than any other with which I am acquainted on the inner nature of the Empire.

any power of direct government in the territories of local kings and potentates in the former cases, princes in the latter ; so the plan by which those who chose Maximilian Emperor sought to strengthen their national monarchy was in substance that which the Popes had followed when they conferred the crown of the world on Charles and Otto. The pontiffs then, like the electors now, finding that they could not give with the title the power which its functions demanded, were driven to the expedient of selecting for the office persons whose private resources enabled them to sustain it with dignity. The first Frankish and the first Saxon Emperors were chosen because they were already the mightiest potentates in Europe; Maximilian because he was the strongest of the German princes. The parallel may be carried one step further. Just as under Otto and his successors the Roman Empire was Teutonized, so now under the Hapsburg dynasty, from whose hands the sceptre departed only once thenceforth, the Teutonic Empire tends more and more to lose itself in an Austrian monarchy.

Of that monarchy and of the power of the house of *Growth of the* Hapsburg, Maximilian was, hardly less than Rudolf his *Hapsburg* ancestor, the founder.[f] Uniting in his person those wide *influence in* domains through Germany which had been dispersed *Germany.* among the collateral branches of his house, and control- ling by his marriage with Mary of Burgundy the richest part of the territories of Charles the Bold, he was a prince greater than any who had sat on the Teutonic throne since the death of Frederick the Second. But it was as arch- duke of Austria, count of Tyrol, duke of Styria and Carinthia, feudal superior of lands in Swabia, Alsace, and

[f] The two immediately preceding Emperors, Albert II and Frederick III (1439-1493), had been Hapsburgs. It is nevertheless from Maximilian and his grandson Charles the Fifth that the ascendancy of that family must be dated.

Switzerland, that he was great, not as Roman Emperor. For just as from him the Austrian monarchy begins, so with him the Holy Empire in its old meaning ends. That strange system of doctrines, half religious, half political, which had supported it for so many ages, was growing obsolete, and the theory which had wrought such changes on Germany and Europe passed ere long so completely from remembrance that we can now do no more than call up a faint and wavering image of what it must once have been.

Character of the epoch of Maximilian.

For it is not only in imperial history that the accession of Maximilian is a landmark. That time — a time of change and movement in every part of human life, a time when printing had become common, and books were no longer confined to the clergy, when drilled troops were replacing the feudal militia, when the use of gunpowder was changing the face of war — was especially marked by one event, to which the history of the world offers no parallel before or since, the discovery of America. The cloud which from the beginning of things had hung thick and dark round the borders of civilization was suddenly lifted.[g] The feeling of mysterious awe with which men had regarded the firm plain of earth and her encircling ocean ever since the days of Homer, vanished when astronomers and geographers taught them that she was an insignificant globe, which, so far from being the centre of the universe, was itself swept round in the motion of one of the least of its countless systems. The notions that had hitherto prevailed regarding the life of man and his relations to nature and the supernatural, were rudely shaken by the knowledge that was soon gained of tribes in every stage of

The discovery of America, A.D. 1492.

[g] The discovery of the sea route to India, an event of scarcely inferior importance, was effected when Bartholomew Diaz rounded the Cape of Good Hope in 1486 and Vasco de Gama reached the Malabar coast in 1493.

culture and living under every variety of condition, who CHAP.
had developed apart from all the influences of the Eastern XVIII.
hemisphere.   In A.D. 1453 the capture of Constantinople
and extinction of the Eastern Empire had dealt a fatal
blow to the prestige of tradition and an immemorial name :
in A.D. 1492 there was disclosed a world whither the eagles
of the all-conquering Rome had never winged their flight,
and in which the name of Christ had never been heard.[h]
No one could now have repeated the arguments of the *De
Monarchia*.

Another influence, too, widely different, but not less *The Re-*
momentous, was beginning to spread from Italy beyond *naissance.*
the Alps.   Since the barbarian tribes settled in the Roman
provinces, no change had come to pass in Europe at all
comparable to that which followed the diffusion of the
New Learning in the latter half of the fifteenth century.
Enchanted by the beauty of the ancient models of art and
poetry, more particularly those of the Greeks, men came
to regard with aversion or contempt all that had been done
or produced from the days of Trajan to those of Pope
Nicholas the Fifth.   To them, the Latin style of the
writers who lived after Tacitus was debased : the architecture of the Middle Ages was barbarous : the scholastic
philosophy was an odious jargon.   Aristotle himself,
Greek though he was, Aristotle who had been for three
centuries more than a prophet or an apostle, was hurled
from his throne, because his name was associated with the
dismal quarrels of Thomists and Scotists.   That spirit,

[h] Nevertheless, fantastic attempts were made by some of the earlier Spanish
ecclesiastics in the New World to connect the native traditions with those
Christian legends which carried some of the Apostles into the Far East.
There may be seen in Tlascala (in Mexico) an ancient picture representing
St. Thomas preaching to the natives in the form of the (so-called) 'Toltec'
deity Quetzalcohuatl, the Feathered Serpent.

whether we call it analytical or sceptical, or earthly, or simply secular, for it is more or less all of these — the spirit which was the exact antithesis of mediaeval mysticism, had swept in and carried men away, with all the force of a pent-up torrent.   People were content to gratify their tastes and their senses, caring little for worship, and still less for doctrine : their hopes and ideas were no longer such as had made their forefathers crusaders or ascetics : their imagination was possessed by associations far different from those which had inspired Dante : they did not revolt against the Church, but they had no enthusiasm for her, and they had enthusiasm for whatever was fresh and graceful and intelligible.   From the gloomy devotion of the cloister, from the rude pleasures of the feudal castle, they turned away, too indifferent to be hostile. And so, in the midst of the Renaissance, so, under the consciousness that former things were passing from the earth, and a new order opening, so, with the other beliefs and memories of the Middle Age, the shadowy rights of the Roman Empire melted away in the fuller modern light.   Here and there a jurist muttered that no neglect could destroy its universal supremacy, or a priest declaimed to listless hearers on its duty to protect the Holy See ; but to Germany it had become an ancient device for holding together the discordant members of her body, to its possessors an engine for extending the power of the house of Hapsburg.

Empire henceforth German.

Henceforth, therefore, we must look upon the Holy Roman Empire as lost in the Germanic ; and after a few faint attempts to resuscitate old-fashioned claims, nothing remains to indicate its origin save a sounding title and a precedence among the states of Europe.   It was not that the Renaissance exerted any direct political influence either against the Empire or for it.   Men were too busy upon statues and coins and manuscripts to care what befel Popes or Emperors. It acted rather by silently withdrawing the whole system of doctrines upon which the Empire had rested, and thus leaving it, since it had previously no support but that of opinion, without any support at all.

During Maximilian's eventful reign several efforts were made to construct a new constitution, but it is to German rather than to imperial history that they properly belong. Here, indeed, the history of the Holy Empire might close, did not the still unchanged title beckon us on, and were it not that the course things took in these later centuries may be traced back to causes dating from those earlier days when the name of Roman was not wholly a mockery. One such event of Maximilian's time proved to have a profound importance for the future. Ever since the age of Conrad III and Frederick I, when the study of the ancient Roman law was revived in Italy, the doctrines of that law had been making way in Germany, partly because it was conceived to have been enacted for all time by the remote predecessors of the Teutonic Emperors, partly because the German students who resorted to the universities of Italy — there was no university in the Transalpine parts of the Empire till Charles IV founded one at Prague in 1347–1348 — brought back with them the legal ideas and rules they had learnt there, and applied these as practitioners or judges at home. Thus, except as regards the law of land rights, which continued to be German, the maxims of Roman law contained in Justinian's *Corpus Iuris* had come to be largely recognized in German courts, though more largely in the South and West than in Saxony, where a native law book (the *Sachsenspiegel*) had obtained much authority. In A.D. 1495 an Imperial Court of Justice ('Reichskammergericht') for the Empire was established : and it is from the declaration then made of the validity of the *Corpus Iuris* as law that the formal acceptance of Roman jurisprudence is usually dated.[1]   In Maximilian's day Germany included the Netherlands : and thus it is that the law of Rome has come to prevail in the Dutch East Indies, in Ceylon, and in South Africa.   The splendid labours of the Dutch jurists in the seventeenth and eighteenth centuries and of the German jurists in the eighteenth and nineteenth have had much to do with the diffusion of this law over the world, for it is not only the basis of all the codes of Southern and Western Europe, as well as of the law of Scotland, but has powerfully influenced the systems of Scandinavia, of Poland, of Hungary, and of the Russian Empire.   It may indeed be said to divide with English law the dominion of the civilized world.

The creation of this Imperial Chamber and the proclamation of a Public Peace did something to secure the preservation of civil order and the better administration of justice.   But schemes still more important failed through the bad constitution of the Diet, and the unconquerable jealousy of the Emperor and the Estates.[j]   Maximilian refused to have his prerogative, indefinite though weak, restricted by the appointment of the administrative council ('Reichsregiment') which had been advocated by the Elector of Mainz, and when the Estates extorted it from him, did his best to ensure its failure.   As a counterpoise he created a sort of Privy Council ('Hofrath') to be dependent on himself and to exercise both administrative

---

[1] The establishment of Roman jurisprudence in Germany was not an unmixed blessing, for it increased the prerogative of the ruler, raising him above the law ; it sanctioned the use of torture in criminal proceedings ; it made the law of high treason more searching and severe.

[j] An account of these attempts at constitutional reform may be found in vol. i of the new *Cambridge Modern History*, chap. ix (by Professor Tout).

and judicial powers.   Abandoned for a time and thereafter Chap.
re-established, this Aulic Council lasted as long as the XVIII.
Empire itself, and was sometimes an effective instrument
in the hands of the Hapsburgs, not so much for carrying
out their own projects as for resisting those of others.   In
the Diet, which consisted of three Colleges, electors,
princes, and cities, the lower nobility and knights of the
Empire were unrepresented, and naturally resented every
decree that affected their position, refusing to pay taxes in
voting which they had no voice.   The interests of the princes
and the cities were often irreconcileable, while the strength
of the crown would not have been sufficient to make its
adhesion to the latter of any effect.   The policy of con-
ciliating the commons, which Sigismund had tried, succeeding Emperors seldom cared to repeat, content to gain their
point by raising factions among the territorial magnates,
and so to stave off the unwelcome demand for reform.
After many earnest attempts to establish a representative
system, such as might resist the tendency to local independence and cure the evils of separate administration, the
hope so often baffled died away.   Forces were too nearly *Causes of*
balanced : the sovereign could not extend his personal *the failure of the projects*
control, nor could the reforming party limit him by a strong *of reform.*
council of government, for such a measure would have
equally trenched on the independence of the states.   So
ended the first great effort for German unity, interesting
from its bearing on the events and aspirations of our own
day ; interesting, too, as giving the most convincing proof
of the decline of the imperial office.   For the projects of
reform did not propose to effect their objects by restoring to Maximilian the authority his predecessors had once
enjoyed, but by setting up a body which would have resem-
bled far more nearly the senate of a federal state than
the council of ministers which surround a monarch.   The

existing system developed itself further : relieved from external pressure, the princes became more despotic in their
own territories : new bodies of law grew up, and new systems of administration were introduced : the insurgent
peasantry were crushed down with more confident harshness. Already had leagues of princes and cities been
formed[k] (that of the Swabian towns was one of the
strongest forces in Germany, and often the monarch's
firmest support); now alliances begin to be contracted by
some princes with foreign powers, and receive a direction
of formidable import from the rivalry which the pretensions
on Naples and Milan of Charles the Eighth and Lewis the
Twelfth of France kindled between their house and the
Austrian. It was no slight gain to have friends in the heart
of the enemy's country, such as French intrigue found in
the Elector Palatine and the count of Würtemberg.

*Germanic
nationality.*

Nevertheless this was also the era of the first conscious
feeling of German nationality, as distinct from imperial.
Driven in on all hands, with Italy and the Slavonic countries and Burgundy hopelessly lost, Teutschland learnt to

*Change of
titles.*

separate itself from Welschland.[1] The Empire became
the representative of a narrower but more practicable
national union. It is not a mere coincidence that at this
date there appear several notable changes of style. 'Na-

[k] Wenzel had encouraged the leagues of the cities, and incurred thereby
the hatred of the nobles.

[1] The Germans, like our own ancestors, called foreign, *i.e.* non-Teutonic
nations, Welsh ; yet apparently not all such nations, but only those which
they in some way associated with the Roman Empire, the Cymry of Roman
Britain, the Romanized Celts of Gaul, the Italians, the Wallachs of Transylvania
and the two Danubian Principalities which are now the kingdom of Roumania.
It does not appear that either the Magyars or any Slavonic people were called
by any form of the name.

In the Icelandic writings of the thirteenth century France (Francia occidentalis) is called 'Valland.'

tionis Teutonicae' (Teutscher Nation) is added to the
simple 'sacrum imperium Romanum.' The title of 'Imperator electus,' which Maximilian obtains leave from Pope
Julius the Second to assume,[m] when the Venetians prevent him from reaching his capital, marks the practical
severance of Germany from Rome. No subsequent Emperor received his crown from the ancient capital (Charles
the Fifth was indeed crowned by the Pope's hands, but
the ceremony took place at Bologna, and was therefore of
at least questionable validity); each assumed after his
German coronation the title of Emperor Elect,[n] and employed this in all documents issued in his name. But the
word 'elect' being omitted when he was addressed by
others, partly from motives of courtesy, partly because the
old rules regarding the Roman coronation were forgotten
or remembered only by antiquaries, he was never called,
even when formality was required, anything but Emperor.
The substantial import of another title now first introduced is the same. Before Otto the First, the Teutonic
king had called himself either 'rex' alone, or 'Francorum
orientalium rex,' or 'Francorum atque Saxonum rex':
after A.D. 962, all lesser dignities had, for the purposes of
titular description, been merged in the 'Romanorum Imperator.'[o] To this Maximilian appended 'Germaniae rex,'
or, adding Frederick the Second's bequest,[p] 'König in
Germanien und Jerusalem.' It has been thought that
from a mixture of the title king of Germany, and that of
Emperor, has been formed the phrase 'German Emperor,'

*The title
'Imperator
Electus.'*

[m] Julius was well pleased to give it, as he had no desire to see Maximilian
in Italy.

[n] See as to the coronation and the title of 'Elected Emperor' (Erwählter
Kaiser) Appendix, Note B.

[o] 'Romanorum rex' (after Henry II) till the coronation at Rome.

[p] But the Emperor was only one of many claimants to this kingdom; they
multiplied as the prospect of regaining it died away.

or less correctly, 'Emperor of Germany.'[q] But more probably these expressions grew up in people's mouths as convenient descriptions of the sovereign who was Emperor but was practically no longer Roman.[r]

That the Empire was thus sinking into a merely German power cannot be doubted. But it was only natural that those who lived at the time should not have fully discerned the tendency of events. Again and again did the restless and sanguine Maximilian propose the recovery of Burgundy and Italy,—his last scheme, perhaps hardly serious, was to adjust the relations of Papacy and Empire by becoming Pope himself: nor were successive Diets less zealous to check private war, still the scandal of Germany, to set right the gear of the imperial chamber, to make the imperial officials permanent, and their administration uniform throughout the country. But while they talked the heavens darkened, and the flood came and destroyed them all.

[q] The term 'Emperor of Germany' does not occur, even in English books, till comparatively recent times. English writers of the seventeenth century always call him 'The Emperor,' pure and simple, just as they invariably say 'the French king,' not 'the king of France' (because the English kings still claimed France). But the phrase 'Empereur d'Almayne' may be found in very early French writers.

[r] See Moser, *Römische Kayser;* Goldast's and other collections of imperial edicts and proclamations.

CHAPTER XIX

THE REFORMATION AND ITS EFFECTS UPON THE EMPIRE

THE Reformation falls to be mentioned here, not as a religious movement, but as the cause of political changes, which still further rent the Empire, and struck at the root of the theory by which it had been created and upheld. Luther completed the work of Hildebrand. Hitherto it had seemed not impossible to strengthen the German state into a monarchy, compact if not despotic; the very Diet of Worms, where the monk of Wittenberg proclaimed to an astonished Church and Emperor that the day of spiritual autocracy was past, had framed and presented a fresh scheme for the construction of a central council of government. The great religious schism put an end to all such hopes, for it became a source of political disunion far more serious and permanent than any that had existed before, and it taught the two sections into which Germany was henceforth divided to regard each other with feelings more bitter than those of hostile nations.

The breach came at the most unfortunate time possible. After an election, more memorable than any preceding, an election in which Francis the First of France and Henry the Eighth of England had been his competitors, a prince had just ascended the imperial throne who united dominions vaster than any Europe had seen since the days of his great namesake. Spain and Naples, Flanders, and other parts of the Burgundian lands, as well as large regions in Eastern Germany, obeyed Charles: he drew inexhaustible

Accession of Charles V (1519–1558).

revenues from a new empire beyond the Atlantic. Such a power, directed by a mind more resolute and profound than that of Maximilian his grandfather, might have well been able, despite the stringency of his coronation engagements[a] and the watchfulness of the electors,[b] to override their extorted privileges, and make himself practically as well as officially the head of the nation. Charles the Fifth, though from the coldness of his manner[c] and his Flemish speech never a favourite among the Germans, was in point of fact far stronger than Maximilian or any other Emperor who had reigned for three centuries. In Italy he succeeded, after long struggles with the Pope and the French, in rendering himself supreme: England he knew how to lead, by flattering Henry and cajoling Wolsey: from no state but France had he serious opposition to fear. To this strength his imperial dignity was indeed a mere ornament: its sources were the infantry of Spain, the looms of Flanders, the barbaric treasures of Mexico and Peru. But a control once re-established would soon have been legitimated by the rights which the imperial title seemed to carry with it; and as the first Charles had veiled the terror of the Frankish sword under the mask of Roman election, so might his successor sway a hundred provinces with the sole name of Roman Emperor, and transmit to his race a dominion as wide and more enduring.

One is tempted to speculate as to what might have hap-

[a] The so-called 'Wahlcapitulation.'

[b] The electors long refused to elect Charles, dreading the power which his hereditary dominions gave him, and were at last induced to do so only by their overmastering fear of the Turks.

[c] Nearly all the Hapsburgs seem to have wanted that sort of genial heartiness which, apt as it is to be stifled by education in the purple, has nevertheless been possessed by several other royal lines, and has often helped them; as for instance by more than one prince of the houses of Brunswick and Hohenzollern.

pened had Charles espoused the reforming cause. His
reverence for the Pope's person is sufficiently seen in the
sack of Rome and the captivity of Pope Clement VII;
the traditions of his office might have led him to tread in
the steps of the Henrys and the Fredericks, into which
even the superstitious Lewis the Fourth and the unstable
Sigismund had sometimes ventured; the awakening zeal
of the German people, exasperated by the exactions of the
Romish court, would have strengthened his hands, and
enabled him, while moderating the excesses of change, to
fix his throne on the deep foundations of national love.
It may well be doubted — Englishmen at least have reason
for the doubt — whether the Reformation would not have
lost as much as it could have gained by being entangled
in the meshes of royal patronage. But, setting aside
Charles's personal leaning to the old faith, and forgetting
that he was king of the most bigoted race in Europe, his
position as Emperor made him almost perforce the Pope's
ally. The Empire had been recalled into being by Rome,
had vaunted the protection of the Apostolic See as its
highest earthly privilege, had latterly been wont, especially
in Hapsburg hands, to lean on the Papacy for support.
Itself founded entirely on prescription and the traditions
of immemorial reverence, how could it abandon the cause
which the longest prescription and the most solemn authority had combined to consecrate? With the German clergy,
despite occasional quarrels, it had been on better terms
than with the lay aristocracy; their heads had been the
chief ministers of the crown; the advocacies of their abbeys
were the last source of imperial revenue to disappear. To
turn against them now, when furiously assailed by heretics; to abrogate claims hallowed by antiquity and a hundred laws, would be to pronounce its own sentence, and
the fall of the eternal city's spiritual dominion must in-

CHAP. XIX.

*Attitude of
Charles to-
wards the
religious
movement.*

volve the fall of what still professed to be her temporal. Charles would have been glad to see some abuses corrected; but a broad line of policy was called for, and he cast in his lot with the Catholics.[d]

Ultimate failure of the repressive policy of Charles.
A.D. 1547.

Of many momentous results only a few need be noticed here. The reconstruction of the old imperial system upon the basis of Hapsburg power, proved in the end impossible. Yet for some years it had seemed actually accomplished. When the Smalkaldic league had been dissolved and its leaders captured, the whole country lay prostrate before Charles. He overawed the Diet at Augsburg by his Spanish soldiery: he forced formularies of doctrine upon the vanquished Protestants: he set up and pulled down whom he would throughout Germany, amid the muttered discontent of his own partizans. Then, as in the beginning of the year 1552 he lay at Innsbruck, fondly dreaming that his work was done, waiting the spring weather to cross to Trent, where the Catholic fathers had again met to settle the faith of the world, news was suddenly brought that North Germany was in arms, and that the revolted Maurice of Saxony had seized Donauwerth, and was hurrying through the Bavarian Alps to surprise his sovereign.[e] Charles rose and fled south over the snows of the Brenner, then eastwards, under the blood-red cliffs of dolomite that wall in the Pusterthal, far away into the silent valleys of

[d] Padre Tosti, *Prolegomeni alla Storia Universale della Chiesa*, suggests that Sigismund may have foreseen this danger: 'Il grido della riforma clericale percuoteva le cime del laicale potere e rimbalzava per tutta la gerarchia sociale. Se l' imperadore Sigismondo nel consilio di Costanza non avesse fiutate queste consequenze nella eresia di Hus e di Girolamo di Praga, forse non avrebbe con tanto zelo mandati alle fiamme que' novatori. Rotto da Lutero il vincolo di suggezione al Papa ed ai preti in fatti di religione, avvenne che anche quello che sommetteva il vassallo al barone, il barone all' imperadore, si allentasse.' — Vol. ii. p. 398.

[e] Maurice is reported to have been just as well pleased at Charles's escape. 'I have no cage big enough,' said he, 'for such a bird.'

Carinthia : the council of Trent broke up in consternation :
Europe saw and the Emperor acknowledged that in his
fancied triumph over the spirit of revolution he had done
no more than block up for the moment an irresistible torrent.   When this last effort to produce religious uniformity
by violence had failed as hopelessly as the previous devices
of holding discussions of doctrine and calling a general
council, a sort of armistice was agreed to in 1555, which
lasted in mutual fear and suspicion for more than sixty
years.   Four years after this disappointment of the hopes
and projects which had occupied his busy life, Charles,
weighed down by cares and with the shadow of coming
death already upon him, resigned the sovereignty of Spain
and the Indies, of Flanders and Naples, into the hands of
his son Philip the Second ; while the imperial sceptre
passed to his brother Ferdinand, who had been some time
before (1531) chosen king of the Romans.   Ferdinand *Ferdinand I,*
was content to leave things much as he found them, and *1558–1564.*
the amiable Maximilian II, who succeeded him, though *Maximilian*
personally well inclined to the Protestants, saw himself *II, 1564–1576.*
fettered by his position and his allies, and could do little *Destruction of the Ger-*
or nothing to quench the flame of religious and political *manic state-*
hatred.   Germany remained divided into two omnipresent *system.*
factions, and so further than ever from harmonious action,
or a tightening of the long-loosened bond of allegiance to
the imperial crown.   The states of each creed being now
gathered into two antagonistic leagues, there could no
longer be a recognized centre of authority for judicial or
administrative purposes.   Least of all could a centre be
sought in the Emperor, the leader of the papal party, the
suspected foe of every Protestant.   Too closely watched
to do anything of his own authority, too much committed
to one party to be accepted as a mediator by the other, he
was driven to attain his own objects by falling in with the

schemes and furthering the selfish ends of his adherents, by becoming the accomplice or the tool of the Jesuits. The Lutheran princes addressed themselves to reduce a power of which they had still an over-sensitive dread, and found when they exacted from each successive sovereign engagements more stringent than his predecessor's, that in this, and this alone, their Catholic brethren were not unwilling to join them. Thus obliged to strip himself one by one of the ancient privileges of his crown, the Emperor came to have little influence on the government except that which his intrigues might exercise. Nay, it became almost impossible to maintain a government at all. For when the Reformers found themselves outvoted at the Diet, they declared that in matters of religion a majority ought not to bind a minority. As the measures were few which did not admit of being reduced to this category, for whatever benefited the Emperor or any other Catholic prince injured the Protestants, nothing could be done save by the assent of two bitterly hostile factions. Thus scarce anything was done; and even the courts of justice were stopped by the disputes that attended the appointment of every judge or assessor.

Alliance of the Protestants with France.

In the foreign politics of Germany another result followed. Inferior in military force and organization, the Protestant princes at first provided for their safety by forming leagues among themselves. The device was an old one, and had been employed by the monarch himself before now, in despair at the effete and cumbrous forms of the imperial system. Soon they began to look beyond the Vosges, and found that France, burning heretics at home, was only too happy to smile on free opinions elsewhere. The alliance was easily struck; Henry the Second assumed in 1552 the title of 'Protector of the Germanic liberties,' and a pretext for interference was never wanting in future.

These were some of the visible political consequences of the great religious schism of the sixteenth century. But beyond and above them there was a change more momentous than any of its immediate results. There is perhaps no event in history which has been represented in so great a variety of lights as the Reformation. It has been called a revolt of the laity against the clergy, or of the Teutonic races against the Italians, or of the kingdoms of Europe against the universal monarchy of the Popes. Some have seen in it only a burst of long-repressed anger at the luxury of the prelates and the manifold abuses of the ecclesiastical system; others a renewal of the youth of the Church by a return to primitive forms of doctrine. All these indeed to some extent it was; but it was also something more profound, and fraught with mightier consequences than any of them. It was in its essence the assertion of the principle of individuality — that is to say, of true spiritual freedom. Hitherto the personal consciousness had been a faint and broken reflection of the universal; obedience had been held the first of religious duties; truth had been conceived as a something external and positive, which the priesthood who were its stewards were to communicate to the passive layman, and in the formal and unquestioning acceptance of which, even if not fully comprehended as truth, there lay a saving virtue. The great principles which mediaeval Christianity still cherished were obscured by the limited, rigid, almost sensuous forms which had been forced on them in times of ignorance and barbarism. That which was in its nature abstract, had been able to survive only by taking a concrete expression. The universal consciousness became the Visible Church : the Visible Church hardened into a government and degenerated into a hierarchy. Holiness of heart and life was sought by outward

CHAP. XIX.   works, by penances and pilgrimages, by gifts to the poor and to the clergy, wherein there might dwell little enough of a charitable mind. The presence of divine truth among men was symbolized under one aspect by the existence on earth of an infallible Vicar of God, the Pope; under another, by the reception of the present Deity in the sacrifice of the mass; in a third, by the doctrine that the priest's power to remit sins and administer the sacraments depended upon a transmission of miraculous gifts unbroken from the time of the Apostles. All this system of doctrine, which might, but for the position of the Church as a worldly and therefore obstructive power, have gradually expanded, renewed, and purified itself during the four centuries that had elapsed since its completion,[f] and thus remained in harmony with the growing intelligence of mankind, was suddenly rent in pieces by the convulsion of the Reformation, and presently flung away by those among the peoples of Europe which have thenceforth been usually, if not always, the foremost in thought and action. The leaders of the new movement sought to supersede that which was external and concrete by that which was inward and spiritual. They proclaimed that the individual spirit, while it continued to mirror itself in the world-spirit, had nevertheless an independent existence as a centre of self-issuing force, and was to be in all things active rather than passive. Truth was no longer to be truth to the soul until it should have been by the soul recognized, and in some measure even created; but when so recognized and felt, it was, under the form of faith, to transcend outward works and to transform the dogmas of the understanding; it was to become the living principle within each man's breast, infinite itself, and expressing

---

[f] The completion can hardly be deemed final until the eleventh century, in which transubstantiation was definitely established as a dogma.

itself infinitely through his thoughts and acts. He who as a spiritual being was no longer to be guided by the priest, but brought into direct relation with the Divinity, needed not, as heretofore, to be enrolled a member of a visible congregation of his fellows, that he might live a pure and useful life among them. Thus among the peoples that accepted the Reformation the Visible Church as well as the priesthood lost that paramount importance which had hitherto belonged to it, and sank from being the depositary of all religious tradition, the source and centre of religious life, the arbiter of eternal happiness or misery, into a mere association of Christian men, for the expression of mutual sympathy and the better attainment of certain common ends. Like those other doctrines which were now assailed by the German, Swiss, and British Reformers, this mediaeval view of the nature of the Visible Church had been naturally, and so, it may be said, necessarily developed between the third and the twelfth century, and must therefore have represented the thoughts and satisfied the wants of those times. By the Visible Church the flickering lamp of knowledge and literary culture, as well as of religion, had been fed and tended through the long night of the Dark Ages. But the form which the Christian Church had taken, though clothed with external splendour and hallowed by immemorial traditions, had now been interpenetrated and overgrown by abuses and corruptions which seemed to have so become a part of its being as to make it capable of no further healthy developement, and unable to satisfy minds which in growing stronger had grown more conscious of their strength. Before the awakened zeal of the Northern nations it stood a cold and lifeless system, whose organization as a hierarchy checked the free activity of thought, whose bestowal of worldly power and wealth on spiritual pastors drew them away from their proper duties, and which by maintaining alongside of the civil magistracy a co-ordinate and rival government, maintained also that view of the separation of the spiritual element in man from the secular, which had been so complete and so pernicious during the Middle Ages, which debases life, and severs religion from morality.

Consequent effect upon the Empire.

To dwell upon this fundamental change in the conception of the Visible Church is not foreign to the present subject. The Holy Empire is but another name for the Visible Church. It has been shewn already how mediaeval theory constructed the civil on the model of the ecclesiastical society; how the Roman Empire was the shadow of the Popedom — designed to rule men's bodies as the pontiff ruled their souls. Both alike claimed obedience on the ground that Truth is One, and that where there is One faith there must be One government.[g] And, therefore, since it was this very principle of Formal Unity that the Reformation overthrew, it became a revolt against the principle of authority in all its forms; it erected the standard of civil as well as of religious liberty, since both of them are needed, though needed in a different measure, for the worthy developement of the individual spirit. The Empire had never been conspicuously the antagonist of popular freedom, and was, even under Charles the Fifth, far less formidable to the commonalty than were the territorial princes of Germany. But submission, and submission on the ground of indefeasible transmitted right, upon the ground of Catholic traditions and the duty of the Christian magistrate to suffer heresy and schism as little as the parallel sins of treason and rebellion, had been its constant claim and watchword. Since the days of Julius Caesar it had passed

[g] See the passage quoted in note ᵐ, p. 99; and see also p. 111.

through many phases, and in so far as it was a Germanic monarchy, it had recognized the rights of the vassals and had admitted the delegates of the cities to a place in the national assembly. But these principles of the mediaeval monarchy, half feudal, half drawn from Teutonic antiquity, principles themselves now decaying, had little to do with the religious conceptions and the Roman traditions on which the theory of the Empire rested. In that theory there was no place for popular rights. And hence the indirect tendency of the Reformation to narrow the province of government and exalt the privileges of the subject was as plainly adverse to what one may call the Imperial Idea as the Protestant claim of the right of private judgement was to the pretensions of the Papacy and the priesthood.

The remark must not be omitted in passing, how much less than might have been expected the religious movement did at first actually effect in the way of promoting either political progress or freedom of conscience. The habits of centuries were not to be unlearnt in a few years, and it was natural that ideas struggling into existence and activity should work erringly and imperfectly for a time. By a few inflammable minds liberty was carried into antinomianism, and produced the wildest excesses of life and doctrine. Several fantastic sects arose, refusing to conform to the ordinary rules without which human society could not subsist. But these commotions neither spread widely nor lasted long. Far more pervading and more remarkable was the other error, if that can be called an error which was the almost unavoidable result of the circumstances of the time. The principles which had led the Protestants to sever themselves from the Roman Church, should have taught them to bear with the opinions of others, and warned them from the attempt to

Immediate influence of the Reformation on political and religious liberty.

Conduct of the Protestant states.

connect agreement in doctrine or manner of worship with the indispensable forms of secular government. Still less ought they to have enforced that agreement by civil penalties; for faith, upon their own shewing, had no value save when it was freely given. A church which does not claim to be infallible is bound to allow that some part of the truth may possibly be with its adversaries. A church which permits or encourages human reason to apply itself to revelation has no right first to argue with people and then to punish them if they are not convinced. But whether it was that men only half saw what they had done, or that finding it hard enough to unrivet priestly fetters, they welcomed all the aid a temporal prince could give, the actual consequence was that religion, or rather theological creeds, began to be involved with politics more closely than had ever been the case before. Through the greater part of Christendom wars of religion raged for a century or more, and down to our own days feelings of religious antipathy continued to affect the relations of the Powers of Europe. In almost every country the form of doctrine which triumphed associated itself with the state, and maintained the despotic system of the Middle Ages, while it forsook the grounds on which that system had been based. It was thus that there arose National Churches, which were to be to the several Protestant countries of Europe that which the Church Catholic had been to the world at large; churches, that is to say, each of which was to be co-extensive with its respective state, was to enjoy landed wealth and exclusive political privilege, and was to be armed with coercive powers against recusants. It was not altogether easy to find a set of theoretical principles on which such churches might be made to rest, for they could not, like the old Church, point to the historical transmission of their doctrines; they could not claim to have in any one man or body of men an infallible organ of divine truth; they could not even fall back upon general councils, or the argument, whatever it may be worth, 'Securus iudicat orbis terrarum.' But in practice these difficulties were soon got over, for the dominant party in each state, if it did not claim to be infallible, was at any rate quite sure that it was right, and could attribute the resistance of other sects to nothing but moral obliquity. The will of the sovereign, as in England, or the will of the majority, as in Holland, the Scandinavian countries and Scotland, imposed upon each country a peculiar form of worship, and kept up the practices of mediaeval intolerance without their justification. Persecution, which might be at least palliated in an infallible Catholic and Apostolic Church, was peculiarly odious when practised by those who were not catholic, who were no more apostolic than their neighbours, and who had just revolted from the most ancient and venerable authority in the name of rights which they now denied to others. If union with the Visible Church by participation in a material sacrament be necessary to eternal life, persecution may be held a duty, a kindness to perishing souls. But if the kingdom of heaven be in every sense a kingdom of the spirit, if saving faith be possible out of one visible body and under a diversity of external forms, if the sense of the written revelation of God be ascertainable by the exercise of human reason, guided by the Divine breath which bloweth where it listeth, persecution becomes at once a crime and a folly. Therefore the intolerance of Protestant rulers, though the forms it took were less cruel than those practised by the Roman Catholics, was also far less defensible; for it had seldom anything better to allege on its behalf than motives of political expediency, or, more often, the headstrong passion of a ruler or a faction to silence the expressions of any opinions but their own. To enlarge upon this theme, did space permit it, would not be to digress from the proper subject of this narrative. For the Empire, as has been said more than once already, was far less an institution than a theory or doctrine. And hence it is not too much to say, that the ideas which have but recently ceased to prevail in Western Europe regarding the duty of the magistrate to compel uniformity in doctrine and worship by the civil arm, may all be traced to the relation which theory established between the Roman Church and the Roman Empire; to the conception, in fact, of an Empire Church itself.

Influence of the Reformation on the name and associations of the Empire.

Two of the ways in which the Reformation affected the Empire have been now described, its immediate political results, and its far more profound doctrinal importance, as implanting new ideas regarding the nature of freedom and the province of government. A third, though apparently almost superficial, cannot be omitted. Its name and its traditions, little as they retained of their former magic power, were still such as to excite the antipathy of the German reformers. The form which the doctrine of the supreme importance of one faith and one body of the faithful had taken was the dominion of the ancient capital of the world through her spiritual head, the Roman bishop, and her temporal head, the Emperor. As the names of Roman and Christian had been once convertible, so long afterwards were those of Roman and Catholic. The Reformation, separating into its parts what had hitherto been one conception, attacked Romanism if not Catholicity, and formed religious communities which, while continuing to call themselves Christian, repudiated the form with which Christianity had been so

long identified in the West.   As the Empire was founded
upon the assumption that the limits of Church and State
are exactly co-extensive, a change which withdrew half
of its subjects from the one body while they remained
members of the other, transformed it utterly, destroyed
the meaning and value of its old arrangements, and forced
the Emperor into a strange and incongruous position.
To his Protestant subjects he was merely the titular head
of the nation, to the Catholics he was also the Defender
and Advocate of their church.   Thus from being chief of
the whole state he became the chief of a party within it,
the Corpus Catholicorum, as opposed to the Corpus
Evangelicorum; he lost what had been hitherto his most
sacred claim to the obedience of the subject; the awakened
feeling of German nationality was driven into hostility to
an institution whose title and history seemed to bind it
to the centre of foreign tyranny.   After exulting for seven
centuries in the heritage of Roman rule, half of the nation
cherished again the feeling with which their ancestors
had resisted Julius Caesar and Germanicus.   Two mutually
repugnant systems could not exist side by side without
striving to destroy one another.   The instincts of theological sympathy overcame the duties of political allegiance, and men who were subjects both of the Emperor
and of their local prince, gave most of their loyalty to
him who professed their doctrines and protected their
worship.   For in North Germany princes as well as
people were mostly Lutheran: in the Southern and
especially the South-eastern lands, where the magnates
held to the old faith, Protestants were scarcely to be
found except in the free cities and a few remote valleys
among the mountains.   The same causes which injured
the Emperor's position in Germany swept away the last
semblance of his authority through other countries.   In

CHAP. XIX.

the religious conflict which rent the Christian world for a century or more after Charles V, the Protestants of England and France, of Holland and Sweden, thought of him as the ally of Spain, of the Vatican, of the Jesuits; and he of whom it had been believed a century before that by nothing but his existence was the coming of Antichrist on earth delayed, was in the eyes of the Northern divines either Antichrist himself or Antichrist's foremost champion. The earthquake that opened a chasm in Germany was felt through Europe; its states and peoples marshalled themselves under two hostile banners, and with the Empire's expiring power vanished that united Christendom it had been created to lead.

Troubles of Germany.

Some of the effects thus sketched began to shew themselves soon after that famous Diet of Worms, from Luther's appearance at which, in A.D. 1521, we may date the beginning of the Reformation. But just as the end of the religious conflict in England can hardly be placed earlier than the Revolution in 1688, nor in France than the Revocation of the Edict of Nantes in 1685, so it was not till after more than a century of doubtful strife that the new order of things was fully and finally established in Germany.[h] The arrangements made at Augsburg in 1530, like most treaties on the basis of *uti possidetis*, were no better than a hollow truce, satisfying no one, and consciously made to be broken. The church lands which Protestants had seized, and Jesuit confessors urged the Catholic princes to reclaim, furnished an unceasing ground of quarrel. Neither party yet knew the strength of its antagonists sufficiently to abstain from in-

Rudolf II, 1576–1612.

Matthias, 1612–1619.

[h] Each German prince claimed, and usually secured, the right of establishing within his territories the creed he adopted, according to the maxim: 'Cuius regio eius religio.' Lutherans and the Calvinists applied this principle against each other.

sulting or persecuting their modes of worship, and the
smouldering hate of half a century was kindled by the
troubles of Bohemia into the Thirty Years' War.

The imperial sceptre held for thirty-six years by the indolent and vacillating Rudolf II (1576–1612), the corrupt
and reckless policy of whose ministers had done much to
exasperate the already suspicious minds of the Protestants,
had now passed, after the short reign of his brother
Matthias, into the firmer grasp of Ferdinand the Second.[i]
Jealous, bigoted, implacable, skilful in forming and con-
cealing his plans, resolute to obstinacy in carrying them
out in action, the house of Hapsburg could have had no
abler and no more unpopular leader in their second
attempt to turn the Germanic Empire into an Austrian
military monarchy. They seemed for a time as near to
the accomplishment of the project as Charles the Fifth
had been. Leagued with Spain, backed by the Catholics
of Germany, served by the genius of Wallenstein, Ferdinand proposed nothing less than the extension of
the Empire to its old limits, and the recovery of his
crown's full prerogative over all its vassals. Denmark and
Holland were to be attacked by sea and land : Italy to
be reconquered with the help of Spain : Maximilian of
Bavaria and Wallenstein to be rewarded with principalities
in Pomerania and Mecklenburg. The latter general was
all but master of Northern Germany when the successful
resistance of Stralsund turned the wavering balance of
the war. Soon after (A.D. 1630), Gustavus Adolphus
crossed the Baltic, and saved Europe from an impend-
ing reign of the Jesuits. Ferdinand's high-handed proceedings had already alarmed even the Catholic princes.
Of his own authority he had put the Elector Palatine
and other magnates to the ban of the Empire : he had

*Thirty
Years' War,
1618–1648.*

*Ferdinand
II,* A.D.
1619–1637.

*Plans of
Ferdinand
II.*

*Gustavus
Adolphus.*

---

[i] Matthias, brother of Rudolf II, reigned from 1612 till 1619.

transferred an electoral vote to Bavaria; had treated the districts overrun by his generals as spoil of war, to be portioned out at his pleasure; had unsettled all possession by requiring the restitution of church property occupied since A.D. 1555. The Protestants were helpless; the Catholics, though they complained of the flagrant illegality of such conduct, did not dare to oppose it; the rescue of Germany was the work of the Swedish king. In four campaigns he destroyed the armies and the prestige of the Emperor; devastated his lands, emptied his treasury, and left him at last so enfeebled that no subsequent successes could make him again formidable. Such, nevertheless, was the selfishness and apathy of the Protestant princes, divided by the mutual jealousy of the Lutheran and the Calvinist party — some, like the Saxon *Ferdinand* Elector, inglorious descendant of the famous Maurice, *III,* bribed by the crafty Austrian; others afraid to stir lest *1637-1658.* a reverse should expose them unprotected to his vengeance — that but for the interference of France the issue of the long-protracted contest would have gone against A.D. 1634. them, although Wallenstein had now fallen by the hand of assassins suborned by Ferdinand II. It was the leading principle of Richelieu's policy to depress the house of Hapsburg and keep Germany disunited: hence he encouraged Protestantism abroad while trampling it down at home. Like Cavour two centuries later, he did *The Peace of* not live to see the triumph his skill had won. That *Westphalia.* triumph was sealed in A.D. 1648, on the utter exhaustion of all the combatants, and the treaties of Münster and Osnabrück were thenceforward the basis of the Germanic constitution.

CHAPTER XX

THE Peace of Westphalia is the first, and, with the CHAP. XX.
possible exception of the Treaties of Vienna in 1815,
the most important of those attempts to reconstruct by
diplomacy the European states-system which have played
so large a part in modern history. It is important, however, less as marking the introduction of new principles,
than as winding up the struggle which had convulsed
Germany since the revolt of Luther, sealing its results,
and closing definitely the period of the Reformation. Although the causes of disunion which the religious movement called into being had now been at work for more
than a hundred years, their effects were not fully seen
till it became necessary to establish a system which should
represent the altered relations to one another of the German states. It may thus be said of this famous peace,
as of the other so-called 'fundamental law of the Empire,' the Golden Bull, that it did no more than legalize
a condition of things already in existence, but which by
being legalized acquired new importance. To all parties
alike the result of the Thirty Years' War was thoroughly
unsatisfactory — to the Protestants, who had lost Bohemia,
and were still obliged to hold an inferior place in the
electoral college and in the Diet : to the Catholics, who
were forced to permit the exercise of heretical worship,
and leave the church lands in the grasp of sacrilegious

spoilers: to the princes, who could not throw off the burden of imperial supremacy: to the Emperor, who could turn that supremacy to no practical account. No other conclusion was possible to a contest in which every one had been vanquished and no one victorious; which had ceased because while the reasons for war continued the means of war had failed. Nevertheless, the substantial advantage remained with the German princes, for they gained the formal recognition of that territorial independence whose origin may be placed as far back as the days of Frederick the Second, and the maturity of which had been hastened by the events of the last preceding century. It was, indeed, not only recognized but justified as rightful and necessary. For while the political situation, to use a current phrase, had changed within the last two hundred years, the eyes with which men regarded it had changed still more. Never by their fiercest enemies in earlier times, not once by Popes or Lombard republics in the heat of their strife with the Franconian and Swabian Caesars, had the Emperors been reproached as mere German kings, or their claim to be the lawful heirs of Rome denied. The Protestant jurists of the seventeenth century were the first persons who ventured to scoff at the pretended lordship of the world, and declare their Empire to be nothing more than a German monarchy, in dealing with which no superstitious reverence need prevent its subjects from making the best terms they could for themselves, and controlling a sovereign whose religious predilections bound him to their ecclesiastical enemies.

The treatise of Hippolytus a Lapide.

It is instructive to turn suddenly from Dante or Peter de Andlau to a book published shortly before A.D. 1648, under the name of Hippolytus a Lapide,[a] and notice the matter-of-fact way, and bitterly contemptuous spirit, in

[a] *De Ratione Status in Imperio nostro Romano-Germanico.*

which, disregarding the traditional glories of the Empire, he comments on its actual condition and prospects. Hippolytus, the pseudonym which the jurist Chemnitz assumed, urges with violence almost superfluous that the Germanic constitution must be treated entirely as a native growth: that the so-called ' lex regia ' and the whole system of Justinianean absolutism which the Emperors had used so dexterously, were in their applications to Germany not merely incongruous but positively absurd. With eminent learning, Chemnitz examines the early history of the Empire, draws from the unceasing contests of the monarch with the nobility the unexpected moral that the power of the former has been always dangerous, and is now more dangerous than ever, and then launches out into a long invective against the policy of the Hapsburgs, an invective which the ambition and harshness of the late Emperor (Ferdinand II) made only too plausible. The one real remedy for the evils that menace Germany he states concisely — ' domus Austriacae extirpatio ': but, failing this, he would have the Emperor's prerogative restricted in every way, and provide means for resisting or dethroning him. It was by these views, which seem to have made a profound impression in Germany, that the states, or rather France and Sweden acting on their behalf, were guided in the negotiations of Osnabrück and Münster. By extorting a full recognition of the sovereignty of all the princes, Catholics and Protestants alike, in their respective territories, they bound the Emperor from any direct interference with the administration, either in particular districts or throughout the Empire. All affairs of public *Rights of the* importance, including the rights of making war or peace, *Emperor and the Diet, as* of levying contributions, raising troops, building fortresses, *settled in* passing or interpreting laws, were henceforth to be left *A.D. 1648.* entirely in the hands of the Diet. The Aulic Council, which had been sometimes the engine of imperial oppression, and always of imperial intrigue, was so restricted as to be comparatively harmless for the future. The '*reservata*' of the Emperor were confined to the rights of granting titles and confirming tolls. In matters of religion, an exact though not perfectly reciprocal equality was established between the two chief ecclesiastical bodies, and the right of 'Itio in partes,' that is to say, of deciding questions in which religion was involved by amicable negotiations between the Protestant and Catholic states, instead of by a majority of votes in the Diet, was definitely conceded. Both Lutherans and Calvinists were declared free from all jurisdiction of the Pope or any Catholic prelate. Thus the last link which bound Germany as a whole to Rome was snapped, the last of the principles by virtue of which the Empire had existed was abandoned. For the Empire now contained and recognized as its members persons who formed a visible body at open war with the Holy Roman Church; and its constitution admitted schismatics to a full share in all those civil rights which, according to the doctrines of the early Middle Age, could be enjoyed by no one who was out of the communion of the Catholic Church. The Peace of Westphalia was therefore an abrogation of the sovereignty of Rome, and of the theory of Church and State with which the name of Rome was associated. And in this light was it regarded by Pope Innocent the Tenth, who commanded his legate to protest against it, and subsequently declared it void by the bull '*Zelo domus Dei.*' [b]

---

[b] Even then the Roman pontiffs had lapsed into that scolding, anile tone (so unlike the fiery brevity of Hildebrand, or the stern precision of Innocent III) which for a long time thereafter characterized their public utterances. Pope Innocent the Tenth pronounces the provisions of the treaty, 'ipso iure nulla, irrita, invalida, iniqua, iniusta, damnata, reprobata, inania, viribusque

The transference of power within the Empire from its head to its members, was a small matter compared with the losses which the Empire suffered as a whole. The real gainers by the treaties of Westphalia were those who had borne the brunt of the battle against Ferdinand the Second and his son. To France were ceded Brisac, the *Loss of* Austrian part of Alsace, and the lands of the three bishop- *imperial* rics in Lorraine — Metz, Toul, and Verdun, which her *territories.* armies had seized in A.D. 1552; to Sweden, Northern Pomerania, Bremen, and Verden. There was, however, this difference between the position of the two, that whereas Sweden became a member of the German Diet for what she received (as the king of Holland was, until 1866, a member for Dutch Luxemburg, and as the king of Denmark, up till the accession of Christian IX in 1863, was for Holstein), the acquisitions of France were delivered over to her in full sovereignty, and for ever (as it then seemed) severed from the Germanic body. And as it was by their aid that the liberties of the Protestants had been won, these two states obtained at the same time what was more valuable than territorial accessions — the right of interfering at imperial elections, and generally whenever the provisions of the treaties of Osnabrück and Münster, which they had guaranteed, might be supposed to be endangered. The bounds of the Empire were further narrowed by the final separation of two countries, once integral parts of Germany, and up to this time legally members of her body. The United Provinces of Holland and the Swiss Confederation were, in A.D. 1648, declared independent.

The Peace of Westphalia is an era in the history of the

---

et effectu vacua, omnino fuisse, esse, et perpetuo fore.' In spite of which they took effect.

This bull may be found in vol. xvii of the *Bullarium Romanum*. It bears date Nov. 20th, A.D. 1648.

Holy Empire not less clearly marked than the coronation of Otto the Great, or the death of Frederick the Second. As from the days of Maximilian I it had borne a mixed or transitional character, well expressed by the name Romano-Germanic, so henceforth it is in everything but title purely and solely a German Empire. Properly, indeed, it was no longer an Empire at all, but a Federation, and that of the loosest sort. For it had no common treasury, no efficient common tribunals,[c] no means of coercing a refractory member ;[d] its states were of different religions, were governed according to different forms, were administered judicially and financially without any regard to each other. The traveller by rail in Central Germany used, up till 1866, to be amused to find, every hour or two, by the change in the soldiers' uniforms, and in the colour of the stripes on the railway fences, that he had passed out of one and into another of its miniature kingdoms. Much more surprised and embarrassed would he have been a

*Number of
petty inde-
pendent
states : effects
of such a
system on
Germany.*

century earlier, when, instead of the present twenty-two, there were three hundred petty principalities between the Alps and the Baltic, each with its own laws, its own court (in which the ceremonious pomp of Versailles was faintly reproduced), its little army, its separate coinage, its tolls and custom-houses on the frontier, its crowd of meddlesome

---

[c] The Imperial Chamber (Kammergericht), instituted in A.D. 1495, continued, with frequent and long interruptions, to sit while the Empire lasted. But its slowness and formality passed that of any other legal body the world has yet seen, and it had no power to enforce its sentences. Till 1689 it sat at Speyer, whence the saying 'Spirae lites spirant et non exspirant'; in that year the French laid Speyer in ashes, and the Chamber was in 1693 established at Wetzlar, where Goethe (who had gone thither as a law student) saw it dawdling over its work in 1772. The house of Charlotte the heroine of the *Sorrows of Werther* is still shewn in this sleepy little city.

[d] The 'matricula' specifying the quota of each state to the imperial army could not be any longer employed.

and pedantic officials, presided over by a prime minister who was often the unworthy favourite of his prince and sometimes the pensioner of a foreign court. This vicious system, which paralyzed the trade, the literature, and the political thought of Germany, had been forming itself for some time, but did not become fully established until the Peace of Westphalia, by finally emancipating the princes from imperial control, had left them masters in their own territories. The impoverishment of the inferior nobility and the decline of the commercial cities caused by a war that had lasted a whole generation, removed every counterpoise to the power of the electors and princes, and made absolutism supreme just where absolutism is least defensible, its states too small to have any public opinion, states in which everything depends on the monarch, and the monarch depends on his favourites. After A.D. 1648 the provincial estates or parliaments became obsolete in most of these principalities, and powerless in the rest. Germany was forced to drink to its very dregs the cup of feudalism, feudalism from which all the sentiment that once ennobled it had departed.

It is instructive to compare the results of the system of *Feudalism* feudality in the three chief countries of modern Europe. *in France,* In France, the feudal head absorbed all the powers of *Germany.* the state, and left to the aristocracy only a few privileges, odious indeed, but politically worthless. In England, the mediaeval system expanded into a constitutional monarchy, where the landholding oligarchy was still strong, but the commons had won the full recognition of equal civil rights. In Germany, everything was taken from the sovereign, and nothing given to the people; the representatives of those who had been fief-holders of the first and second rank before the Great Interregnum were now independent potentates; and what had been once a monarchy was now an aristocratic federation. The Diet, originally an assembly of the whole people, and thereafter of the feudal tenants-in-chief, meeting from time to time like our early English Parliaments, became in A.D. 1654 a permanent body, at which the electors, princes, and cities were represented by their envoys. In other words, it was not so much a national Parliament as an international congress of diplomatists.

Causes of the continued maintenance of the Empire.

Where the sacrifice of imperial, or rather federal, rights to state rights was so complete, we may wonder that the farce of an Empire should have been retained at all. A mere German Empire would probably have perished; but the Teutonic people could not bring itself to abandon the venerable heritage of Rome. Moreover, the Germans were of all European peoples the most slow-moving and long-suffering; and as, if the Empire had fallen, something must have been erected in its place, they preferred to work on with the clumsy machine so long as it would work at all. Properly speaking, it has no history after this; and the history of the particular states of Germany which takes its place is one of the dreariest chapters in the annals of mankind. It would be hard to find, from the Peace of Westphalia to the French Revolution, a single grand character or a single noble enterprise; a single sacrifice made to great public interests, a single instance in which the welfare of the people was preferred to the selfish passions of their princes. One ruler there was indeed of consummate powers, the ruler who by building up a strong and well-administered state became the true founder of that greatness which has enabled the Prussian kingdom to revive the Germanic Empire and to bear its weight. But the policy of Frederick II was throughout a purely Prussian, rather than a German policy, and though he did much for his subjects, he did nothing through or by them, and gave no opportunity for the developement among them of self-government or of the spirit of Germanic nationality. The military history of the seventeenth and eighteenth centuries will always be read with interest; but free and progressive countries have a history of peace not less rich and varied than that of war; and when we ask for an account of the political life of Germany in the eighteenth century, we hear nothing but the scandals of buzzing courts, and the wrangling of diplomatists at never-ending congresses.

Useless and helpless as the Empire had become, it was not without its importance to the neighbouring countries, with whose fortunes it had been linked by the Peace of Westphalia. It was the pivot on which the political sys- *The Empire* tem of Europe was to revolve: the scales, so to speak, *and the* which marked the equipoise of power that had become the *balance* *of power.* grand object of the policy of all states. This modern tra- vesty of the plan by which the theorists of the fourteenth century had proposed to keep the world at peace, used means less noble and attained its end no better than theirs had done. No one will deny that it was and is desirable to prevent a universal monarchy in Europe. But it may be asked whether a system can be considered successful which allowed Frederick of Prussia to seize Silesia, which did not check the aggressions of Russia and France upon their neighbours, which was for ever bartering and ex- changing lands in every part of Europe without thought of the inhabitants, which permitted and was never able to redress such a calamity as the partitionment of Poland. And if it be said that bad as things have been under this system, they would have been worse without it, it is hard to refrain from asking whether any evils could have been greater than those which the people of Europe have suf- fered through constant wars with each other, and through the withdrawal, even in time of peace, of so large a part of their population from useful labour to be wasted in maintaining gigantic standing armies.

The result of the extended relations in which Germany now found herself to Europe, with two foreign kings never wanting an occasion, one of them never the wish, to interfere, was that a spark from her set the Continent ablaze, while flames kindled elsewhere were sure to spread hither. Matters grew worse as her princes inherited or created so many thrones abroad. The Duke of Holstein acquired Denmark, the Elector of Saxony Poland, the Elector of Hanover England, the Archduke of Austria Hungary and Bohemia, while the Elector (originally Margrave) of Brandenburg assumed, on the strength of non-imperial territories to the north-eastward which had come into his hands, the style and title of King of Prussia.[e] Thus the Empire seemed again about to embrace Europe; but in a sense far different from that which those words would have expressed under Charles and Otto. Its history for a century and a half is a dismal list of losses and disgraces. The chief external danger was from French influence, for a time supreme, always menacing. For though Lewis XIV, on whom, in A.D. 1658, half the electoral college wished to confer the imperial crown, was before the end of his life an object of intense hatred, officially entitled 'Hereditary enemy of the Holy Empire,'[f] France had nevertheless a strong party among the princes at her beck. The Rhenish and Bavarian electors were her favourite tools. The '*réunions*' begun in A.D. 1680, a pleasant euphemism for robbery in time of peace, added Strasburg and other places in Alsace, Lorraine, and Franche Comté

[e] A member of the Palatinate family succeeded to the crown of Sweden in 1654.

[f] *Erbfeind des heiligen Reichs.*

to the monarchy of Lewis, and brought him nearer the heart CHAP. XX. of the Empire; his ambition and cruelty were witnessed to by repeated wars, and by the devastation of the Rhine countries; the ultimate though short-lived triumph of his policy was attained when Marshal Belleisle dictated the election of Charles VII in A.D. 1742. In the Turkish wars, when the princes left Vienna to be saved by the Polish king Sobieski, the Empire's weakness appeared in pitiable light. There was, indeed, a complete loss of hope and interest in the old system. The princes had been so long accustomed *Weakness* to consider themselves the natural foes of a central govern- *and stag-* *nation of* ment, that a request made by it was sure to be disregarded; *Germany.* they aped in their petty courts the pomp and etiquette of Vienna or Paris, grumbling that they should be required to garrison the great frontier fortresses which alone protected them from an encroaching neighbour. The Free Cities had never recovered from the famines and sieges of the Thirty Years' War: Hanseatic greatness had waned, and the southern towns had sunk into languid oligarchies. All the vigour of the people in a somewhat stagnant age either found its sphere in rising states like the Prussia of Frederick the Great, or turned away from politics altogether into other channels. The Diet had become contemptible from the slowness with which it moved, and its tedious squabbles on matters the most frivolous. Many sittings were consumed in the discussion of a question regarding the time of keeping Easter, more ridiculous than that which had distracted the Western churches in the seventh century, the Protestants refusing to reckon by the reformed calendar because it was the work of a Pope. Collective action through the old organs was confessed impossible, when the common object of defence against France was sought by forming a league under the Emperor's presidency, and when at European congresses the Empire was

CHAP. XX.

not represented at all.[g] No change could come from the Emperor, whom the capitulation of A.D. 1658 deposed *ipso facto* if he violated its provisions. As Dohm said, to keep him from doing harm, he was kept from doing anything.

Leopold I,
1658–1705.
Joseph I,
1705–1711.
Charles VI,
1711–1740.

Yet little was lost by his inactivity, for what could have been hoped from his action ? From the election of Albert the Second, A.D. 1437, to the death of Charles the Sixth, A.D. 1740, the sceptre had remained in the hands of one family. So far from being fit subjects for undistinguishing invective, the Hapsburg Emperors may be contrasted favourably with the contemporary dynasties of France, Spain, or England. Their policy, viewed as a whole from the days of Rudolf I downwards, had been neither conspicuously tyrannical, nor faltering, nor dishonest. But it had been almost always a selfish family policy. Entrusted with an office which might, if there be any power in those memories of the past to which the champions of hereditary monarchy were wont to appeal, have stirred their sluggish souls with some enthusiasm for the heroes on whose throne they sat, some wish to advance the glory and the happiness of Germany, they had cared for nothing, sought nothing, used the Empire as an instrument for nothing but the attainment of their own personal or dynastic ends. Placed on the eastern verge of Germany, the Hapsburgs had added to their ancient lands in Austria proper, Styria and Tyrol, non-German territories far more extensive, and had thus become the chiefs of a separate and independent state. They endeavoured to reconcile its interests with the interests of the Empire, so long as it seemed possible to recover part of the old imperial prerogative. But when such hopes were dashed by the

The Haps-
burg Em-
perors and
their policy.

[g] Only the envoys of the several states were present at Utrecht in 1713.

defeats of the Thirty Years' War, they hesitated no longer Chap. XX. between an elective crown and the rule of their hereditary dominions, and comported themselves thenceforth in European politics not as the representatives of Germany, but as heads of the great Austrian monarchy. There would have been nothing culpable in this had they not at the same time continued to entangle Germany in wars with which she had no concern: to waste her strength in tedious combats with the Turks, or plunge her into a new struggle with France, not to defend her frontiers or recover the lands she had lost, but that some scion of the house of Hapsburg might reign in Spain or Italy. Watching the whole course of their foreign policy, marking how in A.D. 1736 they had bartered away Lorraine for Tuscany, a German for a non-German territory, and seeing how at home they opposed every scheme of reform which could in the least degree trench upon their own prerogative, how they strove to obstruct the imperial chamber lest it should interfere with their own Aulic council, men were driven to separate the body of the Empire from the imperial office and its possessors,[h] and when plans for reinvigorating the one failed, to leave the others to their fate. Still the old line clung to the crown with that Hapsburg gripe which has almost passed into a proverb. Odious as Austria was, *Causes of* no one could despise her, or fancy it easy to shake her *the long* commanding position in Europe. Her alliances were *retention of the throne* fortunate: her designs were steadily pursued: her dis- *by Austria.* membered territories always returned to her. Though the imperial throne continued strictly elective, it was impossible not to be influenced by long prescription. Projects were repeatedly formed to set the Hapsburgs aside

[h] We have unfortunately no terms to correspond to the distinction expressed by the German 'Reich' and 'Kaiserthum.'

by electing a prince of some other line[i], or by passing
a law that there should never be more than two, or four,
successive Emperors of the same house. France ever
and anon renewed her warnings to the electors, that their
freedom was passing from them, and the sceptre becoming
hereditary in one haughty family.[j] But it was felt that
a change would be difficult and disagreeable, and that the
heavy expense and scanty revenues of the Empire required
to be supported by larger patrimonial domains than most
German princes possessed. The heads of states like
Prussia and Hanover, states whose size and wealth would
have made them suitable candidates, were Protestants,
and thus practically excluded both by the connection of
the imperial office with the Church, and by the majority
of Roman Catholics in the electoral college,[k] who, however jealous they might be of Austria, were led by habit
and by sympathy to rally round her in moments of peril.
The one occasion on which these considerations were

[i] So the elector of Saxony proposed in 1532 that, Albert II, Frederick III,
and Maximilian having been all of one house, Charles V's successor should
be chosen from some other. Moser, *Römische Kayser*. See the various attempts of France in Moser. The coronation engagements (Wahlcapitulation)
of every Emperor bound him not to attempt to make the throne hereditary
in his family.

[j] In 1658 France offered to subsidize the Elector of Bavaria if he would
become Emperor.

[k] Whether an Evangelical was eligible for the office of Emperor was a
question often debated, but never actually raised by the candidature of any
but a Roman Catholic prince. The 'exacta aequalitas' conceded by the
Peace of Westphalia might appear to include so important a privilege. But
it must be remembered that the peculiar relation in which the Emperor stood
to the Holy Roman Church was one which no one out of the communion of
that Church could hold, and that the coronation oaths could not have been
taken by, nor the coronation ceremonies (among which was a sort of ordination) performed upon a Protestant.

The Emperor Sigismund is said to have officiated as a deacon at a solemn
mass at the opening of the Council of Constance, and chanted the Gospel.

disregarded shewed their force. On the extinction of CHAP. XX. the male line of Hapsburg in the person of Charles the Sixth, the intrigues of the French envoy, Marshal Belle-isle, procured the election of the Elector Charles Albert of Bavaria, who stood first among the Catholic princes. His reign was a succession of misfortunes and ignominies. Driven out of Munich by the Austrians, the head of the Holy Empire lived in Frankfort on the bounty of France, cursed by the country on which his ambition had brought the miseries of a protracted war.[1] The choice in 1745 of Duke Francis of Lorraine, husband of the archduchess of Austria and queen of Hungary, Maria Theresa, was meant to restore the crown to the only power capable of wearing it with dignity : in Joseph the Second, her son, it again rested on the brow of a scion of the ancient line.[m] In the war of the Austrian succession,

Charles VII,
1742–1745.

Francis I,
1745–1765.

[1] 'The bold Bavarian, in a luckless hour,
    Tries the dread summits of Caesarean power ;
    With unexpected legions bursts away,
    And sees defenceless realms receive his sway. . . .
    The baffled prince in honour's flattering bloom
    Of hasty greatness finds the fatal doom ;
    His foes' derision and his subjects' blame,
    And steals to death from anguish and from shame.'
                — JOHNSON, *Vanity of Human Wishes.*

[m] The following nine reasons for the long continuance of the Empire in the House of Hapsburg are given by Pfeffinger (*Vitriarius Illustratus*), writing early in the eighteenth century : —

    1. The great power of Austria.
    2. Her wealth, now that the Empire was so poor.
    3. The majority of Catholics among the electors.
    4. Her fortunate matrimonial alliances.
    5. Her moderation.
    6. The memory of benefits conferred by her.
    7. The example of evils that had followed a departure from the blood of former Caesars.
    8. The fear of the confusion that would ensue if she were deprived of the crown.
    9. Her own eagerness to have it.

which followed the death of Charles the Sixth, the Empire as a body took no part; in the Seven Years' War its whole might broke in vain against one resolute member. Under

Frederick the Great Prussia approved herself at least a match for France and Austria leagued against her, and the semblance of unity which the predominance of a single power had hitherto given to the Empire was replaced by

the avowed rivalry of two military monarchies. The Emperor Joseph the Second, a sort of philosopher-king, than whom few have more narrowly missed greatness, made a desperate effort to set things right, striving to restore the disordered finances, to purge and vivify the Imperial Chamber. Nay, he renounced the intolerant policy of his ancestors, quarrelled with the Pope,[n] and presumed to visit Rome, whose streets heard once more the shout that had been silent for three centuries, ' Long live our Emperor! You are in your own house! You are the master!'[o] But his indiscreet haste was met by a sullen resistance, and he died disappointed in plans for which the time was not yet ripe, leaving no result save the league of princes which Frederick the Great had formed

to oppose his designs on Bavaria. His successor, Leopold the Second, abandoned the projected reforms, and a calm, the calm before the hurricane, settled down again upon Germany. The existence of the Empire was almost forgotten by its subjects: there was nothing to remind them of it but a feudal investiture now and then at Vienna (real feudal rights were obsolete, as Joseph II found when he tried to enforce them); a concourse of solemn old lawyers

[n] The Pope undertook a journey to Vienna to mollify Joseph, and met with a sufficiently cold reception. When he saw the famous minister Kaunitz and gave him his hand to kiss, Kaunitz took it and shook it.

[o] Joseph was the first Emperor since Charles the Bald who had kept his Christmas at Rome.

at Wetzlar puzzling over interminable suits,[p] and some CHAP. XX.
thirty diplomatists at Regensburg, the relics of that Imperial Diet where once a hero-king, a Frederick or a *The Diet.*
Henry, enthroned amid mitred prelates and steel-clad
barons, had issued laws for every tribe from the Mediterranean to the Baltic.[q]   The solemn triflings of this so-
called 'Diet of Deputation' — which Frederick the Great
compared to dogs in a yard baying the moon — have
probably never been equalled elsewhere.[r]   Questions of
precedence and title, questions whether the envoys of
princes should have chairs of red cloth like those of the
electors, or only of the less honourable green, whether
they should be served on gold or on silver, how many
hawthorn boughs should be hung up before the door of
each on May-day; these, and such as these, it was their
chief employment not to settle but to discuss.   The
pedantic formalism of old Germany passed that of Spaniards or Turks; it had now crushed under a mountain
of rubbish whatever meaning or force its old institutions
had contained.   It is the penalty of greatness that its form
should outlive its substance: that gilding and trappings
should remain when that which they were meant to deck
and clothe has departed.   So our sloth or our timidity, not
seeing the mischief which a soulless sham can do, main-

[p] Shortly before the Empire ended, there were more than sixty thousand
lawsuits waiting to be heard.

[q] In 1764 the revenue of the Emperor (from the Empire) was estimated
at 13,884 florins and 32 kreutzers.   Some one remarks that one day's journey,
in Germany, might take a traveller through the territories of a free city, a
sovereign abbot, a village belonging to an imperial knight, and the dominions
of a landgrave, a duke, a prince, and a king, so small, so numerous, and so
diverse were the principalities.

[r] He said of the Diet, 'Es ist ein Schattenbild, eine Versammlung aus
Publizisten die mehr mit Formalien als mit Sachen sich beschäftigen, und,
wie Hofhunde, den Mond anbellen.'

tains in being what once was good long after it has become helpless and hopeless: so now at the close of the eighteenth century, strings of sounding titles were all that was left of the Empire which Charles had founded, and Frederick had adorned, and Dante had sung.

Feelings of the German people.

The German mind, just beginning to put forth the first blossoms of its noblest literary epoch, turned away in disgust from the spectacle of ceremonious imbecility more than Byzantine. National feeling seemed gone from princes and people alike. Not to speak of cynical monarchs like Frederick the Great and Joseph II, even Lessing, who did more than any one else to create the German literary spirit, says, 'Of the love of country I have no conception: it appears to me at best a heroic weakness which I am right glad to be without.' There were nevertheless persons who saw how fatal such a system was, lying like a nightmare on the people's soul. Speaking of the Union of Princes (Fürstenbund) formed by Frederick of Prussia to preserve the existing condition of things, Johannes von Müller writes:[8] 'If the German Union serves for nothing better than to maintain the *status quo*, it is against the eternal order of God, by which neither the physical nor the moral world remains for a moment in the *status quo*, but all is life and motion and progress. To exist without law or justice, without security from arbitrary imposts, doubtful whether we can preserve from day to day our children, our honour, our liberties, our rights, our lives, helpless before superior force, without a beneficial connection between our states, without a national spirit at all, this is the *status quo* of our nation. And it was this that the Union was meant to maintain. If it be this and nothing more, then bethink you how when Israel saw that Rehoboam would

[8] *Deutschlands Erwartungen vom Fürstenbunde.*

not hearken, the people gave answer to the king and spake, " What portion have we in David, or what inheritance in the son of Jesse? to your tents, O Israel: David, see to thine own house." See then to your own houses, ye princes.'

Nevertheless, though the Empire stood like a corpse brought forth from some Egyptian sepulchre, ready to crumble at a touch, there seemed no reason why it should not stand so for centuries more. Fate was kind, and slew it in the light.

CHAPTER XXI

FALL OF THE EMPIRE

GOETHE has described the uneasiness with which, in the days of his childhood, the burghers of his native Frankfort saw the walls of the Roman Hall covered with the portraits of Emperor after Emperor, till space was left for few, at last for one.[a] In A.D. 1792 Francis the Second mounted the throne of Augustus, and the last place was filled. Three years before there had arisen on the western horizon a little cloud, no bigger than a man's hand, and now the heaven was black with storms of ruin. There was a prophecy,[b] dating from the first days of the Empire's decline, that when all things were falling to pieces, and wickedness rife in the world, a second Frankish Charles should rise as Emperor to purge and heal, to bring back peace and purify religion. If this was not the mission of the avatar who had risen to be First Consul and thereafter Emperor among the West Franks, he was at least anxious to tread in the steps and revive the glories of the hero whose throne he professed to have again erected. We may smile at the historical parallel with which the Bonapartist courtiers flattered their lord in A.D. 1804, the parallel between the heir of a long line of fierce Teutonic chieftains, whose

[a] *Wahrheit und Dichtung,* bk. i. The Römer Saal is still one of the sights of Frankfort. The portraits, however, which one now sees in it, seem to be all or nearly all of them modern; and few have any merit as works of art.

[b] *Jordanis Chronica,* ap. Schardium, *Sylloge Tractatuum.*

vigorous genius had seized what it could of the monkish learning of the eighth century, and the son of the Corsican lawyer, with all the brilliance of a Frenchman and all the resolute profundity of an Italian, reared in, yet only half believing, the ideas of the Encyclopaedists, swept up into the seat of absolute power by the whirlwind of a revolution. Alcuin and Talleyrand are not more unlike than are their masters. But though in the characters and temper of the men there is little resemblance, though their Empires agree in this only, and hardly even in this, that both were founded on conquest, there is nevertheless a sort of grand historical similarity between their positions. Both were the leaders of fiery and warlike nations, the one still untamed as the creatures of their native woods, the other drunk with revolutionary fury. Both aspired to found, and seemed for a time to have succeeded in founding, universal monarchies. Both were gifted with a strong and susceptible imagination, which if it sometimes overbore their judgement, was yet one of the truest and highest elements of their greatness. As the one looked back to the kings under the Jewish theocracy and the Emperors of Christian Rome, so the other thought to model himself after Julius Caesar and Charlemagne. For, useful as was the fancied precedent of the title and career of the great Carolingian to a chief determined to be king, yet unable to be king after the fashion of the Bourbons, and seductive as was such a connection to the imaginative vanity of the French people, it was no studied purpose or simulating art that led Napoleon to remind his subjects so frequently of the hero he claimed to represent. No one who reads the records of his life can doubt that he believed, as fully as he believed anything, that the same destiny which had made France the centre of the modern world had also appointed him to sit on the throne and carry out the projects of Charles the Frank, to

CHAP. XXI.

Napoleon, Emperor of the West.

Belief of Napoleon that he was the successor of Charlemagne.

rule all Europe from Paris, as the Caesars had ruled it from Rome.[c] Imaginative minds are apt to be swept away by the dreams they have themselves created. Napoleon began by invoking the memories of Charlemagne to serve his purposes: the memories of Charlemagne ended by dominating him. It was in this belief that he went to the ancient capital of the Frankish Emperors to receive there the Austrian recognition of his imperial title: that he talked of 'revendicating' Catalonia and Aragon, because *Attitude of* they had formed a part of the Carolingian realm, though *the Papacy* they had never obeyed any descendant of Hugh Capet: *towards* *Napoleon.* that he undertook a journey to Nimwegen, where he had ordered the ancient palace to be restored, and inscribed on its walls his name below that of Charles: that he summoned Pius VII to attend his coronation, as Pope Stephen had come ten centuries before to instal Pipin in the throne of the last Merovingian. The same desire to be regarded as lawful Emperor of the West shewed itself in his assumption of the Lombard crown at Milan; in the words of the decree by which he annexed Rome to the Empire, 're-voking the donations which my predecessors, the French Emperors, have made';[d] in the title 'King of Rome,' which he bestowed on his ill-fated son, in imitation of the German 'King of the Romans.'[e] So too he called himself 'Emperor of the French,' not 'of France': and as he had brought within his dominions not only parts of North-western Germany but also Rome and the Papal states, 'the Empire' had plainly become much more than French. It was, like the Carolingian realm, not a national monarchy,

[c] See Note XIV at end.

[d] 'Je n'ai pu concilier ces grands intérêts [of political order and the spiritual authority of the Pope] qu'en annulant les donations des empereurs français, mes prédécesseurs, et en réunissant les états romains à la France.'— Proclamation issued in 1809; *Oeuvres*, iv.

[e] See Appendix, Note B.

though one which rested on the dominance of a nation.[f] We are even told that it was at one time his intention to eject the Hapsburgs, and be chosen Roman Emperor in their stead. Had this been done, the analogy would have been complete between the position which the French ruler held to the house of Austria now, and that in which Charles and Otto had stood to the distant Caesars of the East. It was curious to see the spiritual head of the Catholic Church turning away from his ancient ally to the reviving power of France — France, where the Goddess of Reason had been honoured with festivals eight years before — just as his predecessor had sought the help of the first Carolingians against his Lombard enemies.[g] The difference was indeed great between the feelings wherewith Pius the Seventh addressed his 'very dear son in Christ,' and those that had pervaded the intercourse of Pope Hadrian the First with the son of Pipin; just as the contrast is strange between the principles that shaped Napoleon's policy and the vision of a theocracy that had floated before the mind of Charles. Neither comparison is much to the advantage of the modern; but Pius might be pardoned for catching at any help in his distress, and Napoleon found that the protectorship of the Church strengthened his position in France, and gave him dignity in the eyes of Christendom.[h]

[f] He did not annex Spain and Naples to 'the Empire,' but kept them as separate kingdoms under his brothers (the latter ultimately under Murat). There were political reasons for this course, but it is at least an interesting coincidence that neither country had belonged to the Carolingian Empire.

[g] Pope Pius VII wrote to the First Consul, 'Carissime in Christo Fili noster . . . tam perspecta sunt nobis tuae voluntatis studia erga nos, ut *quotiescunque* ope aliqua in rebus nostris indigemus, eam a te fidenter petere non dubitare debeamus.'

[h] Let us place side by side the letters of Hadrian to Charles in the *Codex Carolinus*, and the following preamble to the Concordat of A.D. 1801, be-

The French Empire, A.D. 1804.

A.D. 1805.

A swift succession of triumphs had left only one thing still preventing the full recognition of the Corsican warrior as sovereign of Western Europe, and that one was the existence of the old Romano-Germanic Empire. Napoleon had not long assumed his new title when he began to mark a distinction between 'la France' and 'l'Empire français.' France had, since A.D. 1792, advanced to the Rhine, and, by the annexation of Piedmont, had overstepped the Alps; the French Empire included, besides the kingdom of Italy, a mass of dependent states, Naples, Holland, Switzerland, and many German principalities, the allies of France in the same sense in which the 'socii populi Romani' were allies of Rome. When the last of Pitt's coalitions had been destroyed at Austerlitz, and Austria had made her submission by the peace of Presburg, the conqueror felt that his hour was come. He had now overcome two Emperors, those of Austria and Russia, claiming to represent the old and the new Rome respectively, and had in eighteen months created more kings than had the occupants of the Romano-Germanic throne in as many centuries. It was time, he thought, to sweep away obsolete pretensions, and claim the sole inheritance of that Western Empire, of which the titles and ceremonies of his court presented a grotesque imitation.[1] The task

tween the First Consul and the Pope (which I quote from the *Bullarium Romanum*), and mark the changes of a thousand years.

'Gubernium reipublicae [Gallicae] recognoscit religionem Catholicam Apostolicam Romanam eam esse religionem quam longe maxima pars civium Gallicae reipublicae profitetur.

'Summus pontifex pari modo recognoscit eandem religionem maximam utilitatem maximumque decus percepisse et hoc quoque tempore praestolari ex catholico cultu in Gallia constituto, necnon ex peculiari eius professione quam faciunt reipublicae consules.'

[1] He had arch-chancellors, arch-treasurers, and so forth. The Legion of Honour, which was thought important enough to be mentioned in the coro-

was an easy one after what had been already accomplished.
Previous wars and treaties had so redistributed the territories and changed the constitution of the Germanic Empire that it could hardly be said to exist in anything but
name.   In French history Napoleon appears as the restorer
of peace, the rebuilder of the shattered edifice of social
order, the author of a code and an administrative system
which the Bourbons who dethroned him were glad to
preserve.   Abroad he was the true child of the Revolution, and conquered only to destroy.   It was his mission
—a mission more beneficent in its result than in its intention or its means[j]—to break up in Germany and Italy the
pernicious system of petty principalities, to reawaken the
spirit of the people, to sweep away the relics of an out-
worn feudalism, and leave the ground clear for the growth
of newer and better forms of political life.   Since A.D. 1797,
when Austria at Campo Formio perfidiously exchanged
the Netherlands for the territories of Venice, territories
which she had no more right to receive than the French
Republic had to give, the work of destruction had gone on
apace.   All the German princes west of the Rhine had
been dispossessed, and their territories incorporated with
France, while the rest of the country had been revolu-
tionized by the arrangements of the Peace of Luneville
and the 'Indemnities,' dictated by the French to the Diet
in February 1803.   New kingdoms were erected, electorates created and extinguished, the lesser princes media-
tized, the free cities occupied by troops and bestowed

nation oath, was meant to be something like the mediaeval orders of knighthood, whose connection with the Empire has already been mentioned.

[j] Napoleon's feelings towards Germany may be gathered from the phrase
he once used, 'Il faut dépayser l'Allemagne.'

Again, in a letter to his brother Louis, he says, 'You must know that the
annihilation of German nationality is a necessary leading principle of my
policy.'

on some neighbouring potentate. More than any other change, the secularization of the dominions of the prince-bishops and abbots proclaimed the fall of the old constitution, whose principles had required the existence of a spiritual alongside of the temporal aristocracy. The Emperor Francis, partly foreboding the events that were at hand, partly in order to meet Napoleon's assumption of the imperial name by depriving that name of its special meaning and sanctity, began in A.D. 1805 to style himself 'Hereditary Emperor of Austria,' while not yet abandoning his former title.[k] The next act of the drama was one in which we may more readily pardon the ambition of a foreign conqueror than the selfishness of the German princes, who broke every tie of ancient friendship and

The Confederation of the Rhine. duty to grovel at his throne. By the Act of the Confederation of the Rhine,[l] signed at Paris, July 17, 1806, Bavaria, Würtemberg, Baden, and several other states, sixteen in all, withdrew from the body and repudiated the laws of the Empire, while on August 1st the French envoy at Regensburg announced to the Diet that his master, who had consented to become Protector of the Confederate

[k] Thus in documents issued by the Emperor during these two years he is styled 'Roman Emperor Elect, Hereditary Emperor of Austria' (erwählter Römischer Kaiser, Erbkaiser von Oesterreich).

[l] This Act of Confederation of the Rhine (Rheinbund) is printed in Koch's *Traités* (continued by Schöll), vol. viii, and Meyer's *Corpus Iuris Confoederationis Germanicae*, vol. i. It has every appearance of being a translation from the French, and was no doubt originally drawn up in that language. Napoleon is called in one place 'Der nämliche Monarch, dessen Absichten sich stets mit den wahren Interessen Deutschlands übereinstimmend gezeigt haben.' (The said Monarch, whose views have shewn themselves always in accord with the true interests of Germany.) The phrase 'Roman Empire' does not occur; we hear only of the 'German Empire,' 'body of German states' (Staatskörper), and so forth. This Confederation of the Rhine was eventually joined by every German state except Austria, Prussia, Electoral Hessen, and Brunswick.

princes, no longer recognized the existence of the Empire.
Francis the Second resolved at once to anticipate this new   *Abdication*
Odoacer, and by a declaration, dated August 6th, 1806,   *of the*
resigned the imperial dignity.   The instrument announces   *Francis II.*
that finding it impossible, in the altered state of things, to
fulfil the obligations imposed by the engagements taken
at his election he considers as dissolved the bonds which
attached him to the Germanic body, releases from their
allegiance the states of which it consisted, and retires to
the government of his hereditary dominions under the
title of 'Emperor of Austria.' [m]   Throughout, the term
'German Empire' (*Deutsches Reich*) is employed.   But it
was the crown of Augustus, of Constantine, of Charles,
of Otto, of Maximilian, that Francis of Hapsburg laid
down, and a new era in the world's history was marked
by the fall of its most venerable institution.   One thousand   *End of the*
and six years after Leo the Pope had crowned the Frank-   *Empire.*
ish king in St. Peter's, eighteen hundred and fifty-eight
years after Caesar had conquered at Pharsalia, the Holy
Roman Empire came to its end.

There was a time when this event would have been
thought a sign that the last days of the world were at
hand.   But in the whirl of change that had bewildered
men since A.D. 1789, it passed almost unnoticed.   No one
could yet fancy how things would end, or what sort of a
new order would at last shape itself out of chaos.   When
Napoleon's universal monarchy had dissolved, and the old
landmarks shewed themselves again above the receding

[m] *Histoire des Traités*, vol. viii.   The original may be found in Meyer's
Corpus Iuris Confoederationis Germanicae, vol. i. p. 70.   It is a document
in no way remarkable, except from the ludicrous resemblance which its language suggests to the circular in which a tradesman, announcing the dissolution of an old partnership, solicits, and hopes that by close attention to
business he may merit, a continuance of his customers' patronage to his
business, which will henceforth be carried on under the name of, &c., &c.

CHAP. XXI.

waters, it was commonly supposed that the Empire would be re-established on its former footing.[n] Such was indeed the wish of many states, and among them of Great Britain, whose sovereign was in respect of Hanover a member of the Germanic body.[o] Though a simple revival of the old Romano-Germanic Empire was plainly out of the question, it still appeared to them that Germany would be best off under the presidency of a single head, entrusted with the ancient office of maintaining peace among the members of the confederation. But the new kingdoms, Bavaria especially, were unwilling to admit a superior; Prussia, elated at the glory she had won in the war of independence, would have disputed the crown with Austria; Austria herself cared little to resume an office shorn of much of its dignity, with duties to perform and no resources to enable her to discharge them. Use was therefore made of an expression in the Peace of Paris which spoke of uniting the German states by a federal bond,[p] and the

Congress of Vienna, A.D. 1814–1815.

Congress of Vienna was decided by the wishes of Austria and the difficulty of bringing the various monarchs to agree to anything else, to establish a league of states. Thus was brought into existence the Germanic Confederation — an institution confessed almost from its birth to

---

[n] Koch (Schöll), *Histoire des Traités,* vol. xi. pp. 257 sqq.; Häusser, *Deutsche Geschichte,* vol. iv.

[o] Great Britain had refused in 1806 to recognize the dissolution of the Empire. And it may indeed be maintained that in point of law the Empire was never extinguished at all, but lived on as a sort of disembodied spirit. For it is clear that, technically speaking, the abdication of a sovereign destroys only his own rights, and does not dissolve the state over which he presides. Perhaps the Elector of Saxony might, legally, as imperial Vicar during an interregnum, have summoned the electoral college to meet and choose a new Emperor.

[p] 'Les états d'Allemagne seront indépendans et unis par un lien fédératif.' — *Histoire des Traités,* vol. xi. p. 257.

be a temporary expedient, an unsatisfactory compromise between the reality of local sovereignty and the semblance of national union, which, after an ignoble and often-threatened life of half a century, fell unregretted upon the fields of Königgrätz and Langensalza.

CHAPTER XXII

SUMMARY AND REFLECTIONS

AFTER what has been already said in examining each of the phases through which the Holy Empire passed, only a few concluding pages are needed to describe its character and to sum up the results of its long-continued life. A general character can hardly help being either vague or misleading, for the aspects which the Empire took are as many and as various as the ages and conditions of society during which it continued to exist. Among the peoples around the Mediterranean, whose national feeling had died out, whose national faiths were extinct or had turned to superstition, whose thought and art had lost their force and freshness, there arose a gigantic military power, the power first of a city, then of an administrative system culminating in an irresponsible monarch, which pressing with equal weight on all its subjects, gave them a new imperial nationality, and became to them a religion as well as a government. When this system, weakened by internal decay, was at length beginning to dissolve, the tribes of the North came down, too rude to maintain the elaborate institutions they found subsisting, too few and scattered to introduce their own simpler institutions, and in the weltering confusion that followed, the idea of a civilized commonwealth would have perished, had not the association of a young and vigorous faith with the name and the authority of Rome formed the foundation for a new unity, politically weak, but morally close and durable. Then the strong hand of the first

General summary.

Frankish Emperor raised the fallen image and bade the
nations bow down to it once more.   Under him it was for
some brief space a sort of military theocracy ; under his
German successors the first of feudal kingdoms, the centre
of European chivalry.   As feudalism wanes, the imperial
office, as well as the imperial idea, was again transformed,
and after promising for a time to become an hereditary
Hapsburg monarchy, it sank at last into the presidency, not
more dignified than powerless, of an international league.

To the modern world, penetrated by a critical and prac- *Perpetuation*
tical spirit, a perpetuation under conditions so diverse of *of the name*
of Rome.
the same name and the same pretensions appears at first
sight absurd, a phantom too vain to impress the most
superstitious mind.   Closer examination corrects such a
notion.   No power was ever based on foundations more
sure and deep than those which Rome laid during three
centuries of conquest and four of undisturbed dominion.
If her empire had been an hereditary or local kingdom, it
might have fallen with the extinction of the royal line, the
overthrow of the tribe, the destruction of the city, to which
it was attached.   But it was not so limited.   It was imperishable because it was universal ; and when its power had
ceased, it was remembered with awe and love by the races
whose separate existence it had destroyed, because it had
spared the weak while it smote down the strong ; because
it had granted equal rights to all, and closed against none
of its subjects the path of honourable ambition.   When
the military power of the conquering city had departed,
her sway over the world of thought began.   By her the
Greek theory of a commonwealth of mankind had been
reduced to practice ; the magic of her name remained,
and she held a sway over the imagination which the passing of century after century scarcely reduced.   She had
gathered up and embodied in her literature and institu-

CHAP. XXII. tions all the ideas and all the practical results of ancient thought. Embracing and organizing and propagating the new religion, she made it seem her own. Her language, her theology, her laws, her architecture, made their way where the eagles of war had never winged their flight, and with the spread of civilization have found new homes on the Ganges and the Mississippi.

Parallel instances.

Nor is such a claim of government prolonged under changed conditions by any means a singular phenomenon. Titles sum up the political history of nations, and are as often causes as effects: if significant to-day, how much more so in ages of ignorance when tradition was stronger than reason. Even in our time various pretensions have been put forward to represent the Empire of Rome, all of them without historical foundation, none of them without practical import. Austria clings to a name which seems to perpetuate the primacy held by Charles the Fifth in Europe, and was wont, while she held Lombardy, to justify her position there by invoking the feudal rights of the Franconian and Swabian sovereigns. With no more legal right than a prince of Reuss or a grand duke of Mecklenburg might pretend to, she continued after the disappearance of the old Empire to use its arms and devices, and being almost the youngest of European monarchies, she became respected as the oldest and most conservative. Bonapartean France, as the self-appointed heir of the Carolingians, grasped for a time the sceptre of the West, and under the ruler who fell in 1870 aspired to hold the balance of European politics, and be recognized as the leader and patron of the so-called 'Latin races' on both sides of the Atlantic.[a] Professing the creed of Constanti-

Claims to represent the Roman Empire.

Austria.

France.

---

[a] This was put forward in Louis Napoleon's letter to General Forey, explaining the object of that unlucky expedition to Mexico which helped to undermine his throne.

nople, Russia claims the crown of the Eastern Caesars, CHAP. XXII.
Russia.
and looks forward to the day when the capital which
prophecy has promised for a thousand years will echo to
the tramp of her armies.   The doctrine of Panslavism,
under an imperial head of the Orthodox Eastern Church,
has become a formidable engine of aggression in the hands
of a mighty despotism and a growing race, naturally drawn
to expand its frontiers toward the south.   Another tes- *Greece.*
timony to the enduring influence of old political combi-
nations is supplied by the eagerness with which modern
Hellas embraced the notion of gathering the peoples
of South-eastern Europe and Asia Minor that profess
the Orthodox creed into a revived Empire of the East, *The Turks.*
with its capital on the Bosphorus.   Nay, the intruding
Ottoman himself, different in faith as well as in blood,
long ago declared himself the representative of the Eastern Caesars, whose dominion he extinguished.   Sultan
Suleiman the Magnificent assumed the name of Emperor,
and refused it to Charles the Fifth; his successors were
once preceded through the streets of Constantinople by
twelve officers, bearing straws aloft, a faint semblance of
the consular fasces that had escorted a Quinctius or a
Fabius through the Roman forum.   Yet in no one of
these cases was there that apparent legality of title which
the shouts of the people and the benediction of the pontiff
conveyed to Charles and Otto.[b]

These examples, however, are minor parallels: the com- *Parallel of*
the Papacy.
plement and illustration of the history of the Empire is to

[b] Many other instances might be adduced: consider for instance the perpetuation of the office of consul at Rome and Constantinople for at least five
centuries after it had ceased to carry power ; consider the retention long after
all claims to France had been abandoned of the title ' King of Great Britain,
France, and Ireland ' (its ultimate relinquishment distressed many persons);
consider the retention to-day in Great Britain of the title ' Defender of the

be found in that of the Holy See. The Papacy, whose spiritual power was itself the offspring of Rome's temporal dominion, evoked the phantom of her parent, used it, obeyed it, rebelled and overthrew it, in its old age once more drew it to her bosom, till in its downfall she heard the knell of the old order and saw the end of her own temporal power approaching.

Both Papacy and Empire rose in an age when the human spirit was prostrated before authority and tradition, when the exercise of private judgement was impossible to most and sinful to all. Those who believed the miracles recorded in the *Acta Sanctorum*, and did not question the Pseudo-Isidorian decretals, might well recognize as ordained of God the twofold authority of Rome, founded, as it seemed to be, on so many texts of Scripture, and confirmed by five centuries of undisputed possession.

Both sanctioned and satisfied the passion of the Middle Ages for Unity. Ferocity, violence, disorder, were the conspicuous evils of that time : hence all the aspirations of the good were for something which, breaking the force of passion and increasing the force of sympathy, should teach the stubborn wills to sacrifice themselves in the view of a common purpose. To those men, moreover, unable to rise above the sensuous, seeing with eyes unlike ours both the connection and the difference of the spiritual and the secular elements in life, the idea of the Visible Church was full of awful meaning. Solitary thought was helpless, and strove to lose itself in the aggregate, since it could not create for itself that which was universal.

Faith' (when it had been dropped from a new coin public opinion compelled the renewal of its use); consider the refusal of the Count of Chambord, heir to the throne of France, to accept the crown when it was virtually within his grasp, unless he was permitted to use the white flag of Henry IV instead of the tricolour.

The schism that severed a man from the congregation of the faithful on earth was hardly less dreadful than the heresy which excluded him from the company of the blessed in heaven. He who kept not his appointed place in the ranks of the Church militant had no right to swell the rejoicing anthems of the Church triumphant. Here, as in so many other cases, the continued use of traditional language prevents men from seeing how great is the difference between their own times and those in which the phrases they repeat were first used, and used in full sincerity. Whether the world is better or worse for the change which has passed upon its feelings in these matters is another question : all that is necessary to note here is that the change is a profound and pervading one. Obedience, almost the first of mediaeval virtues, is now often spoken of as if it were fit only for slaves or fools. Instead of praising, men are wont to condemn the submission of the individual will, the surrender of the individual belief, to the will or the belief of the community. Some persons declare variety of opinion to be a positive good. The great mass have little longing for a perfect unity of faith. They have no horror of schism. They cannot understand the fascination which the idea of one all-embracing, all-pervading Church exercised upon their mediaeval forefathers. A life in the Church, for the Church, through the Church ; a life which she blessed in mass at morning and sent to peaceful rest by the vesper hymn ; a life which she supported by the constantly recurring stimulus of the sacraments, relieving it by confession, purifying it by penance, admonishing it by the presentation of visible objects for contemplation and worship — this was the life which they of the Middle Ages conceived of as the rightful life for man ; it was the actual life of many, the ideal of all. The unseen world was so unceasingly pointed to, and its dependence on the seen so intensely felt, that the barrier between the two seemed to disappear. The Church was not merely the portal to heaven; it was heaven anticipated; it was already self-gathered and complete. In one sentence from a singular mediaeval document may be found a key to much which seems strangest to us in the feelings of the Middle Ages: 'The Church is dearer to God than heaven. For the Church does not exist for the sake of heaven, but conversely, heaven for the sake of the Church.' [c]

Again, both Empire and Papacy rested on opinion rather than on material force, and when the struggle which began in the eleventh century came, the Empire succumbed, because its rival's hold over the souls of men was firmer, more direct, enforced by penalties more terrible than the death of the body. The ecclesiastical host which Alexander III and Innocent IV led was animated by a loftier spirit and more wholly devoted to a single aim than the knights and nobles who followed the banner of the Swabian Caesars. Its allegiance was undivided; it comprehended the principles for which it fought. They trembled at even while they resisted the spiritual power.

Papacy and Empire compared as perpetuations of a name. Both sprang from what might seem to be the accident of name. The power of the great Latin patriarchate was a Form: the ghost, it has been said, of the older Empire, favoured in its growth by circumstances, but really vital because capable of wonderful adaptation to the character and wants of the time. So too, though far less perfectly, was the Empire. Its Form was the tradition of the universal rule of Rome; it met the needs of successive cen-

[c] 'Ipsa enim ecclesia charior Deo est quam coelum. Non enim propter coelum ecclesia, sed e converso propter ecclesiam coelum.' From the tract entitled 'A Letter of the four Universities to the Emperor Wenzel and Pope Urban VI,' quoted in chapter VII, p. 105.

turies by civilizing barbarous peoples, by maintaining unity in confusion and disorganization, by controlling brute violence through the sanctions of a higher power, by being made the keystone of a gigantic feudal arch, by becoming in its old age the centre of a European states-system. And its history, as it shews the power of ancient names and forms, shews also how hopeless is the attempt to preserve in life a system which arose out of ideas and under conditions that have passed away, how unreal such a perpetuation may be, and how it may deceive men, by preserving the shadow while it loses the substance. This perpetuation itself, what is it but the expression of the belief of mankind, a belief incessantly corrected yet never weakened, that their old institutions can continue to subsist unchanged, that what has served their fathers will do well enough for them, that it is possible to make a system once for all perfect and abide in it for ever thereafter? Of all political instincts this is perhaps the strongest; often useful, often abused, but never more natural or more fitting than when it led men who felt skill and knowledge slipping from their grasp to seek to save what they could from the wreck of an older and higher civilization. It was thus that both Papacy and Empire were maintained by generations who had no type of greatness and wisdom save that which they associated with the name of Rome. Though it never could have existed save as a prolongation, though it was and remained through the Middle Ages an anachronism, the Empire of the tenth century had changed profoundly from the Empire of the second. Much more was the Papacy, though it too hankered after the forms and titles of antiquity, a truly new creation. And in the same proportion as it was new, and represented the spirit not of a past age but of its own, was it a power stronger and more enduring than the Empire. More enduring, because more lately born, and so in fuller harmony with the ruling spirit and cogent needs of the time, stronger, because at the head of the great ecclesiastical body, in and through which, rather than through secular life, the intelligence and political activity of the Middle Ages sought their expression. The famous simile of Gregory the Seventh is that which best describes the Empire and the Popedom. They were indeed the 'two lights in the firmament of the militant Church,' the lights which illumined and ruled the world all through the Middle Ages. And as moonlight is to sunlight, so was the Empire to the Papacy. The rays of the one were borrowed, feeble, often interrupted: the other shone with an unquenchable brilliance that was all her own.

In what sense was the Empire Roman?   If we analyze the Papacy and the Empire, we shall find that each is old, and each is new. The remark is true in a sense of all institutions, but it applies in a special sense to these two. The Papacy was new in the doctrines and the spirit which it drew from Scripture and Christian tradition. It was old in the form of its government, for this was modelled on the heathen autocracy, old also in the application of compulsive power to matters of opinion and belief, than which nothing could be more opposed to the teachings of Christ. The Empire was new in so far as it was a German kingdom, built up on feudal principles; new also in all that it had imbibed from Christianity — in the sense of its religious mission, and of faith as a bond to unite mankind in one world-embracing state. It was old not only in its name but in the effort to base its universal dominion upon the imprescriptible rights of Rome, and in the autocratic character which its adoption of the ancient Roman law as its own had made it, at least in outward semblance, assume.

This distinction between its component elements may help to supply an answer to the question which the student of its history often puts to himself — 'Was it Roman in anything but name? and was that name anything better than a piece of fantastic antiquarianism?' A comparison might be drawn between the Antonines of the second century and the Ottos of the tenth which should shew nothing but unlikeness. What the Empire was in the second century every student of the ancient classics knows. In the tenth it was a feudal monarchy, resting on a strong territorial oligarchy. Its chiefs were barbarians, the sons of those who had destroyed Varus and baffled Germanicus, sometimes unable even to use the tongue of Rome. Its powers, nominally wide, were limited by custom and the strength of the great vassals. It could scarcely be said to have a governmental organization, whether judicial or administrative. It was consecrated to the defence, nay, it existed by virtue of the religion, which Trajan and Marcus had persecuted. Nevertheless, however strongly the contrast be stated points of resemblance will remain. The Roman idea of universal denationalization survived as an idea, and drew with it that of a certain equality among all free subjects. The world's highest dignity was for many centuries the only civil office to which any free-born Christian was legally eligible. So too there survived the Roman conception of Law, written, settled, scientific law, as the foundation of social order, as the regulator of the relations of members of the community, as the form through which the state must act.

It may be added that there was among the Teutonic Emperors, when one compares them as a whole either with the East Roman monarchs or with the Muslim dynasties, a loftiness of spirit and a sense of duty to the realm they ruled which recalls the old Roman type. Trajan and Marcus might have found their true successors among the woods of Germany rather than in the palaces of Constantinople, where every office and name and custom had floated down from the court of Theodosius in a stream of unbroken legitimacy. The ceremonies of Henry the Seventh's coronation would have been strange indeed to Caius Julius Caesar Octavianus Augustus ; yet they were better than the purple buskins of Byzantium : they had more Roman dignity and force than the fantastic forms with which a Palaeologus was installed ! Of the Germanic Empire in later centuries the same cannot be said. It had lived on, when honour and nature bade it die : it had become what the Empire of the Moguls had then become, and that of the Ottomans still later became, a curious relic of antiquity, on which the philosopher might muse, but from which the vigour of life and all power for good had long since departed. Institutions, however, should, like men, be judged by their prime.

'Imperialism' : Roman, French, and mediaeval.   The word 'Imperialism' has within our own time been used in varying senses and has evoked diverse feelings of attraction and repulsion. From the time when the first Bonaparte took the title of Emperor in France until the fall of Louis Napoleon in 1870, it was used to denote a system intended to imitate that which Julius Caesar and his subtle nephew erected upon the ruins of the republican constitution of Rome. The sacrifice of the individual to the mass, the concentration of all legislative and judicial powers in the person of the sovereign, the centralization of the administrative system, the maintenance of order by a large military force, the substitution of the influence of public opinion for the control of representative assemblies, were commonly taken, whether rightly or wrongly, to characterize that system : and the glory which surrounded

the name of Rome, the peace and order which the sway
of the Roman Caesars had, in its best days, secured for
the world, were used to recommend Napoleonic rule in
France and to justify French predominance in Europe.
That system has passed away, those memories are no
longer invoked.   Neither with Bonapartean imperialism *Essential*
nor with other more recent sense given to the term had *principles of*
the doctrines on which the mediaeval Empire rested any- *the mediaeval*
thing in common.   There was, nevertheless, a thing which *Empire.*
may be called mediaeval imperialism, a theory of the nature
of the state and the best form of government, of which,
since it has been already described,[d] it is enough to say
here, that from three leading principles all its properties
may be derived.   The first and not the most essential was
the existence of the state as a monarchy.   The second
was the exact coincidence of the Holy State's limits, and
the perfect harmony of its workings with the limits and
the workings of Holy Church.   The third was its universality.   These three were vital.   Forms of political organization, the presence or absence of constitutional checks,
the degree of liberty enjoyed by the subject, the rights
conceded to local authorities, all these were matters of
secondary importance.   But although there brooded over
all the shadow of an autocracy, it was an autocracy not of
the sword but of law, itself subject to that Law of Nature
which mediaeval thinkers recognized as the expression of
the will of a righteous God ; an autocracy not chilling and
blighting, but one which, in Germany at least, looked with
favour on municipal freedom, and everywhere did its best
for learning, for religion, for intelligence; an autocracy not
hereditary, but one which maintained in theory the principle that he should rule who was found the fittest.   To
praise or to decry the Empire as a despotic power is to

d See chapters VII and XV, *ante.*

misunderstand it altogether. We need not, because an unbounded prerogative was useful in ages of turbulence, advocate it now; nor need we, with Sismondi, blame the Frankish conqueror because he granted no 'constitutional charter' to all the nations that obeyed him. Like the Papacy, the Empire expressed the political ideas of a time, and not of all time: like the temporal power of the Papacy, it decayed when those ideas changed; when men became more capable of rational liberty, when thought grew stronger, and the spiritual nature shook itself more free from the bonds of sense.

Influence of the Holy Empire on Germany. The influence of the Empire upon Germany may in some aspects appear altogether unfortunate. For many generations the flower of Teutonic chivalry crossed the Alps to perish by the sword of the Lombards, or the deadlier fevers of Rome. Italy terribly avenged the wrongs she suffered. Those who destroyed the national existence of another people forfeited their own. The German kingdom, crushed beneath the weight of the Roman Empire, could never recover strength enough to form a compact and united monarchy, such as arose elsewhere in Europe. The race whom their neighbours had feared and obeyed till the middle of the thirteenth century saw themselves, down even to our own day, the prey of intestine feuds and their country the battlefield of Europe. Spoiled and insulted by a neighbour restlessly active and long superior in the arts of success, they were for a time accustomed to regard France as the downtrodden Slavonic tribes regarded them. The want of national union and political liberty from which Germany used to suffer need not be attributed to the differences of her races; for, conspicuous as that difference was in the days of Otto the Great, it was less conspicuous than in France, where intruding Franks, Goths, Burgundians, and Northmen were mingled with primitive

Celts and Basques; less conspicuous than in Spain, or Italy, or Britain.   Rather was it due to that decline of the central government which was induced by its strife with the Popedom, by its endless Italian wars, by the passion for universal dominion which made it the assailant of all the neighbouring countries.   The absence or the weakness of the embarrassed monarch enabled his feudal vassals to establish petty despotisms, debarring the nation from united political action, and greatly retarding the emancipation of the commons.   Thus, while the princes became shamelessly selfish, justifying their resistance to the throne as the defence of their own liberty — a liberty which included the oppression of their subjects — and ready on the least occasion to throw themselves into the arms of France, the body of the people were deprived of all political training, and found the lack of such experience impede their efforts down to our own time.

For such misfortunes, however, as the Empire entailed upon the nation there was not wanting some compensation.   The inheritance of the Roman Empire made the Germans the ruling race of Europe, and the brilliance of that glorious dawn could never fade entirely from their name.   Even in those later days when they lived as a peaceful people, acquiescent in paternal government, and given to the quiet enjoyments of art, music, and meditation, they delighted themselves with memories of the time when their conquering chivalry was the terror of the Gaul and the Slave, the Lombard and the Saracen.   The national life received a keen stimulus from the sense of exaltation which victory brought, and from the intercourse with countries where the old civilization had not wholly perished.   It was this connection with Italy that raised the German lands out of barbarism, and did for them the work which Roman conquest had performed in Gaul, Spain, and Britain.

From the Empire flowed the richness of their mediaeval life and literature : it first awoke in them a consciousness of national existence ; its history inspired and served as material to their poetry ; to many ardent patriots the splendours of the past became the beacon of the future. There was a bright side even to that long political dis-union, which lasted down till the days when in achieving their national unity they became at the same time a mighty military power. When they complained that they were not a nation, and sighed for the harmony of feeling and singleness of aim which their great rival seemed to display, the example of a wonderful ancient people which never achieved political unity might have brought them some comfort. To the variety of conditions and aptitudes which the existence of so many small governments helped to produce may be partly attributed the breadth of develope-ment in German thought and literature, by virtue of which, in the first half of the nineteenth century, it transcended the French hardly less than the Greek surpassed the Roman. Paris no doubt was great, but a country may lose as well as gain by the predominance of a single city ; and Germany had in those days no cause to lament that she alone among modern states had never possessed a capital.

In the years before 1866 when Austria and Prussia were disputing the headship of Germany, the merits of the old Empire were the subject of a brisk controversy among *Austria as heir of the Holy Empire.* several German professors of history.[e] The spokesmen of the Austrian or Roman Catholic party, a party which was then not less powerful in some of the minor German

---

[e] I have retained (in substance) this and the next following paragraph, written before 1866, because few people, outside Germany, realize to-day the part which the old Empire played in the political controversies of Germany when Austria was still a German power.

States than in Vienna, claimed for the Hapsburg monarchy CHAP. XXII. the honour of being the legitimate representative of the mediaeval Empire, and declared that only by again accepting Hapsburg leadership could Germany win back the glory and the strength that once were hers.[f] The North German liberals ironically applauded the comparison. 'Yes,' they replied, 'your Austrian Empire, as it calls itself, is the true daughter of the old despotism: not less tyrannical, not less aggressive, not less retrograde; like its progenitor, the friend of priests, the enemy of free thought, the trampler upon the national feeling of the peoples that obey it. It is you whose selfish and anti-national policy blasts the hope of German unity now, as Otto and Frederick blasted it long ago by their schemes of foreign conquest. The dream of Empire has been our bane from first to last.'

To an impartial eye, neither of these contending schools seemed entitled to press history into the service of partizan politics. Austria might indeed in those days, when she was ruling over a disaffected Venetia, a disaffected Hungary, a disaffected Galicia, seem to be only too faithfully reproducing the policy of the Saxon and Swabian Caesars. Yet the differences were manifest. If they oppressed the Italian cities they did it in the defence of rights which the Italians themselves admitted. If they lusted after a dominion over the races on their borders, that dominion was to them a means of spreading civilization and religion in savage countries, not of pampering upon their revenues an alien court and aristocracy. They strove to maintain a strong government at home, but they did it when a strong government was the first of political

[f] See especially Von Sybel, *Die deutsche Nation und das Kaiserreich;* and the answers of Ficker and Von Wydenbrugk; also Höfler, *Kaiserthum und Papstthum*, and Waitz, *Deutsche Kaiser von Karl dem Grossen bis Maximilian.*

blessings. They gathered and maintained vast armies; but those armies were composed of knights and barons who lived for war alone, not of peasants torn away from useful labour and condemned to the cruel task of perpetuating their own bondage by crushing the aspirations of another nationality. If Otto and Frederick erred in pursuing the glittering lure of universal dominion, they were the victims of a belief which all the world shared, and they erred in the twilight of a half-barbarous age, not in the noonday blaze of modern civilization. The enthusiasm for mediaeval faith and simplicity which was so fervid in the first half of the nineteenth century has run its course, and is not likely soon to revive. He who reads the history of the Middle Ages will not deny that its heroes, even the grandest of them, were in some respects little better than savages. But when he approaches more recent times, and sees how, during the last three hundred years, kings have dealt with their subjects and with each other, he will forget the ferocity of the Middle Ages, in disgust at the heartlessness, the perfidy, the injustice all the more odious because it sometimes wears the mask of legality, which disgraces the annals of the military monarchies of Europe. And as the Holy Empire of the twelfth and thirteenth centuries cannot fairly be represented as having set a precedent for the later misdeeds of Austria, so neither did its traditions furnish a sufficient basis for the claims she then made to the leadership of the German nation. The day of imperial greatness was already past when Rudolf the first Hapsburg reached the throne; while during the later part of the Austrian period, from Ferdinand II to Francis II, the Holy Empire was to Germany a mere clog and incumbrance, which the unhappy nation bore because she knew not how to rid herself of it.

We are not yet far enough removed from the Empire to

estimate all its influence on European progress, just as he must travel far from the foot of a mountain who would take in at a glance its peaks and slopes and buttresses, appreciate the nobility of its lines, and perceive its relation to the valleys and ranges that fill the landscape on either side of it. But as the revival of the imperial name under Charles and Otto was mainly due to the continuing power of the Roman Law and the Roman Church, we may take note of the relation which it bore to these two great factors in modern civilization. From it came nearly everything in the political and legal institutions of the Middle Ages that was not feudal : and feudalism itself was modified by the notions which the Empire embodied. The conception of royalty which grew up in the thirteenth century and held its ground till recent times, and in particular the singular doctrine of the 'divine right' of a sovereign, belonged originally and properly to the Emperor, and was extended from his office to that of other monarchs. So the existence of the Empire greatly contributed to the prevalence of Roman law as a practical system through Europe, down to our own days. For while in Southern France and Central Italy, where the subject population greatly outnumbered their conquerors, the old system might have in any case survived, it may be conjectured that in other parts of the European continent there would have grown up (as happened in England) bodies of local customary law lacking that symmetry and scientific quality which characterize the law of Rome. The fact that there was still a Roman Emperor, and that the study of the law promulgated by his remote predecessors was renewed under his auspices in countries recognizing his supremacy, gave a life and reality to the ancient texts they could never have possessed, but for the notion that since the German monarch was the legitimate successor of Justinian, the

Corpus Iuris must be binding on all his subjects. This strange idea was received with a faith so unhesitating that even the aristocracy, who naturally disliked a system which the Emperors and the cities favoured, must admit its validity, and by the middle of the sixteenth century Roman law prevailed through Germany.[g] When it is considered how great are the services which German writers have rendered and continue to render to the study of scientific jurisprudence this result will appear far from insignificant. But another of still wider import followed. When by the Peace of Westphalia a crowd of petty principalities were recognized as practically independent states, the need of a body of rules to regulate their relations and intercourse became pressing. Such a code (if one may call it by that name) Grotius and his successors compiled out of the principles which they found in the Roman law, then the private law of the Germanic countries, thus laying the foundation whereon the system of international jurisprudence has been built up during the last three centuries. That system could hardly have arisen in any country where the law of Rome had not been the fountain of legal ideas and the groundwork of positive enactments. In Germany, too, was it first carried out in practice, and with a success which is perhaps the best title of the later Empire to the grateful remembrance of mankind. Under its protecting shade small princedoms and free cities lived, down to Napoleon's day, unmolested beside states like Saxony and Bavaria ; each member of the Germanic body feeling that the rights of the weakest of his brethren were also his own.

The most important chapter in the history of the Empire is that which describes its relation to the Church

[g] Modified of course by the canon law, and not superseding the feudal law relating to land.

CHAP. XXII.

*Influence of
the Empire
upon the
history of the
Church.*

and the Apostolic See. Of the ecclesiastical power it was alternately the champion and the enemy. In the ninth and tenth centuries the Emperors extended the dominion of Peter's chair: in the tenth and eleventh they rescued it from an abyss of guilt and shame to be the instrument of their own downfall. The struggle which began under Gregory the Seventh, although it belonged to the political rather than to the religious sphere, awoke in the Teutonic nations a suspicion of the papal court, and a disposition to resist its pretensions. That struggle ended, with the death of the last Hohenstaufen, in the victory of the priesthood — a victory whose abuse by the arrogant and rapacious pontiffs of the fourteenth and fifteenth centuries made it more ruinous than a defeat. The anger which had long smouldered in the breasts of the Northern peoples burst out in the sixteenth with a violence which alarmed those whom it had hitherto supported, and made the Emperors once more the allies of the Popedom, and the partners of its declining fortunes. But the nature of that alliance and of the hostility which had preceded it must not be misunderstood. It is a natural, but not the less a serious error to suppose, as some modern writers have done, that the pretensions of the Empire and the Popedom were mutually exclusive; that each claimed all the rights, spiritual and secular, of a universal monarch. So far was this from being the case, that we find mediaeval writers and statesmen, even Emperors and Popes themselves, expressly recognizing a divinely appointed duality of government — two potentates, each supreme in the sphere of his own activity, Peter in things eternal, Caesar in things temporal. The relative position of the two does indeed in course of time undergo a signal alteration. In the age of Charles, the barbarous age of modern Europe, when men were and could not but be governed chiefly by

*Nature of the
question at
issue between
the Emperors
and the Popes.*

physical force, the Emperor was practically, if not theoretically, the grander figure. Four centuries later, in the era of Pope Innocent III, when the power of ideas had grown stronger in the world, and was able to resist, or to bend to its service, the arms and the wealth of men, we see the balance inclined the other way. Spiritual authority is conceived of as being of a nature so high and holy that it is entitled to inspire and guide the civil administration. But there was not yet a purpose to supplant that administration or to degrade its head. The great struggle of the eleventh and two following centuries does not aim at the annihilation of one or other power, but turns upon the character of their connection. Hildebrand, the typical representative of the Popedom, requires the obedience of the Emperor on the ground of his own personal responsibility for the souls of their common subjects : he demands, not that the functions of temporal government shall be directly committed to himself, but that they shall be exercised in conformity with the will of God, whereof he is the exponent. The imperialist party, since they could not deny the spiritual supremacy of the Pope, nor the transcendent importance of eternal salvation, could do no more than protest that the Emperor, being also divinely appointed, was directly answerable to God, and remind the Pope that his kingdom was not of this world. There was in truth no way out of the difficulty, for it was caused by the attempt to sever things which, distinguishable in thought, hardly admit of severance in practice, life in the soul and life in the world, life for the future and life in the present. Then the Papacy, embittered by strife and intoxicated by victory, began to advance pretensions so extravagant as to provoke reaction. Frederick II claimed ecclesiastical authority : Lewis IV deposed a reigning Pope and crowned a friar as his successor. Each power had grievously wounded the other; the decline of both had begun, for each was losing its hold upon opinion. Yet for a while neither combatant had pushed his theory to extremities, since he felt that his adversary's title rested on the same foundations as his own. The strife which had been keenest at the time when the world believed fervently in both powers, suddenly died away; and an alliance came when faith had forsaken the one and grown cold towards the other. From the Reformation onwards Empire and Popedom fought no longer against one another for supremacy, but side by side for existence.

Ennobling influence of the conception of the World Empire.

Nor was that which may be called the inner life of the Empire less momentous in its influence upon the minds of men than were its outward dealings with the Roman Church upon the various phases of her fortunes. In the Middle Ages, men conceived of the communion of the saints as the formal unity of an organized body of worshippers, and found the concrete realization of that conception in their universal religious state, which was in one aspect the Church, in another, the Empire. Into the meaning and worth of the conception, into the nature of the connection which subsists or ought to subsist between the Church and the State, this is not the place to inquire. That the form which that connection took in the Middle Ages was always imperfect and became eventually rigid and unprogressive was sufficiently proved by the event. But by it the European peoples were saved from the isolation, and narrowness, and jealous exclusiveness which had checked the growth of the earlier civilizations of the world, and which we see now lying like a weight upon the kingdoms of the East: by it they were brought into that mutual knowledge and co-operation which is the condition if it be not the source of all true culture and progress. For as by the Roman Empire of old the

CHAP. XXII. nations were first forced to own a common sway, so by the Empire of the Middle Ages was preserved the feeling of a brotherhood of mankind, a commonwealth of the whole world, whose sublime unity transcended every minor distinction.

Principles adverse to the Empire.   As despotic monarchs claiming the world for their realm, the Teutonic Emperors strove from the first against three principles, over all of which their forerunners of the elder Rome had triumphed — those of Nationality, Aristocracy, and Popular Freedom. Their early struggles were against the first of these principles, and ended with its victory in the emancipation, one after another, of France, Poland, Hungary, Denmark, Burgundy, and Italy. The second, in the form of feudalism, menaced even when seeming to exalt and obey them, and succeeded, during and after the Great Interregnum, in destroying their effective strength in Germany. Aggression and inheritance turned the numerous independent principalities thus formed out of the greater fiefs, into a few military monarchies, resting neither on reciprocal loyalty, like feudal kingdoms, nor on religious duty and tradition, like the Empire, but on material force, more or less disguised by legal forms. That the hostility to the Empire of the impulse towards free self-government was accidental rather than necessary is seen by this, that the very same monarchs who sought to crush the Lombard and Tuscan cities favoured the growth of the free towns of Germany and sometimes favoured the free rural communities of what afterwards became Switzerland. The theoretical autocracy of Caesar could in practice reconcile itself with civic or cantonal autonomy just as easily as it did with the rights of the feudal vassal in the days when the vassal was content to keep his place. Nevertheless the principles whereon the Holy Empire rested, were in so far incompatible with freedom of judgement, of speech, and of action,

that when the German and Swiss Reformers asserted the
rights of the individual in the sphere of religion, they
weakened the Empire by denying the necessity of external
unity in matters spiritual. The extension of such doctrines
to the secular world would have in like manner struck
at the doctrine of imperial absolutism had it not found a
nearer and deadlier foe in the actual tyranny of the princes.
It is more than a coincidence, that as the proclamation of
the liberty of thought had shaken, so the proclamation of
liberty of action made by the revolutionary movement,
whose beginning the world saw and only half understood
in 1789, should have indirectly become the cause which
overthrew the Holy Empire.

Its fall in the midst of the great convulsion that changed *Change
marked by its
fall.* the face of Europe marks an era in history, an era whose
character the events of the sixty years that followed went
on unfolding : an era of the destruction of old forms and
systems and the building up of new. The latest instances
are the most memorable. Under our eyes, the work which
Theodorich and Lewis the Second, Guido and Ardoin and
the second Frederick, essayed in vain, was achieved by the
steadfast will of the Italian people. The fairest province
of the Empire, for which Franconian and Swabian battled
so long, became at last a single monarchy under the Burgundian count, whom Sigismund created imperial vicar in
Italy, and who, now that he holds the ancient capital, may
call himself 'king of the Romans' more truly than did
ever Greek or Frank or Saxon or Austrian since Constantine forsook the Tiber for the Bosphorus. No longer the
prey of the stranger, Italy could forget the past, and sympathize, as indeed, since the fortunate alliance of 1866, she
began to sympathize, with the efforts after national unity
of her ancient enemy — efforts confronted by so many
obstacles that for many years they seemed all but hope-

less.　On the new shapes that may emerge before the reconstruction of Europe is complete it would be idle to speculate.　Yet one prediction may be ventured.　No universal monarchy is likely to arise.　More frequent intercourse, more rapid communications, the expansion of trade and the progress of thought, though they have effaced some prejudices and given nations a fuller knowledge of one another, have not lessened the strength of national feeling.　The racial or commercial antagonisms of democracies are as fertile in menaces to peace as were ever the dynastic interests of princes.　No one who reads the history of the last three hundred years, no one, above all, who studies attentively the career of Napoleon, can believe it possible for any state, however great her energy and material resources, to repeat in modern Europe the

Relations of the Empire to the nationalities of Europe.

part of ancient Rome : to gather into one vast political body races whose national individuality has grown more and more marked in each successive age.　Nevertheless, it is in great measure due to Rome and to the Roman Empire of the Middle Ages that the bonds of national union are on the whole both stronger and nobler than they were ever before.　The greatest historian of republican Rome, after summing up the results to the world of his hero's career, closes his treatise with these words : 'There was in the world as Caesar found it the rich and noble heritage of past centuries, and an endless abundance of splendour and glory, but little soul, still less taste, and, least of all, joy in and through life.　Truly it was an old world, and even the patriotic genius of Caesar could not make it young again.　The blush of dawn returns not until the night has fully descended.　Yet with him there came to the much-tormented races of the Mediterranean a tranquil evening after a sultry day : and when, after long historical night, the new day broke once more upon the peoples, and fresh nations in free self-guided movement began their course towards new and higher aims, many were found among them in whom the seed of Caesar had sprung up, many who owed him, and who owe him still, their national individuality.' [h] If this be the glory of Julius, the first great founder of the Empire, so is it also the glory of Charles, the second founder, and of more than one amongst his Teutonic successors. The work of the mediaeval Empire was self-destructive; and it fostered, while seeming to oppose, the nationalities that were destined to replace it. It tamed the barbarous races of the North, and forced them within the pale of civilization. It preserved the memory of ancient order and culture. In times of violence and oppression, it set before its subjects the duty of rational obedience to an authority whose watchwords were peace and religion. It kept alive, in the face of national prejudices, the notion of a great European commonwealth. And by doing all this, it was in effect abolishing the need for an all-absorbing autocratic power like itself: it was making men capable of using national independence aright: it was enabling them to rise to the conception of a spontaneous activity, and of a freedom which is above law but not against it, to which national independence itself, if it is to be a blessing, ought to be a means.

In the beginning of the fourteenth century the thoughts and hopes of the purest and most earnest minds were directed to the ideal of a Universal Christian State, by which universal peace should be secured; a lofty ideal, and one never to be forgotten by mankind. In the centuries that followed, other aims, other ideals, inspired the men who led the movement of the world, and five hundred years after Dante's time noble lives were being

[h] Mommsen, *Römische Geschichte*, iii, *sub fin.*

consecrated to the deliverance of every people from alien rule, and the establishment of each as a free self-governing community. This too was a high ideal, and a precious one, for it meant the extinction of many tyrannies and the drying up of many springs of race hatred. No wonder that the principle of nationalities was then advocated with honest devotion as the perfect form of political developement. Yet finality cannot be claimed for this ideal, any more than for those that went before. If all other history did not bid us beware the habit of taking the problems and the conditions of our own age for those of all time, the warning which the history of the Empire gives might alone be warning enough. From the days of Augustus down to those of Charles the Fifth the whole civilized world believed in its existence as a part of the eternal fitness of things, and Christian theologians were not behind heathen poets in declaring that when it perished the world would perish with it. Yet the Empire vanished, and the world remained, and hardly noted the change.

Difficulties arising from the nature of the subject. The highest themes which can occupy the mind are, as Dante has said, those which most transcend the resources of human language. So in parting from a great subject the feeling arises that words fail to convey the ideas it suggests, and that however much may have been said, much must remain unsaid, because incapable of expression. Here one is baffled partly by the magnitude of the subject, for it is a vast one, which needs to be studied as a whole, as an institution which through forty generations of men preserves its name and its claims while its relations to the world around it are constantly changing. But another difficulty lies still deeper. It lies in grasping the essence and spirit of the Holy Empire as it appeared to the saints and poets of the Middle Ages, and in realizing all that it meant to them. Formulas help us little: it is rather through imagination than by logic or analysis that we may succeed in apprehending the true significance of this strange creation of reverent tradition and mystical faith which filled the sky and scarcely touched the earth. A like difficulty meets us when we think of that other still more wonderful child of Rome and of tradition, the Papacy. The Protestants of the seventeenth century, who saw in it nothing but a gigantic upas-tree of fraud and superstition, planted and reared by the enemy of mankind, were hardly further from entering into the mystery of its being than the complacent philosophers of the eighteenth century, who explained in neat phrases the process of its growth, analyzed it as a clever piece of mechanism, enumerating and measuring the interests it appealed to. As there is a sense in which the Papacy is above explanation, because it appeals to emotion, not to reason, to faith, and not to sight, so of the Empire also may this be said, not that it is impossible to discover the beliefs which created and sustained it, but that the power and fascination of those beliefs cannot be adequately apprehended by men whose minds have been differently trained, and whose imaginations are fired by different ideals. Something we should know of it if we knew what were the thoughts of Julius Caesar when he laid the foundations on which Augustus built; of Charles the Great, when he reared anew the majestic pile; of Henry the Third, when he consecrated the strength of his crown to the purification of the Church; of Frederick 'the Wonder of the World,' when he strove to avert the surely coming ruin. Something more succeeding generations will know, who may judge the Middle Ages more fairly than we, still influenced by a reaction against all that is mediaeval, can hope to do, and to whom it will be given to see and understand new forms of political life, whose nature we cannot conjecture. Seeing more than we do, they will also see some things less distinctly. The Empire which to us still looms largely on the horizon of the past, will to them sink lower and lower as they journey onwards into the future. But its importance in universal history it can never lose. For into it all the life of the ancient world was gathered : out of it all the life of the modern world arose.

ADDITIONAL NOTES

I

Note to p. 21

Lact. *Divin. Instit.* vii. 25 : 'Etiam res ipsa declarat lapsum ruinamque rerum brevi fore : nisi quod incolumi urbe Roma nihil istiusmodi videtur esse metuendum. At vero cum caput illud orbis occiderit, et ῥύμη esse coeperit quod Sibyllae fore aiunt, quis dubitet venisse iam finem rebus humanis, orbique terrarum ? Illa, illa est civitas quae adhuc sustentat omnia, precandusque nobis et adorandus est Deus coeli si tamen statuta eius et placita differri possunt, ne citius quam putemus tyrannus ille abominabilis veniat qui tantum facinus moliatur, ac lumen illud effodiat cuius interitu mundus ipse lapsurus est.'

Cf. Tertull. *Apolog.* cap. xxxii : 'Est et alia maior necessitas nobis orandi pro imperatoribus, etiam pro omni statu imperii rebusque Romanis, qui vim maximam universo orbi imminentem ipsamque clausulam saeculi acerbitates horrendas comminantem Romani imperii commeatu scimus retardari.' Also the same writer, *Ad Scapulam*, cap. ii : 'Christianus sciens imperatorem a Deo suo constitui, necesse est ut ipsum diligat et revereatur et honoret et salvum velit cum toto Romano imperio quousque saeculum stabit : tandiu enim stabit.' So too the author — now usually supposed to be Hilary the Deacon — of the Commentary on the Pauline Epistles ascribed to St. Ambrose: 'Non prius veniet Dominus quam regni Romani defectio fiat, et appareat Antichristus qui interficiet sanctos, reddita Romanis libertate, sub suo tamen nomine.' — Ad. II Thess. ii. 4, 7.

II

Note to p. 28

Theodorich (Θευδέριχος, Thiodorich ; in Old German, Dietrich; in Dutch, Dirk ; in French, Thierry) seems to have resided usually at Ravenna, where he died and was buried ; a remarkable building which tradition points out as his tomb, but which cannot belong to his time, stands a little way out of the town, near the railway station. The porphyry sarcophagus, in which his body is supposed to have lain, may be seen built up into the wall of the building called his palace, situated close to the church of Sant' Apollinare in Urbe, and not far from the tomb of Dante. There is no authority for attributing this

building to Ostrogothic times ; it is very different from the representation of
Theodorich's palace which we have in the contemporary mosaics of this
church of Sant' Apollinare at Ravenna.

In the German legends, however, — legends which doubtless led to his being commemorated as a national hero by the superb figure guarding the tomb
of the Emperor Maximilian at Innsbruck, — Theodorich is always the prince of
Verona (Dietrich von Berne), probably because that city was better known
to the Teutonic nations, and because it was thither that he moved his court
when Transalpine affairs required his attention.   His castle there stood in the
old town on the left bank of the Adige, on the height now occupied by the
citadel ; it is doubtful whether any traces of it remain, for the solid foundations which we now see may have belonged to the fortress erected by Gian
Galeazzo Visconti in the fourteenth century.

III

Note to p. 38

A singular account of the origin of the separation of the Greeks from the
Latins occurs in the treatise of Landulfus de Columna (Landolfo Colonna), *De
translatione Imperii Romani* (circa 1320).   'The tyranny of Heraclius,' says
he, 'provoked a revolt of the Eastern nations.   They could not be reduced,
because the Greeks at the same time began to disobey the Roman Pontiff,
receding, like Jeroboam, from the true faith.   Others among these schismatics [apparently with the view of strengthening their political revolt] carried their heresy further and founded Mohammedanism.'   Similarly, Marsilius
of Padua in his revised version of Colonna's book says that Mohammed, 'a
rich Persian,' invented his religion to keep the East from returning to allegiance to Rome.

It is worth remarking that few, if any, of the earlier historians (from the
tenth to the fifteenth century) refer to the Emperors of the West from Constantine to Romulus Augustulus: the transference of the seat of Empire was
deemed to have been effected by Constantine, and the very existence of this
Western line seems to have been even in the eighth or ninth century altogether forgotten.   The first mediaeval writer who mentions Romulus Augus
tulus as the last sovereign reigning at Rome is, according to Döllinger (*Das
Kaiserthum Karls des Grossen und seiner Nachfolger*, p. 111), Matteo Pal-
mieri, who wrote about A.D. 1440.

IV

Note to p. 43 and to p. 101

The original forgery (or rather the extracts which Gratian gives from it)
may be read in the *Corpus Iuris Canonici*, Dist. xcvi. cc. 13, 14 : 'Et sicut

nostram terrenam imperialem potentiam, sic sacrosanctam Romanam ecclesiam decrevimus veneranter honorari, et amplius quam nostrum imperium et terrenum thronum sedem beati Petri gloriose exaltari, tribuentes ei potestatem et gloriae dignitatem atque vigorem et honorificentiam imperialem. . . . Beato Sylvestro patri nostro summo pontifici et universali urbis Romae papae, et omnibus eius successoribus pontificibus, qui usque in finem mundi in sede beati Petri erunt sessuri, de praesenti contradimus palatium imperii nostri Lateranense, deinde diadema, videlicet coronam capitis nostri, simulque phrygium, necnon et superhumerale, verum etiam et chlamydem purpuream et tunicam coccineam, et omnia imperialia indumenta, sed et dignitatem imperialem praesidentium equitum, conferentes etiam et imperialia sceptra, simulque cuncta signa atque banda et diversa ornamenta imperialia et omnem processionem imperialis culminis et gloriam potestatis nostrae. . . . Et sicut imperialis militia ornatur ita et clerum sanctae Romanae ecclesiae ornari decernimus. . . . Unde et pontificalis apex non vilescat sed magis quam terreni imperii dignitas gloria et potentia decoretur, ecce tam palatium nostrum quam Romanam urbem et omnes Italiae seu occidentalium regionum provincias loca et civitates beatissimo papae Sylvestro universali papae contradimus atque relinquimus. . . . Ubi enim principatus sacerdotum et Christianae religionis caput ab imperatore coelesti constitutum est, iustum non est ut illic imperator terrenus habeat potestatem.'

The practice of kissing the Pope's foot was adopted by the Papal in imitation of the ancient imperial court. It was afterwards revived by the Romano-Germanic Emperors.

The spuriousness of the Donation of Constantine was proved by Laurentius Valla in 1440: Nicholas of Cues (1401-1464), afterwards Cardinal, also recognizes its falsity.

V

Note to p. 49

The primitive custom was for the bishop to sit in the centre of the apse, at the central point of the east end of the church (or, as it would be more correct to say, the end furthest from the great door, for the earliest churches do not always run east and west), just as the judge had done in those law courts on the model of which the first basilicas were constructed. This arrangement may still be seen in some of the churches of Rome, as well as elsewhere in Italy; nowhere better than in the churches of Ravenna, particularly the beautiful one of Sant' Apollinare in Classe, and in the very ancient cathedral of Torcello, in the lagoons north-east of Venice.

On the episcopal chair of the Pope were represented the labours of Hercules and the signs of the zodiac. It is believed at Rome to be the veritable chair of the Apostle himself; and whatever may be thought of such an antiquity as this, it can be satisfactorily traced back to the third or fourth century of Christianity. (The story that it is inscribed with verses from the Koran is, I believe, without foundation.) It is of oak and acacia wood, and is now enclosed in a gorgeous casing of bronze, and placed aloft at the eastern extremity of St. Peter's, just over the spot where a bishop's chair would in the old arrangement of the basilica have stood. The Roman sarcophagus in which the body of Charles himself lay, bears reliefs of the rape of Proserpine. It may still be seen in the gallery of the basilica at Aachen.

VI

Note to p. 69

The notion that once prevailed that the Irminsûl was the 'pillar of Hermann,' set up on the spot of the defeat of Varus, is, however, now generally discredited. Some German antiquaries take the pillar to be a rude figure of the native god or hero Irmin, who, as Grimm (*Deutsche Mythologie*, i. 325) thinks, may be an eponym of the Herminones, and was probably worshipped by the Saxons as a warlike representation of Wodan. The omission of their ancestors to commemorate the victory that saved them fròm Rome has been at last supplied by the modern Germans, who in 1875 set up a colossal statue of Arminius or Hermann in the Teutoburger Wald, not far from the reputed scene of the battle. He has in fact become the earliest national hero. A rude ditty, apparently referring to the destruction of the pillar by Charles, still lives in the memory of the Westphalians round Paderborn, and runs thus : —

> ' Hermen sla dermen
> Sla pipen, sla trummen
> De Kaiser wil kummen
> Met hammer un stangen
> Wil Hermen uphangen.'

Mommsen (*Die Oertlichkeit der Varusschlacht*) places the scene of the battle eight or ten miles north of Osnabrück, near a spot called Barenau.

[The name of the deity is preserved in England in the Ermine Street (Eormenstræte), an ancient road which ran north from the Thames Valley into Lincolnshire.]

VII

Note to p. 112

The abbot Engelbert (*De Ortu Progressu et Fine Imperii Romani*) quotes Origen and Jerome to this effect, and proceeds himself to explain, from 2 Thess. ii. 3–9, how the falling away will precede the coming of Antichrist. There will be a triple 'discessio,' of the kingdoms of the earth from the

Roman Empire, of the Church from the Apostolic See, of the faithful from the faith. Of these, the first causes the second; the temporal sword to punish heretics and schismatics being no longer ready to work the will of the rulers of the Church.

St. Thomas Aquinas deals with the same prophecy in a remarkable way, shewing that the falling away is to be understood as referring to a *discessio* from the spiritual power. 'Dicendum quod nondum cessavit, sed est commutatum de temporali in spirituale, ut dicit Leo Papa in sermone de Apostolis: et ideo discessio a Romano imperio debet intelligi non solum a temporali sed etiam a spirituali, scilicet a fide catholica Romanae Ecclesiae. Est autem hoc conveniens signum, nam Christus venit quando Romanum imperium omnibus dominabatur: ita e contra signum adventus Antichristi est discessio ab eo.' — *Comment. ad 2 Thess.* ii.

A full statement of the views that prevailed in the earlier Middle Age regarding Antichrist — as well as of the singular prophecy of the Frankish Emperor who shall appear in the latter days, conquer the world, and then going to Jerusalem shall lay down his crown on the Mount of Olives and deliver over the kingdom to Christ — may be found in the little treatise, *Vita Antichristi*, which Adso, monk and afterwards abbot of Moutier-en-Der, compiled (circa 950) for the information of Queen Gerberga, wife of Louis d'Outremer. Antichrist is to be born a Jew of the tribe of Dan (Gen. xlix. 17), 'non de episcopo et monacha, sicut alii delirando dogmatizant, sed de immundissima meretrice et crudelissimo nebulone. Totus in peccato concipietur, in peccato generabitur, in peccato nascetur.' His birthplace is Babylon: he is to be brought up in Bethsaida and Chorazin.

Adso's book may be found printed in Migne, t. ci. p. 1290. As to the notions current regarding Antichrist (and their supposed derivation from earlier Jewish notions) see Bousset's book on the Antichrist Legend, 1895 (English translation by A. H. Keene, 1896).

No name has been more frequently fitted to different figures than this. Popes as well as Emperors have received it. Everybody in turn has been Antichrist from the Emperor Nero to President Loubet.

VIII

Note to p. 113

A prayer which still keeps its place in the office of the Roman Catholic Church for Good Friday, though it is no longer actually in use, expresses the ancient ideas: 'Oremus pro Christianissimo Imperatore nostro N. ut Deus et Dominus noster subditas illi faciat omnes barbaras nationes ad nostram perpetuam pacem. . . . Omnipotens sempiterne Deus respice ad Romanum imperium ut gentes quae in sua feritate confidunt potentiae Tuae dextera comprimantur.'

IX

Note to p. 117

The ideas expressed in the mosaic of the Lateran triclinium were in substance conveyed by Pope Hadrian I, some twenty-three years before, when writing of Charles as representative of Constantine: ' Et sicut temporibus Beati Sylvestri, Romani pontificis, a sanctae recordationis piissimo Constantino magno imperatore, per eius largitatem sancta Dei catholica et apostolica Romana ecclesia elevata atque exaltata est, et potestatem in his Hesperiae partibus largiri dignatus est, ita et in his vestris felicissimis temporibus atque nostris, sancta Dei ecclesia, id est, beati Petri apostoli, germinet atque exsultet, ut omnes gentes quae haec audierint edicere valeant, "Domine salvum fac regem, et exaudi nos in die in qua invocaverimus te"; quia ecce novus Christianissimus Dei Constantinus imperator his temporibus surrexit, per quem omnia Deus sanctae suae ecclesiae beati apostolorum principis Petri largiri dignatus est.' — *Letter XLIX of Cod. Carol.,* A.D. 777 (in Mur. *Scriptores Rerum Italicarum,* iii. part ii. 195).

This letter is memorable as containing the first allusion, or what seems an allusion, to Constantine's Donation. The document may not yet have been forged, but the legend doubtless existed, and the forger may well have believed it.

X

Note to p. 138

The fevers which prevailed in and near Rome during the summer and autumn were one of the chief causes which baffled the efforts of the Germanic Emperors from the days of Otto the Great to those of Lewis IV.

St. Peter Damiani had, in the eleventh century, noted this when he wrote the lines —

> ' Roma vorax hominum domat ardua colla virorum,
> Roma ferax febrium necis est uberrima frugum,
> Romanae febres stabili sunt iure fideles.'

What we popularly call ' Roman' or malarial fevers are fevers of an intermittent type, due, it is supposed, to haematozoa, spread by a mosquito; and for these intermittent fevers ancient and mediaeval medicine had no remedy. Had quinine been known, the history of those times might have been very different, and many a precious life — Dante's, for instance — might have been prolonged. But cinchona, or, as it used to be called, Peruvian bark or Jesuits' bark, was not introduced into Europe from South America till between 1632 and 1639. Dr. Norman Moore, to whom I owe this date, tells me that the maladies from which armies most usually suffer are dysentery and enteric fever: it may be chiefly from these that the German armies perished, but the prevalence of intermittent fevers would weaken the troops and predispose them to other diseases.

XI

Note to p. 161

Pope Gelasius I wrote to the Emperor Anastasius: 'Duo sunt, Imperator Auguste, quibus principaliter mundus hic regitur, auctoritas sacrata pontificum et regalis potestas. In quibus tanto gravius est pondus sacerdotum quanto etiam pro ipsis regibus hominum in divino reddituri sunt examine rationem. Nosti enim, fili clementissime, quod licet praesideas humano generi dignitate, rerum tamen praesulibus divinarum devotus colla submittis, atque ab eis causas tuae salutis expetis, inque sumendis coelestibus sacramentis eisque (ut competit) disponendis, subdi te debere cognoscis religionis ordine potius quam praeesse, itaque inter haec ex illorum te pendere iudicio, non illos ad tuam velle redigi voluntatem.' — In Migne, vol. lix. ep. viii. p. 42. (Cf. *Corpus Iuris Civilis*, Nov. VI, *principio.*)

These views of Pope Gelasius seem to have exerted much influence in the earlier Middle Ages. They are moderately expressed, and admit the rights of the Emperor in secular affairs, yet in principle they go far. When we reach Gregory VII's time we find Alfanus, archbishop of Salerno, in a poem addressed '*Ad Hildebrandum archidiaconum*' (Migne, vol. cxlvii), treating the spiritual power as the successor and the vindicator of the warlike might of Rome: —

> ' His (*sc.* artibus) et archiapostoli
> Fervido gladio Petri
> Frange robur et impetus
> Illius (*sc.* saeva barbaries) vetus ut iugum
> Usque sentiat ultimum
> Quanta vis anathematis?
> Quidquid et Marius prius
> Quodque Iulius egerint
> Maxima nece militum
> Voce tu modica facis.
> Roma quid Scipionibus
> Caeterisque Quiritibus
> Debuit mage quam tibi
> Cuius est studiis suae
> Nacta via potentiae? '

'Saeva barbaries' seems to mean the Germans.

And in verses addressed to St. Peter he says: —

> Iam cape Romanum consul Caesarque senatum
> Ecce tibi cunctus servit sub sidere mundus.'

But there were in the end of the eleventh century sound churchmen who (like St. Bernard afterwards) held views far more moderate, and desired to restrict the See of Rome to a purely spiritual jurisdiction. Gregorio di Catino (in *Chron. Farfense*, recently edited by Ugo Balzani) writes of the Pope, 'Ipse pastor est animarum, ipse doctor fidei electorum, ipse caput omnium ecclesiarum, in his tamen rebus et causis non quae sunt ad seculum sed quae ad Deum, non enim claves terrae seu regni terrestris sed claves regni caelorum concessit illi omnium Pastor pastorum.'

XII

Note to p. 166

Hohenstaufen is a castle in Swabia (within what is now the kingdom of Würtemberg), about four miles from the Göppingen station of the railway from Stuttgart to Ulm. It stands, or rather stood, on the summit of a steep and lofty conical hill (visible from several points on the line of railway), commanding a boundless view over the great limestone plateau of the Rauhe Alp, the eastern declivities of the Schwartzwald, and the bare and tedious plains of western Bavaria. Of the castle itself, destroyed in the Peasants' War, there remain only fragments of the wall-foundations: in a rude chapel lying on the hill slope below are some strange half-obliterated frescoes: over the arch of the door is inscribed ' Hic transibat Caesar.' Frederick Barbarossa had another famous palace at Kaiserslautern, a small town in the Palatinate, on the railway from Mannheim to Treves, lying in a wide valley at the western foot of the Hardt mountains. It was destroyed by the French, and a house of correction has been built upon its site ; but in a brewery hard by there might be seen (in 1863) some of the huge low-browed arches of its lower story. A third castle where he sometimes dwelt, and in the great Knights' Hall (Rittersaal) of which was held the famous Diet of 1179, was at Geln-hausen, south of Fulda. The ruins stand on an isle in the river Kinzig, and are very picturesque, showing remains of fine Romanesque work. The castle, begun in A.D. 1154 and completed in 1170, was occasionally inhabited by suc-ceeding Emperors down to Sigismund. It suffered severely from the Swedes in the Thirty Years' War.

XIII

Note to p. 222

Marsilius was born in or soon after A.D. 1270 of the burgher family of Raimondini or Mainardini in Padua. He was a man of many accomplishments — John Villani calls him 'grande maestro in natura ed astrologia' — was in orders, though possibly he did not go so far as the diaconate, and at one time seems to have practised medicine. He was for a while with the Della Scala in Verona (where he may have met Dante Alighieri), taught in the University of Paris, whereof he was Rector in A.D. 1312, and immediately after Lewis IV had been excommunicated, departed suddenly thence, and with his friend John of Jandun presented the *Defensor Pacis*, just then composed by him with John's help, to the Emperor. Lewis took them both into Italy with him, and when he left Rome preferred John to the see of Ferrara, which however the latter seems not to have lived to occupy, and Marsilius (who had been accused of wishing to be Pope) to the archbishopric of Milan. Marsilius never entered on that great office (perhaps fortunately for his consistency to his principles) ; and we lose sight of him after 1328, though he was still living in 1336. His ally, possibly his teacher, William of Ockham, seems not to have returned to England ; he died at Munich and was buried in the (now destroyed) Franciscan church there in or soon after 1349 (Reizler, *Literarische Widersacher der Päpste*, p. 126). How much Central and Western Europe was in those days one intellectual community is well illustrated by the fact that the three chief champions of the German Lewis IV in his strife with the Pope were the Italian Marsilius, the Frenchman John of Jandun, and the Englishman William of Ockham.

XIV

Note to p. 231

It is a remarkable evidence of the decline of imperial power after the death of Frederick II, and of the impression which that decline, coupled with the failure of Rudolf, Adolf, and Albert to enter Italy, had made all over Europe, that not only the notion of transferring the crown of the Empire to the kings of France, but also plans for making France predominant in Italy and Rome, were seriously discussed at the beginning of the fourteenth century. One such plan may be found fully stated in the treatise *De Recuperatione Terrae Sanctae* of Peter Du Bois — a man full of bold schemes and novel ideas — who was a royal advocate living at Coutances in Normandy, and a warm partizan of Philip IV in his quarrel with Pope Boniface VIII. He proposes that the Pope should transfer all his temporal and feudal rights to the king of France and should himself come to live in France, the king of France becoming Senator of Rome. The Pope was to have a fixed *pensio* and the Emperor (Albert I) was to be appeased by having the imperial title made hereditary in his family, some compensation being given to the Germanic electors. France was at this time a kingdom practically stronger than the Empire ; and after A.D. 1305 she could generally count on the Papacy: but within forty years the beginning of the great war with England disabled her for more than a century from actively prosecuting schemes in Italy or Germany.

XV

Note to p. 267

The mediaeval practice seems to have been that which still prevails in the Roman Catholic Church — to presume the doctrinal orthodoxy and external conformity of every citizen, whether lay or clerical, until the contrary be proved. Of course when heresy was rife it went hard with suspected men, unless they could either clear themselves or submit to recant. But it was unusual to require any one to pledge himself beforehand, as a qualification for an office, to certain doctrines. And thus, important as an Emperor's orthodoxy was, he does not appear to have been subjected to any test (in the modern sense of the word), although the Pope pretended to the right of catechizing him in the faith and rejecting him if unsound. In the *Ordo Romanus* we find a long series of questions which the pontiff was to administer, but it does not appear, and is in the highest degree unlikely, that such a programme was ever carried out. At the German coronation, however (performed in earlier days at Aachen, afterwards at Frankfort), the custom was for the Emperor before he was anointed to declare his orthodoxy by an oath taken on the famous copy of the Gospels which was held to have been used by Charles the Great, and on a casket containing earth soaked with the blood of the martyr Stephen.

At the coronation of an East Roman Emperor the Patriarch submitted a confession of orthodoxy which the Emperor subscribed.

The charge of heresy was one of the weapons used with most effect against Frederick II (Lewis IV retorted it on Pope John XXII); and as the Popes might hold disobedience to themselves to be virtually heresy, it was a charge easily and often brought against their opponents.

XVI

Note to p. 283

There is a curious seal of the Emperor Otto IV (figured in J. M. Heineccius, *De veteribus Germanorum atque aliarum nationum sigillis*), on which the sun and moon are represented over the head of the Emperor. Heineccius says he cannot explain it, but it may possibly be taken as typifying the accord of the spiritual and temporal powers which were brought about at the accession of Otto, the Guelfic leader, and the favoured candidate of Pope Innocent III.

The analogy between the lights of heaven and the potentates of earth, in which mediaeval writers rejoice, seems to have originated with Gregory VII.

Ockham tries to avoid it by distinguishing between the substance and the accidents of the moon. A gloss upon a letter of Innocent III inserted in the *Corpus Iuris Canonici* (*Decret. Greg. I.* p. 33) says, 'Cum terra sit septies maior luna sol autem octies maior terra, restat ergo ut pontificatus dignitas quadragies septies sit maior regali dignitate.'

This Sun and Moon argument continued to be so frequently used, and was apparently deemed so formidable, that the Parlement of Paris forbade it as late as A.D. 1626. — Friedberg, *Die mittelalterlichen Lehren über das Verhältniss von Staat und Kirche.*

XVII

Note to p. 294

Arnold was born about A.D. 1090 or perhaps a little later; he studied in the University of Paris and was associated with Abelard in the condemnation pronounced on the latter. Driven from France he lived for some time at Zürich, where his preaching made a deep impression, and thence made his way, apparently accompanied by some of his Alemannic followers, to Rome, where Pope Eugenius III permitted him to remain. He is described as not only a powerful and persuasive preacher but also a man of learning.

He appears to have maintained that holy orders were not indelible, and to have denounced the rule of the Pope and cardinals in Rome; 'praeterea non esse homines admittendos qui sedem imperii fontem libertatis Romam mundi dominam volebant subicere servituti' (John of Salisbury). He and his followers mocked at the fable of Constantine's Donation. See a letter in Wibaldi, *Epistolae* (No. 404) in Jaffé, Biblioth. I, quoted by Giesebrecht.

The chief authorities for his Roman career are Otto of Freysing, i. 26 and ii. 20 sqq.; Godfrey of Viterbo, ll. 139 sqq.; and a poem, apparently by a contemporary hand, lately published (under the title *Gesta di Federico imperatore in Italia*) by the Italian Istituto Storico (the volume is edited by E. Monaci). This poem, after describing with sympathy the fortitude of Arnold at the moment of death, adds that Frederick was believed to have repented of the part he played, 'set doluisse datur super hoc rex sero misertus' (line 850). See also his contemporary John of Salisbury, *Histor. Pontif.* ch. 21 (Pertz, *Script.* xx. 537), and Gerhoh prior of Reichersberg, who, though a strong churchman, regrets Arnold's execution, saying that he acted 'zelo forte bono sed minore scientia,' and that he wished the See of Rome was not answerable for his death. (Gerhoh is in Pertz, *Libelli de lite Imperatorum et Pontificum*, vol. iii.) A recent discussion of Arnold's principles and conduct may be found in the interesting book of Ruggiero Bonghi, *Arnaldo da Brescia*, 1895. Brescia has erected a statue to her famous son, but Rome, though now beginning to be filled with such memorials, has not yet paid this honour to the boldest and most disinterested of mediaeval reformers; nor has Padua yet commemorated her Marsilius by any effigy, though she has called a street after him.

XVIII

Note to p. 299

Cola di Rienzo was the son of a man named Laurence, who kept a wine-shop on the edge of the Ghetto near the Tiber. (Can Cola have had some Jewish blood? There are traces in his imagination and behaviour of something not quite Italian, not even Roman.) He gave himself out, in middle life, to be an illegitimate son of the Emperor Henry VII, and tells the story at length in a letter to the Emperor Charles IV, who was Henry's grandson. The tale might possibly have been true, for Henry was in Rome in 1312, but is probably an invention, though Cola says the Romans believed it.

The (apparently contemporary) *Vita di Cola di Rienzo* is one of the most striking among mediaeval biographies, and presents a picture so vivid that one cannot help thinking it life-like. There is much curious matter in his letters, which may be read in the *Epistolario di Cola di Rienzo*, published by the Italian Istituto Storico (ed. A. Gabrielli, 1890).

Cola called himself Augustus as well as tribune; 'tribuno Augusto de Roma.' He cited, on becoming Tribune, the cardinals to appear before the people of Rome and give an account of their conduct; and after them the Emperor. 'Ancora citao lo Bavaro (Lewis the Fourth). Puoi citao li elettori de lo imperio in Alemagna, e disse "Voglio vedere che rascione haco nella elettione," che trovasse scritto che passato alcuno tempo la elettione recadeva a li Romani.' — *Vita*, c. xxvi. His letter to the Commune of Viterbo begins: 'Nicholaus severus et clemens, libertatis pacis iustitiaeque tribunus et sacrae Romanae reipublicae liberator, nobilibus et prudentibus viris potestati capitaneo bonis hominibus sindico consilio et communi civitatis Viterbii in Tuscia.' — Epist. II. p. 6, of *Epistolario*.

XIX

Note to p. 307

The only Teutonic Emperors buried in Italy besides Otto II were, so far as I know, Lewis the Second (whose tomb, with an inscription commemorating his exploits, is built into the wall of the north aisle of the famous church of St. Ambrose at Milan); Henry the Sixth and Frederick the Second, at Palermo; Conrad IV, at Messina; and Henry VII, whose sarcophagus may be seen in the Campo Santo of Pisa, a city always conspicuous for her zeal on the imperial side.

Eight Emperors or German kings (Conrad II, Henry III, Henry IV,

Henry V, Philip, Rudolf I, Adolf, and Albert I) lie in the cathedral of Speyer; five (Charles IV, Wenzel, Ferdinand I, Maximilian II, and Rudolf II) at Prague; two (Charles I and Otto III) at Aachen; two (Henry II and Conrad III) at Bamberg; two (Lewis IV and Charles VII) at Munich; two (Arnulf and his son Lewis the Child) at Regensburg; Lewis the Pious at Metz, Lothar I at Prüm near Treves, Charles the Bald at St. Denis (in France), Charles the Fat at Reichenau on the Lake of Constance, Conrad I at Fulda, Henry I at Quedlinburg, Otto I at Magdeburg, Lothar II at Königslutter near Brunswick, Otto IV at Brunswick, Rupert at Heidelberg, Sigismund at Nagy Várad (Gross Wardein) in Transylvania, Albert II at Stuhlweissenburg in Hungary, Charles V in the Escurial in Spain, Frederick III and most of his successors at Vienna. The bones of Frederick I were interred at Tyre. Of all the tombs the noblest is that of Maximilian I at Innsbruck.

XX

Note to p. 312

Thus in the noble church of San Lorenzo fuori le mura there are several Pointed windows, now bricked up; and similar ones may be seen in the church of Ara Coeli on the summit of the Capitol. So in the apse of St. John Lateran there are three or four windows of Gothic form: and in its cloister, as well as in that of St. Paul without the walls, a great deal of beautiful work in the so-called Lombard style. The elegant porch of the church of Sant' Antonio Abate is Lombard. In the apse of the church of San Giovanni e Paolo on the Coelian hill there is an external arcade exactly like those of the Duomo at Pisa. Nor are these the only instances.

The ruined chapel attached to the fortress of the Caetani family — the family to which Boniface the Eighth belonged, and which still holds a distinguished place among the Roman nobility — is a pretty little building, more like northern Gothic than anything within the walls of Rome. It stands upon the Appian Way, opposite the tomb of Caecilia Metella, which the Caetani used as a stronghold.

XXI

Note to p. 314

The finest of the similar Ravenna mosaics are rather older than these Roman ones: but some there, as well as a few others elsewhere in Italy (e.g. the beautiful ones at Torcello), date from the seventh, eighth, and ninth centuries. The magnificent mosaics of Monreale and Cefalú in Sicily belong to the twelfth century, and were probably executed by artists from Constantinople.

These campaniles are generally supposed to date from the ninth and tenth centuries. Mr. J. H. Parker, however, a competent judge, told me that an examination of their mouldings convinced him that few or none, unless it be that of Santa Prassede, are older than the twelfth century.

This of course applies only to the existing buildings. The type of tower may be, and indeed no doubt is, older.

Somewhat similar towers may be observed in many parts of the Italian Alps, especially in the wonderful mountain land north of Venice, where such towers are of all dates from the eleventh or twelfth down to the nineteenth century, the ancient type having in these remote valleys been adhered to because the builder had no other models before him. In the valley of Cimolais (not very far from Longarone in Val d' Ampezzo) I have seen such a campanile in course of erection, precisely similar to others in the neighbouring villages some eight centuries old.

The very curious round towers of Ravenna, some four or five of which are still standing, seem to have originally had similar windows, though these have been all, or nearly all, stopped up. The Irish round towers were probably copied from these Ravennate towers, or others of the same type. The Roman towers are all square.

XXII

Note to p. 330

The ceremonies of the coronation of an East Roman Emperor took by degrees an ecclesiastical and religious character not less marked than that which belonged to imperial coronations in the West. (Interesting details regarding them may be found in an article by W. Sickel in *Byzantinische Zeitschrift*, vol. vii. pp. 511–557; in another by Mr. Brightman in the *Journal of Theological Studies* for April, 1901.) The first coronation performed by the Patriarch of Constantinople was either that of Marcian (A.D. 450) or that of Leo I, A.D. 457 (after Anastasius it was the usual though not invariable practice); the first performed in a church (the usual place was S. Sophia) was that of Phocas in A.D. 602 ; the first in which the rite of anointing (customary in the West since the time of Pipin and that of Charles the Great) seems to have been used, was that of Basil I (A.D. 886) (Sickel, *ut supra*, p. 524). Brightman, however, puts it as far down as the coronation of (the Latin) Baldwin in 1204. Sometimes an Emperor crowned himself, sometimes when he took a colleague he crowned the person he had chosen. The practice of raising the newly-chosen Emperor on a buckler, which began with the inauguration of Julian in A.D. 361, and was evidently a Teutonic usage familiar to the barbarian troops who acclaimed Julian, continued in the Eastern Empire for some considerable time. The last recorded case seems to be that of Phocas ; but it may well have lasted much longer. At his coronation the Eastern, like the Western, Emperor received the sacramental wine, like a priest, in the chalice, whereas laymen in the East communicated from a spoon containing both kinds (*i.e.* a morsel of bread dipped in wine) (*intincta eucharistia*).. He also took an oath to defend the Church and solemnly professed his orthodoxy, subscribing a confession of faith, reciting the creed, and declaring his assent to the decrees of the seven oecumenical councils.

Neither the diadem nor the assumption of the purple, which was the oldest sign of the imperial dignity, nor the action of the Patriarch, was essential to the authority of an Emperor. He was thus better off than his Western brother, who must receive the imperial crown in Rome and from the Roman bishop.

XXIII

Note to p. 343

'Isaachius a Deo constitutus Imperator, sacratissimus, excellentissimus, potentissimus, moderator Romanorum, Angelus totius orbis, heres coronae magni Constantini, dilecto fratri imperii sui, maximo principi Alemanniae.' A remarkable speech of Frederick's to the envoys of Isaac, who had addressed a letter to him as ' Rex Alemaniae,' is preserved by Ansbert (*Historia de Expeditione Friderici Imperatoris*) : — 'Dominus Imperator divina se illustrante gratia ulterius dissimulare non valens temerarium fastum regis (*sc.* Graecorum) et usurpantem vocabulum falsi imperatoris Romanorum, haec inter caetera exorsus est : — "Omnibus qui sanae mentis sunt constat, quia unus est Monarchus Imperator Romanorum, sicut et unus est pater universitatis pontifex videlicet Romanus; ideoque cum ego Romani imperii sceptrum plusquam per annos XXX absque omnium regum vel principum contradictione tranquille tenuerim et in Romana urbe a summo pontifice imperiali benedictione unctus sim et sublimatus, quia denique Monarchiam praedecessores mei imperatores Romanorum plusquam per CCCC annos etiam gloriose transmiserint utpote a Constantinopolitana urbe ad pristinam sedem imperii, caput orbis Romam, acclamatione Romanorum et principum imperii, auctoritate quoque summi pontificis et S. catholicae ecclesiae translatam, propter tardum et infructuosum Constantinopolitani imperatoris auxilium contra tyrannos ecclesiae, mirandum est admodum cur frater meus dominus vester Constantinopolitanus imperator usurpet inefficax sibi idem vocabulum et glorietur stulte alieno sibi prorsus honore, cum liquido noverit me et nomine dici et re esse Fridericum Romanorum imperatorem semper Augustum." '

Isaac was so far moved by Frederick's indignation that in his next letter he addressed him as 'generosissimum imperatorem Alemaniae,' and in a third thus : —

'Isaakius in Christo fidelis divinitus coronatus, sublimis, potens, excelsus, haeres coronae magni Constantini et Moderator Romeon Angelus nobilissimo Imperatori antiquae Romae, regi Alemaniae et dilecto fratri imperii sui, salutem,' &c., &c. (Ansbert, *ut supra*).

XXIV

Note to p. 410

In an address by Napoleon to the Senate in 1804, bearing date 10th Frimaire (1st Dec.), are the words, 'Mes descendans conserveront longtemps ce trône, le premier de l'univers.' Answering a deputation from the department of the Lippe, Aug. 8th, 1811, 'La Providence, qui a voulu que je rétablisse le trône de Charlemagne, vous a fait naturellement rentrer, avec la Hollande et les villes anséatiques, dans le sein de l'Empire.' — *Oeuvres de Napoléon*, tom. v. p. 521.

'Pour le Pape, je suis Charlemagne, parce que, comme Charlemagne, je réunis la couronne de France à celle des Lombards, et que mon Empire confine avec l'Orient.' (Quoted by Lanfrey, *Vie de Napoléon*, iii. 417.)

'Votre Sainteté est souveraine de Rome, mais j'en suis l'Empereur.' — Letter of Napoleon to Pope Pius, Feb. 13th, 1806. Lanfrey.

'Dites bien,' says Napoleon to Cardinal Fesch, 'que je suis Charlemagne, leur Empereur [of the Papal Court] que je dois être traité de même. Je fais connaître au Pape mes intentions en peu de mots; s'il n'y acquiesce pas, je le réduirai à la même condition qu'il était avant Charlemagne.' — Lanfrey, *Vie de Napoléon*, iii. 420.

Napoleon said on one occasion, 'Je n'ai pas succédé à Louis Quatorze, mais à Charlemagne.' — Bourrienne, *Vie de Napoléon*, vi. 256, who adds that in 1804, shortly before he was crowned, he had the imperial insignia of Charles brought from the old Frankish capital, and exhibited them in a jeweller's shop in Paris, along with those which had just been made for his own coronation. But if there was not in this a trick of Napoleon's, there must be a mistake of Bourrienne's, for these insignia had been removed from Aachen by Austria in 1798. (Cf. Bock, *Die Kleinodien des h. römischen Reiches*, p. 4.) This was done in the same spirit which made him display the Bayeux embroidery, in order to incite his subjects to the conquest of England.

APPENDIX

NOTE A

ON THE BURGUNDIES

It would be hard to mention any geographical name which, by its application at different times to different districts, has caused, and continues to cause, more confusion than this name Burgundy. There may, therefore, be some use in a brief statement of the more important of those applications. Without going into the minutiae of the subject, the following may be given as the ten senses in which the name is most frequently to be met with : —

I. The kingdom of the Burgundians (*regnum Burgundionum*), formed by the settlement of this tribe in Savoy and the lands south-west of the Rhine,[a] A.D. 443–475. At its meridian it included the whole valley of the Saone and Lower Rhone, from Dijon to the Mediterranean, and also the western half of what is now Switzerland. It was overthrown by the sons of Clovis in A.D. 534.

II. The kingdom of Burgundy (*regnum Burgundiae*), mentioned occasionally under the Merovingian kings as a separate principality, confined within boundaries apparently somewhat narrower than those of the older kingdom last named.

III. The kingdom of Provence or Burgundy (*regnum Provinciae seu Burgundiae*) — also, though less accurately,

---

[a] Before this time, the Burgundians had been for a while upon the Middle Rhine. The *Nibelungen-Lied* places them at Worms.

called the kingdom of Cisjurane Burgundy — was founded by Boso in A.D. 877–879, and included Provence, Dauphiné, the southern part of Savoy, and the country between the Saone and the Jura.

IV. The kingdom of Transjurane Burgundy (*regnum Iurense, Burgundia Transiurensis*), founded by Rudolf in A.D. 888, recognized in the same year by the Emperor Arnulf, included the northern part of Savoy, and nearly all that part of Switzerland which lies between the Reuss and the Jura.

V. The kingdom of Burgundy or Arles (*regnum Burgundiae, regnum Arelatense*), formed by the union, under Conrad the Pacific, in A.D. 937, of the kingdoms described above as III and IV. On the death, in 1032, of the last independent king, Rudolf III, it came partly by bequest, partly by conquest, into the hands of the Emperor Conrad II (the Salic), and thenceforward formed a part of the Empire. In the thirteenth century, France began to absorb it, bit by bit (though she did not take Avignon till the Revolution), and she has now (since the annexation of Savoy in 1861) acquired all except the Swiss portion.

VI. The Lesser Duchy (*Burgundia Minor*) (Klein Burgund) corresponded very nearly with what is now Switzerland west of the Reuss, including Canton Valais. It was Transjurane Burgundy (IV) *minus* the parts of Savoy which had belonged to that kingdom. It disappears from history after the extinction of the house of Zähringen in the thirteenth century. Legally it was part of the Empire till A.D. 1648, though practically independent long before that date.

VII. The Free County or Palatinate of Burgundy (Franche-Comté) (Freigrafschaft) (called also Upper Burgundy), to which the name of Cisjurane Burgundy originally and properly belonged, lay between the Saone and the Jura. It formed a part of III and V, and was therefore a fief of the Empire. The French dukes of Burgundy were invested with it in A.D. 1384. Its capital, the imperial city of Besançon, was given to Spain in 1651, and by the treaty of Nimwegen, 1678–1679, it was ceded to the crown of France.

VIII. The Landgraviate of Burgundy (Landgrafschaft) lay in what is now Western Switzerland, on both sides of the Aar, between Thun and Solothurn. It was a part of the Lesser Duchy (VI), and, like it, is hardly mentioned after the thirteenth century.

IX. The circle of Burgundy (Kreis Burgund), an administrative division of the Empire, was established by Charles V in 1548, and included the Free County of Burgundy (VII) and the seventeen provinces of the Netherlands, which Charles inherited from his grandmother Mary, daughter of Charles the Bold.

X. The Duchy of Burgundy (Lower Burgundy) (Bourgogne), the most northerly part of the old kingdom of the Burgundians, was always a fief of the crown of France (*Francia Occidentalis*), and a province of France till the Revolution. It was of this Burgundy that Philip the Good and Charles the Bold were Dukes. They were also Counts of the Free County (VII).

There was very nearly being an eleventh Burgundy. In 1784 Joseph II proposed to the Elector of Bavaria to give him the Austrian Netherlands, except the citadels of Luxemburg and Limburg, with the title of King of Burgundy, in exchange for his Bavarian dominions, which Joseph was anxious to get hold of. The Elector consented, France (bribed by the offer of Luxemburg and Limburg) and Russia approved, and the project was only baffled by the promptitude of Frederick the Great in forming the League of Princes to preserve the integrity of German territories.

The most copious and accurate information regarding the obscure history of the Burgundian kingdoms (III, IV, and V) is to be found in the contributions of Baron Frederic de Gingins la Sarraz, a Vaudois historian, to the *Archiv für Schweizer Geschichte*. Reference may also be made to Mr. E. A. Freeman's *Historical Geography*, and to an essay in his historical essays entitled *The Franks and the Gauls*.

NOTE B

ON CERTAIN IMPERIAL TITLES AND CEREMONIES

THIS subject is a great deal too wide and too intricate to be more than touched upon here. But a few brief statements may have their use; for the practice of the Germanic Emperors varied so greatly from time to time that the reader becomes hopelessly perplexed without some clue. And if there were space to explain the causes of each change of title, it would be seen that the subject, dry as it may appear, is neither barren nor dull.

I. TITLES OF EMPERORS.

Charles the Great styled himself 'Carolus serenissimus Augustus, a Deo coronatus, magnus et pacificus imperator, Romanum (*or* Romanorum) gubernans imperium, qui et per misericordiam Dei rex Francorum et Langobardorum.'

Subsequent Carolingian Emperors were usually entitled simply 'Imperator Augustus.' Sometimes 'rex Francorum et Langobardorum' was added.[a]

Conrad I and Henry I (the Fowler) were only German kings.

A Saxon Emperor was, before his coronation at Rome, 'rex' or 'rex Francorum Orientalium,' or 'Francorum atque Saxonum rex'; after it simply 'Imperator Augustus.' Otto III is usually said to have introduced the form

---

[a] Waitz (*Deutsche Verfassungsgeschichte*) says that the phrase 'semper Augustus' may be found in the times of the Carolingians, but in no official documents.

'Romanorum Imperator Augustus,' but some authorities state that it occurs in documents of the time of Lewis I.

Henry II and his successors, not daring to take the title of Emperor till crowned at Rome (in conformity with the superstitious notion which had begun with Charles the Bald), but anxious to claim the sovereignty of Rome as indissolubly attached to the German crown, began to call themselves 'reges Romanorum.' The title did not, however, become common or regular till the time of Henry IV, in whose proclamations (issued before his Roman coronation) it occurs constantly.

From the eleventh century till the sixteenth, the invariable practice was for the monarch to be called 'Romanorum rex semper Augustus' till his coronation at Rome by the Pope; after it, 'Romanorum Imperator semper Augustus.'

In A.D. 1508, Maximilian I, being refused a passage to Rome by the Venetians, obtained a bull from Pope Julius II permitting him to call himself 'Imperator electus' (erwählter Kaiser). This title Ferdinand I (brother of Charles V) and all succeeding Emperors took immediately upon their German coronation, and it was till A.D. 1806 their strict legal designation,[b] and was always employed by them in proclamations or other official documents. The term 'elect' was however omitted even in formal documents when the sovereign was addressed, or spoken of in the third person; and in ordinary practice he was simply 'Roman Emperor.'

Maximilian added the title 'Germaniae rex,' which had never been known before, although the phrase 'rex Germanorum' may be found employed once or twice in early

[b] There is some reason to think that towards the end of the Empire people had begun to fancy that 'erwählter' did not mean 'elect,' but 'elective.' Cf. note[k], p. 414.

times. ' Rex Teutonicorum,' 'regnum Teutonicum,' [c] occur often in the tenth and eleventh centuries. Henry VI took the title of Rex Siciliae. A great many titles of less consequence were added from time to time. Charles the Fifth had seventy-five, not, of course, as Emperor, but in virtue of his vast hereditary possessions.[d]

It is perhaps worth remarking that the word 'Emperor' has not at all the same meaning now that it had even so lately as two centuries ago. Since a new use began with Napoleon, it has tended to become a title of no special significance, somewhat more pompous than that of King, and supposed to belong especially to despots. It is given to Eastern princes, like those of China, Japan, and Abyssinia, in default of a better name. It was for a time peculiarly affected by new dynasties; and grew so fashionable, that what with Emperors of Brazil, of Hayti, and of

[c] These expressions seem to have been intended to distinguish the kingdom of the Eastern or Germanic Franks from that of the Western or Gallicized Franks (Francigenae), which having been for some time 'regnum Francorum Occidentalium,' grew at last to be simply 'regnum Franciae,' the East Frankish kingdom being no longer so called because swallowed up in the Empire.

It is not very easy to say precisely when the name 'Francia' came to denote, to Europe generally, what we now call France. Bishop Leopold of Bamberg (A.D. 1353) complains that the French kings were then already called 'reges Franciae' instead of 'reges Franciae Occidentalis.' In the thirteenth century Snorri Sturluson speaks of Otto the Great as collecting an army from 'Saxonland, Frakland, Friesland, and Vendland,' apparently denoting by Frakland the old Frankish country (F. orientalis) (*Heimskringla, Olafs Saga Tryggvasonar*). In England the name had no doubt changed its meaning some time earlier.

[d] What is stated above can be taken as only generally and probably true: so great are the discrepancies among even the most careful writers on the subject, and so numerous the forgeries of a later age, which are to be found among the genuine documents of the early Empire. Goldast's Collections, for instance, are full of forgeries and anachronisms. Detailed information may be found in Pfeffinger, Moser, and Pütter, and in the host of writers to whom they refer.

Mexico (countries that have now become republics), the good old title of King seemed in a fair way to become obsolete.[e] But in former times there was, and could be, but one Emperor; he was always mentioned with a certain reverence: his name summoned up a host of thoughts and associations, which moderns do not comprehend or sympathize with. His office, unlike that of modern Emperors, was by its very nature elective and not hereditary; and, so far from resting on conquest or the will of the people, rested on and represented pure legality. War could give him nothing which law had not given him already: the people had delegated all their power to him long ago, and he was now the viceroy of God.

II. THE CROWNS.

Of the four crowns something has been said in the text. They were those of Germany, taken at Aachen (Aix-la-Chapelle) in earlier times,[f] latterly at Frankfort, once or twice at Regensburg; — of Burgundy, at Arles; — of Italy, sometimes at Pavia, more usually at Milan or Monza; — of the world, at Rome.

The German crown was taken by every Emperor after the time of Otto the Great; that of Italy by every one, or

[e] We in England may be thought to have made some slight movement in the same direction, by calling the united great council of the Three Kingdoms the Imperial Parliament.

[f] In the gallery of the basilica in the ancient Frankish capital there may still be seen the marble throne on which the Emperors were crowned from the days of Lewis the Pious to those of Ferdinand the First. It was upon this chair that Otto III had found the body of Charles seated, when he opened his tomb in A.D. 1001. After Ferdinand I, the coronation as well as the election took place at Frankfort. An account of the ceremony may be found in Goethe's *Wahrheit und Dichtung*. Aachen, though it remained and indeed is still a German town, lay in too remote a corner of the country to be a convenient capital, and was moreover in dangerous proximity to the West Franks.

almost every one, who took the Roman down to Frederick III, but by none after him; that of Burgundy, it would appear, by four Emperors only, Conrad II, Henry III, Frederick I, and Charles IV. The imperial crown was received at Rome by most Emperors till Frederick III; after him by none save Charles V, who obtained both it and the Italian at Bologna in a somewhat informal manner. From Ferdinand I onwards the Emperor bound himself by his capitulation, to use all diligence to obtain the imperial crown with reasonable promptitude ('sich zum besten befleissigen zu wollen die kayserliche Cron auch in ziemlich gelegener Zeit zum schiersten zu erlangen'). At the Diet of Ratisbon in 1653 (when Ferdinand archduke of Austria was chosen king of the Romans) the Protestants protested against this article; but the Emperor, appealing to the Golden Bull, insisted on its retention. In the capitulation of Leopold I, however, and his successors down to Francis II, the article was modified so as to bind the new sovereign 'die Römische-Königliche Cron forderlichst zu empfangen, und alles dasjenige dabey zu thun so sich derenthalben gebühret.'

It should be remembered that none of the three inferior crowns were necessarily connected with that of the Roman Empire, which might have been held by a simple knight without a foot of land in the world. For as there had been Emperors (Lothar I, Lewis II, Lewis of Provence, son of Boso, Guy, Lambert, and Berengar) who were not kings of Germany, so there were several (all those who preceded Conrad II) who were not kings of Burgundy, and it is not clear that all were formally crowned or installed as kings of Italy. It is also worth remarking, that although no crown save the German was assumed by the successors of Charles V, their wider rights remained in full force, and were never subsequently relinquished.

There was nothing, except the practical difficulty and absurdity of such a project, to prevent Francis II from having himself crowned at Arles,[g] Milan, and Rome.

III. The King of the Romans (Römischer König).

It has been shewn above how and why, about the time of Henry II, the German monarch began to entitle himself 'Romanorum rex.' Now it was not uncommon in the Middle Ages for the heir-apparent to a throne to be crowned during his father's lifetime, that at the death of the latter he might step at once into his place. (Coronation, it must be remembered, which is now merely a spectacle, was in those days not only a sort of sacrament, but a matter of great political importance.) This plan was specially useful in an elective monarchy, such as Germany was after the twelfth century, for it avoided the delays and dangers of an election while the throne was vacant. But it seemed against the order of nature to have two Emperors at once,[h] and as the sovereign's authority in Germany depended not on the Roman but on the German coronation, the practice came to be that each Emperor during his own life procured, if he could, the election of his successor, who was crowned at Aachen, in later times at Frankfort, and took the title of 'King of the Romans.' During the presence of the Emperor in Germany he exercised (unless by special delegation) no

[g] Although to be sure the Burgundian dominions had all passed from the Emperor to France, the kingdom of Sardinia, and the Swiss Confederation, while Italy had practically been long since separated from the Empire.

[h] Nevertheless, Otto II was crowned Emperor, and reigned for some time along with his father, under the title of 'Co-Imperator.' So Lothar I was associated in the Empire with Lewis the Pious, as Lewis himself had been crowned in the lifetime of Charles. Many analogies to the practice of the Romano-Germanic Empire in this respect might be adduced from the history of the old Roman as well as of the Byzantine Empire.

more authority than a Prince of Wales does in England, but on the Emperor's death he succeeded at once, without any second election or coronation, and assumed (after the time of Ferdinand I) the title of 'Emperor Elect.'[1] Before Ferdinand's time, he would have been expected to go to Rome to be crowned there. While the Hapsburgs held the sceptre, each monarch generally contrived in this way to have his son or other near relative chosen to succeed him. But some were foiled in their attempts to do so; and, in such cases, an election was held after the Emperor's death, according to the rules laid down in the Golden Bull.

The first person who was chosen to be king in the lifetime of an Emperor seems to have been Conrad, son of the Emperor Henry IV.

It was in imitation of this title that Napoleon called his son King of Rome.

There was a certain resemblance between the position in Hindostan of the Mogul monarchs who ruled at Delhi, Lahore, and Agra, from Akbar the Great to Aurungzebe, and that of the earlier Teutonic Emperors in Europe. And the supremacy which the British Crown now holds in India over all or nearly all the native potentates is not unlike that which mediaeval theory assigned to the Emperor among Christian princes. It suggested the creation by statute (39 & 40 Vict. cap. 10) of the title 'Emperor of India' now attached to the king of Great Britain and Ireland.

[1] Maximilian had obtained this title, 'Emperor Elect,' from the Pope. Ferdinand took it as of right, and his successors followed the example. Frederick I appears to have, before his coronation, spoken of himself as 'Imperator Electus.'

NOTE C

LINES CONTRASTING THE PAST AND PRESENT
OF ROME

Dum simulacra mihi, dum numina vana placebant,
  Militia, populo, moenibus alta fui :
At simul effigies arasque superstitiosas
  Deiiciens, uni sum famulata Deo,
Cesserunt arces, cecidere palatia divûm,
  Servivit populus, degeneravit eques.
Vix scio quae fuerim, vix Romae Roma recordor ;
  Vix sinit occasus vel meminisse mei.
Gratior haec iactura mihi successibus illis ;
  Maior sum pauper divite, stante iacens :
Plus aquilis vexilla crucis, plus Caesare Petrus,
  Plus cinctis ducibus vulgus inerme dedit.
Stans domui terras, infernum diruta pulso,
  Corpora stans, animas fracta iacensque rego.
Tunc miserae plebi, modo principibus tenebrarum
  Impero : tunc urbes, nunc mea regna polus.

Written by Hildebert, bishop of Le Mans, and afterwards
archbishop of Tours (born A.D. 1057). Extracted from his
works as printed by Migne, *Patrologiae Cursus Completus.*[a]

a See note d, p. 286.

CHRONOLOGICAL TABLE

OF

EMPERORS AND POPES

Year of Accession	Bishops of Rome	Emperors	Year of Accession
A.D.			B.C.
		Augustus.	27
			A.D.
		Tiberius.	14
		Caligula.	37
		Claudius.	41
42	St. Peter (according to Jerome).		
		Nero.	54
67	Linus (according to Irenaeus, Eusebius, Jerome).		
68	Clement (according to Tertullian and Rufinus).	Galba, Otho, Vitellius, Vespasian.	68
78	Anacletus (?).		
		Titus.	79
		Domitian.	81
91	Clement (according to some later writers).		
		Nerva.	96
		Trajan.	98
100	Evarestus (?).		
109	Alexander (?).		
		Hadrian.	117
119	Sixtus I.		
129	Telesphorus.		
		Antoninus Pius.	138
139	Hyginus.		
143	Pius I.		
157	Anicetus.		
		Marcus Aurelius.	161
168	Soter.		
177	Eleutherius.		
		Commodus.	180
		Pertinax.	193

Year of Accession	Bishops of Rome	Emperors	Year of Accession
A.D.			A.D.
		Didius Julianus.	193
		Niger.	193
193	Victor (?).	Septimius Severus.	193
202	Zephyrinus (?).		
		Caracalla, Geta.	211
		Opilius Macrinus, Diadumenian.	217
		Elagabalus.	218
219	Calixtus I.		
		Alexander Severus.	222
223	Urban I.		
230	Pontianus.		
235	Anterius or Anteros.	Maximin.	235
236	Fabianus.		
		The two Gordians, Maximus Pupienus, Balbinus.	237
		The third Gordian.	238
		Philip.	244
		Decius.	249
251	Cornelius.	Hostilian, Gallus.	251
252	Lucius I.	Volusian.	252
253	Stephen I.	Aemilian, Valerian, Gallienus.	253
257	Sixtus II.		
259	Dionysius.		
		Gallienus alone.	260
		Claudius II.	268
269	Felix.		
		Aurelian.	270
275	Eutychianus.	Tacitus.	275
		Florian.	276
		Probus.	276
		Carus.	282
283	Caius.		
		Carinus, Numerian.	284
		Diocletian.	284
		Maximian, associated with Diocletian.	286
296	Marcellinus.		
304	Vacancy.		
		Constantius, Galerius.	305
		Severus.	306
		Constantine (the Great).	306
		Licinius.	307

Year of Accession	Bishops of Rome	Emperors	Year of Accession
A.D. 308	Marcellus I.	Maximin.	A.D. 308
		Constantine, Galerius, Licinius, Maximin, Maxentius, and Maximian reigning jointly.	309
310	Eusebius.		
311	Melchiades.		
314	Sylvester I.		
		Constantine (the Great) alone.	323
336	Marcus I.		
337	Julius I.	Constantine II, Constantius II, Constans.	337
		Magnentius.	
352	Liberius.		
		Constantius alone.	353
356	(Felix, Anti-pope.)		
		Julian.	361
		Jovian.	363
		Valens and Valentinian I.	364
366	Damasus I.		
		Gratian and Valentinian I.	367
		Gratian and Valentinian II.	375
		Theodosius.	379
384	Siricius.		
		Arcadius (in the East), Honorius (in the West).	395
398	Anastasius I.		
402	Innocent I.		
		Theodosius II. (E)	408
417	Zosimus.		
418	Boniface I.		
418	(Eulalius, Anti-pope.)		
422	Celestine I.		
		Valentinian III. (W)	424
432	Sixtus III.		
440	Leo I (the Great).		
		Marcian. (E)	450
		Maximus, Avitus. (W)	455
		Majorian. (W)	455
		Leo I. (E)	457
461	Hilarius.	Severus. (W)	461
		Vacancy. (W)	465

Year of Accession	Bishops of Rome	Emperors	Year of Accession
A.D.			A.D.
		Anthemius. (W)	467
468	Simplicius.		
		Olybrius. (W)	472
		Glycerius. (W)	473
		Julius Nepos. (W)	474
		Leo II, Zeno, Basiliscus. (All E)	474
		Romulus Augustulus. (W)	475
		(End of the Western line in Romulus Augustulus.)	476
		(*Henceforth, till* A.D. 800, *Emperors reigning at Constantinople.*)	
483	Felix III.*		
		Anastasius I.	491
492	Gelasius I.		
496	Anastasius II.		
498	Symmachus.		
498	(Laurentius, Anti-pope.)		
514	Hormisdas.		
		Justin I.	518
523	John I.		
526	Felix IV.		
		Justinian.	527
530	Boniface II.		
530	(Dioscorus, Anti-pope).		
532	John II.		
535	Agapetus I.		
536	Silverius.		
537	Vigilius.		
555	Pelagius I.		
560	John III.		
		Justin II.	565
574	Benedict I.		
578	Pelagius II.	Tiberius II.	578
		Maurice.	582
590	Gregory I (the Great).		
		Phocas.	602
604	Sabinianus.		
607	Boniface III.		
607	Boniface IV.		
		Heraclius.	610
615	Deus dedit.		
618	Boniface V.		

* Reckoning the Anti-pope Felix (A.D. 356) as Felix II.

Year of Accession	Popes	Emperors	Year of Accession
A.D.			A.D.
625	Honorius I.		
638	Severinus.		
640	John IV.		
		Constantine III, Heracleonas, Constans II.	641
642	Theodorus I.		
649	Martin I.		
654	Eugenius I.		
657	Vitalianus		
		Constantine IV (Pogonatus).	668
672	Adeodatus.		
676	Domnus or Donus I.		
678	Agatho.		
682	Leo II.		
683(?)	Benedict II.		
685	John V.	Justinian II.	685
685(?)	Conon.		
687	Sergius I.		
687	(Paschal, Anti-pope.)		
687	(Theodorus, Anti-pope.)		
		Leontius.	694
		Tiberius III.	697
701	John VI.		
705	John VII.	Justinian II restored.	705
708	Sisinnius.		
708	Constantine.		
		Philippicus Bardanes.	711
		Anastasius II.	713
715	Gregory II.		
		Theodosius III.	716
		Leo III (the Isaurian).	718
731	Gregory III.		
741	Zacharias.	Constantine V (Copronymus).	741
752	Stephen (II).		
752	Stephen II (or III).		
757	Paul I.		
767	(Constantine, Anti-pope.)		
768	Stephen III (IV).		
772	Hadrian I.		
		Leo IV.	775
		Constantine VI.	780
795	Leo III.		
		Deposition of Constantine VI by Irene.	797

Year of Accession	Popes	Emperors	Year of Accession
A.D.			A.D.
		Charles I (the Great). (*Following henceforth the new Western line.*)	800
		Lewis I (the Pious).	814
816	Stephen IV.		
817	Paschal I.		
824	Eugenius II.		
827	Valentinus.		
827	Gregory IV.		
		Lothar I.	840
844	Sergius II.		
847	Leo IV.		
855	Benedict III.	Lewis II (in Italy).	855
855	(Anastasius, Anti-pope.)		
858	Nicholas I.		
867	Hadrian II.		
872	John VIII.		
		Charles II, the Bald (W. Frankish).	875
		Charles III, the Fat (E. Frankish).	881
882	Martin II.		
884	Hadrian III.	*Interval from 888.*	
885	Stephen V.		
891	Formosus.	Guido (in Italy).	891
		Lambert (in Italy).	894
896	Boniface VI.	Arnulf (E. Frankish).	896
896	Stephen VI.		
897	Romanus.		
897	Theodore II.		
898	John IX.		
		*Lewis (the Child).**	899
900	Benedict IV.		
		Lewis III king of Provence (in Italy).	901
903	Leo V.		
903	Christopher.		
904	Sergius III.		
911	Anastasius III.	*Conrad I.*	911
913	Lando.		
914	John X.		
		Berengar (in Italy).	915
		Henry I (the Fowler) of Saxony.	918
928	Leo VI.		

* The names in italics are those of East Frankish or German kings who never made any claim to the imperial title.

Year of Accession	Popes	Emperors	Year of Accession
A.D.			A.D.
929	Stephen VII.		
931	John XI.		
936	Leo VII.	*Otto I (the Great)*, crowned	
939	Stephen VIII.	E. Frankish king at	
941	Martin III.	Aachen.	936
946	Agapetus II.		
955	John XII.	*Saxon House.*	
		Otto I, crowned Emperor	
963	Leo VIII.	at Rome.	962
964	(Benedict V, Anti-pope?)		
965	John XIII.		
972	Benedict VI.		
		Otto II.	973
974	(Boniface VII, Anti-pope?)		
974	Domnus II (?).		
974	Benedict VII.		
983	John XIV.	Otto III.	983
985	John XV.		
996	Gregory V.		
996	(John XVI, Anti-pope?)		
999	Sylvester II.		
		Henry II (the Saint).	1002
1003	John XVII.		
1003	John XVIII.		
1009	Sergius IV.		
1012	Benedict VIII.	*House of Franconia.*	
1024	John XIX.	Conrad II (the Salic).	1024
1033	Benedict IX.		
		Henry III (the Black).	1039
1044	(Sylvester, Anti-pope.)		
1045	Gregory VI.		
1046	Clement II.		
1048	Damasus II.		
1048	Leo IX.		
1054	Victor II.		
		Henry IV.	1056
1057	Stephen IX.		
1058	Benedict X.		
1059	Nicholas II.		
1061	Alexander II.		
1073	Gregory VII (Hildebrand).	(Rudolf of Swabia, rival.)	1077
1080	(Clement, Anti-pope.)		
		(Hermann of Luxemburg,	
1086	Victor III.	rival.)	1081

Year of Accession	Popes	Emperors	Year of Accession
A.D.			A.D.
1087	Urban II.	(Conrad of Franconia, rival.)	1093
1099	Paschal II.		
1102	(Albert, Anti-pope.)		
1105	(Sylvester, Anti-pope.)		
		Henry V.	1106
1118	Gelasius II.		
1118	(Gregory, Anti-pope.)		
1119	Calixtus II.		
1121	(Celestine, Anti-pope.)		
1124	Honorius II.		
		Lothar II (of Saxony).	1125
1130	Innocent II.	*House of Swabia or Hohen-staufen.*	
	(Anacletus, Anti-pope.)	* Conrad III.	1138
1138	(Victor, Anti-pope.)		
1143	Celestine II.		
1144	Lucius II.		
1145	Eugenius III.		
		Frederick I (Barbarossa).	1152
1153	Anastasius IV.		
1154	Hadrian IV.		
1159	Alexander III.		
1159	(Victor, Anti-pope.)		
1164	(Paschal, Anti-pope.)		
1168	(Calixtus, Anti-pope.)		
1181	Lucius III.		
1185	Urban III.		
1187	Gregory VIII.		
1187	Clement III.		
		Henry VI.	1190
1191	Celestine III.		
		* Philip, Otto IV (rivals).	1197
1198	Innocent III.		
		Otto IV (*House of Brunswick*).	1208
		Frederick II.	1212
1216	Honorius III.		
1227	Gregory IX.		
1241	Celestine IV.		
1241	Vacancy.		
1243	Innocent IV.	(Henry Raspe, rival.)	1246
		(William of Holland, rival.)	1246–7

* Those marked with an asterisk were never actually crowned at Rome.

Year of Accession	Popes	Emperors	Year of Accession
A.D.			A.D.
		*Conrad IV.	1250
1254	Alexander IV.	_Interregnum._	1254
		*Richard (earl of Cornwall), *Alfonso (king of Castile) (rivals).	1257
1261	Urban IV.		
1265	Clement IV.		
1269	Vacancy.		
1271	Gregory X.		
		*Rudolf I (of Hapsburg).	1273
1276	Innocent V.		
1276	Hadrian V.		
1277	John XX or XXI.		
1277	Nicholas III.		
1281	Martin IV.		
1285	Honorius IV.		
1289	Nicholas IV.		
1292	Vacancy.	*Adolf (of Nassau).	1292
1294	Celestine V.		
1294	Boniface VIII.		
		*Albert I (of Hapsburg).	1298
1303	Benedict XI.		
1305	Clement V.		
		Henry VII (of Luxemburg).	1308
1314	Vacancy.	Lewis IV (of Bavaria). (Frederick of Austria, rival.)	1314
1316	John XXII.		
1334	Benedict XII.		
1342	Clement VI.		
		Charles IV (of Luxemburg).	
1352	Innocent VI.	(Günther of Schwartzburg, rival.)	1347
1362	Urban V.		
1370	Gregory XI.		
1378	Urban VI. (Clement VII, Anti-pope.) _Beginning of the Great Schism._	*Wenzel (of Luxemburg).	1378
1389	Boniface IX.		
1394	(Benedict, Anti-pope.)	*Rupert (of the Palatinate).	1400
1404	Innocent VII.		
1406	Gregory XII.		
1409	Alexander V.		

* Those marked with an asterisk were never actually crowned at Rome.

Year of Accession	Popes	Emperors	Year of Accession
A.D.			A.D.
1410	John XXIII.	Sigismund (of Luxemburg). (Jobst, of Moravia, rival.)	1410
	End of the Great Schism.		
1417	Martin V.		
1431	Eugene IV.		
		*Albert II (of Hapsburg).†	1438
1439	(Felix V, Anti-pope.)		
		Frederick III.	1440
1447	Nicholas V.		
1455	Calixtus III.		
1458	Pius II.		
1464	Paul II.		
1471	Sixtus IV.		
1484	Innocent VIII.		
1493	Alexander VI.	*Maximilian I.	1493
1503	Pius III.		
1503	Julius II.		
1513	Leo X.		
		‡Charles V.	1519
1522	Hadrian VI.		
1523	Clement VII.		
1534	Paul III.		
1550	Julius III.		
1555	Marcellus II.		
1555	Paul IV.		
		*Ferdinand I.	1558
1559	Pius IV.		
		*Maximilian II.	1564
1566	Pius V.		
1572	Gregory XIII.		
		*Rudolf II.	1576
1585	Sixtus V.		
1590	Urban VII.		
1590	Gregory XIV.		
1591	Innocent IX.		
1592	Clement VIII.		
1604	Leo XI.		
1604	Paul V.		
		*Matthias.	1612
		*Ferdinand II.	1619

* Those marked with an asterisk were never actually crowned at Rome.
† All the succeeding Emperors, except Charles VII and Francis I, belong to the House of Hapsburg.
‡ Crowned Emperor, but at Bologna, not at Rome.

Year of Accession	Popes	Emperors	Year of Accession
A.D.			A.D.
1621	Gregory XV.		
1623	Urban VIII.		
		*Ferdinand III.	1637
1644	Innocent X.		
1655	Alexander VII.		
		*Leopold I.	1658
1667	Clement IX.		
1670	Clement X.		
1676	Innocent XI.		
1689	Alexander VIII.		
1691	Innocent XII.		
1700	Clement XI.		
		*Joseph I.	1705
		*Charles VI.	1711
1720	Innocent XIII.		
1724	Benedict XIII.		
1730	Clement XII.		
1740	Benedict XIV.		
		*Charles VII (of Bavaria).	1742
		*Francis I (of Lorraine).	1745
1758	Clement XIII.		
		*Joseph II.	1765
1769	Clement XIV.		
1775	Pius VI.		
		*Leopold II.	1790
		*Francis II.	1792
1800	Pius VII.		
		ABDICATION OF FRANCIS II.	1806
1823	Leo XII.		
1829	Pius VIII.		
1831	Gregory XVI.		
1846	Pius IX.		
		GERMAN EMPERORS	
		William I.	1871
		Frederick.	1888
		William II.	1888
1878	Leo XIII.		
1903	Pius X.		

* Those marked with an asterisk were never actually crowned at Rome.

CHRONOLOGICAL TABLE OF
IMPORTANT EVENTS IN THE HISTORY
OF THE EMPIRE

B.C. 48 Battle of Pharsalus. Julius Caesar receives the power of a tribune for life, and (B.C. 45) a perpetual dictatorship.

31 Battle of Actium. Octavianus (Augustus) becomes master of the whole dominions of Rome.

A.D. 9 Defeat of the Roman army under Varus in Westphalia: consequent abandonment of the policy of conquering Germany.

64 First persecution of the Christians under Nero.

292 Division of the Empire into four areas of government: first appearance of the East as a separate realm.

313 Recognition of Christianity by Edict of Constantine as a lawful religion.

325 Constantine presides in the First General Council of Nicaea which condemns the Arians and issues the Nicene Creed.

326-8 Constantinople or New Rome, founded by extending the site of the ancient Greek colony of Byzantium, becomes the seat of imperial government.

361 Efforts of Julian to restore pagan worship in the Roman Empire.

364 Division of the Empire by Valentinian I into an Eastern and a Western realm.

376 A large body of Goths permitted to cross the Danube into the Empire: subsequent war between them and the Emperor Valens: he is defeated and killed in the battle of Adrianople in 378.

395 Final Division of the Empire between Arcadius who receives the Eastern and Honorius who receives the Western provinces.

409 Abandonment of Britain by the Roman armies.

410 Capture and sack of Rome by the West Goths under Alarich.

412 Foundation of a West Gothic monarchy in Southern Gaul by Athaulf (who marries Placidia daughter of Theodosius the Great), and (419) by his successor Wallia.

486

395–430 St. Augustine, Bishop of Hippo in Africa: he composes his *De Civitate Dei* between 413 and 426.

429 The Vandals enter Africa, having traversed Gaul and Spain, and found a kingdom there.

443–75 The Burgundians form a monarchy in Southeastern Gaul.

462–72 Euric, king of the West Goths, conquers Spain and establishes there the Gothic monarchy which lasts till the Arab conquest.

455 Invasion of Italy and sack of Rome by the Vandal Gaiserich.

451 Fourth General Council held at Chalcedon: settlement of the doctrine of the Nature of Christ and consequent alienation of the Monophysites of Egypt and Syria.

451–2 Attila invades Gaul and is repulsed near Chalons-sur-Marne. He then enters Italy and destroys Aquileia.

476 Odoacer deposes the Emperor Romulus Augustulus and assumes the rule of Italy, which is however nominally reunited to the Eastern half of the Empire.

481–511 Reign of Clovis king of the Franks: he enters Gaul, overcomes Syagrius, ruling at Soissons, defeats the Burgundians and the West Goths (of Aquitaine), and establishes the Frankish monarchy, which includes Gaul and Western Germany, the Burgundians being reduced to dependence.

489–526 Theodorich the Amal leads the East Goths across the Alps, defeats Odoacer, and reigns over Italy and Sicily.

529–34 The Emperor Justinian revises and consolidates the Roman law and issues the Code Digest and Institutes.

533 Belisarius, sent by Justinian, reconquers Africa from the Vandals for the Roman Empire.

535–53 Long war of Justinian against the East Goths in Italy: Italy and Sicily are reconquered; disappearance of the East Gothic nation.

568 Alboin leads the Lombards into Italy, conquers the Northern part of it and establishes a monarchy there; Lombard chieftains subsequently found the duchies of Spoleto and Benevento.

622 Flight of Mohammed from Mecca to Medina (Era of the Hegira).

622–28 Campaign of the Emperor Heraclius against the Sassanid kings: defeat of the Persians and recovery of the eastern Provinces.

633–52 The Mohammedan Arabs invade Syria, conquer Syria, Egypt, Mesopotamia, and Armenia, and invade Asia Minor.

638 Pipin of Landen, founder of the Carolingian house, rises to power among the Franks as Mayor of the Palace.

688 Pipin (of Heristal), grandson of the first Pipin, becomes virtual ruler of the Franks as Mayor of the Palace.

669–96 The Arabs invade North Africa, and destroy the Roman power there.

711 The Arabs and Berbers invade Spain, defeat Roderich the last of the West Gothic kings in the battle of the Guadalete, and in a few years conquer the whole Iberian peninsula, except the mountains of Asturias and Biscay.

732 The Arab invasions of Gaul are checked in a battle near Poitiers by Charles Martel, Frankish Mayor of the Palace, son of the second Pipin.

726–32 The Emperor Leo III (reigning at Constantinople) issues an Edict forbidding the worship of images and ordering their destruction in the churches. It evokes strong opposition from the Roman church and leads to a revolt of the North Italian subjects of the Empire. The Lombard king, Liudprand, invades the imperial territories in North Italy. Pope Gregory II induces him to withdraw from before Rome.

741 Pope Gregory III, still in conflict with the Emperor and threatened by the Lombards, appeals to Charles Martel and sends him the keys of the tomb of the Apostles.

751 With the authorization of Pope Zacharias, Pipin (the Short), Mayor of the Palace in Gaul, becomes king of the Franks in the place of the Merovingian Childebert III.

753 Pope Stephen II asks help from the Emperor at Constantinople against the Lombard king Aistulf, who is threatening Rome.

754 Pope Stephen goes to Gaul and crowns and anoints Pipin as king. Pipin invades Italy and reduces Aistulf to submission.

756 Pipin, at the call of the Pope, again enters Italy, overcomes the Lombards, bestows on the See of Rome the territories belonging to the Exarchate of Ravenna, and receives the title of Patrician.

758 Charles (the Great), son of Pipin, becomes king of the Franks of Neustria, and after the death of his brother Carloman (in 771) king of the Franks of Austrasia also.

772–803 Wars of Charles against the Saxons, ending in their submission and enforced conversion.

773–4 Charles, at the appeal of the Pope, who is menaced by king Desiderius, attacks and subjects the Lombards, adding North Italy to his dominions, and is recognized as suzerain of Rome.

778 Expedition of Charles into Spain: fight at Roncesvalles between his troops and the Basques.

794 Charles presides in a Church Council held at Frankfort which disapproves of Pope Hadrian's action regarding images.

797 Irene deposes and blinds her son the Emperor Constantine VI.

800 CHARLES IS CROWNED EMPEROR AT ROME.

805 Charles defeats and reduces the Avars.

810–12 Negotiations of Charles with the East Roman Emperors: they ultimately recognize him as Emperor and as ruler of Northern Italy, except Venice. The south of Italy and Sicily remain subject to Constantinople.

814 Death of Charles: he is succeeded by his son Lewis, whom he had crowned as co-Emperor in 813.

817–39 Lewis I makes several divisions of his dominions among his sons: quarrels arise between him and them and between the sons themselves. The administrative system established by Charles falls to pieces. Norse and Danish pirates devastate the coasts of Germany and Gaul.

841 Battle of Fontanetum between Lewis and Charles, the younger sons of Lewis I (who had died in 840) and their brother the Emperor Lothar; defeat of Lothar.

843 Partition treaty of Verdun between the three sons of Lewis I. The East Frankish kingdom assigned to Lewis (the German) is the origin of the German kingdom of later days.

855 Lewis II, reigning in Italy since 844, becomes Emperor. Attacks of the Saracens upon Italy.

866 Dispute between Pope Nicholas I and Photius, Patriarch of Constantinople: it ends in a schism which divides the two churches.

876 Charles the Bald, king of the West Franks, is crowned Emperor at Rome. He dies next year.

877 Boso, husband of Irmingard (daughter of the Emperor Lewis II), founds the kingdom of (Cisjurane) Burgundy or Arles and is recognized as king by Charles the Bald.

888 Death of the Emperor Charles the Fat, who had (during his reign of three years) reunited the dominions of Charles the Great. After him they fall asunder, and the Carolingian Empire disappears. Arnulf, duke of Carinthia (an illegitimate descendant of Charles), is chosen king of the East Franks (subsequently Emperor), and is succeeded by his son Lewis the Child, who dies unmarried, in 911. Rudolf founds the kingdom of Transjurane Burgundy. West France passes to Odo (grand-uncle of Hugh Capet, who becomes king in 987). Odo admits the suzerainty of Arnulf.

891 Guido of Spoleto, having overcome Berengar of Friuli, seizes the throne of Italy and is crowned Emperor at Rome.

894 Arnulf enters Italy, drives Guido from Pavia, and is crowned king of Italy.

896 Arnulf marches to Rome and is crowned Emperor.

901–25 Repeated invasions of Germany and Italy by the Magyars: the Germans pay a sort of tribute to them from 925 to 933: raids continue in Italy.

911 Conrad, duke of Franconia, is chosen king of the East Franks.

919 Henry (the Fowler), duke of the Saxons, is, on Conrad's death, chosen king of the East Franks or Germans. He was, through females, great-great-grandson of Charles the Great, and a man of proved ability and uprightness.

928 Henry the Fowler attacks the Slavs beyond the Elbe, defeats them, and constructs a fort at Brannibor, which grows into the March of Brandenburg: he makes the Czechs of Bohemia his tributaries.

933 Henry, having organized and trained his forces, attacks and defeats the Magyar invaders in Saxony, and strengthens the eastern frontiers of Germany.

936 Death of Henry: his son Otto (the Great) is chosen to succeed him as king of the East Franks, and is crowned at Aachen.

951 Adelheid of Burgundy, widow of Lothar king of Italy, asks help from Otto against Berengar king of Italy: Otto relieves the castle of Canosa, where she had taken refuge, marries her, and makes Berengar his vassal.

955 Great defeat of the Magyars by Otto on the Lech, near Augsburg. He conquers the Slavs between the Elbe and the Oder, and strengthens the East March, afterwards the principality of Austria.

962 Otto, having deposed Berengar and taken to himself the kingdom of Italy, is crowned Emperor at Rome by Pope John XII.

972 The East Roman Emperor John Tzimiskes makes peace with
Otto I and recognizes his title: Theophano (daughter of
the Emperor Romanus II) is married at Rome to Otto I's
son Otto (afterwards the Emperor Otto II): both are crowned
by the Pope.

973 Otto the Great dies and is succeeded by Otto II, in whose
reign the disorders of Germany, repressed by Otto I, grow
worse, and the Slavs again harry the north-eastern borders.

982 War of Otto II against the Saracens in Southern Italy: he is
defeated and escapes with difficulty.

983 Death of Otto II: he is succeeded by his only son Otto III,
who had been chosen in his father's lifetime: the Empress
dowager Theophano acts as regent till her death in 991.

987 Lewis V, king of the West Franks, the last of the Carolingian
line, dies and is succeeded by Hugh Capet, duke of France.

996 Otto III marches to Rome, makes his cousin Bruno Pope
(Gregory V) and is crowned by him. Subsequent revolts
of the Romans against him are suppressed, and on the death
of Gregory V he procures the election of Gerbert as Pope
(Sylvester II) in 999.

1000 The Magyars having now embraced Christianity, Otto gives
his cousin Gisela in marriage to their king Stephen, and
sends him the crown thereafter known as the crown of St.
Stephen.

1002 Death of Otto III at Paterno (under Mount Soracte, near
Rome): his second cousin Henry duke of Bavaria (great-
grandson of Henry the Fowler) succeeds, after some difficulty, in getting himself chosen king of Germany by the
Bavarians, Lotharingians, Swabians, and Saxons successively, and is crowned at Aachen.

1004 Henry enters Italy, defeats Ardoin marquis of Ivrea who had
made himself king there, and is crowned king at Pavia.

1014 Henry re-enters Italy, meeting with little opposition, although
some of the cities had continued to recognize Ardoin, and
is crowned Emperor at Rome by Pope Benedict VIII. The
kingdom of Italy thenceforward goes with the Empire.

1024 Henry II (the Saint) dies (he was canonized in 1152 by Pope
Eugenius III, and his wife Cunigunda was subsequently

canonized by Pope Innocent III) : a great assembly of the German princes held on the banks of the Rhine below Worms chooses Conrad duke of Franconia (surnamed the Salic) to be king. He was a descendant in the female line of Otto the Great.

1026 Conrad (II of Germany) enters Italy, where attempts had been made to set up members of the French royal house as king : he is crowned king of Italy at Pavia.

1027 Conrad is crowned Emperor at Rome, in the presence of Cnut king of England and Denmark and of Rudolf king of Burgundy, who escort him to his lodgings. Quarrel between the German troops and the Romans in which many of the latter are slain.

1032-3 Death of Rudolf king of Burgundy : Conrad II obtains the kingdom in pursuance of arrangements made with Rudolf, and is recognized by the nobles and bishops. The practical independence of the great lay vassals of the Empire and prelates in the Saone and Rhone valleys, and in the country between the Jura and the Pennine Alps, dates from this time, because these districts lay far from the centre of German power.

1035-8 Troubles in Italy : Heribert archbishop of Milan resists the Emperor : Conrad II fails to reduce the rebels, but at Rome restores Pope Benedict IX, whom the Romans had expelled. He loses great part of his army by disease.

1039 Death of Conrad II : he is succeeded by his son Henry (III of Germany), surnamed The Black, who had been chosen king of Germany in his lifetime.

1046 Henry III enters Italy : is crowned at Milan, deposes two rival Popes and obtains the resignation of a third, secures the election of Pope Clement II, and is crowned Emperor by him at Rome.

1041 Norman adventurers under the sons of Tancred of Hauteville begin to carry on war against the East Roman Empire in Southern Italy, and ultimately (1071) win the whole country.

1051 Dispute between Pope Leo IX and the Patriarch of Constantinople, the latter refusing to admit the superiority of the See of Rome. A schism results which lasts till the Council of Florence in 1438-9.

1053 The Normans defeat and capture Pope Leo IX, who had marched against them ; they presently set the Pope free, and restore the lands taken from the See of Rome. In 1059 Robert Wiscard, now the chief of the Normans, who had owned himself vassal to the Chair of St. Peter for his conquests in Calabria and Apulia, is created by Pope Nicholas II duke of Apulia and Calabria.

1056 Death of Henry III : he is succeeded by his son Henry, then six years of age, who had been already chosen and crowned king.

1059 Pope Nicholas II lays down new rules for papal elections, vesting the primary choice in the cardinals, while reserving the rights of the clergy and people of Rome, and of the Emperor Henry IV, to give their consent.

1071 The East Roman Emperor Romanus Diogenes is defeated and captured at Manzikert by the Turkish Sultan Alp Arslan : the Turks begin the conquest of Asia Minor.

1073–4 Great revolt of the Saxons against the Emperor, who after a struggle overcomes them. They revolt again, and peace is not restored till 1097.

1075 Quarrel of Henry with Pope Gregory VII (elected in 1073) over the investiture of clerics. The Pope excommunicates the Emperor (1076).

1077 Henry submits to Gregory at Canosa and is absolved, but soon after strife is renewed ; a rival Emperor (Rudolf of Swabia) is chosen in Germany against Henry, and civil war follows there, while an anti-pope is elected against Gregory.

1081 Henry enters Italy, besieges and after three years captures Rome (except the castle of St. Angelo, where Gregory VII holds out) : he is crowned Emperor by his anti-pope.

1084 Robert Wiscard, summoned by Gregory, enters Rome ; it is subsequently sacked by his troops ; destruction and ultimate desolation of the parts of the city lying on the Aventine and Coelian hills : Gregory returns with Robert to South Italy, and dies at Salerno (1085).

On the death of Rudolf, Hermann of Luxemburg is set up against Henry as ruler in Germany ; he abandons the contest in 1088.

1090 Conquest of Sicily from the Muslims by the Normans is completed ; South Italy and Sicily are ultimately erected into a

kingdom.   Roger is crowned king of Sicily in 1130: Pope
Innocent II yields South Italy by a treaty in 1139.

1096 Beginning of the First Crusade: the Crusaders take Jerusalem
in 1099, and make Godfrey of Bouillon, duke of Lorraine,
king.

1105–6 Henry IV is dethroned by his second son, Henry, who, supported by the papal party, becomes king as Henry V, and is
crowned at Mentz.   (Henry IV dies in 1106.)

1111 Henry V descends into Italy, enters Rome to be crowned,
seizes Pope Paschal II (upon the failure of an agreement by
which the Church was to surrender its possessions, and
Henry consequently his right of investiture) keeps him and
the cardinals prisoners, and extorts a treaty admitting the
Emperor's right of clerical investiture.   He is then crowned
by the Pope, and returns to Germany.   The Pope, when
released, finds that the clergy will not accept the treaty and
is obliged to disavow it.   The contest over the investiture
of ecclesiastics by laymen continues.

1122 Concordat of Worms between Pope Calixtus II and the Emperor, by which the question of investitures is compromised.

1125 Henry V dies, leaving no male heir: Lothar, duke of Saxony,
is chosen to succeed him.   A quarrel breaks out between
Lothar and Frederick of Hohenstaufen, duke of Swabia,
which is the origin of the long strife of the houses of Welf
(so called) and Waiblingen (Waiblingen was a small town
belonging to the Hohenstaufen, whose name is said to have
been on one occasion used as a battle-cry).   Conrad, duke
of Franconia, brother of Frederick of Swabia, disputes the
throne with Lothar, enters Italy, and is crowned at Monza
and Milan.   The hostility of the Pope, however, prevents
him from maintaining authority there, and he and Frederick
ultimately submit.

1133 Lothar II is crowned Emperor in Rome by Pope Innocent II.
He had held the Pope's stirrup at an interview in Germany,
and desiring papal support he took an oath to defend the
Holy See, and acknowledged papal rights over part of the
territories that had belonged to the Countess Matilda.   This
was afterwards represented as a recognition of papal suzerainty; but Lothar maintained the rights secured by the
Concordat of Worms.

1138 Lothar II, after a successful war against the Normans of South Italy, dies in Tyrol: Conrad of Hohenstaufen, duke of Swabia, is chosen king in his stead, to the displeasure of the Saxons and Bavarians, with whom he soon finds himself at war.

1144 Revolt of the Romans against Pope Innocent II: preaching of Arnold of Brescia: republican institutions are reorganized and envoys sent to Conrad III to obtain his support.

1146 Conrad III starts on the Second Crusade, but returns having lost his army and effected little.

1152 Death of Conrad, who had never carried out his intention of receiving the imperial crown at Rome. His nephew Frederick of Hohenstaufen, duke of Swabia, is chosen king and crowned at Aachen with the general approval of the nation.

1154 Frederick enters Italy, where he finds Milan and other Lombard cities disobedient.

1155 Frederick I meets Pope Hadrian IV outside Rome, and after some resistance consents to hold the stirrup for him, and at his demand seizes and puts to death Arnold of Brescia. He is crowned by the Pope in St. Peter's, but is unable to force his way into Rome.

1157 Diet at Besançon, where the great Burgundian vassals do homage to the Emperor. Indignation at the assertion made by the papal legate that the Empire was held from the See of Rome.

1158–62 Frederick carries on war with the recalcitrant Lombard cities and destroys Milan. Diet at Roncaglia.

1160 Double election to the Papacy of Alexander III and Victor IV. Frederick sides with Victor. Long conflict between Alexander and the Empire, the Pope supporting the North Italian cities against Frederick. Alexander, at first driven to take refuge in France, returns to Rome (1165) and deposes the Emperor.

1167–76 Further strife in Italy, ending with the defeat of Frederick's army by the allied cities at Legnano.

1177 Reconciliation of Frederick and Pope Alexander III at Venice.

1180–1 Henry (the Lion) duke of Saxony, who had failed to support Frederick in the campaign of Legnano, is condemned by the Diet at Wurzburg to lose his possessions: he resists by force of arms, but is ultimately obliged to submit, losing his duchies of Saxony and Bavaria, but receiving back some part of his estates.

1183 Peace of Constance between Frederick and the confederated Lombard cities: they secure internal self-government and the right of making peace and war, and are thenceforward practically independent.

1186 Marriage of Henry, eldest son of Frederick, to Constantia, daughter of Roger II king of Sicily, and heiress of the Norman kingdom.

1189 Frederick leads a German host (estimated at 100,000 men) on the Third Crusade. After traversing Bulgaria and Asia Minor, he is drowned in the river Kalykadnus in Cilicia, in 1190 ; and is succeeded by his eldest son, Henry VI, who had been already (as a child) chosen king and crowned at Aachen.

1189 Death of William the Good, king of Sicily. The Sicilian kingdom and South Italy are claimed by Henry in right of his wife: but he is resisted by Tancred (illegitimate son of Roger, son of Roger II), and does not master Sicily till 1194.

1190 Foundation of the Teutonic Order of Knights by Frederick (son of the Emperor Frederick I) while commanding the German Crusaders after his father's death.

1191 Henry VI is crowned Emperor at Rome.

1194 Richard I king of England (made prisoner in 1192 by the duke of Austria) surrenders the kingdom of England to the Emperor and receives it back as a fief on his liberation.

1197 Death of Henry VI at Messina : he had caused his son Frederick, a child of three, to be chosen king two years previously.

1198–1208 Disputed election. Philip of Hohenstaufen, duke of Swabia, brother of Henry VI, had at first tried to rule as regent on behalf of his infant nephew Frederick, but when this proves impossible in face of the opposition of Pope Innocent III, he secures his own election by a large majority of the great princes. The Pope, however, raises up a party against him and procures the election of Otto of Brunswick, son of Henry the Lion (late duke of Saxony) and of Matilda (sister of Richard I of England). Civil war in Germany, terminated by the murder of Philip in 1208.

1204 A French army and Venetian fleet starting for the Fourth
Crusade besiege and take Constantinople, and set up
Baldwin as East Roman Emperor. The East Romans
found an empire at Nicaea which lasts till 1261, when they
recover Constantinople.

1208 Otto, on his rival's death, is formally re-elected Emperor,
and next year visits Rome, and is crowned Emperor by
Innocent III.

1210–18 Otto IV quarrels with Innocent, who encourages Frederick
(son of Henry VI) to put himself at the head of the party
in Germany, which is hostile to Otto IV. Frederick is
elected king and crowned at Mainz (1212) and at Aachen
(1215). Otto IV retires to his dominions in Brunswick,
and dies (1218) after an unsuccessful war against Philip
of France.

1216 The Order of St. Dominic is recognized by the Pope, and in
1223 the Order of St. Francis is also recognized.

1220 Frederick II, by a solemn act (subsequently called a Pragmatic Sanction) issued in a Diet at Frankfort, extends large
powers to the ecclesiastical princes. A similar Sanction
some years later extends the privileges of the secular
princes. He is crowned emperor at Rome. Disputes
soon after arise between him and the Pope, nominally
arising out of his delay in setting out on a crusade.

1226 The Lombard cities renew their league against the Emperor.

1227 Open breach between Frederick and Pope Gregory IX, who
excommunicates him.

1228–9 Frederick II sets out on his Crusade, reaches Jerusalem, and
returns, having made a favourable treaty with the Sultan of
Egypt.

1228–40 Establishment of the Teutonic Knights on the eastern frontier
of Germany and conquest by them of the Lithuanians of
Old Prussia.

1230 Reconciliation of the Pope and Frederick II, who is absolved.

1235 War between the Emperor and the Lombard League, the Pope
supporting the cities. It lasts during the rest of Frederick II's
reign.

1235–40 Strife of Gregory IX and the Emperor, whom he excommunicates (1239), then preaches a crusade against him,
and tries to stir up an insurrection in Germany.

1241 Beginnings of the Hanseatic League of cities.

1242 A Mongol host invades Germany and is defeated in Moravia and Austria.

1243 Election of Pope Innocent IV (a teacher of law at Bologna), who soon resumes hostilities against the Emperor, and in Councils held at Lyons (1244-5) excommunicates and deposes him, and excites some of the German princes to set up Henry of Thuringia, and afterwards (1247) William of Holland, as pretenders to the crown. William is crowned at Aachen, and maintains his pretensions till his death in 1256. Anarchy in Germany.

1250 Frederick II, who had been constantly engaged in fighting the Guelf party in Italy, dies in Apulia. He is succeeded by his son Conrad IV, who had been chosen king in his father's lifetime (1237).

1250-4 Conrad IV, excommunicated by Pope Innocent, enters Italy and maintains the war there against the cities and the papal forces, while William of Holland is generally recognized in northern and middle Germany. Both there and in Italy anarchy continues. There has been, however, during Frederick's reign a great increase in the population and wealth of the German cities, which had been favoured by Frederick I.

1254 Death of Conrad IV: the rights to the German territories of the Hohenstaufen and to the kingdom of Sicily pass to his son Conrad (Conradin), a child of two, while his illegitimate brother Manfred continues the war in South Italy against the Pope and the Guelfs, or papal party, till his death in the battle of Benevento in 1266.

1256-7 An interregnum follows the death of William of Holland, which ends with the double election of Richard earl of Cornwall (brother of the English king Henry III), and, by another section of the electors, a little later, of Alfonso X, king of Castile. Richard crosses to Germany and is crowned at Aachen. Alfonso remains in Spain. Richard retains the title of Emperor till his death in 1271, but is only thrice in Germany and never exercises effective authority there.

1261 Michael Palaeologus recovers Constantinople from the Latin Emperor and re-establishes an Orthodox dynasty there.

1268 Conradin, last male descendant of the Swabian emperors, enters Italy with a German army, but is defeated at Tagliacozzo by the army of Charles of Anjou and beheaded at Naples.

1273 Rudolf count of Hapsburg is chosen king and crowned at Aachen: he conciliates the Pope, and never enters Italy.

1277–82 Rudolf deprives Ottocar king of Bohemia of the Austrian territories and after a time bestows them, as well as Styria and Carniola, on his sons, laying the foundation of the territorial power of the house of Hapsburg.

1291 Death of Rudolf. He had failed to secure the fixing of the imperial crown as hereditary in his house, and even the election of his son Albert; the electors choose Adolf count of Nassau, a man of ability and energy but of slender resources.

1298 A revolt organized by Albert of Hapsburg and the archbishop of Mainz breaks out. Adolf is deposed, but resists: he is killed by the hand of Albert in battle at Göllheim near Worms, having never entered Italy to receive the imperial crown.

Albert of Hapsburg, duke of Austria, is chosen king and crowned at Aachen: Pope Boniface VIII refuses to recognize him.

1302 Dante Alighieri with the party of the White Guelfs is driven into exile from Florence: he writes his *De Monarchia* probably a little before, or in, 1311 or 1312, and dies at Ravenna in 1321.

1303 Boniface VIII, being engaged in a fierce strife with Philip IV of France, becomes reconciled to Albert and invites him to come to Rome to be crowned: which however Albert never does. Boniface is seized at Anagni by an armed band in the service of Philip IV of France, and dies a few days afterwards.

1305 Clement V (a Gascon by birth) becomes Pope. Moved by the constant rebellions and disorders of Rome for a long time previously, he removes the Papal Court to Avignon, where it remains for seventy years.

1307–8 League of the inhabitants of Schwytz Uri and Unterwalden to defend themselves against the oppression of the officers of Albert of Hapsburg: it is the germ of the Swiss Confederation. Albert marches against the Swiss, but is murdered on the banks of the Reuss by his nephew John in 1308.

1308 Henry count of Luxemburg is chosen king: he presently secures the kingdom of Bohemia for his family: and he recognizes the exemption of the three Swiss Cantons from the feudal rights of the counts of Hapsburg.

1310 Henry VII, summoned to put an end to the disorders and civil wars of Italy, where most of the cities had fallen under the dominion of tyrants, crosses the Alps, is crowned king of Italy, fights his way into Rome, where he is resisted by a faction of the nobles and by the troops of the king of Naples, and is crowned Emperor by the legates of Pope Clement V. He carries on war against the Guelfs of Italy till his death in 1313.

1313–14 Double election of Lewis duke of Bavaria and Frederick duke of Austria, followed by a civil war between them.

1315 The Swiss Confederates defeat the Austrian troops at Morgarten, and thereby secure their freedom.

1322 Lewis of Bavaria defeats Frederick at Muhldorf and takes him prisoner: the civil war however continues till 1325.

1324 Open breach between Pope John XXII and Lewis IV. John excommunicates him. Lewis appeals to a General Council. Lewis obtains the support of the English philosopher William of Ockham and other Franciscans, and of Marsilius of Padua: they write treatises against the Pope.

1327–8 Lewis enters Italy, is welcomed at Rome by the citizens; is crowned Emperor by the Syndics whom they appoint for the purpose. In a solemn meeting of the people he deposes John XXII, and crowns a Franciscan friar whom the people had chosen Pope. Finding the Romans fickle and his forces insufficient, he leaves Rome, and, in 1329, returns to Germany, while Rome submits to the Pope. Lewis subsequently endeavours, but in vain, to make peace with John XXII, and afterwards with Benedict XII.

1338 The Germanic Diet at Frankfort solemnly protests against the pretensions of the Pope to supremacy over the Empire and declares that the Empire is held from God alone. The Electors at Rhense issue a similar declaration.

1343 Pope Clement VI renews the decrees of his predecessors against Lewis IV; Lewis sends envoys to Avignon; but the Pope's exorbitant demands are refused by the Germanic Diet: the Pope excommunicates Lewis, and sets up Charles king of Bohemia as rival to the throne. Charles is chosen king by the three ecclesiastical and by two lay electors.

1347–54 Cola di Rienzo effects a revolution at Rome, and is named Tribune with the assent of the papal legate: he falls from power after some months, escapes to the Apennines, goes to Bohemia, is imprisoned there by the Emperor Charles IV, and sent to Avignon, then sent back to Rome by Pope Clement VI with limited powers, and is killed in a popular outbreak in 1354.

1347 Death of Lewis IV: Charles king of Bohemia (grandson of the Emperor Henry VII) is opposed by several of the electors, who choose in succession king Edward III of England, who refuses (his Parliament objecting), Frederick marquis of Meissen (whom Charles buys off), and Gunther of Schwartzburg, who accepts, but dies soon after. Charles then has himself re-chosen and re-crowned at Aachen.

1354 Charles is crowned king of Italy at Milan and afterwards Emperor at Rome by the Cardinal-bishop of Ostia, commissioned thereto by the Pope. He shews himself submissive to the Pope, quits Rome forthwith and returns promptly across the Alps.

1356 Charles IV promulgates in a Diet held at Nürnberg the famous Constitution called the Golden Bull (*Aurea Bulla*), which settles the composition of the Electoral College, the proceedings in imperial elections, and the privileges of the electors.

1365 Charles IV visits the Pope at Avignon and is crowned king of Burgundy. (It is the last Burgundian coronation.) He also visits the king of France.

1378 Death of Charles IV. His son Wenzel king of Bohemia, elected and crowned two years before, succeeds him.

The election of two rival Popes, Urban VI and Clement VII, leads to the Great Schism of the West, which lasts till the Council of Constance.

1384–8 War breaks out between the League of cities (formed in South Germany some years before) and the League of princes: general disorder in Germany.

1395 Wenzel confers the title of Duke of Milan on Gian Galeazzo Visconti, tyrant of that city.

1400 Wenzel's neglect of his imperial duties and dissolute habits having provoked much displeasure, especially that of the clergy, who resent some of his ecclesiastical measures, four electors (the three Rhenish archbishops and the Count

Palatine) pronounce him to be deposed, and choose Rupert (of Wittelsbach), Count Palatine of the Rhine: he is crowned at Cologne, and recognized over most of Germany, but Wenzel retains his title and the kingdom of Bohemia till 1411, when he makes way for his brother Sigismund.

1409 Council of Pisa summoned to endeavour to put an end to the Great Schism.

1410 Death of Rupert, who, like Wenzel, had never been crowned at Rome, though he had made an (unfortunate) expedition into Italy in 1401.

1410–11 Disputed election of Sigismund king of Hungary (brother of Wenzel) and of Jobst margrave of Moravia (cousin of Wenzel). Death of Jobst: Sigismund is again chosen and (in 1414) crowned at Aachen.

1414 Meeting of the Council of Constance: it burns John Huss (although Sigismund had given him a safe-conduct), deposes the rival Popes John XXIII and Benedict XIII, procures the abdication of a third rival Pope, Gregory XII, secures the election of a new Pope, Martin V, and breaks up in 1418.

1415–17 Sigismund confers the Electorate of Brandenburg on Frederick of Hohenzollern, Burggrave of Nürnberg (ancestor of the present house of Prussia).

1431 Sigismund enters Italy, is crowned king at Milan and Emperor at Rome (1433).

1437 Death of Sigismund, who had done something to restore the credit of the Empire, but had not recovered any of its power.

1438 Albert of Hapsburg, duke of Austria, is elected king of the Romans, and soon afterwards becomes king of Hungary and Bohemia.

1438–9 A Council held first at Ferrara, then at Florence, is attended by the East Roman Emperor John Palaeologus: it effects a nominal reconciliation of the Greek and Latin churches. Subsequent efforts of the Easterns to obtain armed help from the West against the Turks prove ineffective.

1439 Death of Albert II. Frederick of Hapsburg, duke of Styria, is elected to succeed him.

1452 Frederick III is crowned Emperor at Rome. It is the last imperial coronation there.

1453 Constantinople taken by the Turks. END OF THE EAST

ROMAN EMPIRE. The (Christian) Empire of Trebizond lingers on till 1460, when it is overthrown by Mohammed II.

1454 A congress at Ratisbon deliberates on the proposal of a crusade against the Turks, but nothing follows.

1477 Marriage of Maximilian, son of Frederick III, to Mary of Burgundy, heiress of Duke Charles the Bold. The Netherlands and Franche Comté are thus acquired by the house of Hapsburg. (Philip, offspring of this marriage, marries Juana of Spain, daughter of Ferdinand of Aragon and Isabella of Castile: their son is Charles, afterwards the Emperor Charles V.)

1485–1512 Efforts to improve the constitution of the Empire, at first led by Berthold Elector of Mainz, are made at successive Diets.

1486 Bartholomew Diaz rounds the Cape of Good Hope.

1489 The Imperial cities are definitely recognized as members of the Germanic Diet.

1492 Discovery of America by Christopher Columbus.

1493 Death of Frederick III: his son, Maximilian of Hapsburg (already elected), succeeds him.

Vasco da Gama reaches India by sea: beginning of the oceanic empire of Portugal.

1508 Maximilian obtains the Pope's permission to call himself Emperor Elect.

1508 Luther begins to teach at Wittenberg.

1518 Zwingli is established as People's Priest at Zurich.

1519 Death of Maximilian I: his grandson Charles (king of Spain) is elected Emperor.

1520–1 Luther, excommunicated by the Pope, burns the Bull: he appears before Charles V at the Diet of Worms, and is put to the ban of the Empire.

1524–5 Insurrection of the peasants in South Germany.

1529 The German Reformers make their 'Protest' in the Diet of Speyer.

1530 Florence captured by the troops of Charles V: the Medici finally established as its rulers.

1531 Battle of Kappel, in which Zwingli is killed.

The leading Protestant princes form the Smalkaldic League against the Emperor.

1534 The Society of Jesus established by Ignatius Loyola.

1545-63 Sittings of the Council of Trent, which are several times suspended for long intervals during these eighteen years.

1546 Death of Martin Luther.

War between the Smalkaldic League and the Emperor: the princes of the League are defeated at Mühlberg (1547) and harshly treated.

1552 The territories of the bishops of Metz, Toul, and Verdun are occupied by France: Charles V attempts in vain to recover them.

Maurice Elector of Saxony attacks the Emperor: chases him out of Tyrol and restores the Protestant cause in Germany.

1555 Charles V abdicates and dies soon after in Spain (1558): he is succeeded by his brother Ferdinand, previously elected.

Proclamation of the so-called 'Religious Peace of Augsburg,' settled at the Diet held there in 1554; it allows each German prince to enforce on his subjects the religion he had adopted: permits the Lutheran princes to retain all ecclesiastical estates occupied before 1552, but strips of his lands and dignities any prelate forsaking the Roman communion.

1560 The Protestants, invited by the Emperor to the Council of Trent, refuse to attend. The Council closes in 1563, having settled and defined the Catholic faith.

1563-8 The Elector of Brandenburg secures for his house the succession of the dukedom of Prussia.

1564 Death of the Emperor Ferdinand I: his son, Maximilian II, previously elected, succeeds, and endeavours to conciliate the Protestants.

1576 Death of Maximilian II: his son, Rudolf II, becomes Emperor.

1608 Formation in Germany of a Protestant Union of Princes and a Catholic League of Princes.

1612 Death of Rudolf II: his brother Matthias becomes Emperor.

1618 A conflict in Bohemia, putting the torch to the inflammable material all over the central and western parts of the Empire, causes the outbreak of the Thirty Years' War.

1619 Death of Matthias: his cousin, Ferdinand of Styria, becomes Emperor.

1621 Frederick the (Protestant) Elector Palatine, who had been chosen king of Bohemia, is driven out, and (1623) deprived of his Electorate, which is given by the Emperor to (the Catholic) Maximilian of Bavaria.

1628 The successes of Wallenstein, Ferdinand II's chief general, against the Protestants are arrested by the resistance of the town of Stralsund.   Sweden prepares to enter the war.

1630 Gustavus Adolphus, king of Sweden, enters Germany and turns the balance of the war in favour of the Protestants.   He defeats Wallenstein at Lützen in 1632, but is himself killed.

1640–88 Reign of Frederick William, 'the Great Elector,' in the Electorate of Brandenburg, the power of which he greatly increases.

1648 The Thirty Years' War is ended, after protracted negotiations, by the Treaties of Osnabrück and Münster (Treaty of Westphalia).

1692 An Electorate of Hanover (the ninth, as the Count Palatine had recovered his electoral rights in 1648) is conferred on the Duke of Brunswick-Lüneburg (father of the English king George I), and the title of Arch Treasurer of the Empire is attached to it.

1700–1 Frederick Elector of Brandenburg becomes King of Prussia by the sanction of the Emperor.

1740 Death of the Emperor Charles VI.   Extinction of the male line of Hapsburg.

Accession of Frederick II (the Great) to the throne of Prussia.

The intrigues of France, pursuing her usual anti-Austrian policy, procure the election as Emperor of Charles, Elector of Bavaria (Charles VII).   A war follows, in which Charles is driven from his dominions.

1745 Death of Charles VII.   Francis, duke of Lorraine, who had married Maria Theresa, daughter of Charles VI, is elected Emperor and crowned at Frankfort.

1756–63 The Seven Years' War, in which Frederick of Prussia successfully resists Austria, France, and Russia.

1765 Death of the Emperor Francis I: his son Joseph, elected in his lifetime, becomes Emperor.

1772 First Partition of Poland between Austria, Russia, and Prussia.

1781 Joseph II, among other reforms, proclaims religious toleration and attempts to reduce clerical power.   The Pope comes next year to Vienna, but effects nothing.   Joseph visits Rome, but is not crowned there.

1786 Death of Frederick the Great of Prussia.

1789 Meeting of the French States General at Versailles: beginning of the Revolution.

1792–5 War between the French Republic and Prussia.

1792–7 War between the French Republic and Austria.   Austria cedes Lombardy and receives the territories of Venice.

1801 By the Peace of Luneville, closing a second war between Austria and the French, the internal constitution of the Empire is completely altered and additional territory taken from it.

1804 Napoleon Bonaparte becomes Emperor; he considers himself the successor of Charlemagne as Emperor of the West.

1805 The overthrow of Austria and Russia by Napoleon at Austerlitz is followed by the formation of the Confederation of the Rhine under the protection of France.

1806 Abdication of the Emperor Francis II. END OF THE HOLY ROMAN EMPIRE.

INDEX

INDEX

SCHOCKEN PAPERBACKS